Pro T-SQL 2005 Programmer's Guide

Michael Coles

Apress®

Pro T-SQL 2005 Programmer's Guide

Copyright © 2007 by Michael Coles

ISBN-13(pbk): 978-1-59059-794-1

ISBN-10(pbk): 1-59059-794-X

Printed and bound in the United States of America 9 8 7 6 5 4 3 2 1

Trademarked names may appear in this book. Rather than use a trademark symbol with every occurrence of a trademarked name, we use the names only in an editorial fashion and to the benefit of the trademark owner, with no intention of infringement of the trademark.

Lead Editor: James Huddleston
Technical Reviewer: Alexzander N. Nepomnjashiy
Editorial Board: Steve Anglin, Ewan Buckingham, Gary Cornell, Jason Gilmore, Jonathan Gennick, Jonathan Hassell, James Huddleston, Chris Mills, Matthew Moodie, Jeff Pepper, Paul Sarknas, Dominic Shakeshaft, Jim Sumser, Matt Wade
Project Manager: Denise Santoro Lincoln
Copy Edit Manager: Nicole Flores
Copy Editor: Jennifer Whipple
Assistant Production Director: Kari Brooks-Copony
Production Editor: Laura Esterman
Compositor: Linda Weidemann, Wolf Creek Press
Proofreaders: Lori Bring and Linda Siefert
Indexer: Broccoli Information Management
Cover Designer: Kurt Krames
Manufacturing Director: Tom Debolski

Distributed to the book trade worldwide by Springer-Verlag New York, Inc., 233 Spring Street, 6th Floor, New York, NY 10013. Phone 1-800-SPRINGER, fax 201-348-4505, e-mail orders-ny@springer-sbm.com, or visit http://www.springeronline.com.

For information on translations, please contact Apress directly at 2560 Ninth Street, Suite 219, Berkeley, CA 94710. Phone 510-549-5930, fax 510-549-5939, e-mail info@apress.com, or visit http://www.apress.com.

The information in this book is distributed on an "as is" basis, without warranty. Although every precaution has been taken in the preparation of this work, neither the author(s) nor Apress shall have any liability to any person or entity with respect to any loss or damage caused or alleged to be caused directly or indirectly by the information contained in this work.

The source code for this book is available to readers at http://www.apress.com in the Source Code/Download section.

For Devoné and Rebecca

Contents at a Glance

Contents

About the Author

MICHAEL COLES is a soldier, a scholar, a software engineer, and a writer. He has worked in the IT industry for more than a decade, with an emphasis on database-enabled applications. He has worked in a wide range of industries, including retail, manufacturing, and technology, to name a few.

After his most recent tour of active duty military service, Michael landed in New Jersey and now works as a senior developer for Barnes & Noble in New York.

About the Technical Reviewer

ALEXZANDER N. NEPOMNJASHIY works as a Microsoft SQL Server DBA with NeoSystems North-West Inc., an ISO 9001:2000–certified software company. As a DBA, he's responsible for drafting design specifications for proposed projects and building database-related applications to spec. As an IT professional, Alexzander has more than 13 years experience in DBMS planning, security, troubleshooting, and performance optimization.

Acknowledgments

There are a lot of people I would like to acknowledge for helping to make this book a reality. First, I'd like to thank the team at Apress. This book would not have been possible without my editor, Jim Huddleston, who set the tone and got the ball rolling. I'd also like to thank the keeper of the schedule, Denise Santoro Lincoln, whose dedication and perseverance kept us all on track.

I'd like to thank my technical reviewer Alexzander Nepomnjashiy for keeping me honest, copy editor Jennifer Whipple for keeping me consistent, production editor Laura Esterman for making it look so good, and everyone else who contributed to this book.

While I'm at it, I'd like to give special thanks to Steve Jones, Andy Warren, and Brian Knight, three of the founders of SQL Server Central. These guys thought enough of my writing to give me my first shot at writing for them. Thanks also to ASP Today editor Simon Robinson for publishing me and for introducing me to the team at Apress.

Thanks to my family, Jennifer, Chris, Deja, Desmond, and, of course, Mom and Eric for your support. I'd also like to thank my good friends Rob and Laura Whitlock, and my Army buddy Joe Johnson.

Thank you to my wonderful girlfriend Donna for all your support.

And most of all, thank you to Devoné and Rebecca for being my little angels.

Introduction

This book examines SQL Server 2005 T-SQL from a developer's perspective. It covers a wide range of developer-specific topics in SQL Server 2005, from an introduction to new developer tools such as SQLCMD and SQL Server Management Studio to new T-SQL functionality such as the xml data type, XQuery support, and T-SQL encryption.

I wrote this book as a practical and useful guide to help you make the most of SQL Server 2005 T-SQL. I provide a generous selection of sample T-SQL and, where appropriate, .NET code to demonstrate specific functionality.

Who This Book Is For

This book is primarily for developers who want to take advantage of the new features in SQL Server 2005 T-SQL. The book assumes a basic knowledge of SQL—preferably a prior version of T-SQL—and builds on that foundation.

How This Book Is Structured

This book is designed so that you can either read it cover to cover, or you can use it as a reference guide to quickly locate just the information you need on any particular topic. It is structured as follows:

Chapter 1: The Role of T-SQL

This chapter provides a brief history of T-SQL and the ANSI SQL standards. It also provides some basic hints and tips for getting the most out of your T-SQL code and maintaining it over the long term. Those readers coming from a background in SQL Server 2000 T-SQL, who are well-versed in T-SQL programming best practices, might choose to skip this chapter.

Chapter 2: Tools of the Trade

SQLCMD and SQL Server Management Studio (SSMS) are new tools designed to replace osql, Enterprise Manager, and Query Analyzer. The online help system and Adventure-Works sample database are also discussed. If you are just beginning to use SQLCMD or SSMS, this chapter provides a solid reference.

Chapter 3: T-SQL for SQL Server 2000 Programmers

SQL Server 2005 provides several enhancements that SQL Server 2000 developers will be able to take advantage of immediately. This chapter covers new SQL Server 2005 data types, Common Table Expressions (CTEs), and new operators, keywords, and functions.

Chapter 4: Control-of-Flow and CASE Expressions

SQL Server T-SQL has always had procedural extensions built right into it. This chapter covers ANSI SQL three-valued logic, T-SQL procedural control-of-flow statements, SQL CASE expressions, and CASE-derivative functions.

Chapter 5: User-Defined Functions

This chapter discusses the three flavors of T-SQL user-defined functions: scalar user-defined functions, multistatement table-valued functions, and inline table-valued functions. Examples are provided, with tips on getting the most out of your own user-defined functions.

Chapter 6: Stored Procedures

SQL Server provides stored procedures, which allow you to create server-side T-SQL modules. This chapter discusses creation and management of stored procedures, stored procedure parameters, recursion, and scope.

Chapter 7: Triggers

SQL Server 2005 supports classic Data Manipulation Language (DML) triggers that perform actions when you insert, update, or delete rows in a table. Data Definition Language (DDL) triggers, which fire in response to DDL events, are new to SQL Server 2005 T-SQL. This chapter discusses both types of triggers.

Chapter 8: T-SQL Encryption

SQL Server 2005 T-SQL includes a whole new set of statements to manage encryption keys and certificates, and a wide range of built-in functions to encrypt and decrypt data. This chapter explores the new T-SQL encryption key management and data encryption and decryption tools.

Chapter 9: Error Handling and Debugging

This chapter discusses methods for handling errors in your T-SQL code, including legacy error handling and the new TRY...CATCH structured error-handling statements. Also discussed is the built-in Visual Studio T-SQL debugging tools.

Chapter 10: Dynamic SQL

The risks (and how to avoid them) and rewards of dynamic SQL are discussed in this chapter. Client-side parameterization, SQL injection, and validation are also covered.

Chapter 11: XML

This chapter begins with a discussion of the enhancements to legacy SQL Server XML functionality provided by SQL Server 2005. The chapter continues with an in-depth discussion of SQL Server's new XML functionality, including the new xml data type and its methods, XML schema collections, typed and untyped XML, XML indexes, and XSL Transformations.

Chapter 12: XQuery and XPath

This chapter expands on the discussion of the enhanced XML functionality that began in Chapter 11 by providing an in-depth discussion of the XPath and XQuery capabilities provided by SQL Server 2005. The information and code samples presented in this chapter are designed to get you up and running with SQL Server 2005 XPath and XQuery quickly.

Chapter 13: SQL Metadata

SQL Server 2005 provides more ways than ever to retrieve metadata about your server and database objects. This chapter covers SQL Server catalog views, compatibility views, ANSI-compatible INFORMATION_SCHEMA views, and system stored procedures.

Chapter 14: SQLCLR Programming

SQL Server 2005's Common Language Runtime integration offers new and exciting possibilities for expanding the power and functionality of your SQL Server–based applications. This chapter will show you how to create and register SQLCLR assemblies that allow access to .NET-based user-defined functions, stored procedures, user-defined aggregates, and user-defined types.

Chapter 15: .NET Client Programming

The best database in the world is only as useful as its client-side application, and the .NET Framework provides several tools for client-side SQL Server connectivity. This chapter discusses ADO.NET, the System.Data.SqlClient namespace and the classes it exposes for querying data and executing T-SQL statements, and the SqlBulkCopy class.

Chapter 16: HTTP Endpoints

SQL Server's new HTTP endpoints allow you to expose stored procedures and user-defined functions as web methods. The new HTTP endpoints feature tight integration with the SQL Server security model, easy setup and configuration, and greater efficiency than other methods of exposing SQL Server procedures as web methods.

Prerequisites

At the time of writing, SQL Server 2005 Service Pack 1 was the latest production release. All of the code samples in the book were developed on SQL Server 2005 Service Pack 1. Because of changes to the SQL Server engine and to T-SQL in general, I cannot guarantee compatibility with previous SQL Server 2005 releases, such as the CTP releases.

Most of the code samples were designed to be run against the AdventureWorks sample database. If you do not have AdventureWorks, I highly recommend that you download it from http://www.microsoft.com/sql.

Many of the code samples will run properly on SQL Server 2005 Express Edition, but some will not due to differences in the available features. For example, SQL Server 2005 Express Edition does not support HTTP endpoints. For complete compatibility, use SQL Server 2005 Standard Edition or better.

Finally, a lot of the code samples in Chapters 14, 15, and 16 are written in VB and C#. These samples require the Microsoft .NET Framework 2.0 to run. If you want to compile and tinker with the code samples, I highly recommend you use Microsoft Visual Studio 2005 for the best overall experience.

Source Code

As you read through the book, you may choose to type in some of the code samples by hand because it provides more familiarity with the techniques and styles used. Or you might want to compile, install, execute, modify, or study the code without entering it manually. Either way, I highly recommend downloading the source and just generally playing with it as you read the book.

All of the code is available in the Source Code/Download section of the Apress website at `http://www.apress.com`.

Errata

Apress and the author have made every effort to ensure that there are no errors in the text or the code for this book. However, to err is human, and as such we recognize the need to keep you informed of any mistakes as they're discovered and corrected. An errata sheet will be made available on this book's main page at `http://www.apress.com`. If you find an error that hasn't already been reported, please let us know.

The Apress website acts as a focus for other information and support, including the code from all Apress books, sample chapters, previews of forthcoming titles, and articles on related topics.

Contacting the Author

You can contact Michael Coles via email at `admin@geocodenet.com`.

CHAPTER 1

■■■

The Role of T-SQL

The history of Structured Query Language (SQL), and its direct descendant Transact-SQL (T-SQL), all began in 1970 when Dr. E. F. Codd published his influential paper, "A Relational Model of Data for Large Shared Data Banks," in the *Communications of the ACM* by the Association for Computing Machinery (ACM). In this paper Dr. Codd introduced the definitive standard for relational databases. IBM went on to create the first relational database management system, known as System R. IBM introduced the Structured English Query Language (SEQUEL, as it was known at the time) to interact with this early database to store, modify, and retrieve data. The name was subsequently changed from SEQUEL to the now-common SQL because of a trademark issue. In 1987 the American National Standards Institute (ANSI) approved a standard for SQL known as the ANSI SQL-86 standard.

Microsoft entered the relational database management system market in 1989 through a joint venture with Sybase and Ashton-Tate (of dBase fame) to create and market SQL Server. Since then, Microsoft, Sybase, and Ashton-Tate have gone their separate ways. Microsoft has introduced several upgrades to Microsoft SQL Server, including Microsoft SQL Server versions 4.2, 4.21, 6.0, 6.5, 7.0, 2000, and 2005. Through it all, T-SQL has remained SQL Server's native tongue and the centerpiece of SQL Server development.

Although based on the ANSI SQL-92 standard, T-SQL has integrated several ANSI SQL:1999 standard features. In addition, T-SQL includes advanced procedural extensions that go above and beyond the ANSI standards. These extensions include control-of-flow statements, transaction control, error handling, SQLCLR integration, and more. With the release of SQL Server 2005, Microsoft has expanded T-SQL to include several new features to support SQLCLR integration, data encryption and decryption, Extensible Markup Language (XML) support, and a wide assortment of additional functionality not available in previous SQL Server releases.

This chapter begins with a discussion of T-SQL ANSI compatibility, then describes declarative programming languages, and concludes with tips to help you create your own T-SQL programming style that will help make maintaining and debugging your T-SQL code as easy as possible.

ANSI SQL Compatibility

Many people see portability as the main advantage of the ANSI SQL standard. Theoretically, you should be able to take your ANSI-compliant SQL Server query and run it without change on Oracle, DB2, or any other SQL-based relational database management system (RDBMS). The key word here is *theoretically*. In practice, enough differences exist between RDBMS platforms to prevent this from being practical. Every vendor implements different ANSI-compliant features, and every vendor provides their own proprietary extensions.

What ANSI compatibility does provide, however, is portability of knowledge. A strong knowledge of the ANSI SQL standard is an excellent starting point for porting SQL code from one RDBMS to another, or even for porting code from one version of SQL Server to the next. An ANSI-compliant LEFT OUTER JOIN, for example, will have similar syntax and produce similar results on any ANSI-compliant RDBMS. The ANSI standard also defines the format and operation of several key functions such as COUNT() and SUM(), which are guaranteed to have similar syntax and produce similar results on any ANSI-compliant RDBMS.

Imperative vs. Declarative Languages

SQL is different from many common programming languages such as C++ and Visual Basic because it is a declarative language. Languages such as C++, Visual Basic, C#, and even assembler are imperative languages. The imperative language model requires the user to determine what the end result should be and also tell the computer step by step how to achieve that result. It's analogous to asking a cab driver to drive you to the airport and then giving him turn-by-turn directions to get there.

Consider Listing 1-1, which is a simple C# code snippet that reads in a flat file of names and displays them on the screen.

Listing 1-1. *C# Snippet to Read a Flat File*

```
StreamReader sr = new StreamReader("Person_Contact.txt");
string FirstName = null;
while ((FirstName = sr.ReadLine()) != null) {
    Console.WriteLine(s);
}
sr.Dispose();
```

The example performs the following functions in an orderly fashion:

1. The code explicitly opens the storage for input (in this example a flat file is used as a "database").

2. It then reads in each record (one record per line), explicitly checking for the end of file.

3. As it reads the data, the code returns each record for display using `Console.WriteLine()`.

4. And finally it closes and disposes of the connection to the data file.

Consider what happens when you want to add or delete a name from the flat-file "database." In those cases, you must write routines to explicitly reorganize all the data in the file so it maintains proper ordering. If you want the names to be listed and retrieved in alphabetical (or any other) order, you must code sort routines as well. Any type of additional processing on the data requires that you implement separate procedural routines.

Declarative languages such as SQL, on the other hand, let you frame problems in terms of the end result. All you have to do is describe what you want from SQL Server via a query and trust the database engine to deliver the correct result as efficiently as possible. To continue the cab driver analogy from earlier, in a declarative language you would tell the cab driver to take you to the airport and then trust that he knows the best route. The SQL equivalent of the C# code in Listing 1-1 might look something like Listing 1-2.

Listing 1-2. *SQL Query to Retrieve Names from a Table*

```
SELECT FirstName
FROM Person.Contact;
```

■**Tip** Unless otherwise specified, you can run all the T-SQL samples in this book in the AdventureWorks sample database using SQL Server Management Studio or SQLCMD.

To sort your data, you can simply add an `ORDER BY` clause to the `SELECT` query in Listing 1-2. With properly designed and indexed tables, SQL Server can automatically reorganize your data for efficient retrieval after you insert, update, or delete rows.

T-SQL includes extensions that allow you to override SQL Server's declarative syntax. In fact, you could rewrite the previous example as a cursor to closely mimic the C# sample code. More often than not, however, trying to force the one-row-at-a-time imperative model on SQL Server hurts performance and makes simple projects more complex than they need to be.

One of the great features of SQL Server is that you can invoke its power, in its native language, from nearly any other programming language. In .NET you can connect and issue SQL queries and T-SQL statements to SQL Server via the `System.Data.SqlClient` namespace, which I will discuss further in Chapter 15. This gives you the opportunity to combine SQL's declarative syntax with the strict control of an imperative language.

Elements of Style

Selecting a particular style and using it consistently helps with debugging and code maintenance. The following sections contain some general recommendations to make your T-SQL code easy to read, debug, and maintain.

Whitespace Is Your Friend

SQL Server ignores extra whitespace between keywords and identifiers in SQL queries and statements. A single statement or query can include extra spaces, can contain tab characters, and can even extend across several lines. You can use this knowledge to great advantage. Consider Listing 1-3, which is adapted from the `HumanResources.vEmployee` view in the AdventureWorks database.

Listing 1-3. *HumanResources.vEmployee View from the AdventureWorks Database*

```
SELECT [HumanResources].[Employee].[EmployeeID], [Person].[Contact].[Title],
[Person].[Contact].[FirstName], [Person].[Contact].[MiddleName],
[Person].[Contact].[LastName], [Person].[Contact].[Suffix],
[HumanResources].[Employee].[Title] AS [JobTitle], [Person].[Contact].[Phone],
[Person].[Contact].[EmailAddress], [Person].[Contact].[EmailPromotion],
[Person].[Address].[AddressLine1], [Person].[Address].[AddressLine2],
[Person].[Address].[City], [Person].[StateProvince].[Name] AS [StateProvinceName],
[Person].[Address].[PostalCode], [Person].[CountryRegion].[Name] AS
[CountryRegionName], [Person].[Contact].[AdditionalContactInfo] FROM
[HumanResources].[Employee] INNER JOIN [Person].[Contact] ON
[Person].[Contact].[ContactID] = [HumanResources].[Employee].[ContactID] INNER JOIN
[HumanResources].[EmployeeAddress] ON [HumanResources].[Employee].[EmployeeID] =
[HumanResources].[EmployeeAddress].[EmployeeID] INNER JOIN [Person].[Address] ON
[HumanResources].[EmployeeAddress].[AddressID] = [Person].[Address].[AddressID]
```

```
INNER JOIN [Person].[StateProvince] ON [Person].[StateProvince].[StateProvinceID] =
[Person].[Address].[StateProvinceID] INNER JOIN [Person].[CountryRegion] ON
[Person].[CountryRegion].[CountryRegionCode] =
[Person].[StateProvince].[CountryRegionCode]
```

This query will run and return the correct result, but it's hard to read. You can use whitespace and table aliases to generate a version that is much easier on the eyes, as demonstrated in Listing 1-4.

Listing 1-4. *HumanResources.vEmployee View Reformatted for Readability*

```
SELECT e.EmployeeID,
    c.Title,
    c.FirstName,
    c.MiddleName,
    c.LastName,
    c.Suffix,
    e.Title AS JobTitle,
    c.Phone,
    c.EmailAddress,
    c.EmailPromotion,
    a.AddressLine1,
    a.AddressLine2,
    a.City,
    sp.Name AS StateProvinceName,
    a.PostalCode,
    cr.Name AS CountryRegionName,
    c.AdditionalContactInfo
FROM HumanResources.Employee e
INNER JOIN Person.Contact c
    ON c.ContactID = e.ContactID
INNER JOIN HumanResources.EmployeeAddress ea
    ON e.EmployeeID = ea.EmployeeID
INNER JOIN Person.Address a
    ON ea.AddressID = a.AddressID
INNER JOIN Person.StateProvince sp
    ON sp.StateProvinceID = a.StateProvinceID
INNER JOIN Person.CountryRegion cr
    ON cr.CountryRegionCode = sp.CountryRegionCode;
```

Notice the ON keywords are indented, associating them visually with the INNER JOIN operators directly before them in the listing. The column names on the lines directly after the SELECT keyword are also indented, associating them visually with the SELECT keyword. This particular style is useful in helping visually break up a query into sections. The personal style you decide upon might differ from this one, but once you have decided on a standard indentation style, be sure to apply it consistently throughout your code.

Code that is easy to read is, by default, easier to debug and maintain. The second version uses table aliases, plenty of whitespace, and the semicolon (;) terminator to mark the end of the SELECT statement in order to make the code more easily readable. Although not always required, it is a good idea to get into the habit of using the terminating semicolon in your SQL queries.

■**Note** Semicolons are required terminators for some statements in SQL Server 2005. Instead of trying to remember all the special cases where they are or aren't required, it is a good idea to get into the habit of using the semicolon statement terminator throughout your T-SQL code. You might notice the use of semicolon terminators in all the examples in this book.

Naming Conventions

SQL Server allows you to name your database objects, such as tables, views, procedures, and so on, using just about any combination of up to 128 characters (116 characters for local temporary table names) as long as you enclose them in double quotes (") or brackets ([ ]). Just because you *can*, however, doesn't necessarily mean you *should*. Many of the allowed characters are hard to differentiate from other similar-looking characters, and some might not port well to other platforms. The following suggestions will help you avoid potential problems:

- Use alphabetic characters (A–Z, a–z, and Unicode Standard 3.2 letters) for the first character of your identifiers. The obvious exceptions are SQL Server variable names that start with the at sign (@), temporary tables and procedures that start with the number sign (#), and global temporary tables and procedures that begin with the double number sign (##).

- Many built-in T-SQL functions and system variables have names that begin with a double at sign (@@), such as @@ERROR and @@IDENTITY. To avoid confusion and possible conflicts, don't use a leading double at sign to name your identifiers.

- Restrict the remaining characters in your identifiers to alphabetic characters (A–Z, a–z, and Unicode Standard 3.2 letters), numeric digits (0–9), and the underscore character (_). The dollar sign ($) character, while allowed, is not advisable.

- Avoid embedded spaces, punctuation marks (other than the underscore character), and other special characters in your identifiers.

- Avoid using SQL Server 2005 reserved keywords as identifiers (Appendix A lists the SQL Server reserved keywords).

- Limit the length of your identifiers. Thirty-two characters or less is a reasonable limit while not being overly restrictive. Much more than that becomes cumbersome to type and can hurt your code readability.

Finally, to make your code more readable, select a capitalization style for your identifiers and code, and use it consistently. My preference is to fully capitalize T-SQL keywords and use mixed case and underscore characters to visually "break up" identifiers into easily readable words. Using all capital characters or inconsistently applying mixed case to code and identifiers can make your code illegible and hard to maintain. Consider the example query in Listing 1-5.

Listing 1-5. *All-Capital SELECT Query*

```
SELECT I.CUSTOMERID, C.TITLE, C.FIRSTNAME, C.MIDDLENAME,
    C.LASTNAME, C.SUFFIX, C.PHONE, C.EMAILADDRESS,
    C.EMAILPROMOTION
FROM SALES.INDIVIDUAL I
INNER JOIN PERSON.CONTACT C
    ON C.CONTACTID = I.CONTACTID
INNER JOIN SALES.CUSTOMERADDRESS CA
    ON CA.CUSTOMERID = I.CUSTOMERID;
```

The all-capital version is difficult to read. It's hard to tell the SQL keywords from the column and table names at a glance. Compound words for column and table names are not easily identified. Basically, your eyes work a lot harder to read this query than they should have to, which makes otherwise simple maintenance tasks more difficult. Reformatting the code and identifiers makes this query much easier on the eyes, as Listing 1-6 demonstrates.

Listing 1-6. *Reformatted "Easy-on-the-Eyes" Query*

```
SELECT i.CustomerID,
    c.Title,
    c.FirstName,
    c.MiddleName,
    c.LastName,
    c.Suffix,
    c.Phone,
    c.EmailAddress,
    c.EmailPromotion
FROM Sales.Individual i
INNER JOIN Person.Contact c
    ON c.ContactID = i.ContactID
INNER JOIN Sales.CustomerAddress ca
    ON ca.CustomerID = i.CustomerID;
```

The use of all capitals for the keywords in the second version makes them stand out from the mixed-case table and column names. Likewise, the mixed-case column and table names make the compound word names easy to recognize. The net effect is that the code is easier to read, which makes it easier to debug and maintain. Consistent use of good formatting habits helps keep trivial changes trivial and makes complex changes easier.

One Entry, One Exit

When writing stored procedures (SPs) and user-defined functions (UDFs), it's good programming practice to use the "one entry, one exit" rule. SPs and UDFs should have a single entry point and a single exit point (RETURN statement). The following stored procedure retrieves the ContactTypeID number from the AdventureWorks Person.ContactType table for the ContactType name passed into it. If no ContactType exists with the name passed in, a new one is created, and the newly created ContactTypeID is passed back. Listing 1-7 demonstrates this simple procedure with one entry point and several exit points.

Listing 1-7. *Stored Procedure Example with One Entry, Multiple Exits*

```
CREATE PROCEDURE dbo.GetOrAdd_ContactType
(
    @Name NVARCHAR(50),
    @ContactTypeID INT OUTPUT
)
AS
    DECLARE @Err_Code AS INT;
    SELECT @Err_Code = 0;

    SELECT @ContactTypeID = ContactTypeID
    FROM Person.ContactType
    WHERE [Name] = @Name;

    IF @ContactTypeID IS NOT NULL
        RETURN;              -- Exit 1: if the ContactType exists

    INSERT
    INTO Person.ContactType ([Name], ModifiedDate)
    SELECT @Name, CURRENT_TIMESTAMP;

    SELECT @Err_Code = @@error;
    IF @Err_Code <> 0
        RETURN @Err_Code;    -- Exit 2: if there is an error on INSERT

    SELECT @ContactTypeID = SCOPE_IDENTITY();

    RETURN @Err_Code;        -- Exit 3: after successful INSERT
GO
```

Listing 1-8 updates the previous example to give it a single entry point and a single exit point, making the logic easier to follow.

Listing 1-8. *Stored Procedure with One Entry, One Exit*

```
CREATE PROCEDURE dbo.GetOrAdd_ContactType
(
    @Name NVARCHAR(50),
    @ContactTypeID INT OUTPUT
)
```

```
AS
    DECLARE @Err_Code AS INT;
    SELECT @Err_Code = 0;

    SELECT @ContactTypeID = ContactTypeID
    FROM Person.ContactType
    WHERE [Name] = @Name;

    IF @ContactTypeID IS NULL
    BEGIN
        INSERT
        INTO Person.ContactType ([Name], ModifiedDate)
        SELECT @Name, CURRENT_TIMESTAMP;

        SELECT @Err_Code = @@error;
        IF @Err_Code = 0          -- If there's an error, skip next
            SELECT @ContactTypeID = SCOPE_IDENTITY();
    END
    RETURN @Err_Code;   -- Single exit point
GO
```

This rule also applies to looping structures, which you implement via the WHILE statement in T-SQL. Avoid using the WHILE loop's CONTINUE and BREAK statements and the GOTO statement; these statements lead to old-fashioned, difficult-to-maintain "spaghetti code."

SQL-92 Syntax Outer Joins

Microsoft has been warning us for a long time, and now it has finally gone and done it. SQL Server 2005 finally eliminates the old-style *= and =* outer join operators. Queries like the one in Listing 1-9 won't work with SQL Server 2005.

Listing 1-9. *Query Using Old-Style Join Operators*

```
SELECT o.name
FROM sys.objects o,
     sys.views v
WHERE o.object_id *= v.object_id;
```

SQL responds to this query with one of the most elaborate error messages ever seen in a Microsoft product:

```
Msg 4147, Level 15, State 1, Line 4
The query uses non-ANSI outer join operators ("*=" or "=*"). To run this query
without modification, please set the compatibility level for current database
to 80 or lower, using stored procedure sp_dbcmptlevel. It is strongly
recommended to rewrite the query using ANSI outer join operators (LEFT OUTER
JOIN, RIGHT OUTER JOIN). In the future versions of SQL Server, non-ANSI join
operators will not be supported even in backward-compatibility modes.
```

As the error message suggests, you can use the sp_dbcmptlevel stored procedure to revert the database compatibility to 80 (SQL Server 2000) to circumvent the problem. As the error message also suggests, the old-style join operators will not be supported in future versions, even in backward-compatibility mode. If you do have old-style joins in your T-SQL code, the best course of action is to convert them to ANSI SQL standard joins as soon as possible. Listing 1-10 updates the previous query to use the current ANSI standard.

Listing 1-10. *ANSI SQL-92 Standard Join Syntax*

```
SELECT o.name
FROM sys.objects o
LEFT JOIN sys.views v
    ON o.object_id = v.object_id;
```

■**Note** You can use sp_dbcmptlevel to revert various SQL Server behaviors to a version prior to SQL Server 2000. Use a compatibility level of 80 for SQL Server 2000, 70 for SQL Server 7.0, 65 for SQL Server 6.5, and 60 for SQL Server 6.0. You should avoid this unless you have a "compelling reason" for reverting to old compatibility modes.

This book uses the ANSI SQL-92 syntax joins in its examples.

Avoid SELECT *

Consider the SELECT * style of querying. In a SELECT clause, the asterisk (*) is a shorthand way of specifying that all columns in a table should be returned. Although SELECT * is a handy tool for ad hoc querying of tables during development and debugging, you should not use it in a production system. One reason to avoid this method of querying is to minimize the amount of data retrieved with each call. SELECT * retrieves all columns, whether or not they are needed by the higher-level applications. For queries that return a large number of rows, even one or two extraneous columns can waste a lot of resources.

Also, if the underlying table or view is altered, your front-end application can receive extra columns in, or columns could be missing from, the result set returned, causing errors that can be hard to locate. By specifying the column names, your front-end application can be assured that only the required columns are returned by a query and that errors caused by missing columns will be easier to locate.

Initializing Variables

When you create stored procedures, user-defined functions, or any script that uses T-SQL user variables, you should initialize those variables before the first use. Unlike other programming languages that guarantee newly declared variables will be initialized to 0 or an empty string (depending on their data types), T-SQL guarantees only that newly declared variables will be initialized to NULL. Consider the code snippet shown in Listing 1-11.

Listing 1-11. *Sample Code Using an Uninitialized Variable*

```
DECLARE @i INT;
SELECT @i = @i + 5;
SELECT @i;
```

The result is NULL, a shock if you were expecting 5. Expecting SQL Server to initialize numeric variables to 0 (like @i in the previous example), or an empty string, will result in bugs that can be extremely difficult to locate in your T-SQL code. To avoid these problems, always explicitly initialize your variables after declaration, as demonstrated in Listing 1-12.

Listing 1-12. *Sample Code Using an Initialized Variable*

```
DECLARE @i INT;
SELECT @i = 0;      -- Added this statement to initialize @i to 0
SELECT @i = @i + 5;
SELECT @i;
```

Summary

This chapter introduced T-SQL. The topics discussed include ANSI SQL:1999 compatibility in SQL Server 2005 and the difference between imperative and declarative languages. You also looked at SQL programming style considerations and how they can make your T-SQL code easy to debug and maintain.

The next chapter provides an overview of the new and improved tools available "out of the box" for developers. Specifically, Chapter 2 will discuss the SQLCMD replacement for osql, as well as SQL Server Management Studio, SQL Server 2005 Books Online, and some of the other tools available for making writing, editing, testing, and debugging easier and faster than ever.

CHAPTER 2

Tools of the Trade

SQL Server 2005 comes with a host of tools and utilities to make development easier. Some of the most important tools for developers include the following:

- The SQLCMD utility

- Microsoft SQL Server Management Studio

- SQL Server 2005 Books Online

This chapter discusses these tools as well as the AdventureWorks sample database, which I use in the examples in this book. Along the way, this chapter will also cover some of the SQL Server connectivity features of Visual Studio 2005.

SQLCMD Utility

The SQLCMD utility is an update to the SQL 2000 `osql` command-line utility. You can use it to execute batches of T-SQL statements from script files, individual queries or batches of queries in interactive mode, or individual queries from the command line.

Command-Line Options

You can run SQLCMD from the command line with the following syntax:

```
sqlcmd [ [-U login_id ] [-P password ] | [-E] ]
    [-S server [\instance] ] [-d db_name] [-H workstation]
    [-l timeout] [-t timeout] [-h headers] [-s column_separator] [-w column_width]
    [-a packet_size] [-I] [-L[c] ] [-W] [-r[0|1]]
    [-q "query"] [-Q "query"] [-c batch_term] [-e]
    [-m error_level] [-V severity_level] [-b]
    [-i input_file [,input_file₂ [, ...] ] ] [-o output_file] [-u]
    [-v var = "value" [,var₂ = "value₂"] [,...] ] [-X[1] ] [-x] [-?]
```

```
[-z new_password] [-Z new_password]
[-f codepage | i:in_codepage [,o:out_codepage] ]
[-k[1|2] ] [-y display_width] [-Y display_width] [-p[1] ] [-R] [-A]
```

The command-line switches are case-sensitive. Table 2-1 lists the SQLCMD command-line options.

Table 2-1. *SQLCMD Command-Line Options*

Option	Description
-?	The -? option displays the SQLCMD help/syntax screen.
-A	The -A option tells SQLCMD to log in to SQL Server with a Dedicated Administrator Connection. This type of connection is usually used for troubleshooting.
-a packet_size	The -a option requests communications with a specific packet size. The default is 4096. packet_size must be from 512 to 32767.
-b	The -b option specifies that SQLCMD exits on an error and returns an ERRORLEVEL value to the operating system. When this option is set, a SQL error of severity 11 or greater will return an ERRORLEVEL of 1; an error or message of severity 10 or less will return an ERRORLEVEL of 0. If the -V option is also used, SQLCMD will report only the errors with a severity greater than or equal to the severity_level (level 11 or greater) specified with the -V option.
-c batch_term	The -c option specifies the batch terminator. By default it is the GO keyword. Avoid using special characters and reserved words as the batch terminator.
-d db_name	The -d option specifies the database to use after SQLCMD connects to SQL Server. Alternatively, you can set this option via the SQLCMDDBNAME environment variable. If the database specified does not exist, SQLCMD exits with an error.
-E	The -E option uses a trusted connection (Windows Authentication mode) to connect to SQL Server. This option ignores the SQLCMDUSER and SQLCMDPASSWORD environment variables, and you cannot use it with the -U and -P options.
-e	The -e option prints (echoes) input scripts to the standard output device (usually the screen by default).

Option	Description
-f *codepage* ∣ i:*in_codepage* [,o:*out_codepage*]	The -f option specifies the code pages for input and output. If i: is specified, the *in_codepage* is the input code page. If o: is specified, *out_codepage* is the output code page. If i: and o: are not specified, *codepage* supplied is the input and output code pages. To specify code pages, use their numeric identifier. The following code pages are supported by SQL Server 2005:

Code Page Number	Code Page Name
1258	Vietnamese
1257	Baltic
1256	Arabic
1255	Hebrew
1254	Turkish
1253	Greek
1252	Latin1 (ANSI)
1251	Cyrillic
1250	Central European
950	Chinese(Traditional)
949	Korean
936	Chinese (Simplified)
932	Japanese
874	Thai
850	Multilingual (MS-DOS Latin1)
437	MS-DOS U.S. English

Option	Description
-H *workstation*	The -H option sets the workstation name. You can use -H to differentiate between sessions with commands such as sp_who.
-h *headers*	The -h option specifies the number of rows of data to print before a new column header is generated. The value must be from −1 (no headers) to 2147483647. The default value of 0 prints headings once for each set of results.
-I	The -I option sets the connection QUOTED_IDENTIFIER option to ON. Turning the QUOTED_IDENTIFIER option on makes SQL Server follow the ANSI SQL-92 rules for quoted identifiers. This option is set to OFF by default.
-i *input_file* [,*input_file2*] [,...]	The -i option specifies SQLCMD should use files that contain batches of T-SQL statements for input. The files are processed in order from left to right. If any of the files don't exist, SQLCMD exits with an error. You can use the GO batch terminator inside your SQL script files.
-k [1∣2]	The -k option removes control characters from the output. If 1 is specified, control characters are replaced one for one with spaces. If 2 is specified, consecutive control characters are replaced with a single space.

Continued

Table 2-1. *Continued*

Option	Description
-L [c]	The -L option returns a listing of available SQL Server machines on the network and local computer. If the -Lc format is used, a "clean" listing is returned without heading information. The listing is limited to a maximum of 3,000 servers. Note that because of the way SQL Server broadcasts to gather server information, any servers that don't respond in a timely manner will not be included in the list. You cannot use the -L option with other options.
-l *timeout*	The -l option specifies the login timeout. The timeout value must be from 0 to 65534. The default value is 8 seconds, and a value of 0 is no timeout (infinite).
-m *error_level*	The -m option defines an error message customization level. Only errors with a severity greater than the specified level are displayed. If *error_level* is -1, all messages are returned, even informational messages.
-o *output_file*	-o specifies the file to which SQLCMD should direct output. If -o is not specified, SQLCMD defaults to standard output (usually the screen).
-P *password*	The -P option specifies a password to log in to SQL Server when using SQL Authentication mode. If -P is omitted, SQLCMD looks for the SQLCMDPASSWORD environment variable to get the password to log in. If the SQLCMDPASSWORD environment variable isn't found, SQLCMD will prompt you for the password to log in using SQL Authentication mode. If neither -P nor -U is specified and the corresponding environment variables aren't set, SQLCMD will attempt to log in using Windows Authentication mode.
-p [1]	The -p option prints performance statistics for each result set. Specifying 1 produces colon-separated output.
-Q *"query"* -q *"query"*	The -Q and -q options both execute a SQL query/command from the command line. -q remains in SQLCMD after query completion. -Q exits SQLCMD after completion.
-R	The -R option specifies client regional settings for currency and date/time formatting.
-r [0|1]	The -r option redirects error message output to the standard error output device, the monitor by default. If 1 is specified, all error messages and informational messages are redirected. If 0 or no number is specified, only error messages with a severity of 11 or greater are redirected. The redirection does not work with the -o option; it does work if standard output is redirected with the Windows command-line redirector (>).
-S *server* [*instance*]	The -S option specifies the SQL Server *server* or named *instance* to which SQLCMD should connect. If this option is not specified, SQLCMD connects to the default SQL Server instance on the local machine.

Option	Description
-s *column_separator*	The -s option sets the column separator character. By default the column separator is a space character. *separator* can be enclosed in quotes, which is useful if you want to use a character that the operating system recognizes as a special character such as the greater-than sign (>).
-t *timeout*	The -t option specifies the SQL query/command timeout in seconds. The timeout value must be from 0 to 65535. If -t is not specified or if it is set to 0, queries/commands do not time out.
-U *login_id*	The -U option specifies the user login ID to log in to SQL Server using SQL Authentication mode. If the -U option is omitted, SQLCMD looks for the SQLCMDUSER environment variable to get the login password. If the -U option is omitted, SQLCMD attempts to use the current user's Windows login name to log in.
-u	The -u option specifies that the output of SQLCMD will be in Unicode format. Use this option with the -o option.
-V *severity_level*	The -V option specifies the lowest severity level that SQLCMD reports back. Errors and messages of severity less than *severity_level* are reported as 0. *severity_level* must be from 1 to 25. In a command-line batch file, -V returns the severity level of any SQL Server errors encountered via the ERRORLEVEL so your batch file can take appropriate action.
-v *var* = *"value"* [, *var2* = *"value2"*] [, ...]]	The -v option sets scripting variables that SQLCMD can use in your scripts to the specified values. I describe scripting variables later in this chapter.
-W	The -W option removes trailing spaces from a column. You can use this option with the -s option when preparing data that is to be exported to another application. You cannot use -W in conjunction with the -Y or -y option.
-w *column_width*	The -w option specifies screen width for output. The width must be from 9 to 65535. The default of 0 is equivalent to the width of the output device. For screen output, the default is the width of the screen. For files, the default width is unlimited.
-X [1]	The -X option disables options that can compromise security in batch files. Specifically, the -X option does the following: • Disables the SQLCMD :!! and :ED commands. • Prevents SQLCMD from using operating system environment variables. • Disables the SQLCMD start-up script. If a disabled command is encountered, SQLCMD issues a warning and continues processing. If the optional 1 is specified with the -X option, SQLCMD exits with an error when a disabled command is encountered. I describe SQLCMD commands, script variables, environment variables, and the start-up script in more detail later in this chapter.
-x	The -x option forces SQLCMD to ignore scripting variables.

Continued

Table 2-1. *Continued*

Option	Description
-Y *display_width*	The -Y option limits the number of characters returned for the char, nchar, varchar (8000 bytes or less), nvarchar (4000 bytes or less), and sql_variant data types.
-y *display_width*	The -y option limits the number of characters returned for variable-length data types such as varchar(max), varbinary(max), xml, text, and fixed-length or variable-length user-defined types (UDTs).
-Z *new_password* -z *new_password*	When used with SQL Authentication (the -U and -P options), the -z and -Z options change the SQL login password. If the -P option is not specified, SQLCMD will prompt you for the current password. -z changes the password and enters interactive mode. -Z exits SQLCMD immediately after the password is changed.

SQLCMD Scripting Variables

SQLCMD has several built-in scripting variables. These SQLCMD scripting variables control various aspects of SQLCMD functionality, such as the login timeout and output width settings. You can use many of these SQLCMD scripting variables in place of, or in conjunction with, various SQLCMD command-line options. When run, SQLCMD performs the following start-up actions:

1. It looks for the appropriate settings on the command line and implicitly sets the appropriate scripting variables based on the command-line switches.

2. SQLCMD then reads the Windows environment settings and sets the SQLCMD scripting variables to the appropriate values, if available.

3. Finally, the SQLCMD initialization/start-up script is run, and :setvar commands in the script set SQLCMD scripting variables as appropriate.

■**Note** The -X and -x options disable start-up script execution and environment variable access, respectively. -x also prevents SQLCMD from dynamically replacing scripting variable references in your code with the appropriate values. This is a feature designed for secure environments where scripting variable usage could compromise security.

Table 2-2 lists the SQLCMD scripting variables, their defaults, and the associated command-line switches.

Table 2-2. *SQLCMD Scripting Variables*

Name	Default	Read/Write	Description
SQLCMDUSER	*<empty string>*	Read-only	SQL Server login username. See the -U command-line switch.
SQLCMDPASSWORD	*<empty string>*	N/A	SQL Server login password. See the -P command-line switch.
SQLCMDSERVER	*server name*	Read-only	SQL Server/instance name. See the -S command-line switch.
SQLCMDWORKSTATION	*<empty string>*	Read-only	SQL Server workstation name. See the -H command-line switch.
SQLCMDDBNAME	*<empty string>*	Read-only	Default database name. See the -d command-line switch.
SQLCMDLOGINTIMEOUT	8	Read/write	Login timeout setting (in secs). See the -l command-line switch.
SQLCMDSTATTIMEOUT	0	Read/write	Query/command timeout setting (in secs). See the -t command-line switch.
SQLCMDHEADERS	0	Read/write	Number of lines to print between result-set headers. See the -h command-line switch.
SQLCMDCOLSEP	*<space>*	Read/write	Column separator character. See the -s command-line switch.
SQLCMDCOLWIDTH	0	Read/write	Output column width. See the -w command-line switch.
SQLCMDPACKETSIZE	4096	Read-only	Packet size being used for SQL communications. See the -a command-line switch.
SQLCMDERRORLEVEL	0	Read/write	Level of error message customization. See the -m command-line switch.
SQLCMDMAXVARTYPEWIDTH	0	Read/write	Variable-length data type display limit. See the -y command-line switch.
SQLCMDMAXFIXEDTYPEWIDTH	256	Read/write	Fixed-width data type display limit. See the -Y command-line switch.
SQLCMDINI	*<empty string>*	Read-only	SQLCMD start-up script.

■**Note** You can set the SQLCMD scripting variables specified as read-only via environment variables (Windows SET command) or via SQLCMD command-line options. You cannot alter them from within a SQLCMD script, however.

You can reference scripting variables set by the command-line -v switch or by the SQLCMD :setvar command (discussed in the next section), the Windows environment variables, or the built-in SQLCMD scripting variables from within SQLCMD scripts. The format to access all these variables is the same: $(*variable_name*). SQLCMD replaces your scripting variables with their respective values during script execution. Here are a few examples:

```
-- Windows environment variable
SELECT '$(PATH)';
```

```
-- SQLCMD scripting variable
SELECT '$(SQLCMDSERVER)';
```

```
-- Command-line scripting variable -v COLVAR= "Name" switch
SELECT $(COLVAR)
FROM Sys.Tables;
```

Because scripting variables are replaced in a script "wholesale," some organizations might consider their use a security risk because of the possibility of SQL Injection–style attacks. The -x command-line option turns this feature off.

The SQLCMDINI scripting variable specifies the SQLCMD start-up script. This script is run every time SQLCMD begins. The start-up script is useful for setting scripting variables with the :setvar command, setting initial T-SQL options such as QUOTED_IDENTIFIERS or ANSI_PADDING, and performing any necessary database tasks before other scripts are run.

SQLCMD Commands

In addition to T-SQL statements, SQLCMD has several commands specific to the application (see Table 2-3). Except for the batch terminator GO, all SQLCMD commands begin with a colon (:).

Table 2-3. *SQLCMD Commands*

Command	Description
:!! *command*	The :!! command invokes the command shell. It executes the specified operating system command in the command shell.
:CONNECT *server* [*instance*] [-l *timeout*] [-U *user* [-P *password*]]	The :CONNECT command connects to a SQL Server instance. The server name (*server*) and instance name (*instance*) are specified in the command. When :CONNECT is executed, the current connection is closed. You can use the following options with the :CONNECT command: • The -l option specifies the login timeout (specified in seconds, 0 = no timeout). • The -U option specifies the SQL Authentication username. • The -P option specifies the SQL Authentication password.
:ED	The :ED command starts the text editor to edit the current batch or the last executed batch. The SQLCMDEDITOR environment variable defines the application used as the SQLCMD editor. The default is the Windows EDIT utility.
:ERROR *destination*	The :ERROR command redirects error messages to the specified *destination*. *Destination* can be a filename, STDOUT for standard output, or STDERR for standard error output.
:EXIT [() I (*query*)]	The :EXIT command has three forms: :EXIT alone immediately exits without executing the batch and with no return code. :EXIT() executes the current batch and exits with no return code. :EXIT(*query*) executes the batch, including the query specified, and returns the value of the first value of the first result row of the query as a 4-byte integer to the operating system.
:HELP	The help command displays a list of SQLCMD commands.
GO [*n*]	GO is the batch terminator. The GO batch terminator executes the statements in the cache. If *n* is specified, GO will execute the statement *n* times.
:LIST	The :LIST list command lists the contents of the current batch of statements in the statement cache.
:LISTVAR	The :LISTVAR command lists all the SQLCMD scripting variables (that have been set) and their current values.
:ON ERROR *action*	The :ON ERROR command specifies the action SQLCMD should take when an error is encountered. action can be one of two values: EXIT stops processing and exits, returning the appropriate error code. IGNORE disregards the error and continues processing.

Continued

Table 2-3. *Continued*

Command	Description
:OUT *destination*	The :OUT command redirects output to the specified destination. *Destination* can be a filename, STDOUT for standard output, or STDERR for standard error output. Output is sent to STDOUT by default.
:PERFTRACE *destination*	The :PERFTRACE command redirects performance trace/timing information to the specified *destination*. *Destination* can be a filename, STDOUT for standard output, or STDERR for standard error output. Trace information is sent to STDOUT by default.
:QUIT	The :QUIT command quits SQLCMD immediately.
:R *filename*	The :R command reads in the contents of the specified file and appends to the statement cache.
:RESET	The :RESET command resets/clears the statement cache.
:SERVERLIST	The :SERVERLIST command lists all SQL Servers on the local machine and servers broadcasting on the local network. If SQLCMD doesn't receive timely responses from all servers on the network, some may not be listed.
:SETVAR *var* [*value*]	The :SETVAR command allows you to set or remove SQLCMD scripting variables. To remove a SQLCMD scripting variable, use the :SETVAR *var* format. To set a SQLCMD scripting variable to a value, use the :SETVAR *var value* format.
:XML ON|OFF	The :XML command indicates to SQLCMD that you expect XML output from SQL Server (that is, the SELECT statement's FOR XML clause). Use :XML ON before your SQL batch is run and :XML OFF after the batch has executed (after the GO batch terminator).

■**Tip** For backward compatibility with older osql scripts, you can enter the following commands without a colon prefix: !!, ED, RESET, EXIT, and QUIT. Also, SQLCMD commands are case-insensitive, they must appear at the beginning of a line, and they must be on their own line. A SQLCMD command cannot be followed on the same line by a T-SQL statement or another SQLCMD command.

SQLCMD Interactive

In addition to its command-line and scripting capabilities, SQLCMD can be run interactively. To start an interactive mode session, run SQLCMD with any of the previous options that do not exit immediately on completion.

■**Note** SQLCMD options such as -Q, -i, -Z, and -? exit immediately on completion. You cannot start an interactive SQLCMD session if you specify any of these command-line options.

During an interactive SQLCMD session, you can run T-SQL queries and commands from the SQLCMD prompt. The interactive screen looks similar to Figure 2-1.

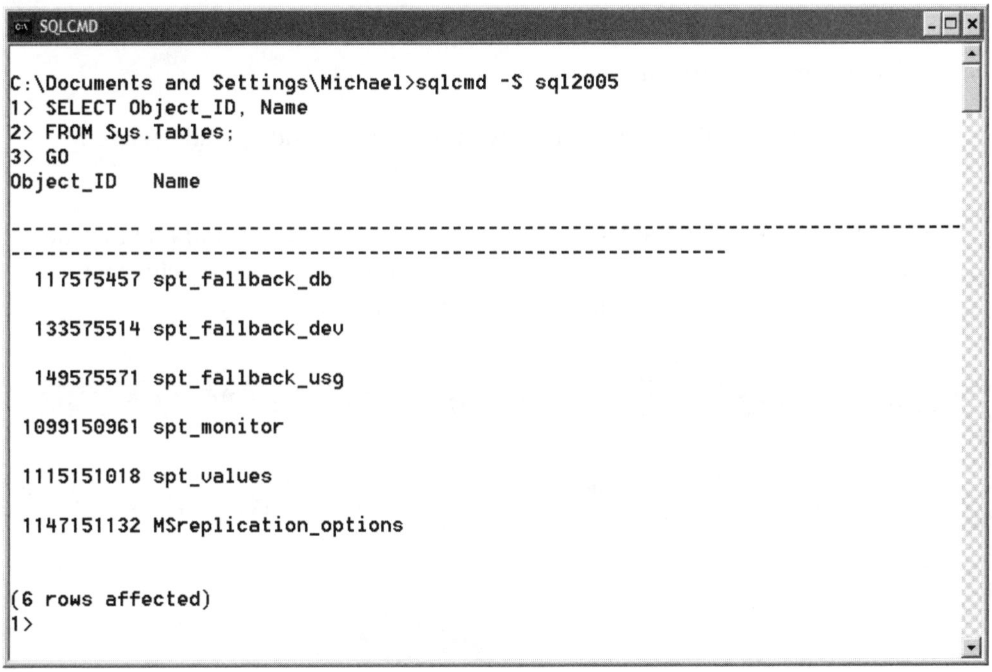

Figure 2-1. *Query run from the SQLCMD interactive prompt*

The SQLCMD prompt indicates the current line number of the batch (1> and so on). You can enter T-SQL statements or SQLCMD commands at the prompt. T-SQL statements are stored in the statement cache as they are entered; SQLCMD commands are executed immediately. Once you have entered a complete batch of T-SQL statements, use the GO batch terminator to process all the statements in the cache.

SQL Server Management Studio

If you're like me, you fire up Enterprise Manager and Query Analyzer in rapid succession whenever you sit down to write T-SQL code on SQL Server 2000. Many SQL Server developers prefer the graphical user interface (GUI) administration and development tools to osql, and on this front SQL Server 2005 doesn't disappoint. Microsoft SQL Server Management Studio (SSMS) was designed as an updated replacement for both Query Analyzer and Enterprise Manager. SSMS offers several features that make development work easier:

- Color coding of scripts

- Context-sensitive help

- Graphical query execution plans

- Project management/code versioning tools

- SQLCMD mode, which allows you to execute SQLCMD and operating system commands

SSMS also includes database and server management features, but I'll limit the discussion of this section to some of the most important developer-specific features. Figure 2-2 shows the SQL Server Management Studio interface.

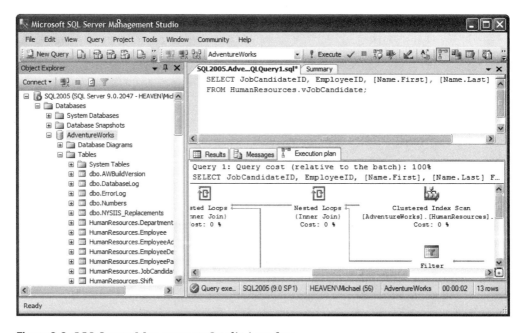

Figure 2-2. *SQL Server Management Studio interface*

Note As of this writing, Query Analyzer version 8.00.2039 (SQL Server 2000 Service Pack 4) can connect to SQL Server 2005. Not all Query Analyzer features are available when connected to SQL Server 2005, though. Earlier versions of Query Analyzer cannot connect to SQL Server 2005, and no versions of Enterprise Manager can.

SSMS Editing Options

SSMS incorporates, and improves on, many of the developer features found in Query Analyzer. You can change the editing options discussed in this section via the Tools ➤ Options menu.

SSMS includes improved script color coding. It allows you to customize the foreground and background colors, font face, size, and style for elements of T-SQL, XML, XSLT, and MDX scripts. Likewise, you can customize just about any feedback that SSMS generates to suit your personal tastes.

You can customize other editing options such as word wrap, line number display, indentation, and tabs for different file types based on file extensions. And like Query Analyzer, you can configure your own keyboard shortcuts in SSMS to execute common T-SQL statements or stored procedures. You can redefine Alt+F1, Ctrl+F1, and all Ctrl+<number> combinations.

By default SSMS displays queries using a tabbed window environment. If you prefer the Query Analyzer style of classic MDI windows, you can switch the environment layout to use that style. You can also change the query results' output style from the default grid output to text or file output.

Context-Sensitive Help

To access context-sensitive help, just highlight the T-SQL or other statement you want help with, and press F1. You can configure Help to use your locally installed copy of SQL Server 2005 Books Online (BOL), or you can specify that Help search MSDN Online for the most up-to-date BOL information. You can add Help pages to your Help Favorites or go directly to the MSDN Community Forums to ask questions with the click of a button.

Help Search rounds out our discussion of the new Help functionality in SSMS. The Help Search function automatically searches several online providers of SQL Server–related information for answers to your questions. Your searches are not restricted to SQL Server keywords or statements; you can search for anything at all, and the Help Search function will scour registered websites and communities for relevant answers. Figure 2-3 shows the Help Search screen in action.

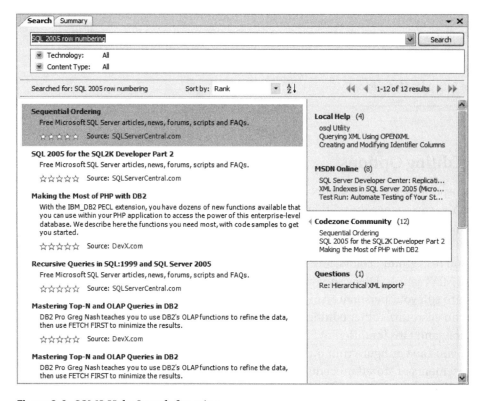

Figure 2-3. *SSMS Help Search function*

Graphical Query Execution Plans

SSMS offers graphical query execution plans similar to the plans available in Query Analyzer. The graphical query execution plan is an excellent tool for optimizing query performance. SSMS allows you to view two types of graphical query execution plans: estimated and actual. The *estimated* query execution plan is SQL Server's cost-based performance estimate of a query. The *actual* execution plan shows the real cost-based performance of the execution plan selected by SQL Server when the query is run. These options are available via the Query menu. Figure 2-4 shows an estimated query execution plan in SSMS.

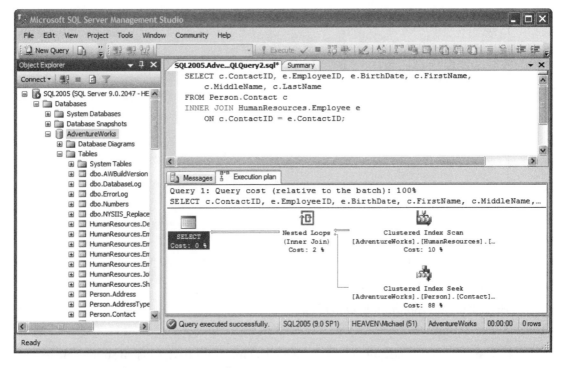

Figure 2-4. *Estimated query execution plan*

Project Management Features

SQL Server Management Studio incorporates new project management features familiar to Visual Studio developers. SSMS supports solution-based development. A solution
in SSMS consists of projects that contain T-SQL scripts, XML files, connection information, and other files. By default, projects and solutions are saved in the My Documents\
SQL Server Management Studio\Projects directory. Solution files have the extension
.ssmssln, and project files are saved in XML format with the .smssproj extension. SSMS
incorporates a Solution Explorer window similar to Visual Studio's Solution Explorer, as
shown in Figure 2-5. You can access it through the View menu.

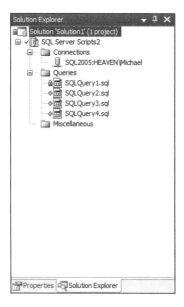

Figure 2-5. *SSMS Solution Explorer*

SSMS can take advantage of source control integration with Visual SourceSafe to help you manage versioning and deployments. After you create a solution and add projects, connections, and SQL scripts, you can add your solution to Visual SourceSafe by right-clicking the solution in the Solution Explorer and selecting Add Solution to Source Control (see Figure 2-6).

Figure 2-6. *Add Solution to Source Control command*

SSMS has several options for checking items out from source control. You can open a local copy and choose Check Out for Edit. You'll find options for checking out items from source control on the File ➤ Source Control menu. After checking out a solution from Visual SourceSafe, a Pending Checkins window appears. The Pending Checkins window lets you add comments to, or check in, individual files or projects, as shown in Figure 2-7.

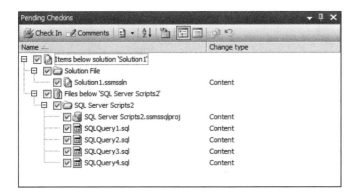

Figure 2-7. *SSMS solution Pending Checkins window*

SQL Server 2005 Books Online

SQL Server 2005 BOL is the primary reference for T-SQL and SQL Server 2005. Updates to your local installation of BOL are available at `http://www.microsoft.com/sql/default.mspx`. The online version of BOL is available at `http://msdn2.microsoft.com/en-us/library/ms130214.aspx`.

Note that you can search online and local versions of BOL, as well as several other SQL resources, via the Help Search function discussed earlier.

AdventureWorks Sample Database

SQL Server 2005 finally puts the good old Northwind sample database to rest. SQL Server 2005 has two main sample databases: the AdventureWorks OLTP and AdventureWorks Data Warehouse databases. In this book, I'll refer to the AdventureWorks OLTP database for most samples. You can download the AdventureWorks databases and the associated "100 SQL Server 2005 Samples" file from `http://www.microsoft.com/sql/downloads/2005/default.mspx`.

Summary

This chapter discussed the primary tools available to SQL Server 2005 developers including the following:

- The SQLCMD utility

- SQL Server Management Studio

- Books Online and the Help Search function

- The AdventureWorks sample databases

Chapter 3 will provide a survey of new SQL Server 2005 features, specifically for SQL Server 2000 programmers.

T-SQL for SQL Server 2000 Programmers

SQL Server 2005 offers several enhancements to T-SQL, but SQL Server 2000 programmers will still feel right at home. As long as legacy SQL Server 2000 scripts were written to follow best practices, most will run with minimal, if any, changes. Converting old scripts to run on SQL Server 2005 is just a starting point. This chapter gives an overview of the exciting new features SQL Server 2005 adds to T-SQL.

■**Caution** You'll find a list of deprecated features in BOL. To locate the list, search for *deprecated* in BOL. The list has deprecated features and the replacement features. Though many of these features are currently supported in SQL Server 2005, they will be removed in a future version of the product.

New Data Types

SQL Server 2005 introduces one new and three enhanced data types: the new xml data type and the varchar(max), nvarchar(max), and varbinary(max) enhanced data types. The enhanced max data types are designed to replace the SQL Server 2000 large object (LOB) data types text, ntext, and image, respectively. The new max data types operate more like their conventional counterparts, exhibiting behavior that more closely resembles these data types.

XML Data Type

SQL Server 2005 expands on the XML functionality introduced in SQL Server 2000 with a new xml data type. You can use the xml data type to store and manipulate XML data. SQL Server 2005 also provides XQuery support for querying XML data. Chapter 11 describes the xml data type in greater detail, along with a discussion of the improved FOR XML clause for SQL Server 2005 SELECT statements.

varchar(max), nvarchar(max), and varbinary(max)

SQL Server 2005 also introduces enhancements to three older data types. If you've ever tried to use the old text, ntext, and image large-value data types, you'll be glad to hear they've been deprecated and replaced with new, easier-to-use types. The varchar(max), nvarchar(max), and varbinary(max) data types completely replace the older LOB data types. Like the older types, each of these new data types can hold up to 2^{31} minus 1 bytes (2.1 billion bytes) of character or binary data. Unlike the old large-object data types, the enhanced max data types are designed to work similarly to the standard varchar, nvarchar, and varbinary data types. This means standard string functions such as LEN and CHARINDEX, which didn't work with SQL Server 2000 large-object data types (or at least didn't work *well* with them), will work as expected with the enhanced max data types. It also means that kludgy solutions involving the TEXTPTR and WRITETEXT statements are no longer needed to manipulate large-object data. The old text, ntext, and image types will be removed from a future version of SQL Server and should not be used in SQL Server 2005.

■**Note** The varchar(max), nvarchar(max), and varbinary(max) data types replace the SQL Server 2000 text, ntext, and image data types completely. The text, ntext, and image data types and their support functions will be removed in a future version of SQL Server. Because they are deprecated, Microsoft recommends you avoid these older LOB data types for new development.

You can also add the .WRITE clause to UPDATE statements of the enhanced max data types. The .WRITE clause allows optimized minimally logged updates and appends to varchar(max), varbinary(max), and nvarchar(max) types. The format is as follows:

```
.WRITE (expression, @offset, @length)
```

To use the new .WRITE clause, just append it to the end of the column name in your UPDATE statement. The example in Listing 3-1 uses the .WRITE clause to update a column.

Listing 3-1. *Minimally Logged .WRITE Method Example*

```
CREATE TABLE #WriteTest ([ID] INT IDENTITY(1,1) NOT NULL PRIMARY KEY,
    BigText NVARCHAR(MAX) NOT NULL);

INSERT
INTO #WriteTest (BigText)
VALUES (N'Transact-SQL Rocks.');

SELECT BigText
FROM #WriteTest;

UPDATE #WriteTest
SET BigText.WRITE(N' and Rolls.', 18, 11);

SELECT BigText
FROM #WriteTest;

DROP TABLE #WriteTest;
```

The key to the sample is the UPDATE statement, which uses the .WRITE clause to update the text in the table from 'Transact-SQL Rocks.' to 'Transact-SQL Rocks and Rolls.', as shown here:

```
UPDATE #WriteTest
SET BigText.WRITE(N' and Rolls.', 18, 11);
```

You should note the following about the .WRITE clause:

- The *@offset* parameter is a zero-based bigint and cannot be negative. The first character of the target string is at offset 0.

- If *@offset* is NULL, the expression is appended to the end of the target string; @length is ignored in this case.

- If *@length* is NULL, SQL Server truncates anything past the end of the .WRITE *expression* after the target string is updated. *@length* is a bigint and cannot be negative.

Data Manipulation Language

SQL Server 2005 includes several DML enhancements. One of the exciting new DML enhancements is the Common Table Expression (CTE), which allows an elegant method of performing recursive queries.

Common Table Expressions

CTEs are an exciting addition to T-SQL. Basically, a CTE generates a temporary virtual table, or *view*, that exists only during the life of a query. CTEs can help make queries easier to read, but they also offer a powerful query recursion facility. The format for declaring a CTE is as follows:

```
WITH CTE_name [ ( column_name [, ...n] ) ]
AS
( CTE_query_definition )
```

CTE_name is the name assigned to the CTE. It can optionally be followed by a list of columns to be returned in parentheses. *CTE_query_definition*, which is the body of the CTE, follows closely behind after the keyword AS.

Consider a recursive CTE to return the chief executive officer and everyone who reports directly to him in the AdventureWorks organization. The CEO has no manager (ManagerID is NULL), and his EmployeeID number is 109. With that in mind, Listing 3-2 demonstrates a simple recursive CTE.

Listing 3-2. *Simple Recursive CTE*

```
WITH OrgChart (EmployeeID, ContactID, ManagerID, Title) AS
(
    SELECT EmployeeID,
        ContactID,
        ManagerID,
        Title
    FROM HumanResources.Employee
    WHERE ManagerID IS NULL
    UNION ALL
    SELECT e.EmployeeID,
        e.ContactID,
        e.ManagerID,
        e.Title
```

```
    FROM HumanResources.Employee e
    INNER JOIN OrgChart o
    ON e.ManagerID = o.EmployeeID
)
SELECT EmployeeID,
    ContactID,
    ManagerID,
    Title
FROM OrgChart
WHERE ManagerID = 109
OR ManagerID IS NULL;
```

The recursive CTE query consists of three distinct parts. First up is the actual CTE, which is enclosed in parentheses and preceded by the keyword WITH:

```
WITH OrgChart (EmployeeID, ContactID, ManagerID, Title) AS
(
    SELECT EmployeeID,
        ContactID,
        ManagerID,
        Title
    FROM HumanResources.Employee
    WHERE ManagerID IS NULL
    UNION ALL
    SELECT e.EmployeeID,
        e.ContactID,
        e.ManagerID,
        e.Title
    FROM HumanResources.Employee e
    INNER JOIN OrgChart o
    ON e.ManagerID = o.EmployeeID
)
```

The recursive CTE comprises two separate queries unioned together. The first query is the *anchor* query, which prevents the CTE from recursively calling itself in an endless loop. The anchor query selects the AdventureWorks CEO as the starting point for the query:

```
WITH OrgChart (EmployeeID, ContactID, ManagerID, Title) AS
(
    SELECT EmployeeID, ContactID, ManagerID, Title
    FROM HumanResources.Employee
    WHERE ManagerID IS NULL
```

The second query is the *recursive* query, which is invoked multiple times recursively. The UNION ALL operator combines the results of the two queries:

```
UNION ALL
SELECT e.EmployeeID,
    e.ContactID,
    e.ManagerID,
    e.Title
FROM HumanResources.Employee e
INNER JOIN OrgChart o
ON e.ManagerID = o.EmployeeID
)
```

Finally, you associate a SELECT query with the CTE by placing it just after the CTE body:

```
SELECT EmployeeID,
    ContactID,
    ManagerID,
    Title
FROM OrgChart
WHERE ManagerID = 109
OR ManagerID IS NULL;
```

As an alternative to the WHERE clause, SQL Server 2005 offers the MAXRECURSION option. To achieve the same results as earlier, you can remove the WHERE clause and add the MAXRECURSION option:

```
SELECT EmployeeID,
    ContactID,
    ManagerID,
    Title
FROM OrgChart
OPTION (MAXRECURSION 1);
```

■**Note** The MAXRECURSION option throws a warning message when it stops query execution. The warning message looks like this:

```
Msg 530, Level 16, State 1, Line 1
The statement terminated. The maximum recursion 2 has been exhausted before
statement completion.
```

You can safely ignore this warning message. Also note that the value for the MAXRECURSION hint must be from 0 to 32767. A value of 0 indicates that no limit should be applied.

This forces the CTE to recurse only once, returning the same result as earlier. The query currently retrieves the CEO and his direct reports. If you wanted to also retrieve the next level of employees who report to them, you could use OPTION (MAXRECURSION 2). The hierarchical modeling of data often requires recursion, and CTEs help ease the pain of retrieving hierarchical data via inefficient cursors and self-joins in a relational database.

OUTPUT Clause

The OUTPUT clause is a new addition to T-SQL. You can apply it to INSERT, UPDATE, and DELETE statements. The OUTPUT clause allows you to return information from DML statements that can be useful to grab the results of an insert or delete or to compare the pre- and post-update data. The OUTPUT clause uses inserted and deleted virtual tables to reference columns inserted and deleted by the DML statement.

You can use the OUTPUT clause to output a SQL result set, like with a SELECT statement, or you can combine it with the INTO clause to output to a table or table variable. The simple example shown in Listing 3-3 inserts and deletes a new work shift into the HumanResources.Shift table. These INSERT and DELETE statements use the OUTPUT clause to return a summary of the changes made.

Listing 3-3. *OUTPUT Clause Example*

```
INSERT INTO HumanResources.Shift ([Name],
    StartTime,
    EndTime)
    OUTPUT 'INSERTED',
        CURRENT_USER,
        INSERTED.ShiftID
SELECT 'Swing Shift', '12:00:00 PM', '8:00:00 PM';

DELETE FROM HumanResources.Shift
    OUTPUT 'DELETED',
        CURRENT_USER,
        DELETED.ShiftID
WHERE [Name] = N'Swing Shift';
```

■**Note** If you use the OUTPUT clause in a trigger, you have to alias the trigger's inserted and deleted virtual tables to prevent conflicts with the OUTPUT clause's inserted and deleted virtual tables.

INTERSECT and EXCEPT

SQL Server 2005 provides two new union-style operators, INTERSECT and EXCEPT. The INTERSECT operator returns any distinct values that are common to the query on the left side of the operator and also the right side of the operator.

EXCEPT returns distinct values from the query on the left side, excluding any results that match the query on the right side. In the example shown in Listing 3-4, EXCEPT returns all contacts whose last name begins with *A* except those whose last name is Adams.

Listing 3-4. *EXCEPT Operator Example*

```
SELECT ContactID,
    LastName,
    FirstName,
    MiddleName
FROM Person.Contact
WHERE LastName LIKE N'A%'
EXCEPT
SELECT ContactID,
    LastName,
    FirstName,
    MiddleName
FROM Person.Contact
WHERE LastName = N'Adams';
```

■**Note** The INTERSECT and EXCEPT operators eliminate duplicate rows from the result set. T-SQL does not support the ANSI INTERSECT ALL and EXCEPT ALL variations of these operators, which do not eliminate duplicate rows from the result set.

The INTERSECT and EXCEPT operators follow a specific set of rules when performing their functions:

- When comparing rows for distinct values, NULLs are considered equal. Usually (and for most SQL operations), NULLs are not considered equal to anything, even other NULLs.

- The number and order of all columns on both sides of the expression have to be the same. The data types of matching columns on both sides of the expression do not have to be the same, but they must be compatible. In other words, they must be able to be compared via implicit conversion.

- The columns on either side of the expression cannot be text, ntext, image, xml, or nonbinary SQLCLR user-defined types.

- The column names returned by the operator are taken from the left side of the operator.

- Just like with the UNION and UNION ALL operators, you can use an ORDER BY clause only on the final result of the operator. The ORDER BY clause must reference column names from the left side of the operator.

- You cannot use GROUP BY and HAVING clauses on the final result of the INTERSECT or EXCEPT queries. You can use them on the individual queries on either side of the operator, though.

TOP Keyword

The TOP keyword has long been a staple of SQL SELECT statements. With SQL Server 2005, TOP has been considerably improved. Now you can use a T-SQL variable to specify the number of rows to return. You can apply this to percentages or actual row counts, as shown in Listing 3-5.

Listing 3-5. *SELECT TOP with Variable*

```
DECLARE @i INT;
SELECT @i = 20;
SELECT TOP (@i) PERCENT FirstName,
    MiddleName,
    LastName
FROM Person.Contact
ORDER BY FirstName,
    MiddleName,
    LastName;
```

Doing something like this in SQL Server 2000 required kludging ugly dynamic SQL or using the SET ROWCOUNT statement. You can also use a subquery to specify the number of rows to return. This example returns half the rows from the Person.Contact table, as shown in Listing 3-6.

Listing 3-6. *SELECT TOP with Subquery*

```
SELECT TOP (SELECT COUNT(*) / 2 FROM Person.Contact)
    FirstName,
    MiddleName,
    LastName
FROM Person.Contact
ORDER BY FirstName,
    MiddleName,
    LastName;
```

You can also use the TOP keyword with a constant value just like in SQL Server 2000. Although you can leave the parentheses off when using SELECT TOP, don't rely on this backward-compatibility feature. With new T-SQL scripts, always use parentheses around the expression to specify the number of rows to return.

■**Note** When you use a variable or subquery with SELECT TOP, you must enclose it in parentheses. For compatibility with SQL Server 2000 scripts, the parentheses aren't required if you specify a constant value with SELECT TOP. This backward-compatibility feature might be removed in future versions of T-SQL, and Microsoft now recommends always using parentheses with TOP.

The TOP keyword was not introduced to T-SQL until SQL Server 7.0. In SQL Server 7.0 and SQL Server 2000, T-SQL allowed the TOP keyword only in a SELECT statement. SQL Server 2005 also allows the TOP keyword in the INSERT, UPDATE, and DELETE Data Manipulation Language (DML) statements. One practical use for TOP with these statements is the development of T-SQL table-based queues, stacks, lists, or other data structures. The example in Listing 3-7 creates a simple table-based queue. It enqueues five names and then dequeues three of them using INSERT and DELETE statements with the TOP keyword. The OUTPUT clause discussed earlier generates instant feedback for each operation.

Listing 3-7. *Using TOP with INSERT and DELETE*

```
CREATE TABLE #Queue (
    [ID] INT IDENTITY(1,1) NOT NULL PRIMARY KEY,
    FirstName NVARCHAR(50) NOT NULL);
```

```
INSERT TOP (5)
INTO #Queue (FirstName)
    OUTPUT N'Enqueued: ' + INSERTED.FirstName
SELECT DISTINCT FirstName
    FROM Person.Contact;

DELETE TOP (3)
FROM #Queue
    OUTPUT N'De-queued: ' + DELETED.FirstName;

DROP TABLE #Queue;
```

This code first creates a temporary table and populates it with five names from the Person.Contact table. Note the use of the OUTPUT clause to display a message for each name added to the queue:

```
CREATE TABLE #Queue (
    [ID] INT IDENTITY(1,1) NOT NULL PRIMARY KEY,
    FirstName NVARCHAR(50) NOT NULL);

INSERT TOP (5)
INTO #Queue (FirstName)
    OUTPUT N'Enqueued: ' + INSERTED.FirstName
SELECT DISTINCT FirstName
    FROM Person.Contact;
```

Then it dequeues the top three names by deleting them. The OUTPUT clause again gives feedback as each item is dequeued. Finally, the temp table is dropped:

```
DELETE TOP (3)
FROM #Queue
    OUTPUT N'De-queued: ' + DELETED.FirstName;

DROP TABLE #Queue;
```

Like SELECT TOP in SQL Server 2005, the INSERT TOP, DELETE TOP, and UPDATE TOP statements can all accept constants, T-SQL variables, or subqueries to specify the number of rows to affect.

CROSS APPLY and OUTER APPLY

Probably one of the most frequently asked questions on the SQL Server newsgroups (`news://microsoft.public.sqlserver.programming`) concerns passing columns as parameters to table-valued functions. In SQL Server 2000, this requires resorting to procedural code or cursors. SQL Server 2005 adds the CROSS APPLY and OUTER APPLY operators that resolve this problem. Like the JOIN operators, APPLY operators take tables on both sides of the operator. The APPLY operators allow columns from the left-side table to be used as parameters for a table-valued function (TVF) on the right side of the operator. As a simple example, Listing 3-8 creates a sample inline TVF that returns the square (n^2) and cube (n^3) of a number passed to it. The CROSS APPLY operator in the example applies the numbers in a table to the TVF.

Listing 3-8. *CROSS APPLY Example*

```
CREATE FUNCTION dbo.fnPowers (@Num INT)
RETURNS TABLE
AS
RETURN
(
    SELECT @Num * @Num AS Squared_Result,
        @Num * @Num * @Num AS Cubed_Result
);
GO

CREATE TABLE #Numbers (Number INT NOT NULL PRIMARY KEY);
INSERT INTO #Numbers (Number) VALUES (1);
INSERT INTO #Numbers (Number) VALUES (2);
INSERT INTO #Numbers (Number) VALUES (3);
SELECT n.Number,
    s.Squared_Result,
    s.Cubed_Result
FROM #Numbers n
CROSS APPLY dbo.fnPowers (n.Number) s;
GO

DROP FUNCTION dbo.fnPowers;
DROP TABLE #Numbers;
```

The sample first creates an inline table-valued function to return the square and cube of a number passed to it:

```
CREATE FUNCTION dbo.fnPowers (@Num INT)
RETURNS TABLE
AS
RETURN
(
    SELECT @Num * @Num AS Squared_Result,
        @Num * @Num * @Num AS Cubed_Result
);
GO
```

Then it creates a temporary table and inserts some numbers to it:

```
CREATE TABLE #Numbers (Number INT NOT NULL PRIMARY KEY);
INSERT INTO #Numbers (Number) VALUES (1);
INSERT INTO #Numbers (Number) VALUES (2);
INSERT INTO #Numbers (Number) VALUES (3);
```

The CROSS APPLY operator used in the SELECT statement takes every row from the temporary table and passes them to the inline TVF. The columns of the temporary table and the columns returned by the inline TVF are all available to the SELECT statement:

```
SELECT n.Number,
    s.Squared_Result,
    s.Cubed_Result
FROM #Numbers n
CROSS APPLY dbo.fnPowers (n.Number) s;
GO
```

Finally, perform a little cleanup:

```
DROP FUNCTION dbo.fnPowers;
DROP TABLE #Numbers;
```

The CROSS APPLY operator returns every row for which the table-valued function returns results for the left table. OUTER APPLY returns all rows, even those for which the function returns no results. If no results are returned by the TVF for a row, OUTER APPLY returns NULL values for the TVF columns. I discuss table-valued functions in detail in Chapter 5.

TABLESAMPLE

Occasionally it's necessary to select a random sample of data from a table. Many people have come up with inventive solutions for this on the SQL Server 2000 platform, including methods based on pregenerated random numbers, procedural code, or globally unique identifiers (GUIDs). SQL Server 2005 includes a new TABLESAMPLE clause for the SELECT statement to make the task of random sampling easier. The TABLESAMPLE clause follows the table name in the WHERE clause and has the following format:

```
TABLESAMPLE [SYSTEM] (sample_number [PERCENT|ROWS])
    REPEATABLE (repeat_seed)
```

TABLESAMPLE accepts a sample_number parameter that specifies a percent or number of rows to return in the sample. The sample method actually randomly samples a percentage of pages, so the number of rows specified might not be the exact number or percent requested.

■**Note** When you specify an exact number of rows, TABLESAMPLE converts the number to a percentage of rows before executing. So even if you specify an exact number of rows, you will still get an approximate number of rows in the result set.

You can use the TOP clause in the SELECT statement to further limit rows to the exact number required. The SYSTEM keyword specifies a system-dependent random sampling method. Since SQL Server 2005 offers only one random sampling method, the SYSTEM keyword has no effect. The random sampling method used by SQL Server 2005 involves retrieving a random number of complete physical pages that make up the specified table. This means the number of rows returned will always be approximate and that tables occupying more storage space and containing more rows will more closely approximate the specified TABLESAMPLE percentage. A small table that takes up only one physical page, for instance, will return either all rows or none.

If you need to repeat the same random sampling multiple times, specify REPEATABLE with repeat_seed, which is a random seed generation number. Specifying the same repeat_seed with the same SELECT statement on the same data produces the same results.

■**Note** The REPEATABLE keyword, even with the same repeat_seed, will produce different results from query to query if the data stored in the table, or the structure of the table, changes.

The SELECT statement shown in Listing 3-9 randomly selects *approximately* ten percent of the rows from the Person.Contact table.

Listing 3-9. *SELECT Example with TABLESAMPLE*

```
SELECT FirstName,
    MiddleName,
    LastName
FROM Person.Contact
TABLESAMPLE (10 PERCENT);
```

■**Tip** TABLESAMPLE always returns an approximate number of rows because of the way it samples data. The required percentage is the number of data pages SQL Server retrieves in full to fulfill your TABLESAMPLE request. The number of rows returned by TABLESAMPLE will often be slightly less, or greater, than the specified amount.

You can use the TABLESAMPLE clause only when querying local tables and locally defined temporary tables. You cannot use it on views, derived tables from subqueries, result sets from table-valued functions and rowset functions, linked server tables, OPENXML, or table variables.

If you need to retrieve a random sampling of rows from a view, derived table, or linked server table, consider using a method like the following, popularized by SQL Server MVP Erland Sommerskag, as shown in Listing 3-10.

Listing 3-10. *Alternate Method of Retrieving Random Rows from a Table*

```
SELECT TOP (10) PERCENT FirstName,
    MiddleName,
    LastName
FROM HumanResources.vEmployee
ORDER BY NEWID();
```

This method works by generating a UNIQUEIDENTIFIER for each row, sorting based on the value generated, and selecting the top ten percent from that result. The result is a random sample of rows from your table. Although not a true statistical sampling, these random sampling methods are adequate for most development and testing purposes.

PIVOT and UNPIVOT

Microsoft Access database users, and even Microsoft Excel spreadsheet users, have long had the ability to generate pivot table reports of their data. Prior to SQL Server 2005, SQL Server users had to use CASE statements and/or dynamic SQL to simulate this functionality. SQL Server 2005 introduces the PIVOT and UNPIVOT operators to generate pivot table–style reports.

The PIVOT operator turns the values of a specified column into column names, effectively rotating a table. You can use PIVOT to sum, count, or otherwise aggregate the values of columns it creates. The PIVOT query shown in Listing 3-11 returns the total number of AdventureWorks customers who live in California, Massachusetts, Texas, and Washington.

Listing 3-11. *PIVOT Operator Test*

```
SELECT [CA],
    [MA],
    [TX],
    [WA]
FROM
(
    SELECT sp.StateProvinceCode
    FROM Sales.CustomerAddress c
    INNER JOIN Person.Address a
        ON c.AddressID = a.AddressID
    INNER JOIN Person.StateProvince sp
        ON a.StateProvinceID = sp.StateProvinceID
  ) p
  PIVOT
  (
    COUNT (StateProvinceCode)
    FOR StateProvinceCode
    IN ([CA], [MA], [TX], [WA])
  ) AS pvt;
```

The first part of the SELECT statement specifies the column names. In this case, the abbreviation codes for the states to include in the result set are as follows:

```
SELECT [CA],
    [MA],
    [TX],
    [WA]
FROM
```

The subquery retrieves all the state codes for AdventureWorks customers:

```
(
    SELECT sp.StateProvinceCode
    FROM Sales.CustomerAddress c
    INNER JOIN Person.Address a
        ON c.AddressID = a.AddressID
    INNER JOIN Person.StateProvince sp
        ON a.StateProvinceID = sp.StateProvinceID
) p
```

The PIVOT operator applies the aggregate COUNT function to each state code and limits the results to the specified states:

```
PIVOT
(
    COUNT (StateProvinceCode)
    FOR StateProvinceCode
    IN ([CA], [MA], [TX], [WA])
) AS pvt;
```

The result is a pivot-style table (see Figure 3-1).

Figure 3-1. *PIVOT query result*

One glaring shortcoming of the PIVOT operator is that you must specify the names of all the columns to be included in the result set. If you want the columns to be dynamically created based on the contents of a column, you'll have to resort to the old-fashioned method of building dynamic SQL statements.

The UNPIVOT operator performs almost—but not exactly—the opposite function of the PIVOT operator. Since PIVOT aggregates results, the original nonaggregated values cannot be returned by UNPIVOT.

Listing 3-12 creates a temporary table containing the results of the previous PIVOT example; it then unpivots the result by rotating the column names into row data.

Listing 3-12. *PIVOT and UNPIVOT Sample*

```
CREATE TABLE #Pvt ([CA] INT NOT NULL,
    [MA] INT NOT NULL,
    [TX] INT NOT NULL,
    [WA] INT NOT NULL,
    PRIMARY KEY ([CA], [MA], [TX], [WA]));

INSERT INTO #Pvt ([CA], [MA], [TX], [WA])
SELECT  [CA],
    [MA],
    [TX],
    [WA]
FROM
(
    SELECT sp.StateProvinceCode
    FROM Sales.CustomerAddress c
    INNER JOIN Person.Address a
        ON c.AddressID = a.AddressID
    INNER JOIN Person.StateProvince sp
        ON a.StateProvinceID = sp.StateProvinceID
) p
PIVOT
(
    COUNT (StateProvinceCode)
    FOR StateProvinceCode
        IN ([CA], [MA], [TX], [WA])
) AS pvt;
```

```
SELECT StateProvinceCode, Customer_Count
FROM
(
    SELECT [CA],
        [MA],
        [TX],
        [WA]
    FROM #Pvt
) t
UNPIVOT
(
    Customer_Count
    FOR StateProvinceCode
        IN  ([CA], [MA], [TX], [WA])
) AS unpvt;

DROP TABLE #Pvt;
```

The first part of this script creates a temporary table and populates it with the results of the pivot query from the previous example:

```
CREATE TABLE #Pvt ([CA] INT NOT NULL,
    [MA] INT NOT NULL,
    [TX] INT NOT NULL,
    [WA] INT NOT NULL,
    PRIMARY KEY ([CA], [MA], [TX], [WA]));

INSERT INTO #Pvt ([CA], [MA], [TX], [WA])
SELECT  [CA],
    [MA],
    [TX],
    [WA]
FROM
(
    SELECT sp.StateProvinceCode
    FROM Sales.CustomerAddress c
    INNER JOIN Person.Address a
        ON c.AddressID = a.AddressID
    INNER JOIN Person.StateProvince sp
        ON a.StateProvinceID = sp.StateProvinceID
) p
```

```
PIVOT
(
    COUNT (StateProvinceCode)
    FOR StateProvinceCode
        IN ([CA], [MA], [TX], [WA])
) AS pvt;
```

The `SELECT` portion of the `UNPIVOT` query defines the columns that will hold the results of the unpivot operation, `StateProvinceCode`, and `Customer_Count`:

```
SELECT StateProvinceCode, Customer_Count
FROM
```

The subquery selects all applicable columns from the pivot table:

```
(
    SELECT [CA],
        [MA],
        [TX],
        [WA]
    FROM #Pvt
) t
```

The `UNPIVOT` operator then rotates the results:

```
UNPIVOT
(
    Customer_Count
    FOR StateProvinceCode
        IN ([CA], [MA], [TX], [WA])
) AS unpvt;

DROP TABLE #Temp;
```

Figure 3-2 shows the result of the `UNPIVOT` operation.

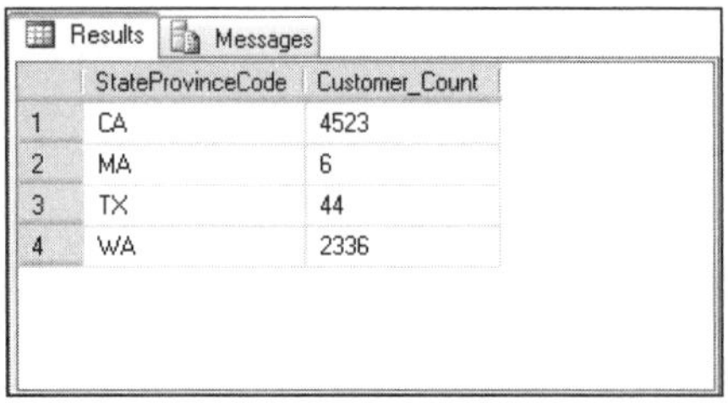

	StateProvinceCode	Customer_Count
1	CA	4523
2	MA	6
3	TX	44
4	WA	2336

Figure 3-2. *UNPIVOT query result*

Ranking Functions

SQL Server 2005 introduces several new functions to allow the dynamic ranking of results. The ROW_NUMBER function numbers all rows in a result set, the RANK and DENSE_RANK functions assign a numeric rank value to each row in a result set, and NTILE assigns an *n*-tile ranking, such as quartile (quarters or 1/4) or quintile (fifths or 1/5) to a result set.

ROW_NUMBER Function

You can use ROW_NUMBER to make light work of paging applications, such as front-end web applications that need to retrieve data ten items at a time. ROW_NUMBER has the following format:

```
ROW_NUMBER() OVER ([PARTITION BY col [,...]] ORDER BY col [,...])
```

The query shown in Listing 3-13 returns ten names from the Person.Contact table beginning at the specified row number.

Listing 3-13. *ROW_NUMBER Function Example*

```
DECLARE @start INT;
SELECT @start = 10;
WITH PageContacts AS
(
    SELECT ROW_NUMBER() OVER
    (
        ORDER BY LastName,
        FirstName,
        MiddleName
    )
    AS PosNo, FirstName, MiddleName, LastName
    FROM Person.Contact
)
SELECT PosNo, FirstName, MiddleName, LastName
FROM PageContacts
WHERE PosNo BETWEEN @start AND @start + 9;
```

The script begins by defining the start position as the tenth row in the result set:

```
DECLARE @start INT;
SELECT @start = 10;
```

To use the `ROW_NUMBER` function to limit the result set to the ten rows beginning at the start position, the sample uses a CTE to wrap the `ROW_NUMBER`–generating query:

```
WITH PageContacts AS
(
    SELECT ROW_NUMBER() OVER
    (
        ORDER BY LastName,
        FirstName,
        MiddleName
    )
    AS PosNo, FirstName, MiddleName, LastName
    FROM Person.Contact
)
```

SQL, and consequently T-SQL, has absolutely no concept of guaranteed row order without an `ORDER BY` clause. The `OVER` keyword provides the mandatory `ORDER BY` clause to guarantee this proper row numbering order. The final step is to select the columns from the CTE and use the `BETWEEN` operator to limit the result set to ten rows:

```
SELECT PosNo,
    FirstName,
    MiddleName,
    LastName
FROM PageContacts
WHERE PosNo BETWEEN @start AND @start + 9;
```

In addition to the `ORDER BY` clause, the `OVER` keyword provides an optional `PARTITION BY` clause that allows you to divide data into numbered subsets. Taking the previous CTE as a starting point, you can modify it to include a `PARTITION BY` clause. Listing 3-14 partitions/divides the data by last name and restarts the count at 1 for each new last name.

Listing 3-14. *ROW_NUMBER with PARTITION BY Clause*

```
DECLARE @start INT;
SELECT @start = 10;
WITH PageContacts AS
(
```

```
    SELECT ROW_NUMBER() OVER
    (
        PARTITION BY LastName
        ORDER BY LastName,
            FirstName,
            MiddleName
    )
    AS PosNo, FirstName, MiddleName, LastName
    FROM Person.Contact
)
SELECT PosNo, FirstName, MiddleName, LastName
FROM PageContacts
WHERE PosNo BETWEEN @start AND @start + 9;
```

The PARTITION BY clause in this example forces the numbering of rows to restart at 1 every time LastName changes.

RANK and DENSE_RANK Functions

The RANK and DENSE_RANK functions are similar to one another. They assign a numeric rank value to each item encountered. RANK and DENSE_RANK have the following formats:

```
RANK() OVER ([PARTITION BY col [,...]] ORDER BY col [,...])

DENSE_RANK() OVER ([PARTITION BY col [,...]] ORDER BY col [,...])
```

Suppose you want to figure out AdventureWorks's best one-day sales dates for the calendar year 2001. RANK can easily give you that information, as shown in Listing 3-15.

Listing 3-15. *One-Day Sales with RANK*

```
WITH TotalSalesBySalesDate (TotalSales, OrderDate)
AS
(
    SELECT SUM(soh.SubTotal) AS TotalSales, soh.OrderDate
    FROM Sales.SalesOrderHeader soh
    WHERE soh.OrderDate >= '2001-01-01'
        AND soh.OrderDate < '2002-01-01'
    GROUP BY soh.OrderDate
)
```

```
SELECT RANK() OVER
(
    ORDER BY TotalSales DESC
)
AS 'Rank', TotalSales, OrderDate
FROM TotalSalesBySalesDate;
```

This query begins by creating a CTE to calculate the total sales for 2001:

```
WITH TotalSalesBySalesDate (TotalSales, OrderDate)
AS
(
    SELECT SUM(soh.SubTotal) AS TotalSales, soh.OrderDate
    FROM Sales.SalesOrderHeader soh
    WHERE soh.OrderDate >= '2001-01-01'
        AND soh.OrderDate < '2002-01-01'
    GROUP BY soh.OrderDate
)
```

The query then ranks the results of the CTE in descending order so that the largest sales days are ranked first:

```
SELECT RANK() OVER
(
    ORDER BY TotalSales DESC
)
AS 'Rank', TotalSales, OrderDate
FROM TotalSalesBySalesDate;
```

Like with the ROW_NUMBER function, you can add a PARTITION BY clause if you want to partition the results. If RANK encounters two equal TotalSales in the previous example, it assigns the same rank number to both and skips the next number in the ranking. In the previous example, the TotalSales value $35,782.70 occurs twice and is given the rank of 14 both times. There is no rank 15 in the result set—RANK skips it because of the duplicate values at rank 14.

DENSE_RANK, like RANK, assigns duplicate values the same rank but with one important difference: it does not skip the next ranking in the list. If you change the RANK function in Listing 3-15 to DENSE_RANK, the rank of 14 is still occupied by two occurrences of $35,782.70, but rank 15 is not skipped by DENSE_RANK, as it was with RANK.

NTILE Function

NTILE is another ranking function that performs a slightly different mission. It divides a result set up into approximate *n*-tiles. An *n*-tile can be a quartile (1/4th, or 25 percent slices), a quintile (1/5th, or 20 percent slices), a percentile (1/100th, or 1 percent slices), or just about any other fractional slices you can imagine. The reason your result set is divided into "approximate" *n*-tiles is that the number of rows returned might not be evenly divisible into the specified number of groups. A table with 27 rows, for instance, is not evenly divisible into quartiles or quintiles. When you query a table with the NTILE function and the number of rows is not evenly divisible by the specified number of groups, NTILE creates groups of two different sizes. The larger groups will all be one row larger than the smaller groups, and the larger groups are numbered first. In the example of 27 rows divided into quintiles (1/5th), the first two groups will have six rows each, and the last three groups will have five rows each.

The format for NTILE is as follows:

```
NTILE (num_groups) OVER ([PARTITION BY col [,...]] ORDER BY col [,...])
```

Like the ROW_NUMBER function, you can include a PARTITION BY clause and an ORDER BY clause after the OVER keyword. NTILE requires the additional *num_groups* parameter, specifying the many groups into which to divide your results.

You can modify the previous example to use NTILE to divide the results into quartiles representing four groups, from the highest 25 percent one-day sales totals to the lowest 25 percent one-day sales totals, as shown in Listing 3-16. Each group is numbered from 1 to 4, respectively.

Listing 3-16. *NTILE Example*

```
WITH TotalSalesBySalesDate (TotalSales, OrderDate)
AS
(
    SELECT SUM(soh.SubTotal) AS TotalSales, soh.OrderDate
    FROM Sales.SalesOrderHeader soh
    WHERE soh.OrderDate >= '2001-01-01'
        AND soh.OrderDate < '2002-01-01'
    GROUP BY soh.OrderDate
)
SELECT NTILE(4) OVER
(
    ORDER BY TotalSales DESC
)
AS 'Rank', TotalSales, OrderDate
FROM TotalSalesBySalesDate;
```

NEWSEQUENTIALID Function

The new NEWSEQUENTIALID function generates GUIDs of T-SQL data type uniqueidentifier. It generates sequential GUIDs in increasing order. You can use the NEWSEQUENTIALID function only as a DEFAULT for a uniqueidentifier-type column of a table, as demonstrated in Listing 3-17.

Listing 3-17. *NEWSEQUENTIALID Usage Example*

```
CREATE TABLE #TestSeqID ([ID] UNIQUEIDENTIFIER
    DEFAULT NEWSEQUENTIALID() PRIMARY KEY NOT NULL,
    Num INT NOT NULL);

INSERT INTO #TestSeqID (Num) VALUES (1);
INSERT INTO #TestSeqID (Num) VALUES (2);
INSERT INTO #TestSeqID (Num) VALUES (3);

SELECT [ID], Num
FROM #TestSeqID;

DROP TABLE #TestSeqID;
```

The sample in Listing 3-17 generates results like the following (note that the GUIDs generated will be different on different systems):

```
ID Num
A4A31F1A-BB4A-DB11-B87E-000FEAE3D7BB 1
A5A31F1A-BB4A-DB11-B87E-000FEAE3D7BB 2
A6A31F1A-BB4A-DB11-B87E-000FEAE3D7BB 3
```

Notice the bold first byte of each GUID, representing the sequentially increasing GUIDs generated by NEWSEQUENTIALID with each INSERT statement.

Synonyms

Synonyms provide a handy way to *alias* database objects. This can help make code easier to read and reduce the number of keystrokes while coding. You create synonyms with the following syntax:

```
CREATE SYNONYM [ syn_schema. ] synonym_name
FOR
{
    [ server_name.] [ database_name. ] [ obj_schema. ] object_name
};
```

In the syntax definition, *syn_schema* is the name of the schema in which to create the synonym. *Synonym_name* is the T-SQL identifier for the synonym. You specify the (up to) four-part name of the object to create a synonym for with *server_name*, *database_name*, *obj_schema*, and *object_name*. Note that four-part names are not supported for function objects.

You can drop synonyms with the DROP SYNONYM syntax:

```
DROP SYNONYM [ schema. ] synonym_name;
```

Also note that synonyms use late binding so that the object a synonym references does not have to exist at creation time. Listing 3-18 demonstrates how to use a synonym to reference an existing table in the AdventureWorks database.

Listing 3-18. *Creating a Synonym for AdventureWorks.Sales.Customer*

```
CREATE SYNONYM AWCust
FOR AdventureWorks.Sales.Customer;

SELECT CustomerID,
    AccountNumber
FROM AWCust;

DROP SYNONYM AWCust;
```

The OVER Clause

As previously discussed, the new ranking functions (ROW_NUMBER, RANK, and so on) all work with the OVER clause to define the order and grouping of the input rows via the ORDER BY and PARTITION BY clauses. The OVER clause also provides *windowing* function-ality to T-SQL aggregate functions such as SUM and COUNT. The OVER clause allows T-SQL to apply the aggregate function to a window, or subset, of the data at a time. For instance, you can apply the OVER clause to the Purchasing.PurchaseOrderDetails table in the AdventureWorks database to retrieve the SUM of the quantities of products ordered, partitioned by ProductId, using the sample query in Listing 3-19.

Listing 3-19. *OVER Clause Example*

```
SELECT PurchaseOrderID,
    ProductID,
    SUM(OrderQty) OVER (PARTITION BY ProductId) AS TotalOrderQty
FROM Purchasing.PurchaseOrderDetail
```

Tip When used with an aggregate function, such as SUM or COUNT, or with a user-defined aggregate, the OVER clause can accept a PARTITION BY clause but not an ORDER BY clause.

This query results in a listing of products, the purchase order ID numbers, and the total quantity of each product. The results look similar to this (only a small sample of the results appears here):

PurchaseOrderID	ProductID	TotalOrderQty
...		
3852	1	154
3931	1	154
79	2	150
158	2	150
...		

Notice that the result of the aggregate function is returned on every row of the result set. In the example given, for instance, a total quantity of 154 of ProductID 1 was ordered. The OVER clause is partitioned by ProductID, so the total quantity of each product is returned on every line. So, every line in the results for ProductID 1 lists the total quantity of 154, and every line in the results for ProductID 2 lists the total quantity of 150. You can achieve the same result via an INNER JOIN and a subquery, as shown in Listing 3-20.

Listing 3-20. *INNER JOIN with Aggregate Function in Subquery*

```
SELECT pod.PurchaseOrderID, pod.ProductID, pqty.TotalOrderQty
FROM Purchasing.PurchaseOrderDetail pod
```

```
INNER JOIN (
    SELECT ProductID, SUM(OrderQty) AS TotalOrderQty
    FROM Purchasing.PurchaseOrderDetail
    GROUP BY ProductID
) pqty
ON pod.ProductID = pqty.ProductID
```

You can use the OVER clause with SQLCLR user-defined aggregates as well.

Other New Features

SQL Server 2005 includes the vast majority of the functionality provided by SQL Server 2000, with several new features as well as enhancements to existing features. You can expect most SQL Server 2000 T-SQL scripts to run on SQL Server 2005 with little or no change, as long as they are "well-written" (see the following tip for more information). In addition to the features listed in this chapter, SQL Server 2005 includes new functionality encompassing encryption, queues, web services, XML, SQLCLR, and several other functional areas that are covered in later chapters.

■Tip How hard will it be to convert your existing SQL Server 2000 scripts to SQL Server 2005? That depends on how closely those scripts followed *best practices* when they were originally written. For example, scripts that rely heavily on undocumented system functions and stored procedures will likely fail outright. Other scripts that rely on undocumented or deprecated features, old-style JOIN operators (*=, =*), or nonstandard settings (such as SET ANSI_NULLS OFF, and so on) may return incorrect results or cause your scripts to fail outright. Additionally, scripts that extensively use dynamic SQL will be harder to troubleshoot and debug during the upgrade process. Be sure to make time to review existing scripts for compliance during the upgrade. A little preparation can save a lot of time and trouble during the process.

Summary

This chapter provided an overview of many of SQL Server 2005's new features for SQL Server 2000 developers in the process of upgrading. These new features include the following:

- The new and enhanced xml, varchar(max), nvarchar(max), and varbinary(max) data types

- Ranking functions including ROW_NUMBER, RANK, DENSE_RANK, and NTILE

- New operators including INTERSECT, EXCEPT, PIVOT, and UNPIVOT

- The new concept of T-SQL synonyms

- The NEWSEQUENTIALID function, which assigns GUIDs to an IDENTITY column of a table in sequential order

- The new OVER clause for aggregate functions

- Improvements to existing T-SQL DML statements such as the OUTPUT clause, the enhanced TOP keyword, CTEs, and the .WRITE clause

In Chapter 4, I will cover T-SQL control-of-flow language statements and begin to lay the groundwork for a detailed discussion of SQL Server 2005 stored procedures, user-defined functions, and triggers.

CHAPTER 4

■ ■ ■

Control-of-Flow and CASE Expressions

T-SQL has always included additional control-of-flow statements useful for writing procedural code. SQL employs a peculiar three-valued logic that is different from most other programming languages' Boolean logic. I begin this chapter with a discussion of SQL three-valued logic, then I move on to the IF...ELSE, WHILE, and other T-SQL control-of-flow constructs, and finish up with a discussion of CASE expressions and CASE-derived functions.

Three-Valued Logic

SQL Server 2005, like all ANSI-compatible SQL database management products, implements a peculiar form of logic known as *three-valued logic* (3VL). Three-valued logic is necessary because SQL introduces the concept of NULL to indicate that values are not known at the time they are stored in the database. Because NULL represents unknown values, comparing anything with NULL produces an UNKNOWN result.

Table 4-1 is a quick reference for SQL Server three-valued logic, where p and q represent Boolean values.

Table 4-1. *SQL Server Three-Valued Logic Table*

p	q	p AND q	p OR q
TRUE	TRUE	TRUE	TRUE
TRUE	FALSE	FALSE	TRUE
TRUE	UNKNOWN	UNKNOWN	TRUE
FALSE	TRUE	FALSE	TRUE
FALSE	FALSE	FALSE	FALSE

Continued

Table 4-1. *Continued*

p	q	p AND q	p OR q
FALSE	UNKNOWN	FALSE	UNKNOWN
UNKNOWN	TRUE	UNKNOWN	TRUE
UNKNOWN	FALSE	FALSE	UNKNOWN
UNKNOWN	UNKNOWN	UNKNOWN	UNKNOWN

p	NOT p
TRUE	FALSE
FALSE	TRUE
UNKNOWN	UNKNOWN

As mentioned previously, comparisons with NULL produce an UNKNOWN result. NULLs are not even equal to other NULLs, and a comparison of two NULLs produces an unknown result when using the standard comparison operators (<, =, >, etc.) The only ANSI-compliant way to test for a NULL is with the IS NULL and IS NOT NULL comparison predicates.

NULL and UNKNOWN are closely related concepts in SQL. It is important, however, to differentiate the two: as mentioned previously NULL is a value that is not known, and an UNKNOWN result is the result of a comparison or operation with NULL. As with most things there are exceptions to the rule: the GROUP BY function treats all NULLs as equivalent by grouping them together in the result set. Additionally the OVER clause, when used with ranking/windowing functions, treats all NULLs as a single *window*. See Chapter 3 for more information on the OVER clause and ranking/windowing functions such as RANK and ROW_NUMBER.

Also keep in mind that NULL requires special handling in almost every situation. Most of the built-in SQL aggregate functions, such as SUM and COUNT, specifically eliminate NULLs during processing (COUNT(*) is an exception). Keep this in mind when using the built-in aggregate functions or creating your own user-defined functions or aggregates.

Control-of-Flow Statements

T-SQL implements procedural language control-of-flow statements including BEGIN...END, IF...ELSE, WHILE, and GOTO statements. T-SQL's control-of-flow statements provide a framework for developing rich server-side procedural code. This section discusses T-SQL's control-of-flow statements as well as the set-based CASE expression.

The following is a list of the T-SQL control-of-flow statements:

- BEGIN...END

- IF...ELSE

- WHILE

- GOTO

- BREAK

- CONTINUE

- WAITFOR

- RETURN

- TRY...CATCH

BEGIN...END Keywords

T-SQL uses the keywords BEGIN and END to group multiple statements together in a statement block. The BEGIN and END keywords don't alter execution order of the statements they contain, nor do they define an atomic transaction or perform any function other than defining a logical grouping of T-SQL statements. The format of BEGIN...END is the following:

```
BEGIN
    { SQL statement | statement block }
END
```

Unlike other languages, such as C++ or C#, which use braces ({ }) to group statements in logical blocks, T-SQL's BEGIN and END keywords do not define or limit scope. The following sample C++ code will not even compile:

```
{
    int j = 10;
}
std::cout << j << "\n";
```

C++ programmers will automatically recognize that the variable j in the previous code is defined inside braces, limiting its scope and making it accessible only inside the braces. T-SQL's roughly equivalent code, however, does not have the same scope definition:

```
BEGIN
    DECLARE @j INT;
    SELECT @j = 10;
END
PRINT @j;
```

The previous T-SQL code executes with no problem, as long as the DECLARE statement is encountered before the variable is referenced, as in the PRINT statement. The scope of variables in T-SQL is defined in terms of command batches and database object definitions (such as stored procedures, user-defined functions, and triggers.) Declaring two or more variables with the same name in one batch or stored procedure will result in errors.

■**Caution** T-SQL's BEGIN...END keywords create a statement block but do not define a scope. Variables declared inside a BEGIN...END block are not limited in scope just to that block, but rather are scoped to the whole batch, stored procedure, or UDF in which they are defined.

IF...ELSE Statement

Like many other procedural languages, T-SQL implements conditional execution of code using the basic procedural IF...ELSE control-of-flow statement. The basic format of the IF...ELSE statement is the following:

```
IF Boolean expression
    { SQL statement | statement block }
[ ELSE
    { SQL statement | statement block } ]
```

If the Boolean expression returns TRUE, the SQL statement or statement block immediately following the IF statement is executed. Otherwise, SQL Server falls through to the ELSE statement. The ELSE statement is executed if the Boolean expression returns FALSE or UNKNOWN.

The example in Listing 4-1 performs up to three comparisons to determine whether a variable is equal to a specified value. Note the second ELSE statement that executes only if the tests for both TRUE and FALSE conditions fail.

Listing 4-1. *Simple IF…ELSE Example*

```
DECLARE @i INT;
SELECT @i = NULL;
IF @i = 10
    PRINT 'THE RESULT OF THE COMPARISON IS TRUE.';
ELSE IF NOT (@i = 10)
    PRINT 'THE RESULT OF THE COMPARISON IS FALSE.';
ELSE
    PRINT 'THE RESULT OF THE COMPARISON IS UNKNOWN.';
```

Because the variable @i is NULL in the sample, SQL Server reports the result is UNKNOWN. If we assign the value 10 to @i, SQL Server will report the result is TRUE; other values will report the result is FALSE.

To create a *statement block* containing multiple T-SQL statements, wrap your statements in the T-SQL BEGIN and END keywords discussed previously. The following simple example of an IF…ELSE statement with statement blocks checks the variable @direction. If @direction is TOP, a message is printed and the top 100 names, in order of last name, are selected from the Person.Contact table. If @direction is not TOP, a different message is printed and the bottom 100 names are selected from the Person.Contact table, as shown in Listing 4-2.

Listing 4-2. *IF…ELSE with Statement Blocks*

```
DECLARE @direction NVARCHAR(6);
SELECT @direction = N'BOTTOM';
IF @direction = N'TOP'
BEGIN
    PRINT 'Start at the top!';

    SELECT TOP 100 FirstName,
        MiddleName,
        LastName
    FROM Person.Contact
    ORDER BY LastName ASC;
END
ELSE
BEGIN
    PRINT 'Start at the bottom!';
```

```
    SELECT TOP 100 FirstName,
        MiddleName,
        LastName
    FROM Person.Contact
    ORDER BY LastName DESC;
END;
```

WHILE, BREAK, and CONTINUE Statements

T-SQL provides looping via the WHILE statement, and the associated BREAK and CONTINUE statements. The format for WHILE is the following:

```
WHILE Boolean expression
    { SQL statement | statement block }
```

The WHILE loop executes the SQL statement or statement block bounded by the BEGIN and END keywords as long as the Boolean expression evaluates to TRUE. If the expression evaluates to FALSE or UNKNOWN, the code in the WHILE loop does not execute and control moves to the next statement after the WHILE loop's SQL statement. The example WHILE loop in Listing 4-3 counts from one to ten.

Listing 4-3. *WHILE Statement Example*

```
DECLARE @i INT;
SELECT @i = 1;
WHILE @i <= 10
BEGIN
    PRINT @i;
    SELECT @i = @i + 1;
END
```

■**Tip** Be sure to update your counter or other flag inside the WHILE loop. The WHILE loop will not exit until the *Boolean expression* evaluates to TRUE, and a mistake could create a nasty infinite loop.

T-SQL also has two additional keywords that can be used with the WHILE statement: BREAK and CONTINUE. The CONTINUE keyword forces the WHILE loop to restart, as in the modified example in Listing 4-4.

Listing 4-4. *WHILE...CONTINUE Example*

```
DECLARE @i INT;
SELECT @i = 1;
WHILE @i <= 10
BEGIN
    PRINT @i;
    SELECT @i = @i + 1;

    CONTINUE; -- Force the WHILE loop to restart

    PRINT 'The CONTINUE keyword ensures that this will never be printed.';
END
```

The BREAK keyword, on the other hand, forces the WHILE loop to terminate. In Listing 4-5, BREAK forces the WHILE loop to exit during the first iteration:

Listing 4-5. *WHILE...BREAK Example*

```
DECLARE @i INT;
SELECT @i = 1;
WHILE @i <= 10
BEGIN
    PRINT @i;
    SELECT @i = @i + 1;

    BREAK; -- Force the WHILE loop to terminate

    PRINT 'The BREAK keyword ensures that this will never be printed.';
END
```

■**Tip** BREAK and CONTINUE can and should be avoided in most cases. Most of the time the BREAK and CONTINUE keywords introduce additional complexity to your logic, causing more problems than they solve.

GOTO Statement

T-SQL also has a GOTO statement. The GOTO statement unconditionally transfers control of your program to a specified label. The format is the following:

```
GOTO label
```

Labels are defined by placing the label identifier on a line followed by a colon (:), as in the example in Listing 4-6.

Listing 4-6. *Simple GOTO Example*

```
PRINT 'Step 1 Complete.';
GOTO Step3_Label;

PRINT 'Step 2 will not be printed.';

Step3_Label:
PRINT 'Step 3 Complete.';
```

The GOTO statement is best avoided, since it can quickly degenerate your programs into unstructured "spaghetti code." Instead of GOTO, use IF...ELSE and WHILE statements.

WAITFOR Statement

The WAITFOR statement suspends execution of a transaction, stored procedure, or T-SQL command batch until a specified time is reached, a time interval is elapsed, or a message is received from Service Broker, a SQL Server messaging system that is not covered in this book. The basic format for WAITFOR is the following:

```
WAITFOR  { DELAY 'time_to_pass'  | TIME 'time_to_execute' }
```

With the WAITFOR statement you can specify that SQL Server block the execution of your transaction, stored procedure, or T-SQL command batch until one of the following criteria is met:

- If the DELAY keyword is specified, SQL Server will wait until the interval *time_to_pass* has elapsed. *Time_to_pass* is specified as a valid time string, in the format hh:mm:ss. *Time_to_pass* cannot contain a date; it must only include the time. *Time_to_pass* can be up to 24 hours.

- If the TIME keyword is used, SQL Server will wait until the appointed time before allowing execution to continue. Datetime variables are allowed, but the date portion is ignored when the TIME keyword is used.

The example of WAITFOR with DELAY in Listing 4-7 blocks execution of the T-SQL command batch for three seconds.

Listing 4-7. *WAITFOR Example*

```
PRINT 'Step 1 complete. ';
GO
DECLARE @time_to_pass NVARCHAR(8);
SELECT @time_to_pass = N'00:00:03';
WAITFOR DELAY @time_to_pass;
PRINT 'Step 2 completed three seconds later. ';
```

■**Note** SQL Server assigns each WAITFOR statement its own thread. If SQL Server determines that it is experiencing *thread starvation*, it can randomly select WAITFOR threads to exit to free up thread resources.

Additionally, if your application is Service Broker-enabled, you can use WAITFOR with a RECEIVE or GET CONVERSATION GROUP statement. The format for WAITFOR with RECEIVE is the following:

```
WAITFOR ( RECEIVE [ TOP ( n ) ] column [ ,...n ]
    FROM queue
    [ INTO table_variable ]
    [ WHERE { conversation_handle = conversation_handle
        | conversation_group_id = conversation_group_id } ] )
    [ , TIMEOUT timeout ]
```

The RECEIVE statement, when used with WAITFOR, waits for receipt of one or more messages from the specified *queue*. TIMEOUT can be used to set the command *timeout*, the length of time WAITFOR should wait for a message from the queue. If TIMEOUT is not specified, or is set to -1, the *timeout* is unlimited.

The format for WAITFOR with the GET CONVERSATION GROUP statement is the following:

```
WAITFOR ( GET CONVERSATION GROUP @conversation_group_id
    FROM queue )
    [ , TIMEOUT timeout ]
```

When WAITFOR is used with GET CONVERSATION GROUP it waits for a conversation group identifier of a message. GET CONVERSATION GROUP allows you to retrieve information about a message and lock the conversation group for the conversation containing the message before retrieving the actual message.

■**Note** The TIMEOUT keyword can only be used by WAITFOR when used with the RECEIVE or
GET CONVERSATION GROUP statements.

A detailed description of Service Broker is beyond the scope of this book, but the
Apress book *Pro SQL Server 2005* (ISBN: 1-59059-477-0) by Thomas Rizzo, et al., gives a
good description of Service Broker functionality and options for SQL Server 2005.

RETURN Statement

The RETURN statement exits unconditionally from a stored procedure or command batch.
The format is the following:

```
RETURN [ integer expression ]
```

The RETURN statement returns the *integer expression* to the calling routine or
batch. If *integer expression* is not specified, a default value of 0 is returned. RETURN is
not normally used to return calculated results, except for UDFs, which offer more
RETURN options described in detail in Chapter 5. For stored procedures and command
batches the RETURN statement is usually used only to return a success or failure indicator or error code.

■**Note** All system stored procedures return zero to indicate success, or a nonzero value to indicate failure
(unless otherwise documented). It is considered bad form to use the RETURN statement to return anything
other than an integer status code from a script or stored procedure.

User-defined functions, on the other hand, have their own rules. UDFs have their own flexible variation of
the RETURN statement, which exits the body of the UDF. In fact, a UDF *requires* the RETURN statement be
used to return scalar or tabular results to the caller. You will see UDFs again in detail in Chapter 5.

TRY...CATCH Statement

The TRY...CATCH statement implements semistructured error handling in T-SQL. Let's
begin with the format for TRY...CATCH:

```
BEGIN TRY
    { SQL statement | statement block }
END TRY
BEGIN CATCH
    { SQL statement | statement block }
END CATCH
```

The TRY...CATCH statement provides error handling similar to C++ and the .NET languages. If one of the statements in the TRY block generates an error, control is passed to the CATCH block. In order for TRY...CATCH to catch errors, the following conditions must be met:

- The error must have a severity higher than 10, but cannot close the database connection.

- The error cannot be a compilation error, such as a syntax error.

- The error cannot have occurred during a statement level recompilation (e.g., name resolution error).

- The error must not have been caused by a broken connection (e.g., KILL statement execution).

- The error must not have been caused by an Attention, such as those sent by Microsoft Distributed Transaction Coordinator.

Unlike C++ and .NET language structured error handling, T-SQL's TRY...CATCH does not allow you to apply multiple CATCH blocks to a single TRY. The TRY...CATCH statement also prevents the error from being automatically passed on to the calling batch, procedure, or front-end application. You can use the RAISERROR statement to rethrow an error or throw a new error from within a CATCH block.

TRY...CATCH blocks can also be nested. If a statement in a nested TRY block throws an error, control is passed to its associated CATCH block. If a statement in a nested CATCH block throws an error, control passes to the containing CATCH block. A nested TRY...CATCH block is useful for capturing potential errors in a CATCH block as well.

In addition, SQL Server 2005 enhances error handling by adding several functions for gathering error information inside a CATCH block:

- ERROR_NUMBER() is the number of the error, which is the same value returned by the @@error function. Unlike @@error, ERROR_NUMBER() is not cleared and reset on each statement executed.

- ERROR_SEVERITY()() is the error severity level.

- ERROR_STATE() is the error state number.

- ERROR_PROCEDURE() is the name of the stored procedure or trigger where the error occurred.

- ERROR_LINE() is the number of the line in the routine that generated the error.

- ERROR_MESSAGE() returns the complete error message text.

The CATCH block functions in the previous list always return NULL when they are accessed outside of a CATCH block. Listing 4-8 shows a simple example of a TRY...CATCH block with code that will generate a primary key constraint violation error, severity 14.

Listing 4-8. *TRY...CATCH Block Error Handling*

```
CREATE TABLE #test_error (i INT NOT NULL PRIMARY KEY);

BEGIN TRY
    INSERT INTO #test_error (i) VALUES (1);
    INSERT INTO #test_error (i) VALUES (1); -- This INSERT causes the error.
END TRY
BEGIN CATCH
    PRINT ERROR_NUMBER();
    PRINT ERROR_SEVERITY();
    PRINT ERROR_STATE();
    PRINT ERROR_LINE();
    PRINT ERROR_MESSAGE();
END CATCH

DROP TABLE #test_error;
```

CASE Expression

The T-SQL CASE function is SQL Server's implementation of the ANSI SQL CASE expression. While the previous T-SQL control-of-flow statements I discussed allow for conditional execution of SQL statements or statement blocks, the CASE expression allows for set-based conditional processing inside a single query. CASE provides two syntaxes, *simple* and *searched*, which I discuss in this section.

Simple CASE Expression

The simple CASE expression returns a *result expression* based on the value of a given *input expression*. Here is the format for a simple CASE expression:

```
CASE input expression
    WHEN when expression1 THEN result expression1
    WHEN when expression2 THEN result expression2
    [ ...n ]
    [ ELSE else result expression ]
END
```

The simple CASE expression compares the *input expression* to the series of *when expressions*. Once a match is encountered, CASE returns the corresponding *result expression*. If no match is found, the *else result expression* is returned. Consider the example in Listing 4-9, which counts all of the AdventureWorks customers on the West Coast:

Listing 4-9. *Simple CASE Expression*

```
SELECT SUM(AllCustomers.NumOfCustomers), AllCustomers.Coast
FROM
(
    SELECT COUNT(*) AS NumOfCustomers,
        sp.CountryRegionCode,
        CASE sp.StateProvinceCode
            WHEN 'CA' THEN 'West Coast'
            WHEN 'WA' THEN 'West Coast'
            WHEN 'OR' THEN 'West Coast'
            ELSE 'Elsewhere'
        END AS Coast
    FROM Sales.CustomerAddress s
        INNER JOIN Person.Address p
            ON s.AddressID = p.AddressID
        INNER JOIN Person.StateProvince sp
            ON p.StateProvinceID = p.StateProvinceID
    WHERE CountryRegionCode = 'US'
    GROUP BY sp.CountryRegionCode,
        sp.StateProvinceCode
) AllCustomers
GROUP BY AllCustomers.Coast;
```

The CASE expression in the subquery returns a value of West Coast where the StateProvinceCode is CA, WA, and OR. For all other states in the United States, it returns a value of Elsewhere:

```
CASE sp.StateProvinceCode
    WHEN 'CA' THEN 'West Coast'
    WHEN 'WA' THEN 'West Coast'
    WHEN 'OR' THEN 'West Coast'
    ELSE 'Elsewhere'
END AS Coast
```

Note If none of the *when expressions* match the *input expression*, the *else result expression* is returned. If no match is found and ELSE is not specified, CASE returns NULL.

Searched CASE Expression

The searched CASE expression provides a mechanism for performing more complex comparisons. The syntax is the following:

```
CASE
    WHEN Boolean expression1 THEN result expression1
    WHEN Boolean expression2 THEN result expression2
        [ ...n ]
    [ ELSE else result expression ]
END
```

The searched CASE evaluates the *Boolean expressions* provided until it encounters one that evaluates to TRUE. At that point it returns the corresponding *result expression*. If none of the *Boolean expressions* evaluates to TRUE, the *else result expression* is returned. The *Boolean expressions* in the searched CASE expression can take advantage of any valid SQL Boolean operators including <, >, =, LIKE, IN, and so on. We can expand the previous simple CASE expression to cover multiple geographic areas using the searched CASE expression with the IN logical operator, as shown in Listing 4-10.

Listing 4-10. *Searched CASE Expression*

```
SELECT SUM(AllCustomers.NumOfCustomers), AllCustomers.Area
FROM
(
    SELECT COUNT(*) AS NumOfCustomers, sp.CountryRegionCode,
        CASE
            WHEN sp.StateProvinceCode IN ('CA', 'WA', 'OR') THEN 'West Coast'
            WHEN sp.StateProvinceCode IN ('HI', 'AK') THEN 'Pacific'
            WHEN sp.StateProvinceCode IN ('CT', 'MA', 'ME',
                'NH', 'RI', 'VT') THEN 'New England'
            ELSE 'Elsewhere'
        END AS Area
    FROM Sales.CustomerAddress s
        INNER JOIN Person.Address p
            ON s.AddressID = p.AddressID
        INNER JOIN Person.StateProvince sp
            ON p.StateProvinceID = p.StateProvinceID
    WHERE CountryRegionCode = 'US'
    GROUP BY sp.CountryRegionCode, sp.StateProvinceCode
) AllCustomers
GROUP BY AllCustomers.Area;
```

The searched `CASE` expression in the example uses the `IN` operator to return the geographical area that `StateProvinceCode` is in: `StateProvinceCode` values of `CA`, `WA`, and `OR` return `West Coast`; `HI` and `AK` return `Pacific`; and `CT`, `MA`, `ME`, `NH`, `RI`, and `VT` return `New England`. If none of the *Boolean expressions* are `TRUE`, the searched `CASE` expression returns `Elsewhere`:

```
    CASE
        WHEN sp.StateProvinceCode IN ('CA', 'WA', 'OR') THEN 'West Coast'
        WHEN sp.StateProvinceCode IN ('HI', 'AK') THEN 'Pacific'
        WHEN sp.StateProvinceCode IN ('CT', 'MA', 'ME',
            'NH', 'RI', 'VT') THEN 'New England'
        ELSE 'Elsewhere'
    END AS Area
```

The `CASE` expression, simple or searched, can be used in `SELECT`, `UPDATE`, `INSERT`, or `DELETE` statements.

Tip If you want to check for a NULL in a CASE expression, you must use the IS NULL or IS NOT NULL keywords in a searched CASE expression. Because of the restrictions on comparisons to NULL, checking directly for NULL with a simple CASE expression is not allowed.

CASE and Pivot Tables

Many times, reporting requirements dictate that a result should be returned in pivot table format. *Pivot table* format simply means that the labels for columns and/or rows are generated from the data contained in the tables. Microsoft Access users have long had the ability to generate pivot tables on their data, and SQL Server 2005 introduces the new PIVOT and UNPIVOT operators (described in Chapter 3). Prior to SQL Server 2005, however, CASE expressions were the only method of generating pivot table type queries. And even though SQL Server 2005 provides the new PIVOT and UNPIVOT operators, truly dynamic pivot tables still require using CASE expressions and dynamic SQL. The static pivot table query shown in Listing 4-11 returns a pivot table style result with the total number of orders for each AdventureWorks sales region in the United States.

Listing 4-11. *CASE-Style Pivot Table*

```
SELECT t.CountryRegionCode,
    SUM (
        CASE
            WHEN t.Name = 'Northwest' THEN 1
            ELSE 0
        END) AS Northwest_US,
    SUM (
        CASE
            WHEN t.Name = 'Northeast' THEN 1
            ELSE 0
        END) AS Northeast_US,
    SUM (
        CASE
            WHEN t.Name = 'Southwest' THEN 1
            ELSE 0
        END) AS Southwest_US,
```

```
    SUM (
        CASE
            WHEN t.Name = 'Southeast' THEN 1
            ELSE 0
        END) AS Southeast_US,
    SUM (
        CASE
            WHEN t.Name = 'Central' THEN 1
            ELSE 0
        END) AS Central_US
FROM Sales.SalesOrderHeader soh
    INNER JOIN Sales.SalesTerritory t
        ON soh.TerritoryID = t.TerritoryID
WHERE t.CountryRegionCode = 'US'
GROUP BY  t.CountryRegionCode
```

Of course this type of static pivot table can also be done with the new SQL Server 2005 PIVOT operator, as shown in Listing 4-12.

Listing 4-12. *PIVOT Operator Pivot Table*

```
SELECT [CountryRegionCode], [Northwest], [Northeast],
    [Southwest], [Southeast], [Central]
FROM
(
    SELECT CountryRegionCode, t.Name
    FROM Sales.SalesOrderHeader soh
        INNER JOIN Sales.SalesTerritory t
            ON soh.TerritoryID = t.TerritoryID
    WHERE t.CountryRegionCode = 'US'
) p
PIVOT
(
    COUNT (Name)
    FOR Name
    IN ([Northwest], [Northeast], [Southwest], [Southeast], [Central])
) AS pvt;
```

See Chapter 3 for more on PIVOT and UNPIVOT. The results of both these methods of generating a pivot table query produce the same results, as shown in Figure 4-1.

Figure 4-1. *PIVOT query result*

On occasion you might need to run a pivot table–style report where you don't know the column names in advance. This is a dynamic pivot table script that uses a temporary table and dynamic SQL to generate a pivot table, without specifying the column names in advance. Listing 4-13 demonstrates one method of generating dynamic pivot tables in T-SQL.

Listing 4-13. *Dynamic Pivot Table Query*

```
DECLARE @sql NVARCHAR(MAX);
CREATE TABLE #temp (TerritoryID INT NOT NULL PRIMARY KEY,
    CountryRegion NVARCHAR(20) NOT NULL,
    CountryRegionCode NVARCHAR(3) NOT NULL);

INSERT INTO #temp (TerritoryID, CountryRegion, CountryRegionCode)
    SELECT DISTINCT TerritoryID,
        Name,
        CountryRegionCode
    FROM Sales.SalesTerritory;

DECLARE @i INT;

SELECT @i = MIN(TerritoryID)
    FROM #temp;

SELECT @sql = N'SELECT ';

WHILE @i <=
    (
        SELECT MAX(TerritoryID)
        FROM #temp
    )
```

```
BEGIN
    SELECT @sql = @sql + N'SUM (CASE ' +
        N'WHEN t.TerritoryID = ' + CAST(TerritoryID AS NVARCHAR(3)) +
        N' ' +N'THEN 1 ELSE 0 END) AS ' + QUOTENAME(CountryRegion +
        N'_' + CountryRegionCode)+
        CASE WHEN @i < (
                SELECT MAX(TerritoryID)
                FROM #temp
            ) THEN N', '
            ELSE N' '
        END
    FROM #temp
    WHERE TerritoryID = @i;

    SELECT @i = @i + 1;
END;


SELECT @sql = @sql + N'FROM Sales.SalesOrderHeader soh ' +
    N'INNER JOIN Sales.SalesTerritory t ' +
    N'ON soh.TerritoryID = t.TerritoryID ' ;

EXEC (@sql);

DROP TABLE #temp;
```

The previous script first declares an nvarchar variable to hold the dynamically generated SQL script. It then creates a temporary table and populates it with all of the column
names that will be generated by the script:

```
DECLARE @sql VARCHAR(MAX);
CREATE TABLE #temp (TerritoryID INT NOT NULL PRIMARY KEY,
    CountryRegion NVARCHAR(20) NOT NULL,
    CountryRegionCode NVARCHAR(3) NOT NULL);

INSERT INTO #temp (TerritoryID, CountryRegion, CountryRegionCode)
    SELECT DISTINCT TerritoryID,
        Name,
        CountryRegionCode
    FROM Sales.SalesTerritory;
```

Next, the script locates the first TerritoryID from the temporary table and initializes
the @sql SELECT statement:

```
DECLARE @i INT;

SELECT @i = MIN(TerritoryID)
    FROM #temp;

SELECT @sql = 'SELECT ';
```

The script then generates the CASE expressions and column names dynamically based on the data stored in the temporary table:

```
WHILE @i <=
    (
        SELECT MAX(TerritoryID)
        FROM #temp
    )
BEGIN
    SELECT @sql = @sql + 'SUM (CASE ' +
        N'WHEN t.TerritoryID = ' + CAST(TerritoryID AS NVARCHAR(3)) +
        N' ' +N'THEN 1 ELSE 0 END) AS ' + QUOTENAME(CountryRegion +
        N'_' + CountryRegionCode)+
        CASE WHEN @i < (
                SELECT MAX(TerritoryID)
                FROM #temp
            ) THEN N', '
            ELSE N' '
        END
    FROM #temp
    WHERE TerritoryID = @i;

    SELECT @i = @i + 1;
END;
```

Finally, you add the FROM clause to the dynamic SQL, execute it (using EXEC), and drop the temporary table:

```
SELECT @sql = @sql + N'FROM Sales.SalesOrderHeader soh ' +
    N'INNER JOIN Sales.SalesTerritory t ' +
    N'ON soh.TerritoryID = t.TerritoryID ' ;

EXEC (@sql);

DROP TABLE #temp;
```

The result of the dynamic pivot table query is shown in Figure 4-2.

	Northwest_...	NortReast_...	Central_...	Southwest_...	Southeast_...	Canada_...	France_...	Germany_...	Australia...	United Kingdom_...
1	4594	352	385	6224	486	4067	2672	2623	6843	3219

Figure 4-2. *Dynamic pivot table query results*

■**Caution** Anytime you use dynamic SQL, make sure that you take precautions against SQL *injection*, that is, malicious SQL code being inserted into your SQL statements. In this instance we're using the QUOTENAME function to quote the column names being dynamically generated to help avoid SQL injection problems.

COALESCE and NULLIF

The COALESCE function takes a list of expressions as arguments and returns the first non-NULL value from the list. The format for COALESCE is the following:

```
COALESCE (expression1, expression2 [ , ...n ])
```

The COALESCE function is defined by ANSI as shorthand for the equivalent searched CASE expression:

```
CASE
    WHEN expression1 IS NOT NULL THEN expression1
    WHEN expression2 IS NOT NULL THEN expression2
    [ ...n ]
END
```

The following COALESCE function call returns the value of MiddleName when MiddleName is not NULL, or the string 'No Middle Name' when MiddleName is NULL:

```
COALESCE (MiddleName, 'No Middle Name')
```

The NULLIF function accepts two arguments. NULLIF returns NULL if the two expressions are equal, or the value of the first expression if they are not equal. The format of NULLIF is the following:

```
NULLIF (expression1, expression2)
```

NULLIF is defined by the ANSI standard as equivalent to the following searched CASE expression:

```
CASE WHEN expression1 = expression2 THEN NULL
ELSE expression1
END
```

NULLIF is often used in conjunction with COALESCE. Consider the following example in Listing 4-14 that combines COALESCE with NULLIF to return the string 'This is NULL or A' if the variable @s is set to 'A' or NULL.

Listing 4-14. *Using COALESCE with NULLIF*

```
DECLARE @s VARCHAR(10);
SELECT @s = 'A';
SELECT COALESCE(NULLIF(@s, 'A'), 'This is NULL or A');
```

T-SQL has long had alternate functionality similar to COALESCE. Specifically the ISNULL function accepts two parameters and returns NULL if they are equal.

■**Tip** COALESCE is more flexible than ISNULL and is ANSI-compliant to boot. This means it is also the more portable option among ANSI-compliant systems. COALESCE also implicitly converts the result to the data type with the highest precedence from the list of expressions. ISNULL implicitly converts the result to the data type of the first expression. The fact of the matter is that the only thing ISNULL has going for it is that it is backward-compatible with SQL 6.5 (COALESCE was introduced with SQL 7.0). Keep this in mind when deciding which function to use.

Summary

This chapter discussed SQL three-valued logic, T-SQL control-of-flow statements, and CASE expressions. The control-of-flow statements discussed include the following:

- BEGIN...END keywords

- IF...ELSE statement

- WHILE, BREAK, and CONTINUE statements

- GOTO statement

- WAITFOR statement

- RETURN keyword

- TRY...CATCH statement

The CASE expression section included discussions of simple CASE expressions, searched CASE expressions, and the COALESCE and NULLIF functions, which are defined as shorthand for common CASE expressions. Also covered was static and dynamic pivot table creation using CASE expressions.

The next chapter begins my discussion of T-SQL programmability features beginning with user-defined functions.

CHAPTER 5

■ ■ ■

User-Defined Functions

Each new version of SQL Server features improvements to T-SQL that make development easier. SQL Server 2000 introduced the concept of user-defined functions (UDFs). Like functions in other programming languages, T-SQL UDFs offer a convenient way for developers to define procedural routines that accept parameters, perform actions based on those parameters, and return data to the caller. T-SQL functions come in three flavors: inline table-valued functions, multistatement table-valued functions, and scalar functions. In this chapter I will talk about T-SQL UDFs. SQL Server 2005 also adds the ability to create SQLCLR UDFs, which I talk about in Chapter 14.

Scalar Functions

The basic form of user-defined functions is the *scalar function*. A scalar function returns a single value as its result. The following is the format of the scalar UDF CREATE FUNCTION statement:

```
CREATE FUNCTION [ schema_name. ] function_name
( [ { @parameter [ AS ] [ data_type_schema. ] parameter_data_type [ = default ] }
    [ , ...n ] ]
)
RETURNS return_data_type
[ WITH function_option [ , ...n ] ]
[ AS ]
BEGIN
    function_body
    RETURN scalar_expression
END;
```

The statement begins with the CREATE FUNCTION keywords followed by the *schema_name* and *function_name* separated by a period, the standard T-SQL two-part naming syntax. The *schema_name* is optional, and if omitted it defaults to the current schema (this will usually be dbo). It's a very good idea to always specify the *schema_name* to ensure your UDF gets created in the correct schema. The *function_name* must follow the standard T-SQL identifier naming conventions.

■**Caution** Always specify the `schema_name` to ensure your UDF gets created in the correct schema.

The *function_name* is immediately followed by the parameter list. Names of parameters in the parameter list follow the convention for T-SQL variable names. Each parameter name begins with the *at* sign (@), and must comply with the rules for T-SQL identifiers. The type of each parameter is specified after the `AS` keyword. The *parameter_data_type* specifies the scalar type of each parameter. The optional *data_type_schema* specifies the schema to which the specified *parameter_data_type* belongs. Each parameter can also have a default value assigned to it by using the optional `=` *default* immediately after the *parameter_data_type*.

■**Note** Not all functions require parameters. The system function `PI()`, which returns the value of the constant π (3.14159265358979), requires no parameters. If your function doesn't require parameters, specify the empty parameter list "`()`" in the definition. When calling a function that doesn't require parameters, the "`()`" are required after the function name.

The `RETURNS` keyword is followed by a valid SQL Server data type, indicating the type of data returned by the UDF.

The optional `WITH` keyword indicates one or more of the following function options. If more than one is specified, they are separated by commas:

- The `ENCRYPTION` option specifies that your UDF will be stored in the database in encrypted format. It also prevents users with no access to the system tables or database files from retrieving the obfuscated text of your UDF.

- The `SCHEMABINDING` option specifies that your UDF will be bound to database objects referenced in the `function_body`. With `SCHEMABINDING` turned on, attempts to change or drop referenced tables and other database objects results in an error. This helps prevent inadvertent changes that can break your UDF. Additionally, `SCHEMABINDING` can improve the performance of UDFs that don't reference other database objects at all.

If your UDF doesn't reference any database tables, you can gain performance benefits from specifying the WITH SCHEMABINDING option. By default SQL Server 2005 sets two extended properties, SYSTEMDATAACCESS and USERDATAACCESS, to 1 indicating that your UDF could potentially
access system catalogs and user tables. By using WITH SCHEMABINDING on a UDF that doesn't
access tables and database objects, SQL Server will reset these properties to 0. This in turn allows
the query optimizer to generate more efficient plans, since it doesn't have to generate the additional protections against data changes that UDFs accessing table data require. You can verify the
values of these extended properties with the OBJECTPROPERTYEX() function:

```
SELECT OBJECTPROPERTYEX(OBJECT_ID('function_name'), 'SYSTEMDATAACCESS');
SELECT OBJECTPROPERTYEX(OBJECT_ID('function_name'), 'USERDATAACCESS');
```

- The RETURNS NULL ON NULL INPUT option indicates to SQL Server that if any of the
  parameters passed in are NULL, the result is NULL. This optimizing option allows SQL
  to skip the body of the function if NULL is passed in as a parameter.

- The CALLED ON NULL INPUT option is the opposite of RETURNS NULL ON NULL INPUT.
  When CALLED ON NULL INPUT is specified, SQL Server executes the body of the function even if the parameters are NULL. CALLED ON NULL INPUT is the default for all
  scalar-valued functions.

- The EXECUTE AS option is specified with the EXECUTE AS clause:

  ```
  { EXEC | EXECUTE } AS { CALLER | SELF | OWNER | 'user_name' }
  ```

  EXECUTE AS can be used on scalar UDFs and multistatement TVFs but cannot be
  used with inline TVFs. This option allows the UDF to run under the context of the
  specified user.

The CALLER keyword specifies the UDF will run under the context of the user executing the function. CALLER is the default if no EXECUTE AS option is specified. SELF specifies
the UDF will run under the context of the user who created (or altered) it. OWNER specifies
the UDF should run in the context of the owner of the function, or the owner of the
schema containing the function if the UDF does not have an owner. Finally, a specific
user can be specified by specifying 'user_name'.

To pull it all together, we'll take a trip back in time to high school geometry class for
a simple scalar UDF demonstration. In accordance with the rules passed down from
Euclid to Miss Kopp (my high-school geometry teacher) this UDF accepts a circle's
radius and returns the area of the circle using the formula area $= \pi \cdot r^2$. Listing 5-1
demonstrates a simple scalar UDF.

Listing 5-1. *Simple Scalar UDF*

```
CREATE FUNCTION dbo.fnCircleArea (@radius FLOAT = 1.0)
RETURNS FLOAT
WITH RETURNS NULL ON NULL INPUT, SCHEMABINDING
AS
BEGIN
    RETURN PI() * POWER(@radius, 2);
END;
```

The first line defines the schema and name of the function (dbo.fnCircleArea) and the single required parameter: the radius of the circle (@radius). I will define @radius as a T-SQL FLOAT type with a default value of 1.0:

```
CREATE FUNCTION dbo.fnCircleArea (@radius FLOAT = 1.0)
```

The next line contains the RETURNS keyword, specifying that the UDF returns a FLOAT result:

```
RETURNS FLOAT
```

The third line contains optional *function_options* following the WITH keyword. In the sample, I use the RETURNS NULL ON NULL INPUT and SCHEMABINDING function options for performance improvements:

```
WITH RETURNS NULL ON NULL INPUT, SCHEMABINDING
```

The AS keyword indicates the start of the function body, which must be enclosed in the T-SQL BEGIN...END keywords for a scalar UDF. Our sample function is very simple, consisting of a single RETURN statement that immediately returns the value of the circle area calculation. Note that the RETURN statement must be the last statement before the END keyword in every scalar UDF:

```
AS
BEGIN
    RETURN PI() * POWER(@radius, 2);
END;
```

You can test this user-defined function with a couple of SELECT statements:

```
SELECT dbo.fnCircleArea(10);
SELECT dbo.fnCircleArea(DEFAULT);
```

Recursion in Scalar UDFs

Now that we have the basics, let's hang out in math class for a few more minutes to talk about recursion. Like most procedural programming languages that allow function definitions, T-SQL allows recursion. There's hardly a better way to demonstrate recursion than the most basic recursive algorithm around: the factorial function.

For those who put factorials out of their minds immediately after graduation, let me give a brief rundown of what they are. A *factorial* is the product of all natural (or counting) numbers less than or equal to n, where $n > 0$. Factorials are represented in mathematics by the *bang* notation: $n!$. As an example, $5! = 1 \cdot 2 \cdot 3 \cdot 4 \cdot 5 = 120$. Our simple scalar UDF will calculate a factorial recursively for an integer parameter passed into it. Listing 5-2 is a recursive scalar UDF.

Listing 5-2. *Recursive Scalar UDF*

```
CREATE FUNCTION dbo.fnFactorial(@n INT = 1)
RETURNS FLOAT
WITH RETURNS NULL ON NULL INPUT
AS
BEGIN
    RETURN
        (CASE
            WHEN @n <= 0 THEN NULL
            WHEN @n > 1 THEN CAST(@n AS FLOAT) * dbo.fnFactorial(@n - 1)
            ELSE 1
        END);
END;
```

This simple UDF calculates the factorial recursively by calling itself. Here we'll step through the code. The first few lines are similar to the previous sample:

```
CREATE FUNCTION dbo.fnFactorial(@n INT = 1)
RETURNS FLOAT
WITH RETURNS NULL ON NULL INPUT
```

This defines the function with the name dbo.fnFactorial, which accepts a single INT parameter. We set the parameter default to 1.

UDF DEFAULT PARAMETERS

Unlike stored procedures, UDFs require that all parameters be specified when calling them, even if you declare default values for those parameters. If you want to use a parameter's default value, you must use the T-SQL keyword DEFAULT as a placeholder for the parameter when calling the UDF. Note that DEFAULT is not a value or a string, but a T-SQL keyword. To call the dbo.fnFactorial UDF with the default parameter value, you would use a statement like the following:

```
SELECT dbo.fnFactorial (DEFAULT);
```

Calling dbo.fnFactorial with no parameters

```
SELECT dbo.fnFactorial();
```

makes SQL Server complain:

```
Msg 313, Level 16, State 2, Line 1
An insufficient number of arguments were supplied for the procedure or
function dbo.fnFactorial.
```

This limits the usefulness of default parameter values in UDFs. I personally recommend accepting NULL values and using the COALESCE function to assign a default value yourself inside the body of the function. This is a much more flexible solution than the DEFAULT keyword.

The dbo.fnFactorial UDF returns a FLOAT result, because the INT type overflows at 13! and BIGINT bombs out at 21!. We also specify RETURNS NULL ON NULL INPUT for increased performance if @n is NULL.

Next we define the body of our UDF. Again, a single RETURN statement, this time with a searched CASE expression, will do the trick:

```
AS
BEGIN
    RETURN
        (CASE
            WHEN @n <= 0 THEN NULL
            WHEN @n > 1 THEN CAST(@n AS FLOAT) * dbo.fnFactorial(@n - 1)
            WHEN @n = 1 THEN 1
        END);
END;
```

The CASE expression checks the value of @n. If @n is 0 or negative, dbo.fnFactorial returns NULL. If @n is greater than 1, dbo.fnFactorial returns @n * dbo.fnFactorial(@n - 1), the recursive part of our UDF. Finally, if @n is 1, it returns 1. This is the part of the dbo.fnFactorial UDF that actually stops the recursion. Without the check for @n = 1, you could theoretically end up in an infinite recursive loop. In practice, however, SQL Server will "save you from yourself" by limiting you to a maximum of 32 levels of recursion. So you can call dbo.fnFactorial with the following parameters:

```
SELECT dbo.fnFactorial(NULL);    -- Returns NULL
SELECT dbo.fnFactorial(-1);      -- Returns NULL
SELECT dbo.fnFactorial(0);       -- Returns NULL
SELECT dbo.fnFactorial(5);       -- Returns 120
SELECT dbo.fnFactorial(32);      -- Returns 2.63130836933694E+35
```

But if you try to do the following

```
SELECT dbo.fnFactorial(33);
```

SQL Server will grumble loudly with the following message:

```
Msg 217, Level 16, State 1, Line 1
Maximum stored procedure, function, trigger, or view nesting level
exceeded (limit 32).
```

Procedural Code in UDFs

So far we've talked about simple functions that demonstrate the basic points of scalar user-defined functions; but in all likelihood, unless we're implementing business logic for a swimming pool installation company, neither you nor I will probably need to calculate the area of a circle in T-SQL.

A common problem that we have a much greater chance of running into is name-based searching. T-SQL offers tools for exact matching, partial matching, and even limited pattern matching. Built-in phonetic matching (*sound-alike matching*) in T-SQL is offered via the SOUNDEX function. The Soundex algorithm itself is nearly 90 years old though, and several improved algorithms have sprung up to replace it. One such improved algorithm, often used by law enforcement due to its increased accuracy, is the New York State Identification and Intelligence System algorithm (NYSIIS). NYSIIS converts groups of one, two, or three alphabetic characters (known as *n-grams*) in names to a phonetic ("sounds like") approximation. This makes it easier to search for names that have similar pronunciations but different spellings, such as *Smythe* and *Smith*.

To demonstrate procedural code in UDFs, we will implement a UDF that phonetically encodes names using NYSIIS encoding rules. The rules of NYSIIS phonetic encoding are relatively simple. In the following rule list, the right-facing arrow (➤) indicates "replace with":

1. The rules to encode the first characters of a name are the following:

MAC ➤ MCC

KN ➤ NN

K ➤ C

PH ➤ FF

PF ➤ FF

SCH ➤ SSS

2. The last characters of the name are encoded according to the following rules:

EE ➤ Y

IE ➤ Y

DT, RT, RD, NT, or ND ➤ D

3. The first character of the encoded value is set to the first character of the name.

4. After the first characters and last characters are encoded, all remaining characters in the name are encoded according to the following rules:

EV ➤ AF else A, E, I, O, U ➤ A

Q ➤ G

Z ➤ S

M ➤ N

KN ➤ N else K ➤ C

SCH ➤ SSS

PH ➤ FF

If previous or next character is a nonvowel, H ➤ previous.

If previous character is a vowel, W ➤ previous.

5. If the last character of the encoded name is S, remove it.

6. If the last characters of the encoded name are AY, replace them with Y.

7. If the last character of the encoded name is A, remove it.

8. Reduce all side-by-side duplicate characters in the encoded name to a single character (e.g., AA ➤ A, and SS ➤ S).

We could use some fairly large CASE expressions to implement these rules, but I've chosen the more flexible option of using a replacement table. This table will contain the majority of the replacement rules in three columns:

- Location, which tells you whether the rule should be applied to the start, end, or middle of the name

- NGram, which is the n-gram, or sequence of characters, you are trying to encode

- Replacement, which represents the replacement value for a given n-gram

The following CREATE TABLE statement builds the NYSIIS phonetic encoding "replacement rules" table:

```
-- Create the NYSIIS replacement rules table
CREATE TABLE dbo.NYSIIS_Replacements
    (Location NVARCHAR(10) NOT NULL,
    NGram NVARCHAR(10) NOT NULL,
    Replacement NVARCHAR(10) NOT NULL,
    PRIMARY KEY (Location, NGram));
```

Several INSERT statements such as the following are used to populate the table with rules for n-grams that appear at the beginning, in the middle, or at the end of words:

```
INSERT INTO NYSIIS_Replacements (Location, NGram, Replacement)
    VALUES (N'End', N'AY', N'YY');
INSERT INTO NYSIIS_Replacements (Location, NGram, Replacement)
    VALUES (N'End', N'DT', N'DD');
INSERT INTO NYSIIS_Replacements (Location, NGram, Replacement)
    VALUES (N'End', N'EE', N'YY');
...
```

■**Note** Because of the length of this example, the full NYSIIS sample code listing is given in Appendix D.

The NYSIIS_Replacements table rules reflect most of the NYSIIS rules described by Robert L. Taft in his famous paper "Name Search Techniques." To remove side-by-side duplicates, you'll use a set-based solution featuring a Numbers table. This is simply a table with the counting numbers in it (from 1 to 10,000 in this case), as shown in Listing 5-3.

Listing 5-3. *Creating a Numbers Table*

```
-- This SELECT INTO statement uses the T-SQL IDENTITY function to quickly
-- build a Numbers table
SELECT TOP 10000 IDENTITY(INT, 1, 1) AS Num
INTO dbo.Numbers
FROM sys.columns a
    CROSS JOIN sys.columns b;

-- A table isn't a table without a Primary Key
ALTER TABLE dbo.Numbers
    ADD CONSTRAINT PK_Num PRIMARY KEY CLUSTERED (Num);
```

■**Tip** The Numbers table is a classic SQL tool useful for converting procedural code to set-based code. A Numbers table is always handy to have around and is, in my opinion, one of the greatest (and cheapest) tools you can add to your T-SQL toolkit. Building one is as simple as the previous two T-SQL statements, and once it's built you never have to change it; just use it to join in other queries.

The remainder of the NYSIIS rules, such as removal of trailing S characters, will be implemented using T-SQL flow-of-control constructs and procedural loops in the function body.

After creating our tables, we'll define our UDF. The complete UDF script is given in Appendix D. Here we will break down the UDF. The UDF accepts a single NVARCHAR(50) parameter and returns an NVARCHAR(50) result. I've chosen to use the RETURNS NULL ON NULL INPUT option to enhance performance when NULL is passed as a parameter:

```
CREATE FUNCTION dbo.fnNYSIIS (@Name NVARCHAR(50))
RETURNS NVARCHAR(50)
WITH RETURNS NULL ON NULL INPUT
```

In the body of the UDF we'll begin by applying some of the previously defined rules for NYSIIS. We'll begin by declaring and initializing a local variable to hold our result. Then we will use a couple of SELECT statements in conjunction with T-SQL's string manipulation functions to replace the start and end n-grams of the name according to our NYSIIS rules table:

```
AS
BEGIN
    DECLARE @Result NVARCHAR(50);    -- This will contain our end result
    SELECT @Result = UPPER(@Name);

    -- Replace the start n-gram
    SELECT TOP 1 @Result = STUFF(@Result, 1, LEN(NGram), Replacement)
    FROM dbo.NYSIIS_Replacements
    WHERE Location = N'Start'
        AND SUBSTRING(@Result, 1, LEN(NGram)) = NGram
    ORDER BY LEN(NGram) DESC;

    -- Replace the end n-gram
    SELECT TOP 1 @Result = STUFF(@Result, LEN(@Result) - LEN(NGram) + 1,
        LEN(NGram), Replacement)
    FROM dbo.NYSIIS_Replacements
    WHERE Location = N'End'
        AND SUBSTRING(@Result, LEN(@Result) - LEN(NGram) + 1, LEN(NGram)) = NGram
    ORDER BY LEN(NGram) DESC;
```

Next we will save the first letter of the name for later use, perform a loop to apply the middle-of-name n-gram rules, and finally we restore the first letter we previously saved:

```
    -- Store the first letter of the name
    DECLARE @first_letter NCHAR(1)
    SELECT @first_letter = SUBSTRING(@Result, 1, 1);

    -- Replace all middle n-grams
    DECLARE @replacement NVARCHAR(10);
    DECLARE @i INT;
    SELECT @i = 1;
    WHILE @i < LEN(@Result)
    BEGIN
        SELECT @replacement = NULL;

        -- Grab the middle-of-name replacement n-gram
        SELECT TOP 1 @replacement = Replacement
        FROM dbo.NYSIIS_Replacements
        WHERE Location = N'Mid'
            AND SUBSTRING(@Result, @i, LEN(NGram)) = NGram
        ORDER BY LEN(NGram) DESC;
```

```
        -- If we found a replacement, apply it
        IF @replacement IS NOT NULL
            SELECT @Result = STUFF(@Result, @i, LEN(@replacement), @replacement);

        -- Move on to the next n-gram
        SELECT @i = @i + COALESCE(LEN(@replacement), 1);
    END;


    -- Replace the first character with the first letter we saved at the start
    SELECT @Result = STUFF(@Result, 1, 1, @first_letter);
```

The next step is to apply the special-case rule handling for the letter H. We will do this in a single SELECT statement using the Numbers table:

```
-- Here we apply our special rules for the 'H' character
SELECT @Result =
    STUFF(@Result, Num, 1,
        CASE SUBSTRING(@Result, Num, 1)
            WHEN N'H'
            THEN
                CASE
                    WHEN SUBSTRING(@Result, Num + 1, 1)
                        NOT IN (N'A', N'E', N'I', N'O', N'U')
                    OR SUBSTRING(@Result, Num - 1, 1)
                        NOT IN (N'A', N'E', N'I', N'O', N'U')
                    THEN SUBSTRING(@Result, Num - 1, 1)
                    ELSE N'H'
                END
            ELSE SUBSTRING(@Result, Num, 1)
        END)
FROM dbo.Numbers
WHERE Num <= LEN(@Result);
```

I'll use a similar SELECT statement to reduce side-by-side duplicate letters to a single letter. The code to replace the duplicates requires two steps: first it replaces the leftmost letter in each series of side-by-side duplicate letters found with a period; it then removes all periods from the result using the T-SQL REPLACE function:

```
-- Here we replace the first letter of any sequence of two
-- side-by-side duplicate letters with a period '.'
SELECT @Result =
    STUFF(@Result, Num, 1,
        CASE SUBSTRING(@Result, Num, 1)
            WHEN SUBSTRING(@Result, Num + 1, 1) THEN N'.'
            ELSE SUBSTRING(@Result, Num, 1)
        END)
FROM dbo.Numbers
WHERE Num <= LEN(@Result);

-- Next we replace all periods '.' with an empty string ''
SELECT @Result = REPLACE(@Result, N'.', N'');
```

The final rules require removing trailing S characters, followed by the removal of trailing A characters:

```
-- Remove trailing 'S' characters
WHILE RIGHT(@Result, 1) = N'S'
    SELECT @Result = STUFF(@Result, LEN(@Result), 1, N'');

-- Remove trailing vowels
WHILE RIGHT(@Result, 1) = N'A'
    SELECT @Result = STUFF(@Result, LEN(@Result), 1, N'');
```

Finally, you end the UDF by returning the calculated result:

```
RETURN @Result;
END;
```

Now that we've built our UDF we can use it to query the Person.Contacts table. The following query retrieves all contacts with the last name *Johnson* and its similar or alternate spellings:

```
SELECT ContactID, FirstName, MiddleName, LastName
FROM Person.Contact
WHERE dbo.fnNYSIIS(LastName) = dbo.fnNYSIIS(N'Johnson');
```

A sample of the results from this query is shown in Figure 5-1.

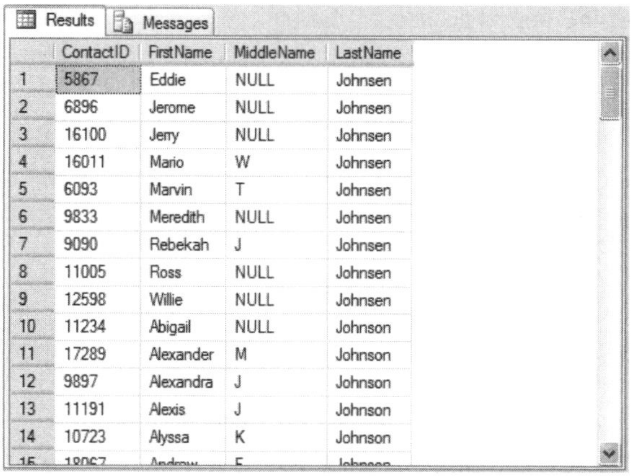

	ContactID	FirstName	MiddleName	LastName
1	5867	Eddie	NULL	Johnsen
2	6896	Jerome	NULL	Johnsen
3	16100	Jerry	NULL	Johnsen
4	16011	Mario	W	Johnsen
5	6093	Marvin	T	Johnsen
6	9833	Meredith	NULL	Johnsen
7	9090	Rebekah	J	Johnsen
8	11005	Ross	NULL	Johnsen
9	12598	Willie	NULL	Johnsen
10	11234	Abigail	NULL	Johnson
11	17289	Alexander	M	Johnson
12	9897	Alexandra	J	Johnson
13	11191	Alexis	J	Johnson
14	10723	Alyssa	K	Johnson

Figure 5-1. *Sample dbo.fnNYSIIS results*

NYSIIS is useful for approximate name-based searches in a variety of applications, including customer service, business reporting, and law enforcement. Note that the sample query is just a demonstration of using the `dbo.fnNYSIIS` function. I highly recommend pre-encoding your name data and storing the encoded values in a table. This will result in much better performance in a production environment.

Multistatement Table-Valued Functions

Multistatement table-valued functions (TVFs) are similar to scalar UDFs but instead of returning a scalar value, they return a table data type. The format for a multistatement TVF declaration is the following:

```
CREATE FUNCTION [ schema_name. ] function_name
( [ { @parameter_name [ AS ] parameter_data_type [ = default ] }
    [ , ...n ] ]
)
RETURNS @return_variable TABLE table_type_definition
[ WITH function_option [ ,...n ] ]
[ AS ]
BEGIN
    function_body
    RETURN;
END
```

The declaration is very similar to that of a scalar UDF, with a few important differences:

- The return type following the RETURNS keyword is actually a table variable declaration, with its structure declared in the *table_type_definition*.

- The RETURNS NULL ON NULL INPUT and CALLED ON NULL INPUT function options are not valid in a table-valued function definition.

- The RETURN statement has no values or variables following it.

Inside the body of the multistatement table-valued function you can use the data-manipulation language (DML) statements INSERT, UPDATE, and DELETE to create and manipulate the return results in the @return_variable table variable.

For the example of a multistatement TVF, we'll create another business application function. Namely we're going to create a product pull list for AdventureWorks. Our TVF will match the AdventureWorks sales orders, namely the Sales.SalesOrderDetail table, against the product inventory in the Production.ProductInventory table. It will effectively create a list for our employees, telling them exactly which inventory bin to go to in order to fill an order. There are some business rules we will need to enforce in this TVF:

- In some cases the number of ordered items might be more than will fit in one bin. In that case our pull list will instruct the employee to grab product from multiple bins.

- Any partial fills from a bin should be reported on the list.

- Any substitution work will be handled by a separate business process and shouldn't be allowed on this list.

- No zero fills will be reported back on the list.

Let's consider an example to demonstrate these rules in action. For purposes of our example we'll say that we have three customers: Jill, Mike, and Dave. Let's say that Jill, Mike, and Dave each order five of item ID number 783, the black Mountain-200 42-inch mountain bike. We will say that we have six of this particular inventory item in Bin 1, Shelf A, Location 7. We also have another three of this particular item in Bin 2, Shelf A, Location 7. Our business rules will create a pull list like the following (also see Figure 5-2):

- *Jill's order*: Pull five of item 783 from Location 7, Shelf A, Bin 1; complete fill.

- *Mike's order*: Pull one of Item 783 from Location 7, Shelf A, Bin 1; partial fill.

- *Mike's order*: Pull three of item 783 from Location 7, Shelf A, Bin 2; partial fill completes the order.

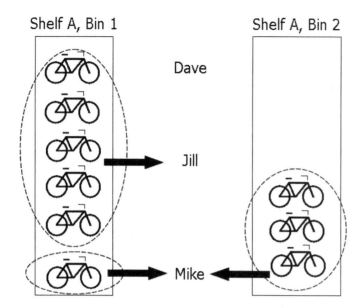

Figure 5-2. *Filling orders from inventory*

Since we ran out of item 783 at this point (we had nine and used all nine to fill Mike's and Jill's orders), we will not even list Dave's order. Also note that this function doesn't concern itself with product substitutions, such as completing Mike's and Dave's orders with a comparable product such as item ID number 780 (the silver Mountain-200 42-inch mountain bike), if we happen to have it in stock.

So with that out of the way, let's dig in (see Listing 5-4).

Listing 5-4. *Creating a Product Pull List*

```
CREATE FUNCTION dbo.fnProductPullList()
RETURNS @result TABLE (
    SalesOrderID INT NOT NULL,
    ProductID INT NOT NULL,
    LocationID SMALLINT NOT NULL,
    Shelf NVARCHAR(10) NOT NULL,
    Bin TINYINT NOT NULL,
    QuantityInBin SMALLINT NOT NULL,
    QuantityOnOrder SMALLINT NOT NULL,
    QuantityToPull SMALLINT NOT NULL,
    PartialFillFlag CHAR(1) NOT NULL,
    PRIMARY KEY (SalesOrderID, ProductID, LocationID, Shelf, Bin))
AS
```

```
BEGIN
    INSERT INTO @result (
        SalesOrderID,
        ProductID,
        LocationID,
        Shelf,
        Bin,
        QuantityInBin,
        QuantityOnOrder,
        QuantityToPull,
        PartialFillFlag)
    SELECT Order_Details.SalesOrderID,
        Order_Details.ProductID,
        Inventory_Details.LocationID,
        Inventory_Details.Shelf,
        Inventory_Details.Bin,
        Inventory_Details.Quantity,
        Order_Details.OrderQty,
        COUNT(*) AS PullQty,
        CASE WHEN COUNT(*) < Order_Details.OrderQty
            THEN 'Y'
            ELSE 'N'
        END AS PartialFillFlag
    FROM
    (
        SELECT ROW_NUMBER() OVER (PARTITION BY i.ProductID
            ORDER BY i.ProductID,
                i.LocationID,
                i.Shelf,
                i.Bin) AS Num,
            i.ProductID,
            i.LocationID,
            i.Shelf,
            i.Bin,
            i.Quantity
        FROM
            (
                SELECT ProductID,
                    LocationID,
                    Shelf,
                    Bin,
                    Quantity
```

```
                      FROM Production.ProductInventory
                      INNER JOIN dbo.Numbers n
                          ON n.Num BETWEEN 1 AND Quantity
                  ) i
              INNER JOIN Production.ProductInventory p
                  ON i.ProductID = p.ProductID
                      AND i.LocationID = p.LocationID
                      AND i.Shelf = p.Shelf
                      AND i.Bin = p.Bin
          ) Inventory_Details
          INNER JOIN
          (
              SELECT ROW_NUMBER() OVER (PARTITION BY o.ProductID
                  ORDER BY o.ProductID,
                      o.SalesOrderID) AS Num,
                  o.ProductID,
                  o.SalesOrderID,
                  o.OrderQty
              FROM
                  (
                      SELECT ProductID,
                          SalesOrderID,
                          SalesOrderDetailID,
                          OrderQty
                      FROM Sales.SalesOrderDetail
                      INNER JOIN dbo.Numbers n
                          ON n.Num BETWEEN 1 AND OrderQty
                  ) o
              INNER JOIN Sales.SalesOrderDetail sod
                  ON o.SalesOrderID = sod.SalesOrderID
                      AND o.SalesOrderDetailID = sod.SalesOrderDetailID
                      AND o.ProductID = sod.ProductID
          ) Order_Details
              ON Inventory_Details.ProductID = Order_Details.ProductID
                  AND Inventory_Details.Num = Order_Details.Num
      GROUP BY Order_Details.SalesOrderID,
          Order_Details.ProductID,
          Inventory_Details.LocationID,
          Inventory_Details.Shelf,
          Inventory_Details.Bin,
          Inventory_Details.Quantity,
          Order_Details.OrderQty;
      RETURN;
END;
```

This one is going to be a bit involved, so let's get the basic stuff out of the way first. In the CREATE FUNCTION statement we begin by defining our multistatement TVF. We specify that it accepts no parameters and that it returns a table. We use the name @result for the table variable that will hold and return our results and define the structure of the table in the RETURNS clause. Note that we define a primary key, which will also serve as the clustered index on @result. Due to limitations in table variables, we can't explicitly specify other indexes on @result:

```
CREATE FUNCTION dbo.fnProductPullList()
RETURNS @result TABLE (
    SalesOrderID INT NOT NULL,
    ProductID INT NOT NULL,
    LocationID SMALLINT NOT NULL,
    Shelf NVARCHAR(10) NOT NULL,
    Bin TINYINT NOT NULL,
    QuantityInBin SMALLINT NOT NULL,
    QuantityOnOrder SMALLINT NOT NULL,
    QuantityToPull SMALLINT NOT NULL,
    PartialFillFlag CHAR(1) NOT NULL,
    PRIMARY KEY (SalesOrderID, ProductID, LocationID, Shelf, Bin))
```

The body of the function begins with the INSERT INTO...SELECT statement, which populates the @result table variable. The only things of note in particular about this portion of the multistatement TVF are the following:

- The COUNT(*) AS PullQty line, which returns the total number of each item to pull from a given bin to fill a specific sales order detail

- The CASE statement, which returns Y for a sales order item partially filled from a particular bin, or N for a sales order item completely filled from a particular bin

The body of the function looks like this:

```
AS
BEGIN
    INSERT INTO @result (
        SalesOrderID,
        ProductID,
        LocationID,
        Shelf,
        Bin,
        QuantityInBin,
        QuantityOnOrder,
```

```
        QuantityToPull,
        PartialFillFlag)
    SELECT Order_Details.SalesOrderID,
        Order_Details.ProductID,
        Inventory_Details.LocationID,
        Inventory_Details.Shelf,
        Inventory_Details.Bin,
        Inventory_Details.Quantity,
        Order_Details.OrderQty,
        COUNT(*) AS PullQty,
        CASE WHEN COUNT(*) < Order_Details.OrderQty
            THEN 'Y'
            ELSE 'N'
        END AS PartialFillFlag
    FROM
```

The SELECT query is composed of two subqueries joined together. The first subquery returns a single row for every item in inventory. Considering the example with Jill, Mike, and Dave, if there are nine black Mountain-200 42-inch mountain bikes in inventory, this query returns nine rows, each with a unique row number starting with 1. The query also returns the LocationID, Shelf, and Bin, where the product is located:

```
    (
        SELECT ROW_NUMBER() OVER (PARTITION BY i.ProductID
            ORDER BY i.ProductID,
                i.LocationID,
                i.Shelf,
                i.Bin) AS Num,
            i.ProductID,
            i.LocationID,
            i.Shelf,
            i.Bin,
            i.Quantity
        FROM
            (
                SELECT ProductID,
                    LocationID,
                    Shelf,
                    Bin,
                    Quantity
```

```
            FROM Production.ProductInventory
            INNER JOIN dbo.Numbers n
                ON n.Num BETWEEN 1 AND Quantity
        ) i
    INNER JOIN Production.ProductInventory p
        ON i.ProductID = p.ProductID
            AND i.LocationID = p.LocationID
            AND i.Shelf = p.Shelf
            AND i.Bin = p.Bin
) Inventory_Details
```

This subquery is inner-joined to a second subquery that likewise breaks up quantities of items in all sales-order details into single rows. Again, looking at the example of Jill, Mike, and Dave, this query will break each of their orders into five rows. The rows are assigned unique numbers for each product; so in the example, the rows for each black Mountain-200 42-inch mountain bike our three customers ordered will be numbered individually from 1 to 15:

```
INNER JOIN
(
    SELECT ROW_NUMBER() OVER (PARTITION BY o.ProductID
        ORDER BY o.ProductID,
            o.SalesOrderID) AS Num,
        o.ProductID,
        o.SalesOrderID,
        o.OrderQty
    FROM
        (
            SELECT ProductID,
                SalesOrderID,
                SalesOrderDetailID,
                OrderQty
            FROM Sales.SalesOrderDetail
            INNER JOIN dbo.Numbers n
                ON n.Num BETWEEN 1 AND OrderQty
        ) o
    INNER JOIN Sales.SalesOrderDetail sod
        ON o.SalesOrderID = sod.SalesOrderID
            AND o.SalesOrderDetailID = sod.SalesOrderDetailID
            AND o.ProductID = sod.ProductID
) Order_Details
    ON Inventory_Details.ProductID = Order_Details.ProductID
        AND Inventory_Details.Num = Order_Details.Num
```

The rows of both subqueries are joined based on their ProductID numbers and the unique row numbers assigned to each row of each subquery. This effectively assigns one item from the inventory to fill exactly one item in each order.

The SELECT statement also requires a GROUP BY since we are counting the total number of items to be pulled from each bin to fill each sales order, as opposed to returning the raw inventory-to-sales order items on a one-to-one basis:

```
GROUP BY Order_Details.SalesOrderID,
    Order_Details.ProductID,
    Inventory_Details.LocationID,
    Inventory_Details.Shelf,
    Inventory_Details.Bin,
    Inventory_Details.Quantity,
    Order_Details.OrderQty;
```

Finally, the RETURN statement returns the @result table back to the caller as the TVF result:

```
    RETURN;
END;
```

The table returned by a table-valued function can be used in the WHERE clause of a SQL SELECT query or in a JOIN clause. Listing 5-5 is a sample query that joins the example TVF to the Production.Product table to get the product names and colors for each product listed in the pull list.

Listing 5-5. *Retrieving a Product Pull List*

```
SELECT p.Name AS ProductName,
    p.ProductNumber,
    p.Color,
    ppl.SalesOrderID,
    ppl.ProductID,
    ppl.LocationID,
    ppl.Shelf,
    ppl.Bin,
    ppl.QuantityInBin,
    ppl.QuantityOnOrder,
    ppl.QuantityToPull,
    ppl.PartialFillFlag
FROM Production.Product p
INNER JOIN dbo.fnProductPullList() ppl
    ON p.ProductID = ppl.ProductID
```

Figure 5-3 shows a sample of output from the previous query.

	ProductName	ProductNumber	Color	SalesOrderID	ProductID	LocationID	Shelf	Bin	QuantityInBin	QuantityOnOrder	QuantityToPull	PartialFillFlag
1	Mountain Bike Socks, M	SO-B909-M	White	43659	709	7	N/A	0	180	6	6	N
2	Sport-100 Helmet, Blue	HL-U509-B	Blue	43659	711	7	N/A	0	216	4	4	N
3	AWC Logo Cap	CA-1098	Multi	43659	712	7	N/A	0	288	2	2	N
4	Long-Sleeve Logo Jersey, M	LJ-0192-M	Multi	43659	714	7	N/A	0	180	3	3	N
5	Long-Sleeve Logo Jersey, XL	LJ-0192-X	Multi	43659	716	7	N/A	0	252	1	1	N
6	Mountain-100 Silver, 38	BK-M82S-38	Silver	43659	771	7	N/A	0	49	1	1	N
7	Mountain-100 Silver, 42	BK-M82S-42	Silver	43659	772	7	N/A	0	88	1	1	N
8	Mountain-100 Silver, 44	BK-M82S-44	Silver	43659	773	7	N/A	0	83	2	2	N
9	Mountain-100 Silver, 48	BK-M82S-48	Silver	43659	774	7	N/A	0	62	1	1	N
10	Mountain-100 Black, 42	BK-M82B-42	Black	43659	776	7	N/A	0	78	1	1	N
11	Mountain-100 Black, 44	BK-M82B-44	Black	43659	777	7	N/A	0	49	3	3	N
12	Mountain-100 Black, 48	BK-M82B-48	Black	43659	778	7	N/A	0	88	1	1	N
13	Road-450 Red, 52	BK-R68R-52	Red	43660	758	7	N/A	0	116	1	1	N
14	Road-650 Red, 44	BK-R50R-44	Red	43660	762	7	N/A	0	75	1	1	N

Figure 5-3. *Sample output from dbo.fnProductPullList join query*

Inline Table-Valued Functions

As if scalar UDFs and multistatement table-valued functions aren't enough to get you excited about T-SQL's user-defined function capabilities, here comes a third form of UDF known as the *inline table-valued function*. Inline table-valued functions are similar to multistatement table-valued functions in that they return a table.

However, where a multistatement TVF can contain multiple SQL statements and control-of-flow statements in the function body, the inline function consists of only a single SELECT query. The inline TVF is literally "inlined" by SQL Server (expanded by the query optimizer as part of the SELECT statement that contains it), much like a view. In fact inline TVFs are sometimes referred to as *parameterized views*. The following is the format for declaring an inline TVF:

```
CREATE FUNCTION [ schema_name. ] function_name
( [ { @parameter_name [ AS ] [ type_schema_name. ] parameter_data_type
    [ = default ] }
    [ , ...n ] ]
)
RETURNS TABLE
[ WITH function_option [ , ...n ] ]
[ AS ]
    RETURN [ ( ] select_stmt [ ) ]
```

Since the inline TVF returns the result of a single SELECT query, you don't need to bother with declaring a table variable or defining its structure. The structure is implied by the *select_stmt* that makes up the function.

The sample inline TVF we'll introduce performs a function commonly implemented by developers in T-SQL using control-of-flow statements. Many times a developer will determine that a function or a stored procedure requires a large, or variable, number of parameters be passed in to accomplish a particular goal. The ideal situation would be to pass an array as a parameter. T-SQL doesn't provide an "array" data type per se, but you can split a comma-delimited list of strings into a table to simulate an array. This gives you the flexibility of an "array" that you can use in SQL joins.

While you could do this using a multistatement table-valued function and control-of-flow statements such as a WHILE loop, you'll get better performance if you let SQL Server do the heavy lifting with a "set-based" version. The sample function will accept a comma-delimited VARCHAR(MAX) string and return a table with two columns:

- The Num column contains a unique number for each element of the array, counting from 1 to the number of elements in the comma-delimited string.

- The Element column contains the substrings extracted from the comma-delimited list.

The sample inline TVF begins much like the others. Listing 5-6 is the full code listing.

Listing 5-6. *Comma-Separated String Splitting Function*

```
CREATE FUNCTION dbo.fnCommaSplit (@String NVARCHAR(MAX))
RETURNS TABLE
AS
RETURN
(
    WITH Splitter(Num, Element)
    AS
    (
        SELECT Num,
            SUBSTRING(@String,
                CASE Num
                    WHEN 1 THEN 1
                    ELSE Num + 1
                END,
                CASE CHARINDEX(N',', @String, Num + 1)
                    WHEN 0 THEN LEN(@String) - Num + 1
                    ELSE CHARINDEX(N',', @String, Num + 1) - Num -
                        CASE
                            WHEN Num > 1 THEN 1
                            ELSE 0
                        END
                END
```

```
            ) AS Element
        FROM dbo.Numbers
        WHERE Num <= LEN(@String)
            AND (SUBSTRING(@String, Num, 1) = N','
                OR Num = 1)
    )
    SELECT ROW_NUMBER() OVER (ORDER BY Num) AS Num,
        Element
    FROM Splitter
);
```

We start by declaring the function name and parameters and specifying that the function returns a TABLE:

```
CREATE FUNCTION dbo.fnCommaSplit (@String VARCHAR(MAX))
RETURNS TABLE
WITH SCHEMABINDING
AS
```

The body of the function is a single RETURN statement followed by a SELECT query. For this example, we will create a CTE (see Chapter 3 for more on CTEs) called Splitter to perform the actual splitting of the comma-delimited list. The query of the CTE returns each substring from the comma-delimited list. CASE expressions are required to handle two special cases:

- The first item in the list because it is not preceded by a comma

- The last item in the list because it is not followed by a comma

```
RETURN
(
    WITH Splitter(Num, Element)
    AS
    (
        SELECT Num,
            SUBSTRING(@String,
                CASE Num
                    WHEN 1 THEN 1
                    ELSE Num + 1
                END,
```

```
            CASE CHARINDEX(N',', @String, Num + 1)
                WHEN 0 THEN LEN(@String) - Num + 1
                ELSE CHARINDEX(N',', @String, Num + 1) - Num -
                    CASE
                        WHEN Num > 1 THEN 1
                        ELSE 0
                    END
            END
        ) AS Element
    FROM dbo.Numbers
```

The query's WHERE clause ensures the function stays within bounds of its comma-delimited string parameter and forces separations on the commas within the string:

```
    WHERE Num <= LEN(@String)
        AND (SUBSTRING(@String, Num, 1) = N','
        OR Num = 1)
)
```

Finally, we select each ROW_NUMBER and Element from the CTE as the result we will return to the caller:

```
SELECT ROW_NUMBER() OVER (ORDER BY Num) AS Num,
    Element
FROM Splitter
);
```

We can use this inline TVF to split up the Jackson family, as shown in Listing 5-7.

Listing 5-7. *Splitting Up the Jacksons*

```
SELECT * FROM dbo.fnCommaSplit
    ('Michael,Tito,Jermaine,Marlon,Rebbie,Jackie,Janet,La Toya,Randy');
```

Or, possibly more usefully, we can use it to pull descriptions for a specific set of AdventureWorks products, good for front-end web page displays or business reports, as shown in Listing 5-8.

Listing 5-8. *Using the fnCommaSplit Function*

```
SELECT n.Num,
    p.Name,
    p.ProductNumber,
    p.Color,
    p.Size,
    p.SizeUnitMeasureCode,
    p.StandardCost,
    p.ListPrice
FROM Production.Product p
INNER JOIN dbo.fnCommaSplit('FR-R38R-52,FR-M94S-52,FR-M94B-44,BK-M68B-38') n
    ON p.ProductNumber = n.Element;
```

Figure 5-4 shows the result of this query.

	Num	Name	ProductNumber	Color	Size	SizeUnitMeasureCode	StandardCost	ListPrice
1	4	Mountain-200 Black, 38	BK-M68B-38	Black	38	CM	1251.9813	2294.99
2	3	HL Mountain Frame - Black, 44	FR-M94B-44	Black	44	CM	699.0928	1349.60
3	2	HL Mountain Frame - Silver, 48	FR-M94S-52	Silver	48	CM	706.811	1364.50
4	1	LL Road Frame - Red, 52	FR-R38R-52	Red	52	CM	187.1571	337.22

Figure 5-4. *Result of dbo.fnCommaSplit inline function sample*

Restrictions on User-Defined Functions

T-SQL imposes some restrictions on user-defined functions. This section discusses these restrictions and some of the reasoning behind them.

Nondeterministic Functions

T-SQL does not allow the use of nondeterministic functions in a user-defined function. A *deterministic* function is one that returns the same value every time when passed a given set of parameters (or no parameters). A *nondeterministic* function can return different results with the same set of parameters passed to it. An example of a deterministic function is ABS, the absolute value function. Every time—and no matter how many times—you call ABS(-10) the result is always 10. This is the basic idea behind determinism.

On the flip side, there are functions that do not return the same value despite the fact that you pass in the same parameters (or no parameters). Built-in functions such as RAND and NEWID are nondeterministic because they return a different result every time they are called. One hack that people sometimes use to try to circumvent this restriction is creating a view that invokes the nondeterministic function and selecting from that view inside their UDFs. While this may work to some extent, it is not recommended, as it could fail to produce the desired results or cause a significant performance hit since SQL won't be able to cache or effectively index the results of nondeterministic functions. Also, if you create a computed column that tries to reference your UDF, the nondeterministic functions you are trying to access via your view can produce unpredictable results. If you need to use nondeterministic functions in your application logic, stored procedures (discussed in the Chapter 6) are probably the better alternative.

■**Note** In SQL Server 2000, the GETDATE could not be used in a user-defined function because it was considered nondeterministic. This restriction has been removed from SQL Server 2005, and GETDATE can now be used in your user-defined functions.

State of the Database

One of the restrictions on UDFs is that they are not allowed to change the state of the database or cause other side effects. The prohibition on side effects in UDFs means that you can't even PRINT from within a UDF. It also means that while you can query database tables and resources, you can't INSERT, UPDATE or DELETE from database tables. Some other restrictions include the following:

- You can't create temporary tables within a UDF. You can, however, create and modify table variables in a UDF.

- You cannot CREATE, ALTER, or DROP regular database tables from within a UDF.

- Dynamic SQL is not allowed, although extended stored procedures (XPs) and SQLCLR functions can be called.

- A table-valued function can return only a single table/result set. If you need to return more than one table/result set, you might be better off with a stored procedure.

■**Caution** Although XPs and SQLCLR functions can be called from a UDF, Microsoft warns against depending on results returned by XPs and SQLCLR functions that cause side effects. If your XP or SQLCLR function modifies tables, alters the database schema, accesses the file system, changes system settings, or utilizes nondeterministic resources external to the database, you might get unpredictable results from your UDF. If you need to change database state or rely on side effects in your server-side code, consider using a SQLCLR function (discussed in Chapter 14), or a regular stored procedure (discussed in Chapter 6).

Variables and table variables created within UDFs have a well-defined scope and cannot be accessed outside of the UDF. Even if you have a recursive UDF, you cannot access the variables and table variables that were previously declared and assigned values by the calling function.

■**Note** The prohibition on UDF side effects extends to the SQL Server display and error systems. This means that you cannot use the T-SQL PRINT or RAISERROR statements within a UDF. The PRINT and RAISERROR statements are useful in debugging stored procedures and T-SQL code batches, but unavailable for use in UDFs. One workaround that I often use is to temporarily move the body of my UDF code to a stored procedure while testing. This gives me the ability to use PRINT and RAISERROR while testing and debugging code in development.

Summary

In this chapter I discussed the three types of T-SQL user-defined functions and provided working examples of the different types:

- Scalar user-defined functions

- Multistatement table-valued functions

- Inline table-valued functions

I also discussed the following:

- Recursion in UDFs

- Procedural code in UDFs

- UDF determinism and side effects

In the next chapter we will look at another tool that allows procedural T-SQL code to be consolidated into procedural units: stored procedures.

CHAPTER 6

■ ■ ■

Stored Procedures

Stored procedures (SPs) have been a part of T-SQL from the beginning. SPs provide a means for creating server-side subroutines written in T-SQL. This chapter begins with a discussion of what SPs are and why you might want to use them, and follows up with how to actually create and use T-SQL SPs.

Introducing Stored Procedures

SPs are code units composed of one or more T-SQL statements and stored on the server. SPs give you the ability to extend the T-SQL language by adding your own procedural subroutines to your SQL Server databases. T-SQL SPs are declared with the CREATE PROCEDURE statement:

```
CREATE PROCEDURE [ schema_name. ] procedure_name [ ;number ]
    [ ( ] [ { @parameter [ type_schema_name. ] data_type }
    [ VARYING ] [ = default ] [ OUT | OUTPUT ] ] [ , ...n ] [ ) ]
[ WITH procedure_option [ , ...n ] ]
[ FOR REPLICATION ]
AS
{ sql_statement [;][ ... n ] }
```

An SP declaration begins with the CREATE PROCEDURE keywords and the name of the SP. The name can specify the *schema_name*, *procedure_name*, and an optional *number*. The *schema_name* should always be included to ensure that your SP is created in the proper schema. The *procedure_name* is the name you assign to the SP. You can add the optional semicolon and *number* after the *procedure_name* to group SPs of the same name.

SP NAMES

Don't use the `sp_` prefix when naming your SPs. SPs that begin with `sp_` follow a different name resolution process than most SPs. SQL Server begins searching for SPs with the `sp_` prefix in the `master` database. Using the `sp_` prefix to name your own SPs will result in *cache misses* as SQL Server tries to locate your SP by name in the cache. This can adversely affect your server's performance.

The optional semicolon (;) and *number* following the *procedure_name* in the SP definition allows you to group SPs of the same name. If you defined two SPs as dbo.MyProc;1 and dbo.MyProc;2, they would belong to the same group. Grouping allows you to drop an entire group of SPs with one DROP PROCEDURE statement. Using this option can be more confusing than it is useful, and I personally recommend naming and managing all of your SPs on an individual basis. Microsoft recommends avoiding this feature, as it will be removed in a future version of SQL Server.

SPs, like the T-SQL user-defined functions discussed in Chapter 5, can accept parameters from the caller. The parameters are specified in a list following the *procedure_name*. Because they can be omitted altogether if they are assigned a default or referenced by name by the caller, SP parameters prove to be far more flexible than UDF parameters. Parameter names are specified by preceding them with an *at* (@) sign. They must follow the normal rules for T-SQL identifiers, which I described in Chapter 1. Parameters can have default values assigned in the declaration, by using = *default* in the declaration.

Each parameter is specified as a specific type and can also be declared as OUTPUT or with the VARYING keyword (for cursor parameters only). When calling SPs, you have two choices: you can specify parameters by position or by name. If you specify an unnamed parameter list, the values are assigned based on position. If you specify named parameters in the format *@parameter = value*, they can be in any order. If your parameter specifies a default value in its declaration, you don't have to pass a value in for that parameter. Unlike user-defined functions, SPs don't require the DEFAULT keyword as a placeholder to specify default values. Just leaving a parameter out when you call the SP will apply the default value to that parameter.

SP OUTPUT PARAMETERS

I previously said that the text, ntext, and image data types should not be used anymore. Here's one more reason to abandon them: they cannot be used as OUTPUT parameters for T-SQL SPs. If you need to use large-object OUTPUT types, use the newer varchar(max), nvarchar(max), and varbinary(max) instead.

Output parameters must be followed by the OUTPUT keyword in the declaration and when calling the SP. If you are passing parameters by name in your SP call, you can use the following format for output parameters:

@parameter = @variable OUTPUT

Regular parameters can be passed by name similarly, but without the OUTPUT keyword:

@parameter = [value | @variable]

Keep these restrictions in mind as you create SPs with OUTPUT parameters.

Unlike user-defined functions that can return results only via the RETURN statement, SPs can communicate with the caller in a variety of ways:

- The SP RETURN statement can return an INT value to the caller. Unlike user-defined functions, SPs do not need a RETURN statement. If the RETURN statement is left out of the SP, zero is returned by default.

Note Since the SP RETURN statement can't return tables, character data, decimal numbers, and so on, it is normally used only to return an INT status or error code. This is a good convention to follow, since most developers who use your SPs will be expecting it. The normal practice is to return a value of zero to indicate success and a nonzero value or error code to indicate an error or failure.

- SPs don't have the same restrictions on database side effects and determinism as do user-defined functions. SPs can read, write, delete, and update permanent tables. The caller and SP can communicate through the use of permanent tables.

- When a temporary table is created in an SP, that temporary table is available to any SPs called from that SP. Furthermore, they are accessible to any SPs subsequently called by those SPs. As an example, if dbo.MyProc1 creates a temporary table named #Temp and then calls dbo.MyProc2, dbo.MyProc2 will be able to access #Temp as well.

If dbo.MyProc2 then calls dbo.MyProc3, dbo.MyProc3 will also have access to the same #Temp temporary table. This provides a useful method of passing an entire table of temporary results to an SP for further processing.

- Output parameters are the primary method of retrieving scalar results from an SP. Parameters are specified as output parameters with the OUTPUT keyword.

- To return table type results from an SP, the SP can return one or more result sets. Result sets are like "virtual tables" that can be accessed by the caller. Unlike views, updates to these result sets by applications do not change the underlying tables used to generate them. Also unlike table-valued functions and inline functions, which return a single table, SPs can return multiple result sets with a single call.

You can call an SP without the EXECUTE keyword if it is the first statement in a batch. For instance, if you have an SP named dbo.MyProc, you can call it like this:

```
dbo.MyProc;
```

You can invoke an SP from anywhere in a batch with the EXECUTE statement. Calling it like this will discard the return value:

```
EXECUTE dbo.MyProc;
```

If you need the return value you can use a variation of EXECUTE to assign the return value to an INT variable:

```
EXECUTE @variable = dbo.MyProc;
```

Listing 6-1 is a simple example to demonstrate SP parameter passing.

Listing 6-1. *Sample SP Parameter Passing and Execution*

```
CREATE PROCEDURE dbo.GetEmployee (@Emp_ID INT = 199,
    @Email_Address NVARCHAR(50) OUTPUT,
    @Full_Name NVARCHAR(100) OUTPUT)
AS
BEGIN
    DECLARE @i INT;
    SELECT @Email_Address = c.EmailAddress,
        @Emp_ID = e.EmployeeID,
        @Full_Name = c.LastName + ' ' + c.MiddleName + ' ' + c.LastName
    FROM HumanResources.Employee e
```

```
    INNER JOIN Person.Contact c
        ON e.ContactID = c.ContactID
    WHERE e.EmployeeID = @Emp_ID;
    RETURN (
        CASE
            WHEN @Email_Address IS NULL THEN 1
            ELSE 0
        END );
END;
GO


DECLARE @Email NVARCHAR(50),
    @Name NVARCHAR(100),
    @Result INT;
EXECUTE @Result = dbo.GetEmployee 123, @Email OUTPUT, @Name OUTPUT;
SELECT @Result AS Result,
    @Email AS Email,
    @Name AS [Name];
```

The SP in the example, dbo.GetEmployee, accepts an employee ID number and retrieves the email address and full name of that employee. If successful, 0 is returned as the SP return value; otherwise 1 is returned. The email address and full name of the employee are returned as output parameters. The sample call retrieves and displays the information for employee number 123.

You can also specify options in your SP declaration by using the WITH keyword. The options that can be used are the following:

- The ENCRYPTION option obfuscates the SP text and helps prevent unauthorized users from accessing the obfuscated text.

- The RECOMPILE option prevents the SQL Server engine from caching the execution plan for the SP. This option forces run-time compilation.

- The EXECUTE AS clause can be used to specify the context that the SP will run under. Valid options for the EXECUTE AS clause are CALLER, SELF, OWNER, or user_name. The EXECUTE AS clause for SP options work the same as the user-defined function EXECUTE AS clause, described in Chapter 5.

Additionally, you can specify FOR REPLICATION to create an SP specifically for replication. An SP created with the FOR REPLICATION option can't be executed on the subscriber. FOR REPLICATION can't be used with the WITH RECOMPILE option.

The body of the SP consists of one or more T-SQL statements following the AS keyword. Unlike scalar or table-valued functions, you don't have to wrap the body of your SP in the BEGIN and END keywords.

Tip You don't *have* to wrap the body of your SP in a BEGIN...END block, but I personally think it makes the code more readable when the body of the SP is wrapped in BEGIN...END.

ALTER PROCEDURE and DROP PROCEDURE

The ALTER PROCEDURE statement allows you to modify the code for an SP without first dropping it. The syntax is the same as the CREATE PROCEDURE statement, except that the keywords ALTER PROCEDURE are used in place of CREATE PROCEDURE. ALTER PROCEDURE, like CREATE PROCEDURE, must be the first statement in a batch.

To delete a procedure from your database, use the DROP PROCEDURE statement. The syntax for DROP PROCEDURE is the following:

```
DROP PROCEDURE { [ schema_name. ] procedure } [ ,...n ] ;
```

Note that you cannot specify the database or server name when dropping an SP. You must be in the database containing the SP in order to drop it.

Why SPs?

Debates have raged through the years over the role and usefulness of SQL Server SPs. SPs cache and reuse query execution plans, which provided significant performance advantages in SQL Server 6.5 and 7.0. Though SQL Server 2000 and 2005 SPs offer the same execution plan caching and reuse, the luster of this benefit faded somewhat. Since SQL Server 2000's release, query optimization and caching and reuse of query execution plans for parameterized queries have been improved. Query optimization has been improved even more in SQL Server 2005. SPs still offer the performance benefit of not having to send large and complex queries over the network, but the primary benefit of query execution plan caching and reuse is not as enticing as it once was.

HOW DOES QUERY EXECUTION PLAN CACHING AND REUSE WORK?

When a query is submitted to SQL Server, the SQL Server engine first checks to see whether a query plan for that exact query already exists. The engine looks for an *exact* match of the query in the cache. By *exact*, I'm referring to the fact that the cache match is case-sensitive and sensitive to whitespace. If any character of the query is different, the engine will not locate the cached execution plan. As an example, the following two queries produce the same results in a database with a case-insensitive collation, but they result in two copies of the query execution plan being compiled and cached because of differences in case:

```
SELECT * FROM humanresources.department;
SELECT * FROM HUMANRESOURCES.DEPARTMENT;
```

When the SQL Server engine can't locate a query execution plan in the cache, it compiles the query into a query execution plan that it then caches for future reuse.

If a matching query plan is found, however, the SQL Server engine will check various counters it stores with each query execution plan to determine whether the tables referenced have reached the *recompilation threshold*, a number indicating the table has changed enough to warrant a recompilation. For regular permanent tables, the recompilation threshold is 500 if the table contains 500 or fewer rows when the query plan is compiled, or 500 + (0.20 *number of rows*) if the number of rows is greater than 500 when the plan is compiled. Other actions that can cause a recompilation of a cached query execution plan include schema changes to objects that are referenced by your query, changes in statistics on a table, and running the `sp_recompile` system stored procedure on a database object. Many T-SQL `SET` options, when changed, will also cause the recompilation of a cached query execution plan.

From the front end, you can help minimize query plan recompilations by parameterizing your queries and SP calls instead of dynamically building them as long strings. When you dynamically build a query string and embed the parameter values as part of that string, you dramatically decrease the odds (to near zero) of SQL Server locating a matching query execution plan in the cache. Chapter 15 discusses query parameterization in .NET code.

So why use SPs? Apart from the performance benefit, which is not as big a factor in these days of highly efficient parameterized queries, SPs offer code modularization. Creating code modules helps reduce redundant code, eliminating potential maintenance nightmares caused by duplicate code stored in multiple locations. SPs also have the advantage of centralized administration of portions of your database code. With SPs you can use SQL Server security to assign rights or deny access to your database code and queries. In addition, SPs can return multiple result sets with a single procedure call, such as the `sp_help` system SP that is demonstrated in Figure 6-1.

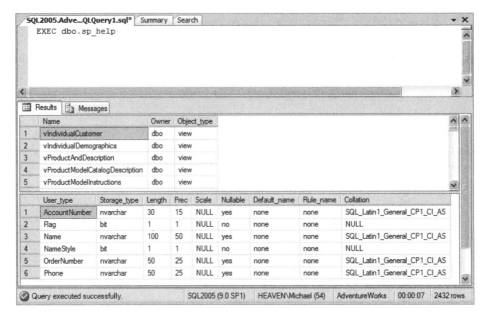

Figure 6-1. *sp_help returns multiple result sets*

Using SPs, you can effectively build an application programming interface (API) for your database. Creation and adherence to such an API can help ensure consistent access across applications and make development easier for front-end and client-side developers who need to access your database.

So what are the arguments against SPs? The major argument tends to be that they "tightly couple your code to the RDBMS." A code base that is tightly integrated with SQL Server 2005 will be more difficult to port over to another RDBMS (such as Oracle, DB2, or MySQL) in the future. A loosely coupled application, on the other hand, is much easier to port to different RDBMSs.

The downside to this portability is that it can result in databases and applications that are slow and inefficient. To get true portability out of any RDBMS system you have to take great care to code everything in *plain vanilla* SQL, meaning that a lot of the platform-specific functionality is off-limits. I'm not going to delve too deeply into a discussion of the pluses and minuses of SPs. In the end, the balance between portability and performance needs to be determined by your business needs and corporate IT policy on a per-project basis.

SPs in Action

A common application of SPs is to create a layer of abstraction for various data manipulation functions. Consider the example in Listing 6-2 of an *upsert* (*update* or *insert*) SP.

Listing 6-2. *Upsert_CountryRegion SP*

```
CREATE PROCEDURE dbo.Upsert_CountryRegion (@Code NVARCHAR(3),
    @Name NVARCHAR(50))
AS
BEGIN
    DECLARE @i INT,
        @err INT;
    SELECT @i = COUNT(*)
    FROM Person.CountryRegion
    WHERE CountryRegionCode = @Code;

    IF @i = 0
    BEGIN
        INSERT INTO Person.CountryRegion (CountryRegionCode,
            [Name],
            ModifiedDate)
        VALUES (@Code, @Name, CURRENT_TIMESTAMP);
        SELECT @err = @@error;
    END
    ELSE
    BEGIN
        UPDATE Person.CountryRegion
        SET [Name] = @Name,
            ModifiedDate = CURRENT_TIMESTAMP
        WHERE CountryRegionCode = @Code;
        SELECT @err = @@error;
    END;
    RETURN @err;
END;
GO
```

■**Note** The ANSI SQL:2003 standard includes a MERGE statement that performs the same function as the *upsert* type of SP. The prerelease versions of SQL Server 2005 included the MERGE statement. Though it was well-publicized during the prerelease period, the MERGE statement was unceremoniously dropped from the production version. We can only hope that Microsoft brings it back sometime in the near future.

The Upsert_CountryRegion SP requires two parameters be passed in: a country/region code and the name of that country. The SP sets the default country code to US and the default country name to United States:

```
CREATE PROCEDURE dbo.Upsert_CountryRegion (@Code NVARCHAR(3) = N'US',
    @Name NVARCHAR(50) = N'United States')
AS
```

The body of the SP first checks to see whether the country/region code passed in already exists in the Person.CountryRegion table:

```
BEGIN
    DECLARE @i INT,
        @err INT;

    SELECT @i = COUNT(*)
    FROM Person.CountryRegion
    WHERE CountryRegionCode = @Code;
```

If the country/region code does not exist yet, the @i variable will be 0. In that case, the SP will INSERT the new country information into the Person.CountryRegion table:

```
    IF @i = 0
    BEGIN
        INSERT INTO Person.CountryRegion (CountryRegionCode,
            [Name],
            ModifiedDate)
        VALUES (@Code, @Name, CURRENT_TIMESTAMP);
        SELECT @err = @@error;
    END
```

Notice the SP grabs the value from the @@error system function immediately after the INSERT statement. This retrieves the error code if the INSERT statement generates an error, or 0 if it succeeds.

If the country/region code already exists in the Person.CountryRegion table, the SP performs an UPDATE on the table:

```
    ELSE
    BEGIN
        UPDATE Person.CountryRegion
        SET [Name] = @Name,
            ModifiedDate = CURRENT_TIMESTAMP
        WHERE CountryRegionCode = @Code;
        SELECT @err = @@error;
    END;
```

Again the SP retrieves the value from `@@error` immediately after the `UPDATE` statement. Finally, it returns the error code generated to the caller (if an error occurs), or 0 if no error occurs:

```
    RETURN @err;
END;
```

To test the SP, AdventureWorks will expand the list of countries it does business in to include the country of Isla de Muerta (a movie reference for all you Captain Jack Sparrow fans out there):

```
DECLARE @result INT;
EXEC @result = dbo.Upsert_CountryRegion @Code = 'IDM',
    @Name = 'Isla de Muerta';

SELECT N'Result Code = ' + CAST(@result AS NVARCHAR(10));

SELECT CountryRegionCode,
    [Name],
    ModifiedDate
FROM Person.CountryRegion;
```

Figure 6-2 shows the results of the `Upsert_CountryRegion` SP example.

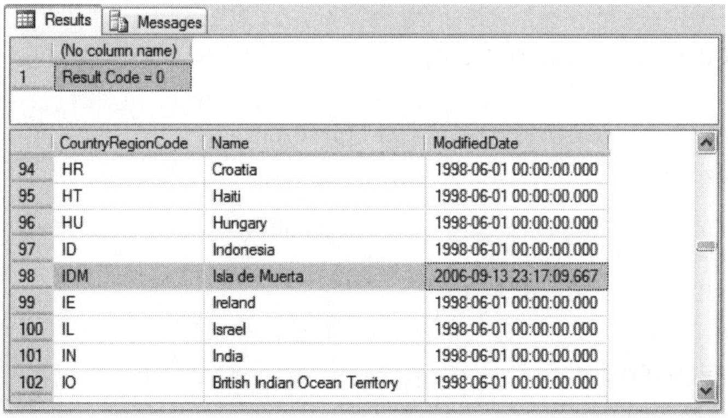

	(No column name)
1	Result Code = 0

	CountryRegionCode	Name	ModifiedDate
94	HR	Croatia	1998-06-01 00:00:00.000
95	HT	Haiti	1998-06-01 00:00:00.000
96	HU	Hungary	1998-06-01 00:00:00.000
97	ID	Indonesia	1998-06-01 00:00:00.000
98	IDM	Isla de Muerta	2006-09-13 23:17:09.667
99	IE	Ireland	1998-06-01 00:00:00.000
100	IL	Israel	1998-06-01 00:00:00.000
101	IN	India	1998-06-01 00:00:00.000
102	IO	British Indian Ocean Territory	1998-06-01 00:00:00.000

Figure 6-2. *AdventureWorks is open for business in Isla de Muerta.*

For the next example, assume that AdventureWorks management has decided to add a database-driven feature to its website. The feature they want is a "recommended products list" that will appear when customers add products to their online shopping carts. Here are the business rules that management has decided you should implement:

- The items that appear on other customer orders should be returned as recommended products.

- Products that are in the same category as the product the customer selected should not be recommended. In other words, if a customer has added a bicycle to his order, other bicycles should not be listed.

- The default ProductID should be 776, a Mountain-100 black 42-inch bike.

- The recommended products should be listed in descending order of the total quantity other customers have ordered. So the best-selling items will be listed first.

Listing 6-3 is the SP that implements all of AdventureWorks's business rules:

Listing 6-3. *Recommended Product List SP*

```
CREATE PROCEDURE dbo.GetProductRecommendations (@ProductID INT = 776)
AS
BEGIN
    WITH RecommendedProducts (TotalQtyOrdered,
        ProductID,
        TotalDollarsOrdered,
        ProductSubCategoryID)
    AS
    (
        SELECT SUM(od2.OrderQty) AS TotalQtyOrdered,
            od2.ProductID,
            SUM(od2.UnitPrice * od2.OrderQty) AS TotalDollarsOrdered,
            p1.ProductSubCategoryID
        FROM Sales.SalesOrderDetail od1
        INNER JOIN Sales.SalesOrderDetail od2
            ON od1.SalesOrderID = od2.SalesOrderID
        INNER JOIN Production.Product p1
            ON od2.ProductID = p1.ProductID
        WHERE od1.ProductID = @ProductID
            AND od2.ProductID <> @ProductID
        GROUP BY od2.ProductID, p1.ProductSubcategoryID
    )
```

```
        SELECT TOP 10 ROW_NUMBER() OVER (ORDER BY rp.TotalQtyOrdered DESC) AS Rank,
            rp.TotalQtyOrdered,
            rp.ProductID,
            rp.TotalDollarsOrdered,
            p.[Name]
        FROM RecommendedProducts rp
        INNER JOIN Production.Product p
            ON rp.ProductID = p.ProductID
        WHERE rp.ProductSubcategoryID <>
            (
                SELECT ProductSubcategoryID
                FROM Production.Product
                WHERE ProductID = @ProductID
            )
        ORDER BY TotalQtyOrdered DESC;
        RETURN 0;
END;
GO
```

The SP begins with a declaration that accepts a single parameter, `@ProductID`. The default `@ProductID` is set to 776, per AdventureWorks management team's rules:

```
CREATE PROCEDURE dbo.GetProductRecommendations (@ProductID INT = 776)
AS
```

Next is a CTE that will return the `TotalQtyOrdered`, `ProductID`, `TotalDollarsOrdered`, and `ProductSubCategoryID` for each product:

```
BEGIN
    WITH RecommendedProducts (TotalQtyOrdered,
        ProductID,
        TotalDollarsOrdered,
        ProductSubCategoryID)
    AS
```

In the body of the CTE the `Sales.SalesOrderDetail` table is joined to itself based on `SalesOrderID`. A join to the `Production.Product` table is also included to get each product's SubcategoryID. The point of the self-join is to grab the total quantity ordered (`OrderQty`) and the total dollars ordered (`UnitPrice * OrderQty`) for each product.

The query is designed to include only orders that contain the product passed in via `@ProductID` in the `WHERE` clause, and it also eliminates results for `@ProductID` itself from the final results. All of the results are grouped by `ProductID` and `ProductSubcategoryID`:

```
(
    SELECT SUM(od2.OrderQty) AS TotalQtyOrdered,
        od2.ProductID,
        SUM(od2.UnitPrice * od2.OrderQty) AS TotalDollarsOrdered,
        p1.ProductSubCategoryID
    FROM Sales.SalesOrderDetail od1
    INNER JOIN Sales.SalesOrderDetail od2
        ON od1.SalesOrderID = od2.SalesOrderID
    INNER JOIN Production.Product p1
        ON od2.ProductID = p1.ProductID
    WHERE od1.ProductID = @ProductID
        AND od2.ProductID <> @ProductID
    GROUP BY od2.ProductID, p1.ProductSubcategoryID
)
```

The final part of the CTE excludes products that are in the same category as the item passed in by `@ProductID`. It then limits the results to the top ten and numbers the results from highest to lowest by `TotalQtyOrdered`. It also joins on the `Production.Product` table to get each product's name:

```
SELECT TOP 10 ROW_NUMBER() OVER (ORDER BY rp.TotalQtyOrdered DESC) AS Rank,
    rp.TotalQtyOrdered,
    rp.ProductID,
    rp.TotalDollarsOrdered,
    p.[Name]
FROM RecommendedProducts rp
INNER JOIN Production.Product p
    ON rp.ProductID = p.ProductID
WHERE rp.ProductSubcategoryID <>
    (
        SELECT ProductSubcategoryID
        FROM Production.Product
        WHERE ProductID = @ProductID
    )
ORDER BY TotalQtyOrdered DESC;
```

Finally, it returns 0 to the caller as the return code:

```
RETURN 0;
END;
```

Figure 6-3 shows the result set of a recommended product list for people who bought a Mountain-100 silver 44-inch bike (`ProductID = 773`):

```
EXECUTE dbo.GetProductRecommendations 773;
```

	Rank	TotalQtyOrdered	ProductID	TotalDollarsOrdered	Name
1	1	878	709	4861.72	Mountain Bike Socks, M
2	2	340	715	9762.4748	Long-Sleeve Logo Jersey, L
3	3	297	712	1538.3157	AWC Logo Cap
4	4	235	711	4743.8275	Sport-100 Helmet, Blue
5	5	201	708	4057.4865	Sport-100 Helmet, Black
6	6	177	707	3573.0105	Sport-100 Helmet, Red
7	7	156	716	4499.1024	Long-Sleeve Logo Jersey, XL
8	8	150	714	4326.06	Long-Sleeve Logo Jersey, M
9	9	148	748	106944.0452	HL Mountain Frame - Silver, 38
10	10	145	741	118711.50	HL Mountain Frame - Silver, 48

Figure 6-3. *Recommended product list for ProductID 773*

Implementing this business logic in an SP provides a layer of abstraction that makes it easier to use from front-end applications. Front-end application programmers don't need to worry about the details of which tables need to be accessed, how they need to be joined, and so on. All your application developers need to know to utilize this logic from the front end is that they need to pass the SP a `ProductID` number and it will return the relevant information in a well-defined result set.

The same interface can be reused if you want to use this same logic elsewhere. Additionally, if you need to change the business logic, it can be done one time, in one place. Consider what happens if the AdventureWorks management decides to make suggestions based on total dollars worth of a product ordered instead of the total quantity ordered. Simply change the `ORDER BY` clause in one place:

```
ORDER BY TotalQtyOrdered DESC;
```

to the following

```
ORDER BY TotalDollarsOrdered DESC;
```

This simple change will do the trick. No additional changes to front-end code or logic are required, since the interface to the SP remains the same.

Recursion in SPs

Like user-defined functions, SPs can call themselves recursively. There is a SQL Server–imposed limit of 32 levels of recursion. To demonstrate recursion, we'll solve a very old puzzle.

The Towers of Hanoi puzzle consists of three pegs and a specified number of discs of varying sizes that slide onto the pegs. The puzzle begins with the discs stacked on top of one another, from smallest to largest, all on one peg. The start position of the puzzle is shown in Figure 6-4.

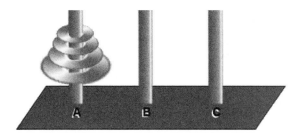

Figure 6-4. *The Towers of Hanoi puzzle start position*

The object of the puzzle is to move all of the discs from Tower A to Tower C. The trick is that you can only move one disc at a time, and no larger disc may be stacked on top of a smaller disc at any time. You can temporarily place discs on Tower B, the intermediate/auxiliary tower, as necessary, but the same rules apply. Towers of Hanoi is often used as an exercise in computer science classes to demonstrate recursion; we'll solve it here to demonstrate T-SQL SP recursion.

Our T-SQL implementation of the Towers of Hanoi puzzle will use five discs and display each move as the computer makes it. This implementation will demonstrate several aspects of SPs discussed in this chapter. The following are some things to note:

- As mentioned previously, SPs can call themselves recursively. This is demonstrated with the dbo.MoveDiscs SP.

- When default values are assigned to parameters in an SP declaration, values do not have to be specified for them when the SP is called. This is demonstrated in dbo.SolveTowers, which calls dbo.MoveDiscs.

- The scope of temporary tables created in an SP include that SP as well as any SPs it calls. This is demonstrated in dbo.SolveTowers, where three temporary tables are created and other SPs are called. The SPs called by dbo.SolveTowers, and those called by those SPs (and so on), can also access these same temporary tables.

- The dbo.MoveDiscs SP demonstrates output parameters. The SP uses an output parameter to update the count of the total number of moves performed after a move.

The T-SQL Towers of Hanoi puzzle solution is shown in Listing 6-4.

Listing 6-4. *The Towers of Hanoi Puzzle*

```
-- This stored procedure displays all the discs in the appropriate
-- towers.
CREATE PROCEDURE dbo.ShowTowers
AS
BEGIN
    -- Each disc is displayed as a series of asterisks (*), centered, with
    -- the appropriate width. Using FULL OUTER JOIN allows us to show all
    -- three towers side by side in a single query.
    SELECT REPLICATE(' ', COALESCE(5 - a.Disc, 0)) +
            REPLICATE('**', COALESCE(a.Disc, 0)) AS Tower_A,
        REPLICATE(' ', COALESCE(5 - b.Disc, 0)) +
            REPLICATE('**', COALESCE(b.Disc, 0)) AS Tower_B,
        REPLICATE(' ', COALESCE(5 - c.Disc, 0)) +
            REPLICATE('**', COALESCE(c.Disc, 0)) AS Tower_C
    FROM #TowerA a
    FULL OUTER JOIN #TowerB b
        ON a.Disc = b.Disc
    FULL OUTER JOIN #TowerC c
        ON a.Disc = b.Disc;
END;
GO


-- This SP moves a single disc from the specified source tower to the
-- specified destination tower.
CREATE PROCEDURE dbo.MoveOneDisc (@Source NCHAR(1),
    @Dest NCHAR(1))
AS
```

```
BEGIN
    -- @Top is the smallest disc on the source tower
    DECLARE @Top INT;
    -- We use IF ... ELSE to get the smallest disc from the source tower
    IF @Source = N'A'
    BEGIN
        -- This gets the smallest disc from Tower A
        SELECT @Top = MIN(Disc)
        FROM #TowerA;
        -- Then we delete it
        DELETE FROM #TowerA
        WHERE Disc = @Top;
    END ELSE IF @Source = N'B'
    BEGIN
        -- This gets the smallest disc from Tower B
        SELECT @Top = MIN(Disc)
        FROM #TowerB;
        -- Then we delete it
        DELETE FROM #TowerB
        WHERE Disc = @Top;
    END ELSE IF @Source = N'C'
    BEGIN
        -- This gets the smallest disc from Tower C
        SELECT @Top = MIN(Disc)
        FROM #TowerC;
        -- Then we delete it
        DELETE FROM #TowerC
        WHERE Disc = @Top;
    END
    -- Print out the disc move performed
    PRINT N'Move Disc #' + CAST(COALESCE(@Top, 0) AS NCHAR(1)) + N' from Tower ' +
        @Source + N' to Tower ' + @Dest;
    -- Perform the move: INSERT the disc from the source tower to the
    -- destination tower
    IF @Dest = N'A'
        INSERT INTO #TowerA (Disc) VALUES (@Top);
    ELSE IF @Dest = N'B'
        INSERT INTO #TowerB (Disc) VALUES (@Top);
    ELSE IF @Dest = N'C'
        INSERT INTO #TowerC (Disc) VALUES (@Top);
    -- Show the towers
```

```
        EXECUTE dbo.ShowTowers;
END;
GO


-- This SP moves multiple discs recursively
CREATE PROCEDURE dbo.MoveDiscs (@DiscNum INT,
    @MoveNum INT OUTPUT,
    @Source NCHAR(1) = N'A',
    @Dest NCHAR(1) = N'C',
    @Aux NCHAR(1) = N'B'
)
AS
BEGIN
    -- If the number of discs to move is 0, we're done
    IF @DiscNum = 0
        PRINT N'Done';
    ELSE
    BEGIN
        -- If the number of discs to move is 1, go ahead and move it
        IF @DiscNum = 1
        BEGIN
            -- Increase the move counter
            SELECT @MoveNum = @MoveNum + 1;
            -- And move one disc from source to destination
            EXEC dbo.MoveOneDisc @Source, @Dest
        END
        ELSE
        BEGIN
            DECLARE @n INT
            SELECT @n = @DiscNum - 1
            -- Move (@DiscNum - 1) discs from Source to Auxiliary tower
            EXEC dbo.MoveDiscs @n, @MoveNum OUTPUT, @Source, @Aux, @Dest;
            -- Move 1 Disc from Source to Destination tower
            EXEC dbo.MoveDiscs 1, @MoveNum OUTPUT, @Source, @Dest, @Aux;
            -- Move (@DiscNum - 1) discs from Auxiliary to Destination tower
            EXEC dbo.MoveDiscs @n, @MoveNum OUTPUT, @Aux, @Dest, @Source;
        END;
    END;
END;
GO
```

```
-- This SP creates the three towers and populates Tower A with 5 discs
CREATE PROCEDURE dbo.SolveTowers
AS
BEGIN
    -- SET NOCOUNT ON to eliminate system messages that will clutter up
    -- the Message display
    SET NOCOUNT ON
    -- Create the three towers: Tower A = Source, Tower B = Auxiliary,
    -- Tower C = Destination
    CREATE TABLE #TowerA (Disc INT PRIMARY KEY NOT NULL);
    CREATE TABLE #TowerB (Disc INT PRIMARY KEY NOT NULL);
    CREATE TABLE #TowerC (Disc INT PRIMARY KEY NOT NULL);
    -- Populate Tower A with 5 discs
    INSERT INTO #TowerA (Disc) VALUES (1);
    INSERT INTO #TowerA (Disc) VALUES (2);
    INSERT INTO #TowerA (Disc) VALUES (3);
    INSERT INTO #TowerA (Disc) VALUES (4);
    INSERT INTO #TowerA (Disc) VALUES (5);
    -- Initialize the move number to 0
    DECLARE @MoveNum INT;
    SELECT @MoveNum = 0;
    -- Show the initial state of the towers
    EXECUTE dbo.ShowTowers;
    -- Solve the puzzle. Notice we don't need to
    -- specify the parameters with defaults
    EXECUTE dbo.MoveDiscs 5, @MoveNum OUTPUT;
    -- How many moves did it take?
    PRINT N'Solved in ' + CAST (@MoveNum AS NVARCHAR(10)) + N' moves.';
    -- Drop the temp tables
    DROP TABLE #TowerC;
    DROP TABLE #TowerB;
    DROP TABLE #TowerA;
    -- SET NOCOUNT OFF before we exit
    SET NOCOUNT OFF
END;
GO
```

To solve the puzzle, just run the following statement:

```
-- Solve the puzzle
EXECUTE dbo.SolveTowers;
```

Figure 6-5 is a screenshot of the processing as the discs are moved from tower to tower.

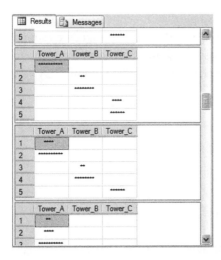

Figure 6-5. *A disc is moved from Tower C to Tower A.*

And now for the code breakdown. The dbo.ShowTowers SP simply displays all of the towers side by side as each disc is moved. The SP uses a couple of FULL OUTER JOINs to generate this side-by-side presentation of the discs:

```
-- This stored procedure displays all the discs in the appropriate
-- towers.
CREATE PROCEDURE dbo.ShowTowers
AS
BEGIN
    -- Each disc is displayed as a series of asterisks (*), centered, with
    -- the appropriate width. Using FULL OUTER JOIN allows us to show all
    -- three towers side by side in a single query.
    SELECT REPLICATE(' ', COALESCE(5 - a.Disc, 0)) +
            REPLICATE('**', COALESCE(a.Disc, 0)) AS Tower_A,
        REPLICATE(' ', COALESCE(5 - b.Disc, 0)) +
            REPLICATE('**', COALESCE(b.Disc, 0)) AS Tower_B,
        REPLICATE(' ', COALESCE(5 - c.Disc, 0)) +
            REPLICATE('**', COALESCE(c.Disc, 0)) AS Tower_C
    FROM #TowerA a
    FULL OUTER JOIN #TowerB b
        ON a.Disc = b.Disc
    FULL OUTER JOIN #TowerC c
        ON a.Disc = b.Disc;
END;
```

As the Towers of Hanoi puzzle involves moving a single disc at a time from tower to tower, the most basic routine you can create simply moves a disc from the specified source tower to the specified destination tower. The code passes the names of the towers (A, B, or C) into the dbo.MoveOneDisc SP, which uses them to decide which tables to modify:

```
-- This SP moves a single disc from the specified source tower to the
-- specified destination tower.
CREATE PROCEDURE dbo.MoveOneDisc (@Source NCHAR(1),
    @Dest NCHAR(1))
AS
BEGIN
    -- @Top is the smallest disc on the source tower
    DECLARE @Top INT;
    -- We use IF ... ELSE to get the smallest disc from the source tower
    IF @Source = N'A'
    BEGIN
        -- This gets the smallest disc from Tower A
        SELECT @Top = MIN(Disc)
        FROM #TowerA;
        -- Then we delete it
        DELETE FROM #TowerA
        WHERE Disc = @Top;
    END ELSE IF @Source = N'B'
    BEGIN
        -- This gets the smallest disc from Tower B
        SELECT @Top = MIN(Disc)
        FROM #TowerB;
        -- Then we delete it
        DELETE FROM #TowerB
        WHERE Disc = @Top;
    END ELSE IF @Source = N'C'
    BEGIN
        -- This gets the smallest disc from Tower C
        SELECT @Top = MIN(Disc)
        FROM #TowerC;
        -- Then we delete it
        DELETE FROM #TowerC
        WHERE Disc = @Top;
    END
```

```
    -- Print out the disc move performed
    PRINT N'Move Disc #' + CAST(COALESCE(@Top, 0) AS NCHAR(1)) + N' from Tower ' +
        @Source + N' to Tower ' + @Dest;
    -- Perform the move: INSERT the disc from the source tower to the
    -- destination tower
    IF @Dest = N'A'
        INSERT INTO #TowerA (Disc) VALUES (@Top);
    ELSE IF @Dest = N'B'
        INSERT INTO #TowerB (Disc) VALUES (@Top);
    ELSE IF @Dest = N'C'
        INSERT INTO #TowerC (Disc) VALUES (@Top);
    -- Show the towers
    EXECUTE dbo.ShowTowers;
END;
```

The routine that is responsible for moving discs recursively is called dbo.MoveDiscs. It accepts several parameters, including the number of discs to move (@DiscNum), the number of the current move (@MoveNum), and the names of the source, destination, and auxiliary/intermediate towers. If the dbo.MoveDiscs procedure is called with @DiscNum = 0, the puzzle is solved. If the procedure is called with @DiscNum = 1, the procedure calls dbo.MoveOneDisc. Other than that, dbo.MoveDiscs calls itself recursively with (@DiscNum - 1):

```
-- This SP moves multiple discs recursively
CREATE PROCEDURE dbo.MoveDiscs (@DiscNum INT,
    @MoveNum INT OUTPUT,
    @Source NCHAR(1) = N'A',
    @Dest NCHAR(1) = N'C',
    @Aux NCHAR(1) = N'B'
)
AS
BEGIN
    -- If the number of discs to move is 0, we're done
    IF @DiscNum = 0
        PRINT N'Done';
    ELSE
    BEGIN
        -- If the number of discs to move is 1, go ahead and move it
        IF @DiscNum = 1
```

```
        BEGIN
            -- Increase the move counter
            SELECT @MoveNum = @MoveNum + 1;
            -- And move one disc from source to destination
            EXEC dbo.MoveOneDisc @Source, @Dest
        END
        ELSE
        BEGIN
            DECLARE @n INT
            SELECT @n = @DiscNum - 1
            -- Move (@DiscNum - 1) discs from Source to Auxiliary tower
            EXEC dbo.MoveDiscs @n, @MoveNum OUTPUT, @Source, @Aux, @Dest;
            -- Move 1 Disc from Source to Destination tower
            EXEC dbo.MoveDiscs 1, @MoveNum OUTPUT, @Source, @Dest, @Aux;
            -- Move (@DiscNum - 1) discs from Auxiliary to Destination tower
            EXEC dbo.MoveDiscs @n, @MoveNum OUTPUT, @Aux, @Dest, @Source;
        END;
    END;
END;
```

Finally, the dbo.SolveTowers SP creates the three temporary tables #TowerA, #TowerB, and #TowerC. It then populates Tower A with five discs. This SP is the entry point for the entire puzzle-solving program, so it displays the start position of the towers and calls dbo.MoveDiscs to "get the ball rolling":

```
-- This SP creates the three towers and populates Tower A with 5 discs
CREATE PROCEDURE dbo.SolveTowers
AS
BEGIN
    -- SET NOCOUNT ON to eliminate system messages that will clutter up
    -- the Message display
    SET NOCOUNT ON
    -- Create the three towers: Tower A = Source, Tower B = Auxiliary,
    -- Tower C = Destination
    CREATE TABLE #TowerA (Disc INT PRIMARY KEY NOT NULL);
    CREATE TABLE #TowerB (Disc INT PRIMARY KEY NOT NULL);
    CREATE TABLE #TowerC (Disc INT PRIMARY KEY NOT NULL);
    -- Populate Tower A with 5 discs
    INSERT INTO #TowerA (Disc) VALUES (1);
    INSERT INTO #TowerA (Disc) VALUES (2);
    INSERT INTO #TowerA (Disc) VALUES (3);
    INSERT INTO #TowerA (Disc) VALUES (4);
    INSERT INTO #TowerA (Disc) VALUES (5);
```

```
    -- Initialize the move number to 0
    DECLARE @MoveNum INT;
    SELECT @MoveNum = 0;
    -- Show the initial state of the towers
    EXECUTE dbo.ShowTowers;
    -- Solve the puzzle. Notice we don't need to
    -- specify the parameters with defaults
    EXECUTE dbo.MoveDiscs 5, @MoveNum OUTPUT;
    -- How many moves did it take?
    PRINT N'Solved in ' + CAST (@MoveNum AS NVARCHAR(10)) + N' moves.';
    -- Drop the temp tables
    DROP TABLE #TowerC;
    DROP TABLE #TowerB;
    DROP TABLE #TowerA;
    -- SET NOCOUNT OFF before we exit
    SET NOCOUNT OFF
END;
```

TOWERS OF HANOI AND THE END OF THE WORLD

The minimum number of moves required to solve the Towers of Hanoi puzzle increases exponentially as you add discs to the puzzle. For instance, the five-disc example requires a minimum of 31 moves to solve. Ten discs require 1,023 moves. With sixty-four discs, the required minimum number of moves jumps to 18,446,744,073,709,552,000 moves. And that assumes that every single move you make is perfect.

There is a legend that a group of monks has been working on solving the puzzle with sixty-four discs since ancient times. According to the legend, when they complete the puzzle the world will end. At a rate of 1 move per second, it will take about 600 billion years to solve the sixty-four-disc puzzle, so we're probably safe . . . for now.

Temporary Stored Procedures

In addition to normal SPs, T-SQL provides what are known as *temporary stored procedures*. These SPs are created just like any other SP; the only difference is that the SP name must begin with a number sign (#) for a local temporary stored procedure, or two number signs (##) for a global temporary stored procedure.

While a normal SP remains a part of the database and schema it was created in until it is explicitly dropped via the DROP PROCEDURE statement, temporary SPs are dropped automatically. A local temporary stored procedure is visible only to the current session and is dropped when the current session ends (normally when the database connection is closed). A global temporary stored procedure is visible to all connections and is automatically dropped when the last session using it ends.

Normally, temporary stored procedures are used only for specialized solutions such as database drivers. Open Database Connectivity (ODBC) drivers, for instance, make use of temporary stored procedures to implement SQL Server connectivity functions.

Summary

This chapter discussed T-SQL SPs. Topics covered include the following:

- How to pass scalar values to an SP via input parameters

- SP execution query plan caching and the affects of recompilation on performance

- Retrieving data from SPs via return values, output parameters, and result sets

- SP recursion and the SQL Server-imposed 32-level limitation

- Using a temporary table to pass a table of data between SPs

- The difference between normal SPs and local and global temporary stored procedures

While some of the performance and other advantages provided by SPs in previous releases of SQL Server are not as pronounced in SQL Server 2005, the ability to modularize server-side code, administer your T-SQL code base in a single location, and ease front-end programming development still make SPs a powerful development tool in any T-SQL developer's toolkit.

The samples provided in this chapter are designed to demonstrate several aspects of SP functionality in SQL Server 2005.

The next chapter covers another important part of T-SQL programming: triggers.

CHAPTER 7

Triggers

SQL Server provides triggers as a means of detecting database events and executing T-SQL code in response. SQL Server 2005 implements two types of triggers: classic T-SQL DML triggers that fire in response to INSERT, UPDATE, and DELETE statements, and new DDL triggers that fire in response to CREATE, ALTER, DROP, and some stored procedures that perform DDL-like operations.

Triggers are similar in form to stored procedures, but they are closely tied to your data and database objects. In the past DML triggers were used to enforce various aspects of business logic, such as foreign key and other constraints on data and other more complex business logic. Declarative Referential Integrity (DRI) and robust check constraints in T-SQL have supplanted DML triggers in many areas, but they are still useful in their own right. In this chapter we will discuss how triggers work, how to use them, and when they are most appropriate.

DML Triggers

DML triggers are blocks of code that are executed (fired) in response to an INSERT, UPDATE, or DELETE statement on a table or view. To create a DML trigger, use the CREATE TRIGGER statement:

```
CREATE TRIGGER [ schema_name. ] trigger_name
ON { table | view }
[ WITH <dml_trigger_option> [ ,...n ] ]
{ FOR | AFTER | INSTEAD OF }
{ [ INSERT ] [ , ] [ UPDATE ] [ , ] [ DELETE ] }
[ WITH APPEND ]
[ NOT FOR REPLICATION ]
AS { sql_statement [ ,...n ] |
    EXTERNAL NAME assembly_name.class_name.method_name } ;
```

The first part of the CREATE TRIGGER statement specifies the *trigger_name*. The *schema_name* can be added in front of the *trigger_name* to specify the schema in which to create the trigger. As I mentioned with user-defined functions and stored procedures, it's recommended that DML trigger names also be specified with a *schema_name*. The *trigger_name* must be unique to the schema where it is created, and it must follow the standard rules for T-SQL identifiers.

The ON keyword is used to specify the *table* or *view* on which the trigger executes. Only an INSTEAD OF trigger can be created on a view. The WITH keyword is used to specify additional *dml_trigger_options*, which can include the following:

- The ENCRYPTION option obfuscates the trigger code in the database and prevents unauthorized users from accessing the obfuscated code directly.

- The EXECUTE AS option allows you to specify the context the trigger will execute under. Valid options are CALLER, SELF, OWNER, and *user_name*. Each of these options have the same effect as the user-defined function EXECUTE AS options described in Chapter 5. The default execution context is CALLER.

■**Caution** DML triggers have some restrictions on their creation that you should keep in mind. For one, DML triggers cannot be defined on global or local temporary tables. Also DML triggers cannot be declared on table variables. Finally, as mentioned previously, only INSTEAD OF triggers can be used on views.

The trigger can be defined as an AFTER (FOR) or INSTEAD OF trigger. The AFTER trigger fires after a DML statement completes execution. The INSTEAD OF trigger is a replacement for the normal INSERT, UPDATE, or DELETE action, and it fires before the change occurs on the underlying table or view. In both cases you will rely on the inserted and deleted virtual tables within the body of your trigger to determine what changes have, or are supposed to, occur on the underlying table or view. We discuss the differences between AFTER and INSTEAD OF triggers, and the inserted and deleted virtual tables, later in this section.

To finish defining the type of trigger, you specify the action that fires the trigger following the AFTER or INSTEAD OF keywords. You can specify INSERT, DELETE, UPDATE, or a combination of these actions.

The WITH APPEND keywords tell SQL Server that you are adding additional triggers of the same type to a table.

■**Caution** WITH APPEND is a backward-compatibility feature (SQL Server 6.5) and will be removed from a future version of SQL Server. Do not use this feature; if you are currently using it in your older scripts, update them to remove this feature.

Specifying NOT FOR REPLICATION in the trigger definition informs SQL Server that the trigger should not be fired when a replication agent modifies the data in the table.

The final option, EXTERNAL NAME, allows you to bind a method in a SQLCLR assembly to a trigger. The specified *assembly_name* must exist in SQL Server; the *class_name* must exist in the specified assembly; and the *method_name* must specify a method that takes no arguments and returns nothing (void in C# or Sub in VB 2005).

The body of the trigger is composed of one or more T-SQL statements after the AS keyword in the trigger declaration. Just like stored procedures it's not mandatory to enclose the body of the trigger with the BEGIN and END keywords. As always, my personal style is to wrap the body in BEGIN and END to improve readability.

■**Note** A CREATE TRIGGER or ALTER TRIGGER statement must be the first statement in a batch.

When to Use DML Triggers

Way back in the day, triggers were the best (and sometimes only) way to perform a variety of tasks such as ensuring referential integrity, validating data before storing it in tables, auditing changes, and enforcing complex business logic. Newer versions of SQL Server have added functionality that more closely integrates many of these functions into the core database engine. In most cases, for instance, you can use SQL Server's built-in declarative referential integrity (DRI) to ensure referential integrity and check constraints for simple validations. Triggers are still an excellent choice when simple auditing tasks or validations with complex business rules are required.

■**Note** DRI is not enforced across databases. What this means is that you cannot reference a table in a different database in a DRI/foreign key constraint. Because they can reference objects such as tables and views in other databases, triggers are still a good option when this type of referential integrity enforcement is necessary.

Whenever a trigger fires, it is automatically wrapped in a transaction. This has big implications for your database. What it means is that whatever your trigger does, it should do it as quickly and efficiently as possible. The T-SQL statements in your trigger body can potentially create locks on tables throughout your database, and it is not unheard of for inefficient triggers to cause blocking problems.

There are some steps you can take to ensure your triggers are efficient. First, you can check the @@ROWCOUNT function at the start of your trigger. If @@ROWCOUNT is 0, it means that no rows were inserted, updated, or deleted by the DML statement that fired the trigger.

This means your trigger has no work to do and can exit immediately. You should also minimize the amount of work done inside the trigger and optimize the operations it does have to perform.

We will look at a trigger already defined on the HumanResources.Department table. The trigger HumanResources.uDepartment simply updates the ModifiedDate column of the HumanResources.Department table with the current date and time whenever a row is updated. Listing 7-1 shows this trigger.

Listing 7-1. *HumanResources.uDepartment Trigger Code*

```
CREATE TRIGGER [HumanResources].[uDepartment]
ON [HumanResources].[Department]
AFTER UPDATE
NOT FOR REPLICATION
AS
BEGIN
    SET NOCOUNT ON;

    UPDATE [HumanResources].[Department]
    SET [HumanResources].[Department].[ModifiedDate] = GETDATE()
    FROM inserted
    WHERE inserted.[DepartmentID] = [HumanResources].[Department].[DepartmentID];
END;
```

The first part of the CREATE TRIGGER statement defines the name of the trigger and specifies that it will be created on the HumanResources.Department table. The definition also specifies that the trigger will fire AFTER UPDATE, and the NOT FOR REPLICATION keywords prevent replication events from firing the trigger:

```
CREATE TRIGGER [HumanResources].[uDepartment]
ON [HumanResources].[Department]
AFTER UPDATE
NOT FOR REPLICATION
AS
```

The body of the trigger begins with the SET NOCOUNT ON statement to keep the trigger from reporting *n Rows Affected* after the UPDATE statement within the trigger. The UPDATE statement uses the inserted virtual table and the GETDATE function to set the ModifiedDate of each affected row to the current date/time:

```
BEGIN
    SET NOCOUNT ON;

    UPDATE [HumanResources].[Department]
    SET [HumanResources].[Department].[ModifiedDate] = GETDATE()
    FROM inserted
    WHERE inserted.[DepartmentID] = [HumanResources].[Department].[DepartmentID];
END;
```

■**Tip** Any SET statement (such as SET ROWCOUNT ON) can be used in a trigger. The statement remains in effect while the trigger executes, and reverts to its former setting when the trigger completes.

Testing the trigger is as simple as using SELECT and UPDATE. The following sample changes the name of the *Information Services* department to *Information Technology* as a demonstration. The first step is to determine what's in the table for this department with a SELECT statement:

```
SELECT DepartmentID, Name, GroupName, ModifiedDate
FROM HumanResources.Department
WHERE DepartmentID = 11;
```

The result looks something like Figure 7-1 (notice the ModifiedDate column):

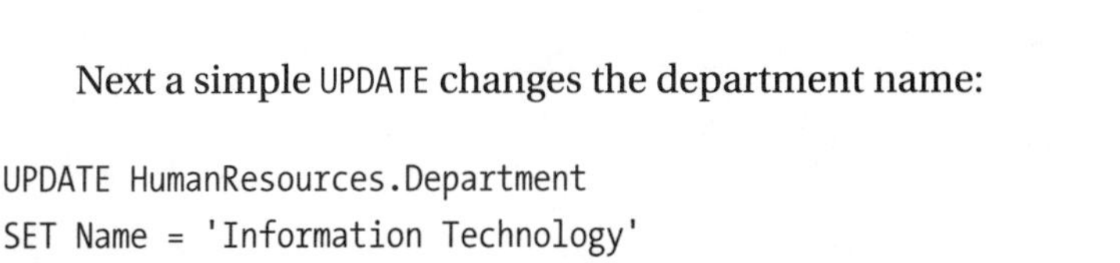

	DepartmentID	Name	GroupName	ModifiedDate
1	11	Information Services	Executive General and Administration	1998-06-01 00:00:00.000

Figure 7-1. *Information Services Department at AdventureWorks*

Next a simple UPDATE changes the department name:

```
UPDATE HumanResources.Department
SET Name = 'Information Technology'
WHERE DepartmentID = 11;
```

Finally, running the previous SELECT statement proves the trigger properly updated the ModifiedDate as shown in Figure 7-2.

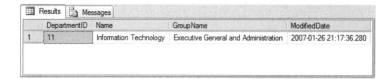

Figure 7-2. *Department name changed to Information Technology*

Triggers can also be used for auditing of tables, as the example in Listing 7-2 demonstrates.

Listing 7-2. *Audit Logging Trigger Example*

```
CREATE TABLE HumanResources.ActionLog (
    EntryNum INT IDENTITY(1, 1) PRIMARY KEY NOT NULL,
    TableName NVARCHAR(200) NOT NULL,
    ActionType NVARCHAR(10) NOT NULL,
    ActionDML NVARCHAR(500) NOT NULL,
    UserID NVARCHAR(50) NOT NULL,
    ActionDate DATETIME NOT NULL);
GO

CREATE TRIGGER HumanResources.Trg_DepartmentChangeAudit
ON HumanResources.Department
AFTER INSERT, UPDATE, DELETE
NOT FOR REPLICATION
AS
BEGIN
    -- First make sure rows were actually affected
    IF (@@ROWCOUNT > 0)
    BEGIN
        SET NOCOUNT ON;
        DECLARE @inserted_count INT;
        DECLARE @deleted_count INT;
        SELECT @inserted_count = COUNT(*)
        FROM inserted;
        SELECT @deleted_count = COUNT(*)
        FROM deleted;
```

```
-- First scenario: 1 or more rows inserted and
-- no deletes = INSERT statement
IF (@inserted_count > 0) AND (@deleted_count = 0)
BEGIN
    INSERT INTO HumanResources.ActionLog (TableName,
        ActionType,
        ActionDML,
        UserID,
        ActionDate)
    SELECT N'HumanResources.Department',
        N'INSERT',
        N'INSERT INTO HumanResources.Department (Name, GroupName) ' +
            N'VALUES (N''' + REPLACE(name, N'''', N'''''') + N''', N''' +
            REPLACE(groupname, N'''', N'''''') + N''');',
        USER_NAME(),
        CURRENT_TIMESTAMP
    FROM inserted;
END
-- Second scenario: no inserted rows and
-- 1 or more rows deleted = DELETE statement
ELSE IF (@inserted_count = 0) AND (@deleted_count > 0)
BEGIN
    INSERT INTO HumanResources.ActionLog (TableName,
        ActionType,
        ActionDML,
        UserID,
        ActionDate)
    SELECT N'HumanResources.Department',
        N'DELETE',
        N'DELETE FROM HumanResources.Department ' +
            N'WHERE name = N''' + REPLACE(name, N'''', N'''''') + N''';',
        USER_NAME(),
        CURRENT_TIMESTAMP
    FROM deleted;
END
```

```
            -- Third scenario: 1 or more inserted rows and
            -- 1 or more deleted rows = UPDATE statement
            ELSE IF (@inserted_count > 0) AND (@deleted_count > 0)
            BEGIN
                INSERT INTO HumanResources.ActionLog (TableName,
                    ActionType,
                    ActionDML,
                    UserID,
                    ActionDate)
                SELECT N'HumanResources.Department',
                    N'UPDATE',
                    N'UPDATE HumanResources.Department ' +
                        N'name = N''' + REPLACE(name, N'''', N'''''') + N''', ' +
                        N'groupname = ''' + REPLACE(groupname, N'''', N'''''') +
                        N''' ' + N'WHERE DepartmentID = ' +
                        CAST(DepartmentID AS NVARCHAR(10)) + N';',
                    USER_NAME(),
                    CURRENT_TIMESTAMP
                FROM inserted;
            END
        END
END;
GO
```

The audit logging example begins by creating an audit logging table called
HumanResources.ActionLog. This table will keep audit information for INSERT, UPDATE, and
DELETE statements on the HumanResources.Department table. The information we will audit
includes the table affected (TableName), the type of DML action performed (ActionType),
the ID of the user performing the action (UserID), the date the action was performed
(ActionDate), and finally a recreation of the DML statement that caused the trigger to fire
(ActionDML). Although we are only auditing a single table here, by adding the TableName
column, this example could be extended easily to audit additional tables:

```
CREATE TABLE HumanResources.ActionLog (
    EntryNum INT IDENTITY(1, 1) PRIMARY KEY NOT NULL,
    TableName NVARCHAR(200) NOT NULL,
    ActionType NVARCHAR(10) NOT NULL,
    ActionDML NVARCHAR(500) NOT NULL,
    UserID NVARCHAR(50) NOT NULL,
    ActionDate DATETIME NOT NULL);
GO
```

The trigger itself is created on the HumanResources.Department table. The definition begins with the name of the trigger, Trg_DepartmentChangeAudit, to be created in the HumanResources schema. The trigger will fire after INSERT, UPDATE, and DELETE actions are performed on the data in the table. Finally, the NOT FOR REPLICATION keywords specify that replication events will not cause the trigger to fire:

```
CREATE TRIGGER HumanResources.Trg_DepartmentChangeAudit
ON HumanResources.Department
AFTER INSERT, UPDATE, DELETE
NOT FOR REPLICATION
AS
```

The first part of the trigger body begins by setting NOCOUNT ON to prevent the trigger from reporting n Rows Affected after each DML statement in the trigger. The trigger then checks @@ROWCOUNT to make sure that rows were actually affected. If one or more rows were affected by the event that fired the trigger, the trigger will determine how many rows were inserted, deleted, or both by querying the inserted and deleted virtual tables:

```
BEGIN
    -- First make sure rows were actually affected
    IF (@@ROWCOUNT > 0)
    BEGIN
        SET NOCOUNT ON;
        DECLARE @inserted_count INT;
        DECLARE @deleted_count INT;
        SELECT @inserted_count = COUNT(*)
        FROM inserted;
        SELECT @deleted_count = COUNT(*)
        FROM deleted;
```

The trigger deals with three scenarios. The first is the simple INSERT. If an INSERT event fires the trigger, the inserted virtual table will have one or more rows in it and the deleted virtual table will have zero rows in it. In the case of an INSERT event, the trigger inserts the appropriate INSERT action information in the audit table. This includes a recreation of the DML statement that inserted the data in the HumanResources.Department table:

```
        -- First scenario: 1 or more rows inserted and
        -- no deletes = INSERT statement
        IF (@inserted_count > 0) AND (@deleted_count = 0)
```

```
    BEGIN
        INSERT INTO HumanResources.ActionLog (TableName,
            ActionType,
            ActionDML,
            UserID,
            ActionDate)
        SELECT N'HumanResources.Department',
            N'INSERT',
            N'INSERT INTO HumanResources.Department (Name, GroupName) ' +
                N'VALUES (N''' + REPLACE(name, N'''', N'''''') + N''', N''' +
                REPLACE(groupname, N'''', N'''''') + N''');',
            USER_NAME(),
            CURRENT_TIMESTAMP
        FROM inserted;
    END
```

The second scenario handles DELETE events. In this scenario, the deleted virtual table contains one or more rows and the inserted virtual table contains no rows. When a DELETE event fires the trigger, the DELETE action information is stored in the audit table. As with the INSERT action information, a recreation of the DELETE statement is also included:

```
    -- Second scenario: no inserted rows and
    -- 1 or more rows deleted = DELETE statement
    ELSE IF (@inserted_count = 0) AND (@deleted_count > 0)
    BEGIN
        INSERT INTO HumanResources.ActionLog (TableName,
            ActionType,
            ActionDML,
            UserID,
            ActionDate)
        SELECT N'HumanResources.Department',
            N'DELETE',
            N'DELETE FROM HumanResources.Department ' +
                N'WHERE name = N''' + REPLACE(name, N'''', N'''''') + N''';',
            USER_NAME(),
            CURRENT_TIMESTAMP
        FROM deleted;
    END
```

The third and final scenario handles UPDATE events. When an UPDATE occurs, both the inserted and deleted virtual tables contain rows. As in the other two scenarios, UPDATE events insert UPDATE action information with a recreation of the UPDATE statement:

```
        -- Third scenario: 1 or more inserted rows and
        -- 1 or more deleted rows = UPDATE statement
        ELSE IF (@inserted_count > 0) AND (@deleted_count > 0)
        BEGIN
            INSERT INTO HumanResources.ActionLog (TableName,
                ActionType,
                ActionDML,
                UserID,
                ActionDate)
            SELECT N'HumanResources.Department',
                N'UPDATE',
                N'UPDATE HumanResources.Department ' +
                    N'name = N''' + REPLACE(name, N'''', N'''''') + N''', ' +
                    N'groupname = ''' + REPLACE(groupname, N'''', N'''''') +
                    N''' ' + N'WHERE DepartmentID = ' +
                    CAST(DepartmentID AS NVARCHAR(10)) + N';',
                USER_NAME(),
                CURRENT_TIMESTAMP
            FROM inserted;
        END
    END
END;
GO
```

VIRTUAL TABLES IN THE TRIGGER

The `inserted` and `deleted` virtual tables are available within the scope of a trigger. They are read-only tables with the same structure as the table the trigger was created on. You cannot perform INSERT, UPDATE, or DELETE statements against the `inserted` and `deleted` virtual tables—only SELECT statements are allowed on them. The `inserted` and `deleted` virtual tables can be used to determine the type of event that fired a trigger:

- For an INSERT event, the `inserted` table contains one or more rows; the `deleted` table contains no rows.

- For DELETE events, the `deleted` table contains one or more rows; the `inserted` table contains no rows.

- For UPDATE events, the `deleted` table contains one or more rows—a snapshot of the data before the change—and the `inserted` table contains one or more rows reflecting the updated data.

The `inserted` and `deleted` virtual tables are extremely useful in triggers, as demonstrated in the audit trigger sample in Listing 7-2.

You can easily verify the trigger with a few simple DML statements, as shown in Listing 7-3.

Listing 7-3. *Testing the Audit Trigger*

```
INSERT INTO HumanResources.Department (Name, GroupName)
VALUES (N'Customer Service', N'Sales and Marketing');

INSERT INTO HumanResources.Department (Name, GroupName)
VALUES (N'Regulatory Compliance', N'Executive General and Administration');

DELETE FROM HumanResources.Department
WHERE Name = N'Regulatory Compliance';

UPDATE HumanResources.Department
SET Name = N'Customer Relations'
WHERE Name = N'Customer Service';

SELECT EntryNum,
    TableName,
    ActionType,
    UserId,
    ActionDate,
    ActionDML
FROM HumanResources.ActionLog;
```

The results returned show that all events were logged in the `HumanResources.ActionLog` table:

```
EntryNum     TableName     ActionType  UserId   ActionDate     ActionDML
-----------  -----------   ----------  -------  -------------  --------------------------
1            HumanRes...   INSERT      dbo      2006-08-19...  INSERT INTO HumanResour...
2            HumanRes...   INSERT      dbo      2006-08-19...  INSERT INTO HumanResour...
3            HumanRes...   DELETE      dbo      2006-08-19...  DELETE FROM HumanResour...
4            HumanRes...   UPDATE      dbo      2006-08-19...  UPDATE HumanResources.D...
5            HumanRes...   UPDATE      dbo      2006-08-19...  UPDATE HumanResources.D...

(5 row(s) affected)
```

Nested Triggers

In the sample trigger, you might have noticed that a single UPDATE event appears to be audited twice. This happened because of the HumanResources.uDepartment trigger that was already on the HumanResources.Department table. This trigger performs an UPDATE on the table, which in turn fires the HumanResources.Trg_DepartmentChangeAudit trigger. SQL Server supports triggers firing other triggers via the concept of *nested triggers*. Triggers can be nested up to 32 levels deep, although if you find your triggers nested several levels deep it will affect performance and you might want to reconsider your trigger design.

NESTED TRIGGER TIPS

Nested triggers are triggers that are fired by the action of other triggers. In the sample code, the HumanResources.uDepartment trigger updates the HumanResources.Department table. This update by the trigger causes the HumanResources.Trg_DepartmentChangeAudit trigger to fire. Triggers can be nested up to 32 levels deep, the same as the limitation on nested stored procedures. Keep in mind, however, that nested triggers can affect performance. Very rarely will you want (or need) to nest triggers more than one or two levels deep.

Nested triggers can also fire across tables. For instance, if *Table A* and *Table B* both have triggers, and the trigger on *Table A* updates *Table B*, it can fire the trigger on *Table B*. Again you are limited to a maximum of 32 levels of nesting.

SQL Server 2005 trigger nesting is controlled by the nested triggers configuration option. By default this option is set to 1, meaning nested triggers are enabled. To disable nested triggers set this option to 0 with the sp_configure system stored procedure, like the following:

```
EXEC sp_configure 'nested triggers', 0;
RECONFIGURE;
GO
```

This option disables nesting of AFTER triggers only. INSTEAD OF triggers can be nested regardless of this setting.

Triggers can also be called recursively. There are two types of recursion:

- *Direct recursion* is when a trigger performs an action that causes it to recursively fire itself.

- *Indirect recursion* is when a trigger fires another trigger (which can fire another trigger, etc.), which eventually fires the first trigger.

Direct and indirect recursion of triggers applies only to triggers of the same type. As an example, an INSTEAD OF trigger call is considered direct recursion even if one or more AFTER triggers are called between the first and second call to the same INSTEAD OF trigger. Indirect recursion occurs when a trigger of the same type is called in between firings of the same trigger.

The ALTER DATABASE *database_name* SET RECURSIVE_TRIGGERS OFF statement turns off direct recursion of AFTER triggers. Setting the nested triggers option to 0 with sp_configure turns off indirect AFTER trigger recursion.

The UPDATE and COLUMNS_UPDATED Functions

Triggers use two system functions, UPDATE and COLUMNS_UPDATED, to tell you which columns are affected by the INSERT or UPDATE statement that fires the trigger in the first place. UPDATE takes the name of a column as a parameter and returns TRUE if the column is updated or inserted, or FALSE otherwise. COLUMNS_UPDATED returns a bit pattern indicating which columns are affected by the INSERT or UPDATE.

The sample trigger in Listing 7-4 demonstrates the use of the UPDATE function to determine if either of two particular columns are affected by an INSERT or UPDATE statement.

Listing 7-4. *Trigger to Enforce Standard Sizes*

```
CREATE TRIGGER Production.Trg_EnforceStandardSizes
ON Production.Product
AFTER INSERT, UPDATE
NOT FOR REPLICATION
AS
BEGIN
    -- Make sure at least one row was affected and the Size
    -- column was changed
    IF (@@ROWCOUNT > 0) AND (UPDATE(SizeUnitMeasureCode) OR UPDATE(Size))
    BEGIN
        SET NOCOUNT ON;
        -- Only accept valid UOM codes
        IF EXISTS(SELECT SizeUnitMeasureCode
            FROM inserted
            WHERE SizeUnitMeasureCode
            NOT IN (N'M', N'DM', N'CM', N'MM', N'IN'))
        BEGIN
            RAISERROR ('Invalid Size Unit Measure Code.', 14, 127);
            ROLLBACK TRANSACTION;
        END
```

```
        ELSE
        BEGIN
            UPDATE Production.Product
            SET SizeUnitMeasureCode = N'CM',
                Size = CAST(CAST(CASE i.SizeUnitMeasureCode
                    WHEN N'M' THEN CAST(i.Size AS FLOAT) * 100.0
                    WHEN N'DM' THEN CAST(i.Size AS FLOAT) * 10.0
                    WHEN N'CM' THEN CAST(i.Size AS FLOAT)
                    WHEN N'MM' THEN CAST(i.Size AS FLOAT) * 0.10
                    WHEN N'IN' THEN CAST(i.Size AS FLOAT) * 2.54
                    END
                AS INTEGER) AS NCHAR(5))
            FROM inserted i
            WHERE Production.Product.ProductID = i.ProductID;
        END
    END
END;
GO
```

This trigger enforces the simple business logic of enforcing standard size codes on the `Production.Product` table. The trigger restricts inserted and updated units of measure to five standard units: M = meters, DM = decimeters, CM = centimeters, MM = millimeters, and IN = inches. No matter which unit of measure is used, the size is automatically converted to centimeters by the trigger.

The first part of the trigger definition gives the trigger its name, `Production.Trg_EnforceStandardSizes`, and creates it on the `Production.Product` table. It is specified as an AFTER INSERT, UPDATE trigger, and is declared as NOT FOR REPLICATION:

```
CREATE TRIGGER Production.Trg_EnforceStandardSizes
ON Production.Product
AFTER INSERT, UPDATE
NOT FOR REPLICATION
AS
```

The code in the body of the trigger checks @@ROWCOUNT to make sure at least one row is affected. It also uses the UPDATE function to check that at least one of either the `SizeUnitMeasureCode` or `Size` columns is updated. If so, the trigger sets NOCOUNT ON to prevent the *n Rows Affected* messages from being generated. The IF EXISTS statement checks to make sure that a valid unit of measure code is used. If not, the trigger raises a custom error and rolls back the transaction:

```
BEGIN
    -- Make sure at least one row was affected and the Size
    -- column was changed
    IF (@@ROWCOUNT > 0) AND (UPDATE(SizeUnitMeasureCode) OR UPDATE(Size))
    BEGIN
        SET NOCOUNT ON;
        -- Only accept valid UOM codes
        IF EXISTS(SELECT SizeUnitMeasureCode
            FROM inserted
            WHERE SizeUnitMeasureCode
            NOT IN (N'M', N'DM', N'CM', N'MM', N'IN'))
        BEGIN
            RAISERROR ('Invalid Size Unit Measure Code.', 14, 127);
            ROLLBACK TRANSACTION;
        END
```

▓**Tip** Remember, every trigger is part of a transaction. Issuing a ROLLBACK TRANSACTION inside a trigger rolls back the transaction and cancels the entire batch that the trigger is fired from. In addition, a ROLLBACK TRANSACTION prevents further triggers from being fired by the current trigger.

Finally, if all checks are passed, the SizeUnitMeasureCode is set to centimeters (CM) and the Size is converted to centimeters for each inserted or updated row:

```
        ELSE
        BEGIN
            UPDATE Production.Product
            SET SizeUnitMeasureCode = N'CM',
                Size = CAST(CAST(CASE i.SizeUnitMeasureCode
                    WHEN N'M' THEN CAST(i.Size AS FLOAT) * 100.0
                    WHEN N'DM' THEN CAST(i.Size AS FLOAT) * 10.0
                    WHEN N'CM' THEN CAST(i.Size AS FLOAT)
                    WHEN N'MM' THEN CAST(i.Size AS FLOAT) * 0.10
                    WHEN N'IN' THEN CAST(i.Size AS FLOAT) * 2.54
                    END
                AS INTEGER) AS NCHAR(5))
            FROM inserted i
            WHERE Production.Product.ProductID = i.ProductID;
        END
    END
END;
GO
```

This trigger enforces the simple business logic of enforcing standard size codes on the Production.Product table. The trigger restricts inserted and updated units of measure to five standard units: M = meters, DM = decimeters, CM = centimeters, MM = millimeters, and IN = inches. No matter which unit of measure is used, the size is automatically converted to centimeters by the trigger.

The first part of the trigger definition gives the trigger its name, Production.Trg_EnforceStandardSizes, and creates it on the Production.Product table. It is specified as an AFTER INSERT, UPDATE trigger, and is declared as NOT FOR REPLICATION:

```
CREATE TRIGGER Production.Trg_EnforceStandardSizes
ON Production.Product
AFTER INSERT, UPDATE
NOT FOR REPLICATION
AS
```

The code in the body of the trigger checks @@ROWCOUNT to make sure at least one row is affected. It also uses the UPDATE function to check that at least one of either the SizeUnitMeasureCode or Size columns is updated. If so, the trigger sets NOCOUNT ON to prevent the *n Rows Affected* messages from being generated. The IF EXISTS statement checks to make sure that a valid unit of measure code is used. If not, the trigger raises a custom error and rolls back the transaction:

```
BEGIN
    -- Make sure at least one row was affected and the Size
    -- column was changed
    IF (@@ROWCOUNT > 0) AND (UPDATE(SizeUnitMeasureCode) OR UPDATE(Size))
    BEGIN
        SET NOCOUNT ON;
        -- Only accept valid UOM codes
        IF EXISTS(SELECT SizeUnitMeasureCode
            FROM inserted
            WHERE SizeUnitMeasureCode
            NOT IN (N'M', N'DM', N'CM', N'MM', N'IN'))
        BEGIN
            RAISERROR ('Invalid Size Unit Measure Code.', 14, 127);
            ROLLBACK TRANSACTION;
        END
```

Tip Remember, every trigger is part of a transaction. Issuing a ROLLBACK TRANSACTION inside a trigger rolls back the transaction and cancels the entire batch that the trigger is fired from. In addition, a ROLLBACK TRANSACTION prevents further triggers from being fired by the current trigger.

Finally, if all checks are passed, the SizeUnitMeasureCode is set to centimeters (CM) and the Size is converted to centimeters for each inserted or updated row:

```
        ELSE
        BEGIN
            UPDATE Production.Product
            SET SizeUnitMeasureCode = N'CM',
                Size = CAST(CAST(CASE i.SizeUnitMeasureCode
                    WHEN N'M' THEN CAST(i.Size AS FLOAT) * 100.0
                    WHEN N'DM' THEN CAST(i.Size AS FLOAT) * 10.0
                    WHEN N'CM' THEN CAST(i.Size AS FLOAT)
                    WHEN N'MM' THEN CAST(i.Size AS FLOAT) * 0.10
                    WHEN N'IN' THEN CAST(i.Size AS FLOAT) * 2.54
                    END
                AS INTEGER) AS NCHAR(5))
            FROM inserted i
            WHERE Production.Product.ProductID = i.ProductID;
        END
    END
END;
GO
```

To test the trigger, you can insert a row into the Production.Product table. Listing 7-5 adds a new Gold-Plated King Roadster bike to the Production.Product table. The size is entered as 18.9 inches, which is converted to centimeters by the trigger.

Listing 7-5. *Testing the Trigger by Adding a New Product*

```
INSERT INTO Production.Product(Name,
    ProductNumber,
    Size,
    SizeUnitMeasureCode,
    SafetyStockLevel,
    ReorderPoint,
    StandardCost,
    ListPrice,
    DaysToManufacture,
    SellStartDate)
```

```
VALUES ('King Roadster-1000 Gold Plated, 48',
    N'BK-K20Z-48',
    N'18.9',
    N'IN',
    1000,
    750,
    1412.50,
    2639.99,
    2,
    N'2006-08-19');

SELECT Name,
    ProductNumber,
    Size,
    SizeUnitMeasureCode
FROM Production.Product
WHERE ProductNumber = N'BK-K20Z-48';
```

As you can see in the results, the trigger converts the size to centimeters:

Name	ProductNumber	Size	SizeUnitMeasureCode
King Roadster-1000 Gold Plated, 48	BK-K20Z-48	48	CM

(1 row(s) affected)

While the UPDATE function accepts a column name and returns TRUE if the column is affected, UPDATED_COLUMNS accepts no parameters and returns a varbinary with a single bit representing each column. You use the logical AND operator (&) and a bit mask to test which columns are affected. The bits are set from left to right, in the same ordinal positions as the columns. To create your bit mask, you must use 2^0 (= 1) to represent the first column, 2^1 (= 2) to represent the second column, and so on. To test the MakeFlag and FinishedGoodsFlag of the Production.Product table (columns four and five, respectively), you would use a bit mask of 24 ($24 = 2^3 + 2^4$) in an IF statement of this form:

```
IF (UPDATED_COLUMNS() & 24 = 24)
```

Because UPDATED_COLUMNS returns a varbinary result, the column indicator bits can be spread out over several bytes. To test columns beyond the first eight, like the Size and SizeUnitMeasureCode columns in the example code (columns 11 and 12), you can use the SUBSTRING function like this:

```
IF (SUBSTRING(UPDATED_COLUMNS(), 2, 1) & 12 = 12)
```

The UPDATED_COLUMNS function will not return correct results if the ordinal positions of the table are changed. If the table is dropped and recreated with columns in a different order, or if new columns are added between existing columns, you will need to change your triggers that use UPDATED_COLUMNS to reflect the changes.

Tip The UPDATED_COLUMNS function's reliance on the ordinal positions of columns can cause problems if your table structure changes in the future. Avoid using UPDATED_COLUMNS and use the UPDATE function in your triggers instead.

Triggers and Identity Columns

There are several ways to retrieve the values inserted into identity columns from within triggers. One recommended method is to use the SCOPE_IDENTITY function to retrieve the last identity value generated in any table within the current session and scope. Another method is to retrieve the values inserted into the identity column from the inserted virtual table. Finally, the OUTPUT clause can be used within a trigger to retrieve the identity value at INSERT time.

Caution The other methods of retrieving identity column values include the @@IDENTITY function and IDENT_CURRENT. @@IDENTITY returns the last inserted identity value in any table during the current session. It is not limited to a particular table and can be the source of hard-to-locate errors if used within a trigger. IDENT_CURRENT is not limited to scope or session; it is limited to a particular table. Use care with these functions.

Altering, Dropping, and Disabling Triggers

The ALTER TRIGGER statement allows you to change the definition of a trigger. The syntax is similar to that of the CREATE TRIGGER statement, except that the ALTER keyword is used in place of CREATE. The trigger specified in the ALTER TRIGGER statement must already exist.

The DROP TRIGGER syntax allows you to remove a previously created trigger. The syntax for DROP TRIGGER is the following:

```
DROP TRIGGER schema.trigger_name [ , ...n ];
```

DROP TRIGGER permanently removes the specified trigger from your database. If you just want to disable a DML trigger without deleting it permanently, use the DISABLE TRIGGER statement:

```
DISABLE TRIGGER { [ schema. ] trigger_name [ , ... n ] | ALL }
ON { table | view } ;
```

You can specify triggers by name in the DISABLE TRIGGER statement, or specify the keyword ALL to disable all triggers on the specified *table* or *view*. The trigger must exist on the specified *table* or *view*. To enable a trigger, use the ENABLE TRIGGER statement:

```
ENABLE TRIGGER { [ schema. ] trigger_name [ , ... n ] | ALL }
ON { table | view } ;
```

MORE TRIGGER CONSIDERATIONS

There are many considerations and options to take into account when designing and creating triggers. These include the following:

- Constraints on tables are checked before an AFTER trigger is fired. If a constraint violation occurs the trigger will not be fired. On very rare occasions you might wish to disable a constraint until after a trigger has finished. You can use the ALTER TABLE statement to disable and reenable constraints.

- An AFTER trigger can only be specified on a table. An INSTEAD OF trigger can be specified on a table or view.

- When cascaded DRI DELETEs occur, any triggers are fired in reverse order. For instance if deleting a row from Table A causes DRI to automatically delete a row (or rows) from Table B, the trigger on Table B will fire first, followed by the trigger on Table A.

- INSTEAD OF DELETE and INSTEAD OF UPDATE triggers cannot be defined on tables with a foreign key delete or update cascade action specified.

- When you create an INSTEAD OF trigger, the trigger must perform the action it is replacing. For instance, if you create an INSTEAD OF INSERT trigger it must perform the actual INSERT that updates the table.

- Unlike older versions of SQL Server, SQL 2005 allows you to select TEXT, NTEXT, and IMAGE column values from the inserted and deleted virtual tables. If compatibility is set to 70 or lower, you cannot access TEXT, NTEXT, or IMAGE columns in the inserted or deleted tables. If the compatibility is 80 or higher you can update columns of these data types in an INSTEAD OF trigger. Fortunately, these data types are deprecated and should be avoided in favor of the new VARCHAR(max), NVARCHAR(max), and VARBINARY(max) data types.

- The TRUNCATE TABLE statement is useful for quickly removing all rows from a table; however, it does not fire DML DELETE triggers on a table. Similarly, the deprecated WRITETEXT and UPDATETEXT statements do not fire triggers.

- Triggers can return result sets in a fashion similar to stored procedures. This functionality is deprecated and will be removed in a future version of SQL Server, however. Plan to change any triggers that return result sets and don't design new triggers to return result sets. You can set the disallow results from triggers option to 0 to prevent triggers from returning result sets. In order to set this option, you must set the show advanced options option to 1:

```
EXEC sp_configure 'show advanced options', 1;
RECONFIGURE;
EXEC sp_configure 'disallow results from triggers', 0;
RECONFIGURE;
EXEC sp_configure 'show advanced options', 0;
RECONFIGURE
GO
```

- The following statements are not allowed in the body of a DML trigger: ALTER DATABASE, CREATE DATABASE, DROP DATABASE, LOAD DATABASE, LOAD LOG, RECONFIGURE, RESTORE DATABASE, and RESTORE LOG. Additional restrictions are introduced on T-SQL statements against the table or view that fired the trigger: ALTER/CREATE/DROP INDEX, DROP TABLE, ALTER PARTITION FUNCTION, and DBCC DBREINDEX. ALTER TABLE cannot be used to add, modify, or drop columns, add or drop PRIMARY KEY or UNIQUE constraints, or switch partitions on the table or view that fired the trigger.

- Creation of a DML trigger requires ALTER permission on the table or view on which it is being created.

Additionally you can set the first and last AFTER triggers that fire on a table with the sp_settriggerorder system stored procedure. The order of firing for any triggers between the first and last triggers is always unspecified. The format of sp_settriggerorder for DML triggers is the following:

```
sp_settriggerorder [ @triggername = ] '[ schema. ] trigger_name',
    [ @order = ] [ 'First' | 'Last' | 'None' ],
    [ @stmt_type = ] 'statement_type'
    [ , @namespace = NULL]
```

The *schema* and *trigger_name* specify the trigger you want to set the order for. The *@order* parameter can be set to First or Last if you want the trigger to fire first or last, respectively. It should be None if you don't want to specify the order of firing for this trigger. The first and last triggers must have different names, and the *statement_type* is used to specify the type of statement for which this trigger fires first or last. *Statement_type* can be INSERT, DELETE, or UPDATE for DML triggers. The *@namespace* parameter is optional, and should be set to NULL if used, for a DML trigger.

DDL Triggers

Prior to SQL Server 2005, T-SQL programmers had only one type of trigger to work with: DML triggers. SQL Server 2005 adds additional trigger functionality in the form of DDL triggers that fire when DDL events occur within a database or server. In this section we will discuss DDL triggers and the events that fire them.

The format of the CREATE TRIGGER statement for DDL triggers is only slightly different from the DML trigger syntax:

```
CREATE TRIGGER trigger_name
ON { ALL SERVER | DATABASE }
[ WITH [ ENCRYPTION ] [ [ , ] EXECUTE AS context ] ]
{ FOR | AFTER } { event_type | event_group } [ , ... n ]
AS { sql_statement  [ ; ] [ , ... n ] } ;
```

The CREATE TRIGGER statement for DDL triggers begins by specifying the *trigger_name*. The *trigger_name* must follow the specifications for T-SQL identifiers. DDL triggers are specified with ALL SERVER or DATABASE scope. DATABASE scope causes the DDL trigger to fire if the specified event_type or event_group occurs within the current database. ALL SERVER scope causes the DDL trigger to fire if the event_type or event_group occurs anywhere on the current server.

The optional WITH keyword can specify either ENCRYPTION or the EXECUTE AS clause, or any combination of these.

The ENCRYPTION keyword obfuscates the text of the CREATE TRIGGER statement, just like with CREATE PROCEDURE or CREATE FUNCTION.

The EXECUTE AS clause specifies the security context the trigger will run under. For all DDL triggers the *context* can be CALLER to specify the context of the calling module or SELF to specify the context of the person creating or altering the trigger. For DDL triggers with

ALL SERVER scope only you can specify *login_name* to indicate that the trigger will run under the context of a specific SQL Server login. For DDL triggers with DATABASE scope only you can specify the context of a particular user by using *user_name*.

▪Note If using EXECUTE AS *user_name* on a DDL trigger with DATABASE scope, *user_name* must exist in the current database and cannot be a group, role, built-in account, certificate, or key. If using EXECUTE AS *login_name* on a DDL trigger with ALL SERVER scope, similar restrictions apply.

DDL triggers can only be specified as FOR or AFTER (there's no INSTEAD OF option). The *event_types* that can fire a DDL trigger are generally of the form CREATE, ALTER, DROP, GRANT, DENY, REVOKE, and UPDATE STATISTICS. Some system stored procedures that perform DDL functions also fire DDL triggers.

▪Caution Not all system stored procedures that perform DDL functions fire DDL triggers. If you are unsure whether a system stored procedure that you need to execute will fire a DDL trigger, you should test your trigger's response to the system stored procedure in question. Also, DDL triggers do not fire in response to DDL events on temporary tables and temporary stored procedures.

DDL triggers are useful when you want to prevent changes to your database schema, perform actions in response to a change to the database schema, or audit changes to the database schema. Which DDL statements can fire a DDL trigger depends on the scope of the trigger. Table 7-1 is a list of the *event_types* for DDL triggers with DATABASE scope:

Table 7-1. *Database Scoped DDL Trigger Event Types*

• ALTER_APPLICATION_ROLE	• ALTER_ASSEMBLY
• ALTER_AUTHORIZATION_DATABASE	• ALTER_CERTIFICATE
• ALTER_FUNCTION	• ALTER_INDEX
• ALTER_MESSAGE_TYPE	• ALTER_PARTITION_FUNCTION
• ALTER_PARTITION_SCHEME	• ALTER_PROCEDURE
• ALTER_QUEUE	• ALTER_REMOTE_SERVICE_BINDING
• ALTER_ROLE	• ALTER_ROUTE
• ALTER_SCHEMA	• ALTER_SERVICE
• ALTER_TABLE	• ALTER_TRIGGER
• ALTER_USER	• ALTER_VIEW

- ALTER_XML_SCHEMA_COLLECTION
- CREATE_APPLICATION_ROLE
- CREATE_ASSEMBLY
- CREATE_CERTIFICATE
- CREATE_CONTRACT
- CREATE_EVENT_NOTIFICATION
- CREATE_FUNCTION
- CREATE_INDEX
- CREATE_MESSAGE_TYPE
- CREATE_PARTITION_FUNCTION
- CREATE_PARTITION_SCHEME
- CREATE_PROCEDURE
- CREATE_QUEUE
- CREATE_REMOTE_SERVICE_BINDING
- CREATE_ROLE
- CREATE_ROUTE
- CREATE_SCHEMA
- CREATE_SERVICE
- CREATE_STATISTICS
- CREATE_SYNONYM
- CREATE_TABLE
- CREATE_TRIGGER
- CREATE_TYPE
- CREATE_USER
- CREATE_VIEW
- CREATE_XML_SCHEMA_COLLECTION
- DENY_DATABASE
- DROP_APPLICATION_ROLE
- DROP_ASSEMBLY
- DROP_CERTIFICATE
- DROP_CONTRACT
- DROP_EVENT_NOTIFICATION
- DROP_FUNCTION
- DROP_INDEX
- DROP_MESSAGE_TYPE
- DROP_PARTITION_FUNCTION
- DROP_PARTITION_SCHEME
- DROP_PROCEDURE
- DROP_QUEUE
- DROP_REMOTE_SERVICE_BINDING
- DROP_ROLE
- DROP_ROUTE
- DROP_SCHEMA
- DROP_SERVICE
- DROP_STATISTICS
- DROP_SYNONYM
- DROP_TABLE
- DROP_TRIGGER
- DROP_TYPE
- DROP_USER
- DROP_VIEW
- DROP_XML_SCHEMA_COLLECTION
- GRANT_DATABASE
- REVOKE_DATABASE
- UPDATE_STATISTICS

Table 7-2 shows the *event_groups* for DDL triggers with DATABASE scope.

Table 7-2. *Database Scoped DDL Trigger Event Groups*

```
DDL_DATABASE_LEVEL_EVENTS

  DDL_TABLE_VIEW_EVENTS

      DDL_TABLE_EVENTS (CREATE/ALTER/DROP TABLE)

      DDL_VIEW_EVENTS (CREATE/ALTER/DROP VIEW)

      DDL_INDEX_EVENTS (CREATE/ALTER/DROP INDEX, CREATE XML INDEX)

      DDL_STATISTICS_EVENTS (CREATE/UPDATE/DROP STATISTICS)

  DDL_SYNONYM_EVENTS (CREATE SYNONYM, DROP SYNONYM)

  DDL_FUNCTION_EVENTS (CREATE/ALTER/DROP FUNCTION)

  DDL_PROCEDURE_EVENTS (CREATE/ALTER/DROP PROCEDURE)

  DDL_TRIGGER_EVENTS (CREATE/ALTER/DROP TRIGGER)

  DDL_EVENT_NOTIFICATION_EVENTS (CREATE/DROP EVENT NOTIFICATION)

  DDL_ASSEMBLY_EVENTS (CREATE/ALTER/DROP ASSEMBLY)

  DDL_TYPE_EVENTS (CREATE/DROP TYPE)

  DDL_DATABASE_SECURITY_EVENTS

      DDL_CERTIFICATE_EVENTS (CREATE/ALTER/DROP CERTIFICATE)

      DDL_USER_EVENTS (CREATE/ALTER/DROP USER)

      DDL_ROLE_EVENTS (CREATE/ALTER/DROP ROLE)

      DDL_APPLICATION_ROLE_EVENTS (CREATE/ALTER/DROP APPROLE)

      DDL_SCHEMA_EVENTS (CREATE/ALTER/DROP SCHEMA)

      DDL_GDR_DATABASE_EVENTS (GRANT/DENY/REVOKE DATABASE)

      DDL_AUTHORIZATION_DATABASE_EVENTS (ALTER AUTHORIZATION DATABASE)

  DDL_SSB_EVENTS

      DDL_MESSAGE_TYPE_EVENTS (CREATE/ALTER/DROP MSGTYPE)

      DDL_CONTRACT_EVENTS (CREATE/DROP CONTRACT)

      DDL_QUEUE_EVENTS (CREATE/ALTER/DROP QUEUE)

      DDL_SERVICE_EVENTS (CREATE/ALTER/DROP SERVICE)

      DDL_ROUTE_EVENTS (CREATE/ALTER/DROP ROUTE)

      DDL_REMOTE_SERVICE_BINDING_EVENTS (CREATE/ALTER/DROP REMOTE SERVICE BINDING)

  DDL_XML_SCHEMA_COLLECTION_EVENTS (CREATE/ALTER/DROP XML SCHEMA COLLECTION)

  DDL_PARTITION_EVENTS

      DDL_PARTITION_FUNCTION_EVENTS (CREATE/ALTER/DROP PARTITION FUNCTION)

      DDL_PARTITION_SCHEME_EVENTS (CREATE/ALTER/DROP PARTITION SCHEME)
```

Table 7-3 is a list of the DDL *event_types* with ALL SERVER scope:

Table 7-3. *Server Scoped DDL Event Types*

• ALTER_AUTHORIZATION_SERVER	• ALTER_DATABASE
• ALTER_ENDPOINT	• ALTER_LOGIN
• CREATE_DATABASE	• CREATE_ENDPOINT
• CREATE_LOGIN	• DENY_SERVER
• DROP_DATABASE	• DROP_ENDPOINT
• DROP_LOGIN	• GRANT_SERVER
• REVOKE_SERVER	

Table 7-4 shows the DDL *event_groups* with ALL SERVER scope.

Table 7-4. *Server Scoped DDL Event Groups*

```
DDL_SERVER_LEVEL_EVENTS (CREATE/ALTER/DROP DATABASE)
    DDL_ENDPOINT_EVENTS (CREATE/ALTER/DROP ENDPOINT)
    DDL_SERVER_SECURITY_EVENTS
        DDL_LOGIN_EVENTS (CREATE/ALTER/DROP LOGIN)
        DDL_GDR_SERVER_EVENTS (GRANT/DENY/REVOKE SERVER)
        DDL_AUTHORIZATION_SERVER_EVENTS (ALTER AUTHORIZATION SERVER)
```

If you specify an *event_group*, any events specified within that group will fire the DDL trigger. In Tables 7-2 and 7-4, the trigger event groups included in higher-level groups are indicated by indentation beneath the groups that include them.

As with DML triggers, the DDL trigger body contains *sql_statements* after the AS keyword. The *sql_statements* perform actions in response to the trigger firing. Like the DML triggers and stored procedures, the trigger body code does not have to be wrapped in the BEGIN...END keywords (but as with stored procedures, I personally prefer to use them for readability).

The ALTER TRIGGER, DROP TRIGGER, DISABLE TRIGGER, and ENABLE TRIGGER work for DDL triggers just as they do for DML triggers. Creation of a DDL trigger with ALL SERVER scope requires CONTROL SERVER permission on the server. Creating a DDL trigger with DATABASE scope requires ALTER ANY DATABASE DDL TRIGGER permissions.

Once the DDL trigger fires, you can access metadata about the event that fired the trigger with the EVENTDATA function. EVENTDATA returns information such as the time, connection, and type of event that fired the trigger. The results are returned as SQL Server xml data. You can use the xml data type's value() method to retrieve a specific node from the result. The sample DDL trigger in Listing 7-6 creates a DDL trigger that fires on CREATE TABLE in the AdventureWorks database.

Listing 7-6. *CREATE TABLE DDL Trigger Example*

```
CREATE TRIGGER Trg_CreateTable
ON DATABASE
FOR CREATE_TABLE
AS
BEGIN
    DECLARE @event_data XML;
    SELECT @event_data = EVENTDATA();
    DECLARE @event_type NVARCHAR(2000);
    DECLARE @firing_command NVARCHAR(2000);
    SELECT @event_type = @event_data.value(N'(/EVENT_INSTANCE/EventType)[1]',
        N'NVARCHAR(2000)');
    SELECT @firing_command = @event_data.value(
        N'(/EVENT_INSTANCE/TSQLCommand/CommandText)[1]', N'NVARCHAR(2000)');
    PRINT N'Event type = ' + @event_type;
    PRINT N'Command that fired this trigger = ' + @firing_command;
    PRINT N'Event data = ' + CAST(@event_data AS NVARCHAR(MAX));
END;
GO


--Test the trigger.
CREATE TABLE NewTable (Column1 INT NOT NULL PRIMARY KEY);
GO


-- Drop the table.
DROP TABLE NewTable;
GO


--Drop the trigger.
DROP TRIGGER Trg_CreateTable
ON DATABASE;
GO
```

The results will look similar to the following (the XML results formatted for easy readability):

```
Event type = CREATE_TABLE
Command that fired this trigger = CREATE TABLE NewTable (Column1
INT NOT NULL PRIMARY KEY);
Event data =
<EVENT_INSTANCE>
    <EventType>CREATE_TABLE</EventType>
    <PostTime>2006-08-20T15:44:17.267</PostTime>
    <SPID>53</SPID>
    <ServerName>SQL2005\SQL2K5</ServerName>
    <LoginName>SQL2005\Michael</LoginName>
    <UserName>dbo</UserName>
    <DatabaseName>AdventureWorks</DatabaseName>
    <SchemaName>dbo</SchemaName>
    <ObjectName>NewTable</ObjectName>
    <ObjectType>TABLE</ObjectType>
    <TSQLCommand>
        <SetOptions ANSI_NULLS="ON"
            ANSI_NULL_DEFAULT="ON"
            ANSI_PADDING="ON"
            QUOTED_IDENTIFIER="ON"
            ENCRYPTED="FALSE"/>
        <CommandText>
            CREATE TABLE NewTable (Column1 INT NOT NULL PRIMARY KEY);&#xOD;
        </CommandText>
    </TSQLCommand>
</EVENT_INSTANCE>
```

The trigger definition begins with the name Trg_CreateTable scoped to the DATABASE. The action that fires this trigger is the CREATE TABLE event:

```
CREATE TRIGGER Trg_CreateTable
ON DATABASE
FOR CREATE_TABLE
AS
```

The body of the trigger begins by declaring an xml variable, @event_data. This variable holds the results of the EVENTDATA function:

```
BEGIN
    DECLARE @event_data XML;
    SELECT @event_data = EVENTDATA();
```

Next, the trigger uses the value() method of the @event_data xml variable to extract the event type and the command that fired the trigger from @event_data:

```
DECLARE @event_type NVARCHAR(2000);
DECLARE @firing_command NVARCHAR(2000);
SELECT @event_type = @event_data.value(N'(/EVENT_INSTANCE/EventType)[1]',
    N'NVARCHAR(2000)');
SELECT @firing_command = @event_data.value(
    N'(/EVENT_INSTANCE/TSQLCommand/CommandText)[1]', N'NVARCHAR(2000)');
```

Finally, the trigger prints the results to the display:

```
PRINT N'Event type = ' + @event_type;
PRINT N'Command that fired this trigger = ' + @firing_command;
PRINT N'Event data = ' + CAST(@event_data AS NVARCHAR(MAX));
END;
GO
```

The CREATE TABLE statement tests the trigger and produces the results. Finally, the DROP TABLE and DROP TRIGGER statements are used to clean up after the test:

```
--Test the trigger.
CREATE TABLE NewTable (Column1 INT NOT NULL PRIMARY KEY);
GO

-- Drop the table.
DROP TABLE NewTable;
GO

--Drop the trigger.
DROP TRIGGER Trg_CreateTable
ON DATABASE;
GO
```

Summary

This chapter discussed triggers, including traditional DML triggers and the new SQL Server 2005 DDL triggers. The following topics were covered:

- DML triggers are tied to tables and views and are fired in response to INSERT, UPDATE, and DELETE DML statements.

- DDL triggers are scoped to a database or server and are fired in response to DDL statements, such as CREATE, ALTER, and DROP.

- The UPDATE and UPDATED_COLUMNS system functions can be used in triggers to identify columns that were affected by DML statements.

- The EVENTDATA function can be used to retrieve data about the event that fired a DDL trigger.

- The differences between AFTER and INSTEAD OF triggers were discussed.

- The inserted and deleted virtual tables were described.

- Trigger nesting and recursion were explained.

Much of the functionality that DML triggers were used for in the past, such as enforcing referential integrity, have been supplanted by newer and more efficient T-SQL functionality over the years, like DRI. DML triggers do provide an excellent means of simple auditing of data and enforcing complex business logic on the server side. DDL triggers provide new functionality that extends the ability to audit server and database events and provide protections against accidental or malicious changes to, or destruction of, database objects.

In the next chapter I will discuss one of the most exciting new aspects of SQL Server 2005 and one of my favorite topics, T-SQL encryption.

CHAPTER 8

■■■

T-SQL Encryption

One of the new exciting features of SQL Server 2005 is its built-in T-SQL encryption functionality. Previous versions of SQL Server offered no built-in encryption functionality for data. In order to encrypt sensitive data, database administrators and developers had to turn to third-party tools or write their own extended procedures. Even with these tools in place various aspects of the system, such as encryption key management, left many databases in a vulnerable state.

SQL Server 2005's integrated encryption security model takes advantage of the Windows CryptoAPI to secure your data. With built-in encryption key management and facilities to handle encryption, decryption, and one-way hashing with built-in T-SQL statements, SQL 2005 encryption is an excellent choice for securing sensitive data. In this chapter we will discuss SQL 2005's built-in encryption, decryption, key management, and one-way hashing.

The Encryption Hierarchy

SQL Server 2005 offers a layered approach to encryption key management, similar to the method described in the ANSI X9.17 "Financial Institution Key Management (Wholesale)" standard (http://www.x9.org). The standard describes three levels of encryption key management: Master Keys, Key Encrypting Keys, and Data Keys. According to the ANSI standard, *Master Keys* are used to encrypt Key Encrypting Keys, and *Key Encrypting Keys* are used to encrypt Data Keys. *Data Keys* are used in turn to encrypt actual data. The advantage to this system is that when a Master Key or Key Encrypting Keys are changed to maintain security, large amounts of data do not need to be decrypted and reencrypted. Only the keys encrypted by the Master Key or Key Encrypting Keys need to be decrypted and reencrypted. When a Data Key is changed, however, all of the data it is securing needs to be decrypted and reencrypted. The ANSI standard specifies Triple DES as the means of securing data and keys.

SQL Server 2005 takes this model a step further by allowing several levels of Key Encrypting Keys between the Master Key and Data Keys. SQL Server also allows for encryption by certificates, symmetric keys, and asymmetric keys. The SQL 2005 encryption model is hierarchical as shown in Figure 8-1.

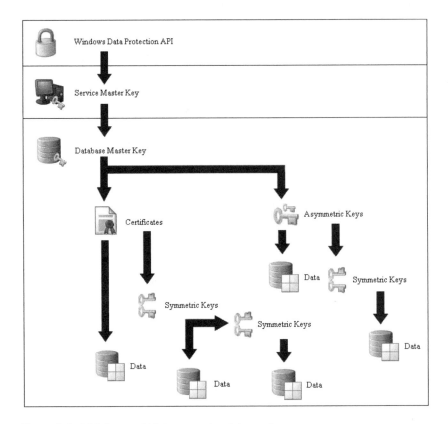

Figure 8-1. *SQL Server 2005 encryption hierarchy*

At the top of the SQL 2005 encryption hierarchy is the granddaddy of all SQL 2005 encryption keys: the *service master key* (SMK). This key is automatically generated by SQL Server the first time it is needed to encrypt another key. The SMK is encrypted by the operating system with the Windows Data Protection API (DPAPI). There is only one SMK per SQL Server instance, and it directly or indirectly secures all keys on the server. The SMK is analogous to the ANSI X9.17 Master Key.

While each SQL Server instance has only a single SMK, each database can have a *database master key* (DMK). The DMK is encrypted by the SMK. The DMK is used to encrypt lower-level keys and certificates. The DMKs and other intermediate layers of symmetric keys, asymmetric keys, and certificates are roughly analogous to ANSI standard Key Encrypting Keys.

At the bottom of the SQL Server 2005 key hierarchy are the certificates, symmetric keys, and asymmetric keys used to encrypt data. These are synonymous with the ANSI Data Keys.

Service Master Key

As mentioned, the SMK is automatically generated by SQL Server the first time it is needed. Because the SMK is generated automatically and managed by SQL Server, there are only a couple of administrative tools needed to BACKUP and RESTORE it on a server:

```
BACKUP SERVICE MASTER KEY TO FILE = 'path_to_file'
   ENCRYPTION BY PASSWORD = 'password'

RESTORE SERVICE MASTER KEY FROM FILE = 'path_to_file'
   DECRYPTION BY PASSWORD = 'password' [ FORCE ]
```

The BACKUP SERVICE MASTER KEY statement backs up the SMK to the file specified. The *path_to_file* can be a local path or a UNC path to a file. *Password* specifies the password to use to encrypt or decrypt the SMK. The RESTORE SERVICE MASTER KEY statement can include the optional keyword FORCE to force the SMK to restore even if there is a data decryption failure. If you have to use the FORCE keyword you can expect to lose data, so use this option with care and only as a last resort. Backing up and restoring an SMK requires CONTROL SERVER permissions.

■**Tip** After installing SQL Server 2005 you should immediately back up your SMK and store a copy of it in a secure offsite location. If your SMK becomes corrupted or is otherwise compromised, you could lose all of your encrypted data if you don't have it backed up.

In addition, the ALTER SERVICE MASTER KEY statement allows you to change the SMK for an instance of SQL Server. The format for this statement is the following:

```
ALTER SERVICE MASTER KEY [ [ FORCE ] REGENERATE ] |
   [ WITH OLD_ACCOUNT = 'account_name', OLD_PASSWORD = 'password' ] |
   [ WITH NEW_ACCOUNT = 'account_name', NEW_PASSWORD = 'password' ] |
   [ { ADD | DROP } ENCRYPTION BY MACHINE KEY ]
```

The REGENERATE keyword regenerates the SMK. When used with the FORCE keyword, the SMK is regenerated even at the risk of data loss. The SMK is encrypted by the DPAPI, using the SQL Server service account credentials, or by the local machine key. If the service account credentials are changed, you can use the WITH OLD_ACCOUNT or WITH NEW_ACCOUNT options to enable encryption under the new service account. The WITH NEW_ACCOUNT option tells SQL Server to impersonate the specified new account user and encrypt the SMK using that user's credentials. The WITH OLD_ACCOUNT option tells SQL Server to impersonate the old account user to decrypt the SMK using that user's credentials.

The ADD ENCRYPTION BY MACHINE KEY specifies that the SMK is encrypted by the local machine key. If you DROP ENCRYPTION BY MACHINE KEY, the SMK is encrypted using the SQL Server service account credentials.

When you regenerate the SMK, all keys that are encrypted by it must be decrypted and reencrypted. This operation can be resource-intensive and should be scheduled during off-peak time periods.

■**Caution** When restoring or regenerating the SMK, SQL Server will stop if it encounters an error during the decryption process. Using the FORCE option causes SQL Server to continue despite decryption errors. If the FORCE option is required, you can expect data loss.

Database Master Key

Each database can have a single DMK, which is used to encrypt certificate and asymmetric key private keys in the current database. The DMK is created with the CREATE MASTER KEY statement:

```
CREATE MASTER KEY ENCRYPTION BY PASSWORD = 'password' ;
```

The CREATE MASTER KEY statement creates the DMK and uses Triple DES to encrypt it with the supplied *password*. If the *password* supplied does not meet Windows' complexity requirements, SQL Server will complain with an error message like the following:

```
Msg 15118, Level 16, State 1, Line 1
Password validation failed. The password does not meet Windows policy requirements
because it is not complex enough.
```

SQL 2005 automatically encrypts a copy of the DMK with the SMK. This feature is known as *automatic key management*. With this feature turned on, SQL Server can decrypt your DMK when needed. Automatic key management allows SQL Server to automatically open and decrypt your DMK as necessary. Without automatic key management you must issue the OPEN MASTER KEY statement and supply the same *password* initially used to encrypt it when you need to use it. The potential downside to automatic key management is that any member of the sysadmin server role can decrypt the DMK. You can use the ALTER MASTER KEY statement to add or remove automatic key management for a DMK or to regenerate it. The format for ALTER MASTER KEY is the following:

```
ALTER MASTER KEY
    [ [ FORCE ] REGENERATE WITH ENCRYPTION BY PASSWORD = 'password' ] ] |
    [ ADD ENCRYPTION BY [ SERVICE MASTER KEY | PASSWORD = 'password' ] ] |
    [ DROP ENCRYPTION BY [ SERVICE MASTER KEY | PASSWORD = 'password' ] ] ;
```

The specific format to turn off automatic key management is the following:

```
ALTER MASTER KEY DROP ENCRYPTION BY SERVICE MASTER KEY
```

To regenerate a DMK, use the REGENERATE option:

```
ALTER MASTER KEY REGENERATE WITH ENCRYPTION BY PASSWORD = 'password'
```

When the DMK is regenerated, all the keys it protects are decrypted and reencrypted with the new DMK. The FORCE keyword is used to force SQL Server to regenerate even if there are decryption errors. As with the SMK, the FORCE keyword should be used only as a last resort. You can expect to lose data if you have to use FORCE.

You can also back up and restore a DMK with the BACKUP and RESTORE statements:

```
BACKUP MASTER KEY TO FILE = 'path_to_file'
    ENCRYPTION BY PASSWORD = 'password' ;

RESTORE MASTER KEY FROM FILE = 'path_to_file'
    DECRYPTION BY PASSWORD = 'password'
    ENCRYPTION BY PASSWORD = 'password'
    [ FORCE ] ;
```

The BACKUP MASTER KEY statement backs up your DMK to the specified file. The path_to_file can be a local file or network path. The supplied password is used to encrypt the DMK in the file.

The RESTORE MASTER KEY statement restores a previously backed up DMK from a file. The DECRYPTION BY PASSWORD is the same password supplied to the BACKUP MASTER KEY statement. This password is used to decrypt the DMK from the file. The ENCRYPTION BY PASSWORD specifies the password that should be used to encrypt the DMK on the server. Again, the FORCE keyword should only be used as a last resort, as it will probably result in lost data.

The DROP MASTER KEY statement is used to remove a DMK from the database. The format is simple:

```
DROP MASTER KEY ;
```

DROP MASTER KEY will not remove a DMK if it is currently being used to encrypt other keys in the database. If you want to drop a DMK that is protecting other keys in the database, the protected keys must be altered to remove their encryption by DMK first.

> **Tip** Always make backups of your DMKs immediately upon creation and store them in a secure location.

If you chose to disable automatic key management with the ALTER MASTER KEY statement, you will need to use the OPEN MASTER KEY and CLOSE MASTER KEY statements every time you wish to perform encryption and decryption in a database. The formats of these statements are as follows:

```
OPEN MASTER KEY DECRYPTION BY PASSWORD = 'password' ;
CLOSE MASTER KEY ;
```

OPEN MASTER KEY requires you to supply the same password used to encrypt the DMK when it is created or restored from backup. This password is used to decrypt the DMK, a required step when you are encrypting and decrypting data. When finished using the DMK, issue the CLOSE MASTER KEY statement. If you have automatic key management enabled (it is by default), you do not need to use the OPEN MASTER KEY and CLOSE MASTER KEY statements; SQL Server will handle that task for you automatically.

> **Tip** Automatic key management allows SQL Server to automatically decrypt your DMK whenever you need to encrypt and decrypt data, eliminating the need to use the OPEN MASTER KEY and CLOSE MASTER KEY statements. It also prevents you from having to reveal the plain-text password encrypting your DMK inside your code.

Certificates

Certificates are asymmetric encryption keys with additional metadata, such as subject and expiration date, in the X.509 certificate format. You can think of a certificate as a wrapper for a private key/public key pair for asymmetric encryption. The CREATE CERTIFICATE statement can be used to either install an existing certificate or create a new certificate on SQL Server. The format to create a brand new certificate is the following:

```
CREATE CERTIFICATE certificate_name [ AUTHORIZATION user_name ]
  {
    [ ENCRYPTION BY PASSWORD = 'password' ]
    WITH SUBJECT = 'certificate_subject_name'
    [ , START_DATE = 'mm/dd/yyyy' | EXPIRY_DATE = 'mm/dd/yyyy' ]
  }
[ ACTIVE FOR BEGIN_DIALOG = { ON | OFF } ] ;
```

The details for this format include the following:

- *Certificate_name* is the name of the certificate in the database.

- *User_name* is the name of the user who owns this certificate.

- ENCRYPTION BY PASSWORD specifies a password to be used to encrypt the certificate's private key. If this optional clause is left out, the private key will be encrypted with the DMK. The password can be up to 128 characters in length.

- WITH SUBJECT specifies a subject, an X.509-defined metadata field (as mentioned in the first paragraph of this section) of up to 4,096 bytes, for your certificate.

- The optional START_DATE and EXPIRY_DATE identify the certificate start and expiration dates. If omitted, START_DATE is set to the current date and EXPIRY_DATE is set to one year after the START_DATE.

- ACTIVE FOR BEGIN_DIALOG makes the certificate available to a Service Broker dialog conversation initiator. The default is ON.

The following is the format to load an existing certificate:

```
CREATE CERTIFICATE certificate_name [ AUTHORIZATION user_name ]
  {
    FROM ASSEMBLY assembly_name |
    {
        [ EXECUTABLE ] FILE = 'path_to_file'
        [ WITH PRIVATE KEY
            ( FILE = 'path_to_private_key'
              [ , DECRYPTION BY PASSWORD = 'password' ]
              [ , ENCRYPTION BY PASSWORD = 'password' ]
            ) ]
    }
  }
[ ACTIVE FOR BEGIN_DIALOG =  { ON | OFF } ] ;
```

The details for this CREATE CERTIFICATE statement are the following:

- *Certificate_name* and *user_name* specify the name of the certificate in the database and the certificate owner, respectively.

- FROM ASSEMBLY specifies that the certificate will be loaded from a signed assembly that has already been loaded into the database.

- The FILE option specifies the complete path and file name to a Distinguished Encoding Rules (DER)–encoded X.509 file containing a certificate. If the EXECUTABLE keyword is used, the file should be a certificate-signed DLL.

- The WITH PRIVATE KEY clause allows you to specify that the certificate's private key will be loaded into SQL Server. The FILE keyword of this clause specifies the file containing the private key. Note that ALTER CERTIFICATE is required to load a private key from a .NET assembly. DECRYPTION BY PASSWORD in this clause specifies the *password* needed to decrypt the private key from the file. ENCRYPTION BY PASSWORD indicates that the private key should be encrypted in SQL Server with the specified *password*. If ENCRYPTION BY PASSWORD is left out, the private key is encrypted by the DMK.

- ACTIVE FOR BEGIN_DIALOG makes the certificate available to a Service Broker dialog conversation initiator. The default is ON.

■**Note** SQL Server generates private keys that are 1,024 bits in length. If you import a private key from an external source, it must be a multiple of 64 bits, between 384 and 3,456 bits in length.

After creating a certificate or any other SQL Server encryption securable you should immediately make a backup and store it in a secure location. The following is the format of the BACKUP statement:

```
BACKUP CERTIFICATE certificate_name TO FILE = 'path_to_file'
    [ WITH PRIVATE KEY
      (
        FILE = 'path_to_private_key_file' ,
        ENCRYPTION BY PASSWORD = 'password'
        [ , DECRYPTION BY PASSWORD = 'password' ]
      ) ] ;
```

The *certificate_name* specifies the name of the certificate in the database, and *path_to_file* indicates the file to back the certificate up to. To back up the certificate's private key, include the WITH PRIVATE KEY clause. When you use WITH PRIVATE KEY, use the FILE keyword to specify the file to store the private key in. You must also specify ENCRYPTION BY PASSWORD to encrypt the private key in the file. DECRYPTION BY PASSWORD is used to indicate the *password* used to decrypt the private key in the database. If DECRYPTION BY PASSWORD is left out, the private key is decrypted with the DMK. Use the CREATE CERTIFICATE statement to restore a backed-up certificate.

Note There is no RESTORE CERTIFICATE statement in T-SQL. Use the CREATE CERTIFICATE statement (install an existing certificate form) to restore a backed-up certificate.

T-SQL also has an ALTER CERTIFICATE statement that allows you to make changes to an existing certificate. The format is the following:

```
ALTER CERTIFICATE certificate_name
    REMOVE PRIVATE KEY |
    WITH PRIVATE KEY
    (
       FILE = 'path_to_private_key'
       [ , DECRYPTION BY PASSWORD = 'password'  ]
       [ , ENCRYPTION BY PASSWORD = 'password' ]
    ) |
    WITH ACTIVE FOR BEGIN_DIALOG = [ ON | OFF ]
```

The options for ALTER CERTIFICATE include the following:

- The *certificate_name* is the name of the certificate in the database.

- REMOVE PRIVATE KEY can be used to prevent the private key from being stored in the database. You can use this option when a private key is not required, such as for signature verification.

- WITH PRIVATE KEY allows you to store the private key for the certificate in the database. The FILE keyword specifies the path and file that contains the private key. DECRYPTION BY PASSWORD specifies the password used to decrypt the private key from the file. ENCRYPTION BY PASSWORD specifies the password used to encrypt the private key in the database. If left out, the DMK is used to encrypt the private key.

- WITH ACTIVE FOR BEGIN_DIALOG allows you to make the certificate available to a Service Broker dialog conversation initiator.

Note In addition to the previous options, the ALTER CERTIFICATE includes the options ATTESTED BY and REMOVE ATTESTED OPTION. These options are currently undocumented by Microsoft and, in fact, Microsoft has stated that references to these particular options should not have been included in BOL.

You can use certificates to encrypt and decrypt data directly with the certificate encryption/decryption functions. The EncryptByCert function encrypts the given cleartext with the specified certificate:

```
EncryptByCert ( certificate_id , 'cleartext' )
```

The EncryptByCert function returns a varbinary up to a maximum of 432 bytes in length. The length of the result depends on the length of the key. See the following note for specifics on EncryptByCert limitations. The *certificate_id* is the integer ID number of the certificate in the database. This ID number can be retrieved with the Cert_ID function described later in this section. The *cleartext* is the string to be encrypted. It can be a char, varchar, binary, nchar, nvarchar, or varbinary constant, column, or variable.

THE 421-BYTE LIMIT

The length of the *cleartext* strings accepted and *ciphertext* results returned by EncryptByCert are limited by the length of the certificate's asymmetric key. The maximum is 421 bytes of *cleartext*, which results in a 432-byte *ciphertext* result. The default for the 1,024-bit key modulus in SQL Server–generated certificates is 117 bytes of *cleartext* (a maximum of 58 characters for nchar and nvarchar) with a 128-byte *ciphertext* result. The formula for calculating the maximum size of your *cleartext* and the size of your encrypted *ciphertext* result for a certificate is the following:

```
Max. size of cleartext = (size of encryption key modulus in bits / 8) - 11
Size of ciphertext = (size of encryption key modulus in bits / 8)
```

DecryptByCert decrypts text previously encrypted with EncryptByCert. The following is the format for DecryptByCert:

```
DecryptByCert ( certificate_id , ciphertext [ , 'cert_password' ] )
```

DecryptByCert requires the *certificate_id* of the certificate used to encrypt the *ciphertext*. The *ciphertext* is the varbinary result of the EncryptByCert function and *cert_password* is the password used to encrypt the certificate if one is specified when it is created. If no password was specified when the certificate was created the DMK will be used to decrypt it.

Tip Because certificates encrypt and decrypt using asymmetric encryption, they are slower and use more resources than symmetric encryption functions. Of course, symmetric encryption algorithms have shorter keys and require a single key to encrypt and decrypt. SQL Server 2005 uses asymmetric keys and certificates to encrypt symmetric keys, which can be used to encrypt data directly. This is a well-established design that provides the best of both worlds: the security of asymmetric encryption and the speed of symmetric encryption. To maximize speed, you'll generally want to use symmetric encryption on your data and save certificates and asymmetric encryption for securing encryption keys.

The Cert_ID function can be used to retrieve the ID number of a certificate by name at encryption and decryption time. Cert_ID accepts the name of the certificate and returns the integer ID of the certificate. Use Cert_ID to retrieve the ID numbers of certificates for use by EncryptByCert and DecryptByCert. The following is the format for Cert_ID:

```
Cert_ID( 'certificate_name' )
```

Certificate_name is the name of the certificate as specified when it is created. Listing 8-1 demonstrates encryption and decryption with a certificate.

Listing 8-1. *Sample Encryption and Decryption by Certificate*

```
CREATE MASTER KEY ENCRYPTION BY PASSWORD = 'Test_P@ssw0rd';

CREATE CERTIFICATE TestCertificate
    WITH SUBJECT = 'Adventureworks Test Certificate',
    EXPIRY_DATE = '10/31/2026';

DECLARE @s NVARCHAR(58);
SELECT @s = N'This is a test string to encrypt';
SELECT @s;

DECLARE @e VARBINARY(128);
SELECT @e = EncryptByCert(Cert_ID('TestCertificate'), @s);
SELECT @e;

DECLARE @d NVARCHAR(58);
SELECT @d = DecryptByCert(Cert_ID('TestCertificate'), @e);
SELECT @d;

DROP CERTIFICATE TestCertificate;

DROP MASTER KEY;
```

The sample code first creates a DMK and a test certificate:

```
CREATE MASTER KEY ENCRYPTION BY PASSWORD = 'Test_P@sswOrd';

CREATE CERTIFICATE TestCertificate
    WITH SUBJECT = 'Adventureworks Test Certificate',
    EXPIRY_DATE = '10/31/2026';
```

The next lines assign a test string to an nvarchar variable, encrypt it with the EncryptByCert function, and then decrypt it again with the DecryptByCert function:

```
DECLARE @s NVARCHAR(58);
SELECT @s = N'This is a test string to encrypt';
SELECT @s;

DECLARE @e VARBINARY(128);
SELECT @e = EncryptByCert(Cert_ID('TestCertificate'), @s);
SELECT @e;

DECLARE @d NVARCHAR(58);
SELECT @d = DecryptByCert(Cert_ID('TestCertificate'), @e);
SELECT @d;
```

Finally, a little cleanup, as the sample drops the test certificate and DMK it created:

```
DROP CERTIFICATE TestCertificate;

DROP MASTER KEY;
```

You can also use a certificate to generate a signature for plain text. This allows you to detect whether your plain text has been tampered with. The format for the SignByCert function is the following:

```
SignByCert ( certificate_id, plaintext [ ,'password' ] )
```

SignByCert accepts a *certificate_id* and *plaintext* to sign. The *password* is the nvarchar password, up to 128 characters in length, used when the certificate is created. If no *password* is specified the DMK is used to decrypt the certificate. Listing 8-2 demonstrates the SignByCert function.

Listing 8-2. *The SignByCert Function*

```
CREATE MASTER KEY ENCRYPTION BY PASSWORD = 'Test_P@ssw0rd';

CREATE CERTIFICATE TestCertificate
    WITH SUBJECT = 'Adventureworks Test Certificate',
    EXPIRY_DATE = '10/31/2026';

DECLARE @speech NVARCHAR(4000);
SELECT @speech = N'Four score and seven years ago, our fathers brought ' +
    N'forth on this continent a new nation, conceived in Liberty, ' +
    N'and dedicated to the proposition that all men are created ' +
    N'equal. ';
SELECT @speech;

SELECT SignByCert(Cert_ID(N'TestCertificate'), @speech);

DROP CERTIFICATE TestCertificate;

DROP MASTER KEY;
```

Asymmetric Keys

Asymmetric keys are actually composed of two separate keys: a *public key* that is publicly accessible, and a *private key* that is kept secret. The mathematical relationship between the public and private keys allows for encryption and decryption without revealing the private key. T-SQL includes statements for creating, altering, and dropping asymmetric keys. The CREATE ASYMMETRIC KEY statement has two formats. The first format allows you to install an existing public/private key pair:

```
CREATE ASYMMETRIC KEY key_name [ AUTHORIZATION user_name ]
    FROM [ EXECUTABLE ] FILE = 'path_to_file' | ASSEMBLY assembly_name
    [ ENCRYPTION BY PASSWORD = 'password' ]
```

When creating an asymmetric key you can specify installation of a key pair from an external strong-name file using the FILE option (add the EXECUTABLE keyword to specify an executable assembly). Use the ASSEMBLY keyword to specify installation of a key pair from an assembly that is installed on the server. The AUTHORIZATION keyword specifies the owner of the asymmetric key, which cannot be a role or group. If AUTHORIZATION is omitted, the current user is the owner. The second format creates a new asymmetric key:

```
CREATE ASYMMETRIC KEY key_name [ AUTHORIZATION user_name ]
    WITH ALGORITHM = { RSA_512 | RSA_1024 | RSA_2048 }
    [ ENCRYPTION BY PASSWORD = 'password' ]
```

Use the WITH ALGORITHM keywords to tell SQL Server to generate a new key pair for the specified RSA encryption algorithm. If you include ENCRYPTION BY PASSWORD, SQL Server will encrypt the asymmetric key private keys in the database with the specified password. Otherwise the asymmetric key will be encrypted by the DMK.

To alter an existing asymmetric key, use the ALTER ASYMMETRIC KEY statement:

```
ALTER ASYMMETRIC KEY key_name
    REMOVE PRIVATE KEY |
    WITH PRIVATE KEY
    (
        [ ENCRYPTION BY PASSWORD = 'password' ]
        [ , DECRYPTION BY PASSWORD = 'old_password' ]
    )
```

Use REMOVE PRIVATE KEY to remove the private key from the asymmetric public/private key pair. The WITH PRIVATE KEY option changes the method used to protect the private key. Use the ENCRYPTION BY PASSWORD option alone to change the protection method from DMK encryption to password encryption. Specify DECRYPTION BY PASSWORD alone to change from password encryption to DMK encryption. To change the password used to encrypt the private key, specify both options.

Use DROP ASYMMETRIC KEY to remove an asymmetric key from the database:

```
DROP ASYMMETRIC KEY key_name
```

The EncryptByAsymKey and DecryptByAsymKey functions allow you to encrypt and decrypt data with an asymmetric key:

```
EncryptByAsymKey ( asym_key_id, plaintext )
DecryptByAsymKey ( asym_key_id, ciphertext [ , 'password' ] )
```

Asym_key_id is the asymmetric key ID. Use the AsymKey_ID function to retrieve asymmetric key IDs by name. Plaintext is the text to encrypt and ciphertext is the encrypted text to decrypt. Password is the nvarchar password used to encrypt the asymmetric key. Omit password if the asymmetric key is encrypted with the DMK.

Note that asymmetric key encryption and decryption has limitations similar to the certificate encryption and decryption functions. The limits on plaintext parameters and ciphertext results are listed in Table 8-1.

Table 8-1. *Size Limits of T-SQL Asymmetric Encryption*

Algorithm	Plaintext	Ciphertext	Signature
RSA_512	53 bytes	64 bytes	64 bytes
RSA_1024	117 bytes	128 bytes	128 bytes
RSA_2048	245 bytes	256 bytes	256 bytes

The AsymKey_ID function accepts the name of an asymmetric key as a parameter and returns the integer ID of the asymmetric key. Use this function to retrieve asymmetric key IDs by name for the encryption and decryption functions. The following is the format for AsymKey_ID:

```
AsymKey_ID ( 'asym_key_name' )
```

Listing 8-3 demonstrates the use of T-SQL asymmetric key encryption and decryption functions.

Listing 8-3. *Asymmetric Key Encryption/Decryption Example*

```
CREATE MASTER KEY ENCRYPTION BY PASSWORD = 'Test_P@ssw0rd';

CREATE ASYMMETRIC KEY TestAsymKey
WITH ALGORITHM = RSA_512

DECLARE @credit_card NVARCHAR(26);
SELECT @credit_card = N'9000 1234 5678 9012';
SELECT @credit_card;

DECLARE @enc_credit_card VARBINARY(64);
SELECT @enc_credit_card = EncryptByAsymKey(AsymKey_ID(N'TestAsymKey'),
    @credit_card);
SELECT @enc_credit_card;

DECLARE @dec_credit_card NVARCHAR(26);
SELECT @dec_credit_card = DecryptByAsymKey(AsymKey_ID(N'TestAsymKey'),
    @enc_credit_card);
SELECT @dec_credit_card;

DROP ASYMMETRIC KEY TestAsymKey;

DROP MASTER KEY;
```

This example first creates a DMK and an RSA asymmetric key with a 512-bit private key modulus:

```
CREATE MASTER KEY ENCRYPTION BY PASSWORD = 'Test_P@ssw0rd';

CREATE ASYMMETRIC KEY TestAsymKey
WITH ALGORITHM = RSA_512
```

Next, it encrypts a fake credit card number with the EncryptByAsymKey function:

```
DECLARE @credit_card NVARCHAR(26);
SELECT @credit_card = N'9000 1234 5678 9012';
SELECT @credit_card;

DECLARE @enc_credit_card VARBINARY(64);
SELECT @enc_credit_card = EncryptByAsymKey(AsymKey_ID(N'TestAsymKey'),
    @credit_card);
SELECT @enc_credit_card;
```

It then decrypts the encrypted credit card number using the DecryptByAsymKey function:

```
DECLARE @dec_credit_card NVARCHAR(26);
SELECT @dec_credit_card = DecryptByAsymKey(AsymKey_ID(N'TestAsymKey'),
    @enc_credit_card);
SELECT @dec_credit_card;
```

The sample finishes up with a little cleanup:

```
DROP ASYMMETRIC KEY TestAsymKey;

DROP MASTER KEY;
```

Like certificates, asymmetric keys offer a function to generate digital signatures for plain text. The following is the format for the SignByAsymKey function:

```
SignByAsymKey( asym_key_id, plaintext [ , 'password' ] )
```

The SignByAsymKey function accepts a string up to 8,000 bytes in length and returns a varbinary signature for the string. The length of the signature is dependent on the key modulus (see Table 8-1 for the result lengths). The SignByASymKey function is demonstrated in Listing 8-4.

Listing 8-4. *SignByAsymKey Function Sample*

```
CREATE MASTER KEY ENCRYPTION BY PASSWORD = 'Test_P@ssw0rd';

CREATE ASYMMETRIC KEY TestAsymKey
WITH ALGORITHM = RSA_512

DECLARE @quote NVARCHAR(4000);
SELECT @quote = N'Alas, poor Yorick!';
SELECT @quote;

SELECT SignByAsymKey(AsymKey_ID(N'TestAsymKey'), @quote);

DROP ASYMMETRIC KEY TestAsymKey;

DROP MASTER KEY;
```

Symmetric Keys

Symmetric keys are at the bottom of the encryption hierarchy. In the SQL Server 2005 encryption model, symmetric keys are encrypted by certificates or asymmetric keys and they can be used in turn to encrypt raw data or other symmetric keys. To create a symmetric key use the CREATE SYMMETRIC KEY statement:

```
CREATE SYMMETRIC KEY key_name [ AUTHORIZATION user_name ]
    WITH ALGORITHM =
      {
          DES | TRIPLE_DES | RC2 | RC4 | RC4_128 | DESX |
          AES_128 | AES_192 | AES_256
      }
    KEY_SOURCE = 'pass_phrase'  |
    [ IDENTITY_VALUE = 'identity_phrase' ] |
    ENCRYPTION BY
      {
          CERTIFICATE certificate_name |
          PASSWORD = 'password' |
          SYMMETRIC KEY symmetric_key_name |
          ASYMMETRIC KEY asym_key_name
      }
```

The *key_name* is the name of the symmetric key in the database, and *user_name* specifies the owner of the symmetric key. You can create temporary symmetric keys by prefixing the *key_name* with the number sign (#). A temporary symmetric key exists only during the current session and is automatically removed when the current session ends. In addition, it is not accessible to any sessions outside of the session it is created in. When referencing a temporary symmetric key, the number sign (#) prefix must always be used. The WITH clause specifies how the symmetric key should be created. The options are the following:

- KEY_SOURCE designates a *pass_phrase* to be used as key material to derive the symmetric key from.

- ALGORITHM specifies the encryption algorithm the symmetric key will be used with.

- IDENTITY_VALUE specifies an *identity_phrase* that is used to generate a GUID that can be used to "tag" data encrypted with this key.

- The ENCRYPTION BY clause specifies the method used to encrypt this symmetric key in the database. You can specify encryption by a certificate, password, asymmetric key, or another symmetric key.

■**Caution** Microsoft recommends avoiding the RC4 and RC4_128 encryption algorithms when creating a symmetric key. Unlike the other encryption algorithms, RC4 and RC4_128 don't add a random salt value to the encryption process. Salting the encryption helps remove recognizable patterns from the encrypted *ciphertext*. It's important to remove these patterns, as they can aid cryptanalysts trying to hack encrypted data. Also note that AES encryption is not supported on Windows 2000 or Windows XP.

In addition to creating a symmetric key, you can alter or drop it using the ALTER SYMMETRIC KEY and DROP SYMMETRIC KEY statements. The following is the ALTER statement format:

```
ALTER SYMMETRIC KEY key_name
    ADD ENCRYPTION BY
      {
          CERTIFICATE certificate_name |
          PASSWORD = 'password' |
          SYMMETRIC KEY symmetric_key_name |
          ASYMMETRIC KEY asym_key_name
      } [ , ... n ] |
```

```
DROP ENCRYPTION BY
  {
      CERTIFICATE certificate_name |
      PASSWORD = 'password' |
      SYMMETRIC KEY symmetric_key_name |
      ASYMMETRIC KEY asym_key_name
  } [ , ... n ]
```

The ALTER statement allows you to add or remove encryption methods on a symmetric key. This allows you to change the encryption method used for a key. For instance, if you have a symmetric key encrypted by password but wish to change it to encryption by certificate, first ADD ENCRYPTION BY CERTIFICATE and then DROP ENCRYPTION BY PASSWORD.

The DROP SYMMETRIC KEY statement allows you to remove a symmetric key from the database:

```
DROP SYMMETRIC KEY symmetric_key_name
```

Once you have created a symmetric key and wish to use it, you must first open it with the OPEN SYMMETRIC KEY statement. Any keys used to encrypt the symmetric key must be opened before you open the symmetric key in question. The following is the format for the OPEN statement:

```
OPEN SYMMETRIC KEY key_name
    DECRYPTION BY
      {
          CERTIFICATE certificate_name [ WITH PASSWORD = 'password' ] |
          ASYMMETRIC KEY asym_key_name [ WITH PASSWORD = 'password' ] |
          SYMMETRIC KEY symmetric_key_name |
          PASSWORD = 'password'
      }
```

The key_name in the OPEN statement is the name of the symmetric key to open. The DECRYPTION BY clause specifies the method to use to decrypt the symmetric key for use. You can specify decryption by certificate, asymmetric key, symmetric key, or password. If you specify by certificate or asymmetric key, you can specify the password used to encrypt the certificate or asymmetric key with the WITH PASSWORD clause. If the DMK was used to encrypt the certificate or asymmetric key, leave off the WITH PASSWORD clause.

When you have finished using a symmetric key, issue the CLOSE SYMMETRIC KEY statement:

```
CLOSE { SYMMETRIC KEY key_name | ALL SYMMETRIC KEYS }
```

You can specify a single symmetric key to close by name or use CLOSE ALL SYMMETRIC KEYS to close all open symmetric keys.

■Note Opening and closing a symmetric key affects only the current session on the server. All open symmetric keys available to the current session are automatically closed when the current session ends.

The EncryptByKey and DecryptByKey functions use a symmetric key to encrypt and decrypt data. The format of EncryptByKey is the following:

```
EncryptByKey ( key_guid, 'cleartext' [ , add_authenticator, authenticator ] )
```

In this function, the *key_guid* is the GUID of the symmetric key. This value can be retrieved by the key name using the Key_GUID function described next:

```
Key_GUID ( 'key_name' )
```

This function accepts one parameter, *key_name*, which is the name of the key for which the *key_guid* is to be retrieved. The *key_guid* is the MD5 hash value of the IDENTITY_VALUE option specified when the symmetric key is created. If no IDENTITY_VALUE is specified at creation time, the *key_guid* is a GUID that is automatically generated by the server. *Cleartext* is the plain text that is to be encrypted by the EncryptByKey function. It can be a char, varchar, binary, varbinary, nchar, or nvarchar constant, column, or T-SQL variable. The result is the encrypted data in varbinary format with a maximum length of 8,000 bytes.

You cannot specify an initialization vector (IV) when encrypting data. An IV is automatically generated randomly by SQL Server. The IV is used to further obfuscate the encrypted result of block ciphers such as AES and DES. The obfuscation provided by an IV helps further eliminate patterns from encrypted data that cryptanalysts can use in attempts to hack encrypted data.

■Note The IV is an important aspect of block cipher encryption algorithms like DES and AES. Although T-SQL does not allow you to specify your own IV, it automatically generates a random IV that helps further obfuscate the result. This randomly generated IV also means that adding an index to a column in a table that contains encrypted data is useless.

The *add_authenticator* parameter allows you to add an authenticator to prevent wholesale substitution of values. When *add_authenticator* is set to 1, SQL Server derives an authentication value from the *authenticator* parameter passed in. The *authenticator* is a varbinary value. To further explain the functionality of this option, consider Table 8-2, which contains bank account information.

Table 8-2. *Sample Bank Account Table*

Name	Account Number	Balance
Gates, Bill	9872	^#eQrT\&0yU8!@-=
Thomas, John	9928	&3!@-+=!Rt}l;2-A
Ellison, Larry	9964	%^~!)*p:x3K9l?>.

In this example, the bank balances are encrypted. However, if hacker extraordinaire (and customer) John Thomas gains access to this table, he might recognize that both Bill Gates and Larry Ellison have larger balances in their accounts than he. In this case he would not even need to decrypt the balances—he would just copy either Larry's or Bill's balance into his account in encrypted form. Adding an *authenticator* (the Account Number column could be used in this instance) prevents this type of whole value substitution attack. When data is encrypted with an *authenticator*, the *authenticator* is hashed and applied to the data during encryption. The same *authenticator* must be supplied to decrypt the data, or decryption will fail.

When SQL Server encrypts by symmetric key, it adds metadata to the encrypted result, as well as padding, making the encrypted result larger (sometimes significantly larger) than the unencrypted plain text. The format for the encrypted result with metadata follows this format:

- The first 16 bytes of the encrypted result represent the GUID of the symmetric key used to encrypt the data.

- The next 4 bytes represent a version number, currently hard-coded as "01000000."

- The next 8 bytes for DES encryption (16 bytes for AES encryption) represent the randomly generated initialization vector.

- The next 8 bytes are header information representing the options used to encrypt the data. If the authenticator option is used, this header information includes a 20-byte SHA1 hash of the authenticator, making the header information 28 bytes in length.

- The last part of the encrypted data is the actual data and padding itself. For DES algorithms, the length of this encrypted data will be a multiple of 8 bytes. For AES algorithms, the length will be a multiple of 16 bytes.

BLOCK CIPHERS AND PADDING

Block cipher algorithms must pad their result to the size of their blocks. For algorithms that encrypt data in 8-byte blocks (such as DES and Triple DES) the result will be padded out to an 8-byte boundary. If you encrypt data that is already a multiple of 8 bytes in length, an additional 8 bytes of padding will be added. For AES and other algorithms that encrypt in 16-byte blocks, the result will be padded to a 16-byte boundary. If the length of your plain text is already a multiple of 16 bytes, an additional 16 bytes of padding are added.

The length of the encrypted data is limited to 8,000 bytes. To calculate the length of the cipher text your plain text will generate on SQL Server, use one of the following two formulas.

For 8-byte block ciphers like the DES family, use the following:

```
Length of ciphertext = 8 * ( ( Length of plaintext + 8 ) / 8 ) + 36
```

For 16-byte block ciphers like AES, use the following:

```
Length of ciphertext = 16 * ( ( Length of plaintext + 16 ) / 16 ) + 44
```

For either algorithm, add an additional 20 bytes for the SHA1 hash of the authenticator if the *add_authenticator* option is used. Note that the length of the encrypted result generated might change in the future if Microsoft modifies this format.

Use the DecryptByKey function to decrypt data previously encrypted by symmetric key:

```
DecryptByKey ( ciphertext [ , add_authenticator, authenticator ] )
```

Because the GUID of the key used to encrypt the data is stored with the encrypted data, it is not necessary to supply the symmetric key GUID when decrypting data. The *ciphertext* is the varbinary encrypted result of the EncryptByKey function. If an authenticator is used with EncryptByKey, the *add_authenticator* option of DecryptByKey must be set to 1 and the *authenticator* value must be the same value used with EncryptByKey.

Listing 8-5 demonstrates the EncryptByKey and DecryptByKey functions.

Listing 8-5. *EncryptByKey and DecryptByKey Demonstration*

```
CREATE MASTER KEY ENCRYPTION BY PASSWORD = 'Test_P@ssw0rd';

CREATE CERTIFICATE TestCertificate
    WITH SUBJECT = 'AdventureWorks Test Certificate',
    EXPIRY_DATE = '10/31/2036';
```

```
CREATE SYMMETRIC KEY TestSymmetricKey
    WITH ALGORITHM = TRIPLE_DES
    ENCRYPTION BY CERTIFICATE TestCertificate;

OPEN SYMMETRIC KEY TestSymmetricKey
    DECRYPTION BY CERTIFICATE TestCertificate;

CREATE TABLE #Temp (ContactID    INT PRIMARY KEY,
    FirstName    NVARCHAR(200),
    MiddleName   NVARCHAR(200),
    LastName     NVARCHAR(200),
    eFirstName   VARBINARY(200),
    eMiddleName  VARBINARY(200),
    eLastName    VARBINARY(200));

INSERT
    INTO #Temp (ContactID, eFirstName, eMiddleName, eLastName)
    SELECT ContactID,
        EncryptByKey(Key_GUID('TestSymmetricKey'), FirstName),
        EncryptByKey(Key_GUID('TestSymmetricKey'), MiddleName),
        EncryptByKey(Key_GUID('TestSymmetricKey'), LastName)
FROM Person.Contact
    WHERE ContactID <= 100;

UPDATE #Temp
    SET FirstName = DecryptByKey(eFirstName),
        MiddleName = DecryptByKey(eMiddleName),
        LastName = DecryptByKey(eLastName);

SELECT ContactID,
    FirstName,
    MiddleName,
    LastName,
    eFirstName,
    eMiddleName,
    eLastName
FROM #Temp;

DROP TABLE #Temp;
CLOSE SYMMETRIC KEY TestSymmetricKey;
```

```
DROP SYMMETRIC KEY TestSymmetricKey;
DROP CERTIFICATE TestCertificate;
DROP MASTER KEY;
```

The sample begins by creating the necessary DMK, certificate, and TRIPLE_DES algorithm symmetric key. It then creates a temporary table to hold the results of encryption and decryption:

```
CREATE MASTER KEY ENCRYPTION BY PASSWORD = 'Test_P@ssw0rd';

CREATE CERTIFICATE TestCertificate
    WITH SUBJECT = 'AdventureWorks Test Certificate',
    EXPIRY_DATE = '10/31/2036';

CREATE SYMMETRIC KEY TestSymmetricKey
    WITH ALGORITHM = TRIPLE_DES
    ENCRYPTION BY CERTIFICATE TestCertificate;

OPEN SYMMETRIC KEY TestSymmetricKey
    DECRYPTION BY CERTIFICATE TestCertificate;

CREATE TABLE #Temp (ContactID    INT PRIMARY KEY,
    FirstName    NVARCHAR(200),
    MiddleName  NVARCHAR(200),
    LastName    NVARCHAR(200),
    eFirstName  VARBINARY(200),
    eMiddleName VARBINARY(200),
    eLastName   VARBINARY(200));
```

The next step uses EncryptByKey to encrypt the names of 100 contacts from the Person.Contact table and store the result in the temporary table:

```
INSERT
    INTO #Temp (ContactID, eFirstName, eMiddleName, eLastName)
    SELECT ContactID,
        EncryptByKey(Key_GUID('TestSymmetricKey'), FirstName),
        EncryptByKey(Key_GUID('TestSymmetricKey'), MiddleName),
        EncryptByKey(Key_GUID('TestSymmetricKey'), LastName)
FROM Person.Contact
    WHERE ContactID <= 100;
```

Then the temporary table is updated with the decrypted form of the encrypted data it contains, via the DecryptByKey function:

```
UPDATE #Temp
    SET FirstName = DecryptByKey(eFirstName),
        MiddleName = DecryptByKey(eMiddleName),
        LastName = DecryptByKey(eLastName);
```

Finally, the results are displayed with a SELECT statement and some cleanup is performed, including dropping the temporary table and removing the keys and certificates:

```
SELECT ContactID,
    FirstName,
    MiddleName,
    LastName,
    eFirstName,
    eMiddleName,
    eLastName
FROM #Temp;

DROP TABLE #Temp;
CLOSE SYMMETRIC KEY TestSymmetricKey;

DROP SYMMETRIC KEY TestSymmetricKey;
DROP CERTIFICATE TestCertificate;
DROP MASTER KEY;
```

In addition to DecryptByKey, SQL Server 2005 offers the following additional symmetric key decryption functions:

```
DecryptByKeyAutoAsymKey ( asym_key_id, password, ciphertext
    [ , add_authenticator, authenticator ] )

DecryptByKeyAutoCert ( certificate_id, password , ciphertext
    [ , add_authenticator, authenticator ] )
```

DecryptByKeyAutoAsymKey automatically opens the asymmetric key protecting the symmetric key used to encrypt the *ciphertext*. If a *password* is used to encrypt the asymmetric key, that same *password* must be passed to the function. If the asymmetric key is encrypted with the DMK, pass NULL as the *password*. If an authenticator was used to encrypt the *ciphertext*, set *add_authenticator* to 1 and pass the *authenticator* value to the function.

If the symmetric key is protected by certificate, you can use the `DecryptByKeyAutoCert` function. This function automatically opens the certificate protecting the symmetric key and decrypts the *ciphertext* with the symmetric key. As with `DecryptByKeyAutoAsymKey`, you must specify the *password* used to protect the certificate, or `NULL` if it is protected by the DMK. If an *authenticator* was specified when *ciphertext* was encrypted, *add_authenticator* should be set to 1 and the *authenticator* value must be passed in.

Hashing and Encryption Without Keys

SQL Server 2005 provides a few additional functions for encryption and decryption without keys and for one-way hashing:

```
EncryptByPassPhrase ( passphrase, plaintext
    [ , add_authenticator, authenticator ] )
```

```
DecryptByPassPhrase ( passphrase, ciphertext
    [ , add_authenticator, authenticator ] )
```

`EncryptByPassPhrase` encrypts the *plaintext* passed in with the *passphrase*. The function derives a temporary encryption key from the *passphrase* and uses it to encrypt the *plaintext*. If an authenticator is desired, set *add_authenticator* to 1 and pass in an authenticator value. `EncryptByPassPhrase` uses the `TRIPLE_DES` algorithm to encrypt the *plaintext* passed in.

`DecryptByPassPhrase` performs the opposite function. It uses the *passphrase* passed in to generate a temporary encryption key that it then uses to decrypt the *ciphertext* passed in. If an *authenticator* was used to encrypt the *ciphertext*, set *add_authenticator* to 1 and pass in an *authenticator* value.

The `HashBytes` function performs a one-way hash on the data passed to it and returns the hash value. A hash value is like a "fingerprint" for any given data. The `HashBytes` function has the following form:

```
HashBytes ( { 'MD2' | 'MD4' | 'MD5' | 'SHA' | 'SHA1' }, input )
```

The first parameter specifies the hash algorithm to use. The input parameter is the data to hash. The MD2, MD4, and MD5 algorithms produce a 128-bit (16-byte) hash result. The SHA and SHA1 algorithms produce a 160-bit (20-byte) hash result. The result of the `HashBytes` function is `varbinary`. Listing 8-6 demonstrates the `EncryptByPassPhrase`, `DecryptByPassPhrase`, and `HashBytes` functions.

■**Caution** For highly secure applications, the MD2, MD4, and MD5 series of hashes should be avoided. Researchers have over the past couple of years produced *meaningful hash collisions* with these algorithms that have revealed their vulnerability to hacker attacks. A *hash collision* is a string of bytes that produces a hash value that is identical to another string of bytes. A *meaningful* hash collision is one that can be produced with meaningful (or apparently meaningful) strings of bytes. Generating a hash collision by modifying the content of a certificate would be an example of a meaningful hash collision.

Listing 8-6. *Encryption and Decryption by Passphrase and Byte Hashing*

```
DECLARE @plaintext NVARCHAR(256)
DECLARE @enctext VARBINARY(512)
DECLARE @dectext NVARCHAR(256)

SELECT @plaintext = N'To be, or not to be: that is the question: ' +
    N'Whether ''tis nobler in the mind to suffer ' +
    N'The slings and arrows of outrageous fortune, ' +
    N'Or to take arms against a sea of troubles '

SELECT @enctext = EncryptByPassPhrase (N'Shakespeare', @plaintext);
SELECT @dectext = CAST (DecryptByPassPhrase (N'Shakespeare', @enctext) AS
    NVARCHAR(128));

SELECT @plaintext;
SELECT @enctext;
SELECT @dectext;
SELECT HashBytes ('SHA1', @plaintext);
```

Summary

Prior to SQL Server 2005, database encryption functionality could be achieved only through third-party tools or by creating your own encryption and decryption functions. SQL 2005 T-SQL adds encryption and decryption functionality that you can use directly in your databases. The tight integration of Windows secure encryption functionality with T-SQL means that data encryption in a database is now easier and more secure than ever.

This chapter discussed the SQL Server hierarchical encryption model. SMKs, DMKs, certificates, asymmetric keys, and symmetric keys were all covered. In addition, the functions that encrypt and decrypt data using these securables were discussed. Finally this chapter ended with a discussion of encryption and decryption by `passphrase` and the one-way hash function.

The next chapter will cover the art of T-SQL debugging and error handling.

CHAPTER 9

■ ■ ■

Error Handling and Debugging

In prior versions of SQL Server, error handling was limited to the @@error system function. T-SQL in SQL Server 2005 still has this system function available but also adds structured error handling similar to that offered by other high-level languages such as C++, C#, and VB. This chapter discusses legacy T-SQL error handling functionality and the new structured error handling model in T-SQL. This chapter also introduces tools useful for debugging server-side code including T-SQL statements and the Visual Studio IDE.

Legacy Error Handling

In prior versions of SQL Server, the primary method of handling errors was the @@error system function. This function returns an int value representing the current error code. An @@error value of 0 means no error occurred. One of the major limitations of this function is that it is automatically reset to 0 after every successful statement. So you cannot have any statements between the code that you expect to produce an error and the code that checks the value of @@error. This also means that after @@error is checked, it is automatically reset to 0, so you can't both check the value of @@error and RETURN @@error from within a stored procedure. Listing 9-1 demonstrates a stored procedure that generates an error and attempts to print the error code from within the procedure and return the value of @@error to the caller.

Listing 9-1. *Incorrect Error Handling Sample with @@error*

```
CREATE PROCEDURE dbo.TestError
AS
BEGIN
    INSERT INTO Person.Address (AddressID)
    VALUES (1);
    PRINT N'Error Code = ' + CAST(@@error AS NVARCHAR(10));
    RETURN @@error;
```

```
END
GO


DECLARE @ret INT;
EXEC @ret = dbo.TestError;
PRINT N'Return value = ' + CAST(@ret AS NVARCHAR(10));
```

The TestError procedure in Listing 9-1 demonstrates the problem with @@error. The result of executing the procedure should be similar to the following:

```
Msg 544, Level 16, State 1, Procedure TestError, Line 4
Cannot insert explicit value for identity column in table 'Address' when
IDENTITY_INSERT is set to OFF.
Error Code = 544
Return value = 0
```

As you can see, the error code is 544, but a value of 0 (no error) is returned to the caller. The problem is with the following line in the stored procedure:

```
PRINT N'Error Code = ' + CAST(@@error AS NVARCHAR(10));
```

The PRINT statement automatically resets the value of @@error after it executes, meaning you can't test or retrieve the same value of @@error afterward (it will be 0 every time). The workaround is to store the value of @@error in a local variable immediately after the statement you suspect might fail (in this case the INSERT statement). Listing 9-2 demonstrates this method of using @@error.

Listing 9-2. *Corrected Error Handling with @@error*

```
CREATE PROCEDURE dbo.TestError2
AS
BEGIN
    DECLARE @e INT;
    INSERT INTO Person.Address (AddressID)
    VALUES (1);
    SELECT @e = @@error;
    PRINT N'Error Code = ' + CAST(@e AS NVARCHAR(10));
    RETURN @e;
END
GO
```

```
DECLARE @ret INT;
EXEC @ret = dbo.TestError2;
PRINT N'Return value = ' + CAST(@ret AS NVARCHAR(10));
```

By storing the value of `@@error` in a variable immediately after the statement you suspect might cause an error, you can test or retrieve the value as often as you need for further processing. The following is the result of the new procedure:

```
Msg 544, Level 16, State 1, Procedure TestError2, Line 5
Cannot insert explicit value for identity column in table 'Address' when
IDENTITY_INSERT is set to OFF.
Error Code = 544
Return value = 544
```

In this case, the proper `@@error` code is both printed and returned to the caller.

TRY...CATCH

SQL Server 2005 adds the `TRY...CATCH` model of error handling common in modern languages such as C# and VB. With `TRY...CATCH` you wrap the code you suspect could cause an error in a `BEGIN TRY...END TRY` block. This block is immediately followed by a `BEGIN CATCH...END CATCH` block that will be invoked only if the statements in the `TRY` block cause an error. The following is the precise syntax for the T-SQL `TRY...CATCH` statement:

```
BEGIN TRY
    sql_statement; [ ...n ]
END TRY
BEGIN CATCH
    sql_statement; [ ...n ]
END CATCH;
```

The *sql_statements* in the `BEGIN TRY...END TRY` block execute normally. If the block completes without error, the *sql_statements* between the `BEGIN CATCH...END CATCH` block are skipped. If an error does occur while the `BEGIN TRY...END TRY` block is executing, control transfers to the *sql_statements* in the `BEGIN CATCH...END CATCH` block.

The `CATCH` block exposes several functions for determining exactly what error occurred and where it occurred. These functions are available only between the `BEGIN CATCH...END CATCH` keywords, and only during error handling when control has been transferred to it from an error in a `TRY` block. The functions are the following:

- `ERROR_LINE()` is the line number on which the error occurred.

- `ERROR_MESSAGE()` is the complete text of the error message generated.

- `ERROR_PROCEDURE()` is the name of the stored procedure or trigger where the error occurred.

- `ERROR_NUMBER()` is the error number.

- `ERROR_SEVERITY()` is the severity level of the error.

- `ERROR_STATE()` is the state number of the error.

These functions are limited in scope and only return meaningful values inside of a CATCH block. If you try to use them outside of a CATCH block, they return NULL. Listing 9-3 demonstrates what the previous sample code might look like in TRY...CATCH form.

Listing 9-3. *Sample TRY...CATCH Error Handling*

```
CREATE PROCEDURE dbo.TestError3
AS
BEGIN
    DECLARE @e INT;
    SELECT @e = 0;
    BEGIN TRY
        INSERT INTO Person.Address (AddressID)
        VALUES (1);
    END TRY
    BEGIN CATCH
        SELECT @e = ERROR_NUMBER();
        PRINT N'Error Code = ' + CAST(@e AS NVARCHAR(10));
        PRINT N'Error Procedure = ' + ERROR_PROCEDURE();
        PRINT N'Error  Message = ' + ERROR_MESSAGE();
    END CATCH
    RETURN @e;
END
GO

DECLARE @ret INT;
EXEC @ret = dbo.TestError3;
PRINT N'Return value = ' + CAST(@ret AS NVARCHAR(10));
```

The result is similar to Listing 9-2, but TRY...CATCH gives you more control and flexibility over the output:

```
Error Code = 544
Error Procedure = TestError3
Error Message = Cannot insert explicit value for identity column in table
'Address'
when IDENTITY_INSERT is set to OFF.
Return value = 544
```

TRY...CATCH blocks can be nested. You can have TRY...CATCH blocks within other TRY blocks or CATCH blocks to handle errors that might be generated within them. You can also test the state of transactions within a CATCH block by using the XACT_STATE function. Table 9-1 lists the return values for XACT_STATE and how you should handle each in your CATCH block.

Table 9-1. *XACT_STATE Function Return Values*

XACT_STATE	Meaning
-1	There is an uncommittable transaction pending. Issue a ROLLBACK TRANSACTION statement.
0	There is no transaction pending. No action is necessary.
1	There is a committable transaction pending. Issue a COMMIT TRANSACTION statement.

The T-SQL TRY...CATCH method of error handling has certain limitations attached to it. For one, TRY...CATCH can only capture errors that have a severity higher than 10 that do not close the database connection. The following errors are not caught:

- Any errors with a severity of 10 or lower will not be caught.

- Severity levels of 20 or higher are also not caught because they close the database connection immediately.

- Compile-time errors, such as syntax errors, are not caught by TRY...CATCH.

- Statement-level recompilation errors, such as object-name resolution errors, are not caught due to SQL Server's deferred-name resolution.

Also, errors captured by a TRY...CATCH block are not returned to the caller. You can, however, use the RAISERROR statement described in the next section to return the error to the caller.

RAISERROR

The `RAISERROR` statement is a legacy T-SQL statement that allows you to generate an error at run time. It is similar to the `throw` functions used in languages such as C++ and C# that throw or rethrow exceptions. The following is the format of the `RAISERROR` statement:

```
RAISERROR ( { msg_id | msg_str }, severity, state
    [ , argument [ , ... n ] ] )
    [ WITH { LOG | NOWAIT | SETERROR } [ , ... n ] ]
```

`RAISERROR` takes several parameters that I describe here:

- *Msg_id* is an int ID number for a user-defined error message. User-defined error messages can be added with the `sp_addmessage` system stored procedure.

- *Msg_str* is a user-supplied ad hoc error message. If *msg_str* is used instead of *msg_id*, the error generated will have an ID of 50000.

- *Severity* is the severity level of the error message. Severity levels between 0 and 10 are considered informational messages. Levels from 11 to 18 are considered errors, and levels from 19 to 25 are considered fatal errors. Only `sysadmin` users or users with `ALTER TRACE` permissions can specify `RAISERROR` severity levels higher than 18, and the `WITH LOG` option must be specified.

- *State* is a user-defined informational value from 1 to 127 that can help in locating the specific errors within code.

- The optional *argument* parameters are values that are substituted for special for-matting codes in the error message.

- The `WITH` keyword specifies one or more options that can be set for `RAISERROR`. These options are the following:

    - The `LOG` option logs the error in the application log and SQL error log. Only a `sysadmin` or user with `ALTER TRACE` permissions can specify this option.

    - The `NOWAIT` option sends the message immediately to the client.

    - The `SETERROR` option sets the `@@error` and `ERROR_NUMBER` functions to *msg_id*, for any severity level.

`RAISERROR` can be used within a `TRY` or `CATCH` block to generate errors. Within the `TRY` block, if `RAISERROR` generates an error with severity between 11 and 19, control passes to the `CATCH` block. For errors with severity of 10 or lower, processing continues in the `TRY` block. For errors with severity of 20 or higher, the client connection is terminated and control does not pass to the CATCH block. For these high-severity errors, the error is returned to the caller.

Debugging Tools

The PRINT statement demonstrated in Listing 9-3 is a simple and useful server-side debugging tool. It simply prints constants or variable values to standard output. When errors or unexpected results are being returned by a stored procedure or script, some well-placed PRINT statements can often help to quickly and easily locate the cause of the problem. PRINT works from within stored procedures and batches, but does not work inside of user-defined functions because of built-in restrictions on function side effects.

While SSMS doesn't offer much in the way of debugging tools, Visual Studio Pro and Team editions have an excellent facility for stepping through stored procedures and user-defined functions just like any VB or C# application. The following describes how it works.

In Visual Studio, select Tools ➤ Connect to Database to create a new database connection, as shown in Figure 9-1.

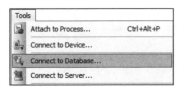

Figure 9-1. *Connect to Database on the Tools menu*

In the Add Connection window select the proper connection settings to connect to your server and database as shown in Figure 9-2.

The Visual Studio Server Explorer will appear with your new connection in it. Open up the Stored Procedures folder under your server and locate the stored procedure you wish to debug, as shown in Figure 9-3.

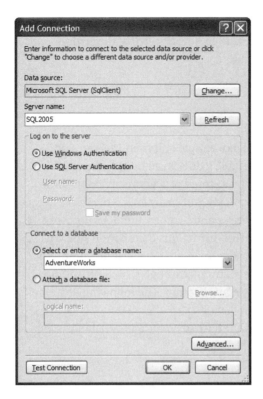

Figure 9-2. *The Add Connection window*

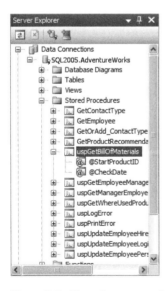

Figure 9-3. *Choosing a stored procedure to debug in the Server Explorer*

The next step is to right-click the stored procedure and select Step Into Stored Procedure from the pop-up menu as shown in Figure 9-4.

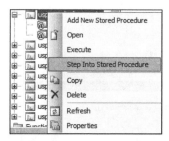

Figure 9-4. *Step Into Stored Procedure from Server Explorer*

If your stored procedure requires parameters, the Run Stored Procedure window pops up and asks you to enter values for those parameters. In this example we'll enter **770** for the @StartProductID and **7/10/2001** as the @CheckDate. Figure 9-5 demonstrates this.

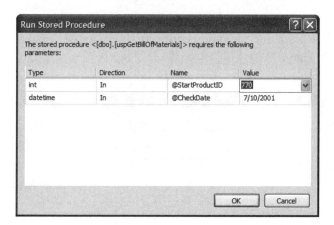

Figure 9-5. *Entering parameter values in the Run Stored Procedure window*

After you enter the parameters, the procedure will begin running in debug mode in Visual Studio. Visual Studio shows the script and highlights each line in yellow as you step through it. Visual Studio debug mode is shown in Figure 9-6. Just as when debugging other Visual Studio programs, you can set breakpoints by clicking the left border and using the Visual Studio Continue (F5), Stop Debugging (Shift + F5), Step Over (F10), Step Into (F11), and Step Out (Shift + F11) commands. You can also add Watches and view Locals to inspect parameter and variable values as your code executes.

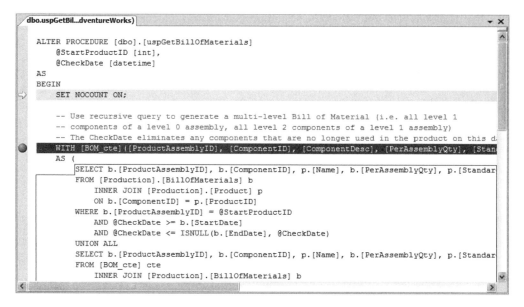

Figure 9-6. *Stepping through a stored procedure in Visual Studio debug mode*

Any result sets and return values from the stored procedure are shown in the Visual Studio Output window as shown in Figure 9-7.

```
Output                                                                            ▼ ⤢ ✕
Show output from: Debug                    ▼  🔲  🔲 🔲  | 🗐  🔲
Running [dbo].[uspGetBillOfMaterials] ( @StartProductID = 770, @CheckDate = 7/10/2001 ).

ProductAssemblyID ComponentID ComponentDesc                          TotalQuantity   StandardC
----------------- ----------- -------------------------------------- --------------- ---------
770               517         LL Road Seat Assembly                  1               98.77
770               738         LL Road Frame - Black, 52              1               204.6251
770               806         ML Headset                             1               45.4168
```
🔲 Error List 📋 Breakpoints 🖳 Immediate Window 📄 Output 📋 Pending Checkins

Figure 9-7. *The Visual Studio Output window*

You can use Visual Studio to debug stored procedures and user-defined functions in this manner.

■**Note** If you are debugging on a remote server, you may have to have your database administrator set up debugging on the server and apply the correct permissions so you can access debugging functionality. This process is described in several documents on MSDN: http://msdn.microsoft.com/library/default. asp?url=/library/en-us/vsdebug/html/vxlrfsettingupsqldebugging.asp.

Summary

SQL Server 2005 includes legacy error-handling functionality via the @@error system function and the RAISERROR statement. It also includes new structured error handling in the form of TRY...CATCH error-handling blocks.

SQL Server 2005 also provides debugging functionality that includes tools as simple as the basic T-SQL PRINT statement and the more advanced T-SQL debugging capabilities available in Visual Studio Pro and Team editions. This chapter introduced Visual Studio debugging functionality and how to use it to step through your server-side code.

The next chapter discusses dynamic SQL and what it can do for you.

CHAPTER 10

■ ■ ■

Dynamic SQL

SQL Server MVP Erland Sommarskog said it best: dynamic SQL is a curse and a blessing. Put simply, dynamic SQL is a means of constructing SQL statements as strings in your server-side applications and executing them dynamically ("on the fly"). When used properly, dynamic SQL can be used to generate complex queries at run time, in some cases improve performance, and do tasks that just aren't doable (or are extremely difficult) in nondynamic T-SQL. The downside is that there are numerous ways to shoot yourself in the foot with dynamic SQL. If not done properly, dynamic SQL can open up security holes in your system big enough to drive a truck through. In this chapter I will discuss the various methods of executing dynamic SQL, as well as some of its risks and rewards.

The EXECUTE Statement

The most basic form of dynamic SQL is achieved by simply passing a SQL query or other instruction as a string to the EXECUTE statement (often abbreviated EXEC). The following is the format of the dynamic SQL EXECUTE statement:

```
EXECUTE (sql_statement)
```

The *sql_statement* is a char, varchar, nchar, or nvarchar constant or variable, including the (max) data types. Listing 10-1 shows the most basic form of dynamic SQL with an EXECUTE statement and a string constant.

Listing 10-1. *Basic EXECUTE Statement Dynamic SQL*

```
EXECUTE (N'SELECT ProductID FROM Production.Product')
```

As you can see there is no real advantage to performing dynamic SQL on a string constant. A simple SELECT statement without the EXECUTE would perform the same function and return the same result. The true power of dynamic SQL is that you can build a SQL statement or query dynamically and execute it. Listing 10-2 demonstrates how this can be done.

Listing 10-2. *More Complex Example of Dynamic SQL with EXECUTE*

```
DECLARE @min_product_id INT;
SELECT @min_product_id = 500;
DECLARE @sql_stmt NVARCHAR(128);
SELECT @sql_stmt = N'SELECT ProductID ' +
    N'FROM Production.Product ' +
    N'WHERE ProductID >= ' + CAST(@min_product_id AS  NVARCHAR(10));
EXECUTE (@sql_stmt);
```

SQL Injection and Dynamic SQL

In Listing 10-2 the variable @sql_stmt contains the dynamic SQL query. The query is built dynamically by appending the minimum product ID to the WHERE clause. This is not the recommended method of performing this type of query, and is only shown here to demonstrate how this type of dynamic query is often built.

One of the problems with this method is that you lose some of the benefits of cached query plan execution. SQL Server 2005 has some features that can help in this area, including parameter sniffing, but there's no guarantee (especially for complex queries) that SQL Server will be able to reuse cached query execution plans as your query changes.

Another major problem is SQL injection. Although not really a problem when appending an integer value to the end of a dynamic query as done previously, SQL injection can provide a back door for hackers trying to access or destroy your data when you append strings to the end of your dynamic SQL queries. Take a look at the innocent-looking dynamic SQL query in Listing 10-3. I discuss how a hacker could wreak havoc with this query after the listing.

Listing 10-3. *Basic Dynamic SQL Query with a String Appended*

```
DECLARE @product_name NVARCHAR(50);
SELECT @product_name = N'Mountain';
DECLARE @sql_stmt NVARCHAR(128);
SELECT @sql_stmt = N'SELECT ProductID, Name ' +
    N'FROM Production.Product ' +
    N'WHERE Name LIKE ''' +
    @product_name + N'%''';
EXECUTE (@sql_stmt);
```

SINGLE QUOTES IN DYNAMIC SQL

When you want to include single quotes in a dynamic SQL query, you must *escape* them since single quotes are string delimiters in T-SQL. To escape single quotes in a string is fairly simple in theory: just double them up. In practice, however, trying to read a complex dynamic SQL query with a lot of escaped quotes can become confusing and is often a source of errors in dynamic SQL. Escaped quotes can make dynamic SQL very difficult to read and can easily be mismatched and have the effect of making your dynamic SQL hard to follow and debug.

One method of handling single-quote escaping is to use the REPLACE string function to escape single quotes in strings at run time. The format to escape single quotes with REPLACE is *string* = REPLACE (*string*, '''', ''''''). This can be further abstracted and your other code simplified by coding the REPLACE function once in a user-defined function. An example of a user-defined function to escape quotes is given here:

```
CREATE FUNCTION dbo.fnEscapeQuotes(@string NVARCHAR(4000))
RETURNS NVARCHAR(4000)
AS
BEGIN
    RETURN REPLACE(@string, '''', '''''');
END;
```

This query simply returns all product IDs and names of all products that begin with the string Mountain. The problem is with how SQL Server interprets the concatenated string. The EXECUTE statement sees the following string:

```
SELECT ProductID, Name
FROM Production.Product
WHERE Name LIKE 'Mountain%'
```

A simple substitution for @product_name can execute other unwanted statements on your server. This is especially true with data coming from an external source (i.e., the front end or application layer). Consider the following change to Listing 10-3:

```
SELECT @product_name = N''''; SELECT * FROM Production.ProductInventory; --'
```

The following is the new statement EXECUTE sees:

```
SELECT ProductID, Name
FROM Production.Product
WHERE Name LIKE '';
SELECT *
FROM Production.ProductInventory; --%'
```

The hacker has now turned your SQL query into two queries, effectively bypassing the first query and running his own afterward. The hacker could be even more malicious and issue INSERT, UPDATE, DELETE, DROP TABLE, TRUNCATE TABLE, or other statements to destroy data or open himself a back door into your system. Depending on how secure your server is, a hacker could grant himself administrator rights, retrieve and modify data stored in your server's file system, or even take control of your server.

The only justification for using the string concatenation method with EXECUTE is if you have to dynamically name the tables or columns in your statements. And that is far rarer than most people think. In fact, the only time this is usually necessary is if you need to dynamically generate SQL statements around database, table, or column names—if you are creating a dynamic pivot table type query or if you are coding an administration tool for SQL Server, for instance.

If you must use the string-concatenation and EXECUTE method, be sure to take the following precautions with the strings being passed in from the front end:

- Don't ever trust data from the front end. Always validate the data. If you are expecting only the letters A–Z and the numbers 0–9, reject all other characters in the input data.

- If you allow apostrophes in your data, escape them (double them up) before using them.

- Don't allow semicolons, parentheses, and double dashes (--) in the input if possible. These characters have special significance to SQL Server and should be avoided when possible. If you must allow these characters, scrutinize the input thoroughly before using it.

- Reject strings that contain binary data, escape sequences, and multiline comment markers (/* and */).

- Validate XML input data against a schema.

- Take extra special care when input data contains xp_ or sp_, as it may be an attempt to run procedures or extended stored procedures on your server.

More on Validation

Usually data validation is performed client-side, on the front end, in the application layer, or in the middle tiers of n-tier systems. In critical situations it is important to also perform server-side validation of some sort. Triggers and check constraints can perform this type of validation on data before it's inserted into a table, and you can create user-defined functions or stored procedures to perform this type of validation on dynamic SQL before executing it. Listing 10-4 is a UDF that uses the Numbers table created in

Chapter 5 to perform basic validation on a string, ensuring that it contains only the let-ters A–Z, digits 0–9, and the underscore character (_), which is a common validation used on usernames, passwords, and other simple data.

Listing 10-4. *Simple T-SQL String Validation Function*

```
CREATE FUNCTION dbo.fnValidateString (@string NVARCHAR(4000))
RETURNS INT
AS
BEGIN
    RETURN (
        SELECT SUM (
            CASE
                WHEN SUBSTRING(@string, n.Num, 1) LIKE N'[A-Z0-9\_]' ESCAPE '\'
                    THEN 0
                ELSE 1
            END)
        FROM dbo.Numbers n
        WHERE n.Num <= LEN(@string)
    )
END
```

The function in Listing 10-4 uses the Numbers table created in Chapter 5 to validate each character in the given string. The result is the number of invalid characters in the string: a value of 0 indicates all characters in the string are valid. More complex valida-tions can be performed with the LIKE operator or procedural code to ensure data is in a prescribed format as well.

Troubleshooting Dynamic SQL

One of the main disadvantages to dynamic SQL is in debugging and troubleshooting code. Complex dynamic SQL queries can be difficult to troubleshoot, and very simple syntax or other errors can be difficult to locate. Fortunately there is a fairly simple fix for that: write your troublesome query directly in T-SQL, replacing parameters with potential values. Highlight the code, and parse—or execute—it. Any syntax errors will be detected and described by SQL Server immediately. Fix the errors and repeat until all errors have been fixed. Then, and only then, revert the values back to their parameter names and put it in a SQL statement. Another handy method of troubleshooting is to PRINT the dynamic SQL statement before executing it. Highlight, copy, and attempt to parse or run it in SQL Server Management Studio. You should be able to quickly and easily locate any problems and fix them as necessary.

One of the restrictions on dynamic SQL is that it cannot be executed in a user-defined function. This restriction is in place because user-defined functions cannot produce side effects that change the database. Dynamic SQL offers opportunities to circumvent this restriction, so it is simply not allowed.

sp_executesql

The sp_executesql stored procedure is a second method of executing dynamic SQL. When used correctly, it is safer than the simple EXECUTE method of concatenating strings and executing them. The following is the format for sp_executesql:

```
sp_executesql [ @stmt = ] sql_statement
[
    { , [ @params= ] N'@parameter_name data_type [ OUT | OUTPUT ][ , ... n]' }
    { , [ @parameter_name= ] 'value' [ , ... n ] }
]
```

Like EXECUTE, sp_executesql takes a string constant or variable as a SQL statement to execute. Unlike EXECUTE the sql_statement must be an NCHAR or NVARCHAR. The sp_executesql procedure offers another advantage over the EXECUTE method: you can specify your parameters separately from the statement. When you specify the parameters separately instead of concatenating them, SQL Server passes the parameters to sp_executesql separately. It then substitutes the values of the parameters in the sql_statement. It does not concatenate the parameters into the sql_statement, and in that way it protects against SQL injection attacks. A limitation to this approach is that you cannot use the parameters in your sql_statement in place of table, column, or other object names. Sp_executesql parameterization also improves query execution plan cache reuse, which can help performance. Listing 10-5 shows how to parameterize the previous sample.

Listing 10-5. *Dynamic SQL sp_executesql Parameterized Method*

```
DECLARE @product_name NVARCHAR(50);
SELECT @product_name = N'Mountain%';
DECLARE @sql_stmt NVARCHAR(128);
SELECT @sql_stmt = N'SELECT ProductID, Name ' +
    N'FROM Production.Product ' +
    N'WHERE Name LIKE @name';
EXECUTE  sp_executesql @sql_stmt,
    N'@name NVARCHAR(50)',
    @name = @product_name;
```

Dynamic SQL and Scope

Dynamic SQL executes in its own scope. What this means is that variables and temporary tables created in a dynamic SQL statement or statement batch are not directly available to the calling routine. Consider the example in Listing 10-6.

Listing 10-6. *Limited Scope of Dynamic SQL*

```
DECLARE @sql_stmt NVARCHAR(512);
SELECT @sql_stmt = N'CREATE TABLE #Temp_ProductIDs ' +
    N'(ProductID INT NOT  NULL PRIMARY KEY); ' +
    N'INSERT INTO #Temp_ProductIDs (ProductID) ' +
    N'SELECT ProductID ' +
    N'FROM Production.Product;' ;

EXECUTE (@sql_stmt);

SELECT ProductID
FROM #Temp_ProductIDs;
```

The sample in Listing 10-6 generates the following error message:

```
(506 row(s) affected)
Msg 208, Level 16, State 0, Line 10
Invalid object name '#Temp_ProductIDs'.
```

The message (506 row(s) affected) indicates that the temporary table creation and INSERT INTO statement of the dynamic SQL executed properly and without error. The problem is with the SELECT statement after the EXECUTE. Since the #Temp_ProductIDs table was created within the scope of the dynamic SQL statement, once the dynamic SQL statement completed, the temporary table was dropped. Once SQL Server reaches the SELECT statement, the #Temp_ProductIDs table no longer exists. One way to work around this issue is to create the temporary table before the dynamic SQL executes. The dynamic SQL is able to access and update the temporary table created by the caller, as shown in Listing 10-7.

Listing 10-7. *Creating a Temp Table Accessible to Dynamic SQL and the Caller*

```
CREATE TABLE #Temp_ProductIDs
    (ProductID INT NOT NULL PRIMARY KEY);

DECLARE @sql_stmt NVARCHAR(512);
SELECT @sql_stmt = N'INSERT INTO #Temp_ProductIDs (ProductID) ' +
    N'SELECT ProductID ' +
    N'FROM Production.Product;' ;

EXECUTE (@sql_stmt);

SELECT ProductID
FROM #Temp_ProductIDs;
```

Table variables and other variables declared by the caller are not accessible to dynamic SQL, however. Variables and table variables have well-defined scope. They are only available to the batch, function, or procedure in which they are created and are not available to dynamic SQL or other called routines.

Client-Side Parameterization

Parameterization of dynamic SQL queries is not just a good idea server-side; it's also a great idea to parameterize queries instead of building dynamic SQL strings on the front end. Apart from the security implications, query parameterization provides cached query execution plan reuse, making queries more efficient than their concatenated string counterparts. Microsoft .NET languages provide the tools necessary to parameterize queries from the application layer in the System.Data.SqlClient and System.Data namespaces. Although this book is not a .NET application programming book per se, this topic is important enough to warrant further explanation.

In the old days (before .NET), ASP, VB 6, and SQL 6.5 application programmers often created SQL queries in their client-side applications by simply concatenating parameter values into SQL query strings. Unfortunately, this exposes the same security and performance problems that occur when you concatenate strings together to generate server-side dynamic SQL. A lot of application programmers carried this string concatenation approach to building SQL queries forward with them to the newer generations of SQL Server and the .NET programming languages, but there is a better way. Listing 10-8 demonstrates simple client-side parameterization in VB 2005. To keep the code simple I've eliminated the exception handling that I would normally include. Always use Try...Catch exception handling in production .NET code. To use the sample code you must Import the System.Data.SqlClient and System.Data namespaces (see the MSDN library for more details).

Listing 10-8. *Sample VB 2005 Client-Side Parameterized Query*

```
Dim SqlCon As New SqlConnection("SERVER=(local);INITIAL " & _
    "CATALOG=AdventureWorks;INTEGRATED SECURITY=SSPI;")
SqlCon.Open()

Dim SqlCmd As New SqlCommand("SELECT  ProductId, Name FROM " & _
    "Production.Product WHERE Name LIKE @name", SqlCon)

SqlCmd.Parameters.Add("@name", SqlDbType.NVarChar, 50).Value = "Mountain%"

Dim SqlDr As SqlDataReader = SqlCmd.ExecuteReader()
While (SqlDr.Read())
    Console.WriteLine("Item {0} = {1}", SqlDr.Item("ProductId"), SqlDr.Item("Name"))
End While

SqlDr.Close()
SqlCmd.Dispose()
SqlCon.Dispose()
```

The code in Listing 10-8 sets up a new SqlConnection to the SQL Server and connects to the AdventureWorks database using Windows integrated security. Of course, you'll need to modify the connection string to suit your needs:

```
Dim SqlCon As New SqlConnection("SERVER=(local);INITIAL " & _
    "CATALOG=AdventureWorks;INTEGRATED SECURITY=SSPI;")
SqlCon.Open()
```

Next, the sample creates a simple SqlCommand. Notice the @name parameter in the query string itself. This is the indicator to SQL Server that it should use a parameterized value in the query:

```
Dim SqlCmd As New SqlCommand("SELECT ProductId, Name FROM " & _
    "Production.Product WHERE Name LIKE @name", SqlCon)
```

Then the @name parameter is actually added to the SqlCommand Parameters collection. I assign the string value Mountain% to the parameter with the same statement:

```
SqlCmd.Parameters.Add("@name", SqlDbType.NVarChar, 50).Value = "Mountain%"
```

Finally the code uses a SqlDataReader to loop through the results, prints the results to standard output, and performs a little cleanup:

```
Dim SqlDr As SqlDataReader = SqlCmd.ExecuteReader()
While (SqlDr.Read())
    Console.WriteLine("Item {0} = {1}", SqlDr.Item("ProductId"), SqlDr.Item("Name"))
End While

SqlDr.Close()
SqlCmd.Dispose()
SqlCon.Dispose()
```

Because the query is parameterized, the parameters are handled separately from the query string by SQL Server; just like when you use sp_executesql with server-side parameterized queries. Also like sp_executesql, client-side parameterization protects you against SQL injection attacks and provides the performance benefits of cached query execution plan reuse. Listing 10-9 is a C# 2005 version of the code in Listing 10-8. In C# you must use the using statement to use the System.Data.SqlClient and System.Data namespaces (see the MSDN Library for details).

Listing 10-9. *C# Version of Client-Side Query Parameterization*

```
SqlConnection SqlCon = new SqlConnection("SERVER=(local);INITIAL " & _
    "CATALOG=AdventureWorks;INTEGRATED SECURITY=SSPI;");
SqlCon.Open();

SqlCommand SqlCmd = new SqlCommand("SELECT ProductId, Name FROM " & _
    "Production.Product WHERE Name LIKE @name", SqlCon);

SqlCmd.Parameters.Add("@name", SqlDbType.NVarChar, 50).Value = "Mountain%";

SqlDataReader SqlDr = SqlCmd.ExecuteReader();
while (SqlDr.Read())
{
    Console.WriteLine("Item {0} = {1}", SqlDr.GetValue(0), SqlDr.GetValue(1));
}

SqlDr.Close();
SqlCmd.Dispose();
SqlCon.Dispose();
```

Finally, I end with a VB 2005 code sample showing how *not* to build query strings on the client side, demonstrated in Listing 10-10.

Listing 10-10. *How Not to Build a Client-Side Query String*

```
Dim SqlCon As New SqlConnection("SERVER=(local);INITIAL " & _
    "CATALOG=AdventureWorks;INTEGRATED SECURITY=SSPI;")
SqlCon.Open()

Dim Name As  String = "Mountain%"
Dim SqlCmd As New SqlCommand("SELECT ProductId, Name FROM " & _
    "Production.Product WHERE Name LIKE '" & Name & "'", SqlCon)

Dim SqlDr As SqlDataReader = SqlCmd.ExecuteReader()
While (SqlDr.Read())
    Console.WriteLine("Item {0} = {1}", SqlDr.Item("ProductId"), SqlDr.Item("Name"))
End While

SqlDr.Close()
SqlCmd.Dispose()
SqlCon.Dispose()
```

As you can see, the parameter in this last sample is concatenated into the query string. This leaves the query wide open to SQL injection as described previously. Avoid this method of building query strings and instead parameterize your queries.

Summary

Dynamic SQL can be a very useful tool, but it is often incorrectly used. Misuse of dynamic SQL can have serious implications for the security of your server and databases. Improper use of dynamic SQL can also impact application performance. I discussed SQL injection and query performance as two of the most compelling reasons to take extra care when using dynamic SQL.

This chapter presented the different approaches to performing server-side dynamic SQL, including the following:

- The EXECUTE statement

- The sp_executesql system stored procedure

I also talked about dynamic SQL scope, including the following:

- Dynamic SQL access to temporary tables

- Dynamic SQL with variables and table variables

In addition to server-side query parameterization, client-side parameterized queries were also introduced with .NET code samples.

The next chapter will delve into SQL Server 2005 XML integration and support. I will review the legacy SQL Server XML functionality, the new `xml` data type, and the additional XML functionality built into SQL Server 2005.

CHAPTER 11

■■■

XML

In SQL Server 2005, XML support has been improved with much tighter T-SQL to XML integration, a new xml data type, and new functionality to take advantage of XML directly from your T-SQL code.

SQL Server 2005's tight XML integration and new xml data type provide streamlined methods of performing dozens of tasks that used to require clunky code to interface with COM objects and other tools external to the SQL Server engine. This chapter discusses the new xml data type and the new XML tools built into T-SQL to take advantage of SQL Server's XML functionality.

This chapter discusses the following:

- SQL Server 2005 XQuery support

- The new xml data type and its methods

- FOR XML enhancements and XPath support

- XML indexes

- XSL transformations

- Legacy (SQL Server 2000) XML support

Legacy XML

SQL Server XML functionality was introduced in T-SQL with SQL Server 2000. The main tools provided to implement this functionality were the FOR XML clause of the SELECT statement, the OPENXML rowset provider, and the sp_xml_preparedocument and sp_xml_removedocument system stored procedures. Though the functionality still exists in SQL Server 2005 and can be useful in some situations, it can be somewhat awkward to use.

FOR XML RAW

The FOR XML clause appears at the end of the SELECT statement and can take one of several formats. The first is the FOR XML RAW clause, shown here:

```
FOR XML RAW [ ( element_name ) ] [ , BINARY BASE64 ] [ , TYPE ]
    [ , ROOT [ ( 'root_name' ) ] ]
    [ , { XMLDATA | XMLSCHEMA [ ( 'target_namespace_uri' ) ] } ]
    [ , ELEMENTS [ XSINIL | ABSENT ] ]
```

If the RAW format is used, data is returned in XML format with each row represented as a node with attributes representing each column. You can specify the *element_name* (if you leave it off the default name, row is used). The query in Listing 11-1 demonstrates.

Listing 11-1. *Sample FOR XML RAW Clause in a SELECT Statement*

```
SELECT ProductID,
    Name,
    ProductNumber
FROM Production.Product
WHERE ProductID = 770
    FOR XML RAW;
```

The following is the result of the query (reformatted for easier reading) in Listing 11-1.

```
<row ProductID="770"
        Name="Road-650 Black, 52"
        ProductNumber="BK-R50B-52"/>
```

You can specify several additional options in FOR XML RAW mode, including the following:

- BINARY BASE64 returns binary data in Base-64 encoded form.

- TYPE returns the results as an xml type.

- ROOT adds a single top-level root element to the results.

- XMLDATA appends an XML-Data Reduced (XDR) schema to the beginning of your XML result.

- XMLSCHEMA returns an inline XSD (the W3C standard for XML Schema is available at http://www.w3.org/XML/Schema).

- The ELEMENTS keyword indicates that column data should be returned as subelements instead of attributes. The ELEMENTS keyword can have the following additional options as well:

  - XSINIL specifies that columns with NULL values are included in the result with an xsi:nil attribute set to true.

  - ABSENT specifies that no elements are created for NULL values. ABSENT is the default action.

FOR XML AUTO

For a query against a single table, the AUTO keyword retrieves data in a format similar to RAW mode, but the XML node name is the name of the table and not the more generic row. For queries that join multiple tables, however, rows of the tables on the right-hand side of the join are generated as subelements in the XML data. The following is the format of the FOR XML AUTO clause:

```
FOR XML AUTO [ , BINARY BASE64 ] [ , TYPE ] [ , ROOT [ ( 'root_name' ) ] ]
    [ , { XMLDATA | XMLSCHEMA [ ( 'target_namespace_uri' ) ] } ]
    [ , ELEMENTS [ XSINIL | ABSENT ] ]
```

Listing 11-2 demonstrates the FOR XML AUTO clause on a single table.

Listing 11-2. *Sample FOR XML AUTO Clause in a SELECT Statement on a Single Table*

```
SELECT ProductID,
    Name,
    ProductNumber
FROM Production.Product
WHERE ProductID = 770
FOR XML AUTO;
```

The following is the result of the query in Listing 11-2:

```
<Production.Product
        ProductID="770"
        Name="Road-650 Black, 52"
        ProductNumber="BK-R50B-52"/>
```

Listing 11-3 demonstrates using FOR XML AUTO in a SELECT statement that joins two tables.

Listing 11-3. *Sample FOR XML AUTO Clause in a SELECT Statement on Multiple Tables*

```
SELECT Product.ProductID,
    Product.Name,
    Product.ProductNumber,
    Inventory.Quantity
FROM Production.Product Product
INNER JOIN Production.ProductInventory Inventory
    ON Product.ProductID = Inventory.ProductID
WHERE Product.ProductID = 770
    FOR XML AUTO;
```

The XML result of this query takes the following form:

```
<Product ProductID="770"
        Name="Road-650 Black, 52"
        ProductNumber="BK-R50B-52">
    <Inventory Quantity="104"/>
    <Inventory Quantity="123"/>
</Product>
```

The FOR XML AUTO clause can be further refined by adding the ELEMENTS keyword. Just as with the FOR XML RAW clause, this keyword transforms the XML column attributes into subelements, as in Listing 11-4.

Listing 11-4. *FOR XML AUTO Sample with ELEMENTS Keyword*

```
SELECT ProductID,
    Name,
    ProductNumber
FROM Production.Product
WHERE ProductID = 770
    FOR XML AUTO, ELEMENTS;
```

The result of the query in Listing 11-4 looks like this:

```
<Production.Product>
    <ProductID>770</ProductID>
    <Name>Road-650 Black, 52</Name>
    <ProductNumber>BK-R50B-52</ProductNumber>
</Production.Product>
```

The additional options of the FOR XML AUTO clause are the same as those of the FOR XML RAW clause.

FOR XML EXPLICIT

The EXPLICIT keyword is flexible but complex. It allows you to specify the exact hierarchy of XML elements and attributes. This structure is specified in the SELECT statement itself using the Element!Tag!Attribute!Directive notation. The SELECT query must return data in a *universal* relational format that includes a Tag column defining the level of the current tag and a Parent column defining the parent level of the current tag. The remaining columns are the actual data columns. The FOR XML EXPLICIT clause takes the following format:

```
FOR XML EXPLICIT [ , BINARY BASE64 ] [ , TYPE ]
    [ , ROOT [ ( 'root_name' ) ] ]
    [ , XMLDATA ]
```

Listing 11-5 demonstrates this type of query.

Listing 11-5. *FOR XML EXPLICIT Sample*

```
SELECT 1 AS Tag,
    NULL AS Parent,
    ProductID AS [Products!1!ProductID!element],
    Name AS [Products!1!ProductName],
    ProductNumber AS [Products!1!ProductNumber],
    NULL AS [Products!2!Quantity]
FROM Production.Product
WHERE ProductID = 770
UNION ALL
```

```
SELECT 2 AS Tag,
    1 AS Parent,
    NULL,
    NULL,
    NULL,
    Quantity
FROM Production.ProductInventory
WHERE ProductID = 770
    FOR XML EXPLICIT;
```

The results of the query in Listing 11-5 are the following:

```
<Products ProductName="Road-650 Black, 52"
        ProductNumber="BK-R50B-52">
    <ProductID>770</ProductID>
    <Products Quantity="104"/>
    <Products Quantity="123"/>
</Products>
```

The FOR XML EXPLICIT query defines the top-level items as Tag = 1 and Parent = NULL. The next level defines the Tag = 2 and Parent = 1, referencing back to the top level. Additional levels can be added by using the UNION keyword with additional queries that increment the Tag and reference the next higher level as the Parent. Each column of the query must be named with the Element!Tag!Attribute!Directive format mentioned previously. In this format, Element is the name of the XML element, in this case Products. Tag is the level of the element, which is 1 for top-level elements. Attribute is the name of the attribute if you want the data in the column to be returned as an XML attribute. If you want the item to be returned as an XML element, use Attribute to specify the name of the attribute, and specify a Directive of element. The Directives that can be specified include the following:

- The hide directive, which is useful when you want to retrieve values for sorting purposes but do not want the specified node included in the resulting XML

- The element directive, which generates an XML element instead of an attribute

- The elementxsinil directive, which generates an element for NULL column values

- The xml directive, which generates an element instead of an attribute, but does not encode entity values

- The cdata directive, which wraps the data in a CDATA section and does not encode entities

- The xmltext directive, which wraps the column content in a single tag integrated with the document

- The id, idref, and idrefs directives, which allow you to create internal document links

The additional options of the FOR XML EXPLICIT clause are BINARY BASE64, TYPE, ROOT, and XMLDATA. These options operate the same as they do in the FOR XML RAW clause.

FOR XML PATH

The FOR XML PATH clause is a new feature of SQL Server 2005. It provides an easier way to generate results similar to the FOR XML EXPLICIT clause. Like FOR XML EXPLICIT you have to define the structure of the resultant XML, but unlike FOR XML EXPLICIT, FOR XML PATH allows you to use a subset of the well-documented and much more intuitive XPath syntax to define that structure. The following is the format of FOR XML PATH:

```
FOR XML PATH [ ( 'element_name' ) ] [ , BINARY BASE64 ] [ , TYPE ]
    [ , ROOT [ ( 'root_name' ) ] ]
    [ , ELEMENTS [ XSNIL | ABSENT ] ]
```

With the FOR XML PATH clause, column names are used to name the data as with FOR XML EXPLICIT. Any columns that do not have names are *inlined*. This is useful if you want to include an xml data type column in your result. In keeping with the XML standard, column names in the SELECT statement with a FOR XML PATH clause are case-sensitive. A column named Name is different from a column named NAME. The other rules for column names are the following:

- If a column name begins with an *at* sign (@) and does not contain a slash mark (/), the value of the column is mapped as an attribute of the *element_name* element for each corresponding row.

- If a column name does not start with an *at* sign (@) and does not contain a slash mark (/), the value of the column is mapped as a subelement of the *element_name* element for each row.

- If a column name does not start with an *at* sign (@) and contains one or more slash marks (/), the item is mapped as a subelement in a hierarchy below the *element_name* element for each row. What this means is if a column name such as Product/ID is used, and *element_name* is the default value row, the value of that element will be mapped in a hierarchy like this:

```
<row>
    <Product>
        <ID>value</ID>
    </Product>
</row>
```

- If multiple columns have the same prefix, they will be grouped together as elements under the same subelement. For instance, if there are three columns named Product/ID, Product/Price, and Product/Name, and *element_name* is the default value row, the resulting hierarchy might look like this:

```
<row>
    <Product>
        <ID>value</ID>
        <Price>value</Price>
        <Name>value</Name>
    </Product>
</row>
```

However, if a column with a different prefix appears between the columns with the same prefix, it breaks the grouping. SQL Server will generate multiple subelements with the same name. As an example, if there were four columns named Product/ID, Product/Price, Quantity, and Product/Name in that order, the resulting hierarchy might look like this:

```
<row>
    <Product>
        <ID>value</ID>
        <Price>value</Price>
    </Product>
    <Quantity>value</Quantity>
    <Product>
        <Name>value</Name>
    </Product>
</row>
```

- If the wildcard character (*) or the name node() is used as a column name, the value of the column is inserted inline under the *element_name* element. If the column is a non-xml data type, it is inserted as a text value. When a value is inserted inline, or *inlined*, its value is inserted directly as a text node, except for XML itself, which is inserted in the current position as XML.

Additionally, you can use certain XPath node tests as column names. Table 11-1 is a summary of column naming conventions, including XPath node tests.

Table 11-1. *FOR XML PATH Column Naming Conventions*

Column Name	Result
text()	The string value of the column is added as a text node.
comment()	The string value of the column is added as an XML comment.
node()	The string value of the column is inserted inline under the *element_name* element.
*	This is the same as node().
data()	The string value of the column is inserted as an atomic value. Spaces are inserted between atomic values in the resulting XML.
processing-instruction(*name*)	The string value of the column is inserted as an XML processing instruction named *name*.
@name	The string value of the column is inserted as an attribute of the *element_name* element.
name	The string value of the column is inserted as a subelement of the *element_name* element.
elem/name	The string value of the column is inserted as a subelement of the specified element hierarchy, under *element_name*.
elem/@name	The string value of the column is inserted as an attribute of the last element in specified hierarchy, under *element_name*.

Listing 11-6 demonstrates the use of the FOR XML PATH clause in a SELECT statement.

Listing 11-6. *FOR XML PATH Clause Example*

```
SELECT p.ProductID AS "Product/@ID",
    p.Name AS "Product/Name",
    p.ProductNumber AS "Product/Number",
    i.Quantity AS "Product/Quantity"
FROM Production.Product p
INNER JOIN Production.ProductInventory i
    ON p.ProductID = i.ProductID
WHERE p.ProductID = 770
FOR XML PATH;
```

The result of this sample FOR XML PATH query looks like this:

```
<row>
    <Product ID="770">
        <Name>Road-650 Black, 52</Name>
        <Number>BK-R50B-52</Number>
        <Quantity>104</Quantity>
    </Product>
</row>
<row>
    <Product ID="770">
        <Name>Road-650 Black, 52</Name>
        <Number>BK-R50B-52</Number>
        <Quantity>123</Quantity>
    </Product>
</row>
```

The additional FOR XML PATH options operate the same as they do for the FOR XML AUTO clause.

OPENXML

OPENXML is a legacy XML function that provides a rowset view of XML data. It is technically a *rowset provider*, which means its contents can be queried and accessed like a table. The legacy SQL Server XML functionality requires the sp_xml_preparedocument and sp_xml_removedocument system stored procedures to parse text into an XML document and to clean up afterward. These procedures are used in conjunction with the OPENXML function to move XML data from its textual representation into a parsed XML document, and from there to a database table.

This method is rather clunky compared to the newer methods introduced by SQL Server 2005, but you might need it if you're writing code that needs to work on both SQL Server 2000 as well as 2005. The first step in using OPENXML is to use the sp_xml_preparedocument stored procedure to convert an XML-formatted string into an XML document. The following is the format for sp_xml_preparedocument:

```
sp_xml_preparedocument hdoc OUTPUT [ , xmltext ] [ , xpath_namespaces ]
```

- The *hdoc* parameter is an int OUTPUT parameter that contains a handle to the XML document created by the stored procedure.

- The *xmltext* parameter is the original XML document in string format. It can be a char, nchar, varchar, nvarchar, text, ntext, or xml data type. If NULL is passed in, or *xmltext* is omitted, an empty XML document is created. The default for this parameter is NULL.

- The *xpath_namespaces* parameter specifies the namespace declarations used in XPath expressions in OPENXML. Like *xmltext*, the *xpath_namespaces* parameter can be a char, nchar, varchar, nvarchar, text, ntext, or xml data type. The default *xpath_namespaces* value is <root xmlns:mp="urn:schemas-microsoft-com:➥ xml-metaprop">.

The sp_xml_preparedocument procedure invokes the MSXML parser to parse your XML document into an internal tree representation of the nodes. The resulting document is cached and will continue to take up SQL Server memory until it is explicitly removed with the sp_xml_removedocument procedure. The following is the format for sp_xml_removedocument:

```
sp_xml_removedocument hdoc
```

The sp_xml_removedocument procedure only takes one parameter. The *hdoc* parameter is the int handle previously returned by the sp_xml_preparedocument procedure.

The final piece of the puzzle is the OPENXML rowset provider itself. Because it is a rowset provider, OPENXML can be queried like a table or view. The following is the format for OPENXML:

```
OPENXML(hdoc, rowpattern [ , flags ])
    [ WITH ( SchemaDeclaration | TableName ) ]
```

OPENXML takes up to three parameters:

- The *hdoc* parameter is the integer XML document handle returned by the sp_xml_preparedocument procedure.

- The *rowpattern* is an nvarchar XPath query pattern that determines which nodes of the XML document are returned as rows.

- The optional *flags* parameter is a tinyint value that specifies the type of mapping to be used between the XML data and the relational rowset. If specified, *flags* can be a combination of the values listed in Table 11-2.

Table 11-2. *OPENXML Flags Parameter Options*

Value	Name	Description
0	DEFAULT	A *flags* value of 0 tells OPENXML to default to attribute-centric mapping.
1	XML_ATTRIBUTES	A *flags* value of 1 indicates that OPENXML should use attribute-centric mapping.
2	XML_ELEMENTS	A *flags* value of 2 indicates that OPENXML should use element-centric mapping.
3	XML_ATTRIBUTES | XML_ELEMENTS	Combining XML_ATTRIBUTES with XML_ELEMENTS (logical OR) indicates that attribute-centric mapping should be applied first, and element-centric mapping should be applied to all columns not yet dealt with.
8		The *flags* value of 8 indicates that the consumed data should not be copied to the overflow property @mp:xmltext. This value can be combined (logical OR) with *flags* 1, 2, or 3.

The optional WITH clause of OPENXML provides a format for the returned rowset. The WITH clause can specify a *SchemaDeclaration* or an existing *TableName*. If the WITH clause isn't specified, the results are returned in *edge table* format. According to Microsoft SQL Server 2005 BOL, "Edge tables represent the fine-grained document structure . . . in a single table" (http://msdn2.microsoft.com/en-us/library/ms186918.aspx). Basically an edge table is Microsoft's default format for representing XML data that has been *shredded*, or converted to relational format. The format for edge tables is given in Table 11-3.

Table 11-3. *Edge Table Format*

Column Name	Data Type	Description
id	bigint	The unique ID of the document node. The root element ID is 0.
parentid	bigint	The identifier of the parent of the node. If the node is a top-level node, the parentid is NULL.
nodetype	int	The column that indicates the type of the node. It can be 1 for an element node, 2 for an attribute node, or 3 for a text node.
localname	nvarchar	The local name of the element or attribute, or NULL if the DOM object does not have a name.
prefix	nvarchar	The namespace prefix of the node.
namespaceuri	nvarchar	The namespace URI of the node, or NULL if no namespace.
datatype	nvarchar	The data type of the element or attribute row, which is inferred from the inline DTD or the inline schema.
prev	bigint	The XML ID of the previous sibling element, or NULL if there is no direct previous sibling.
text	ntext	The attribute value or element content.

The sample query in Listing 11-7 pulls this together with a simple demonstration of OPENXML without the WITH clause.

Listing 11-7. *Sample OPENXML Query; No WITH Clause*

```
DECLARE @docHandle INT;
DECLARE @xmlDocument NVARCHAR(MAX);
SELECT @xmlDocument =
N'<Customers>
    <Customer CustomerID="1234" ContactName="Larry" CompanyName="APress">
        <Orders>
            <Order OrderDate="2006-04-25T13:22:18"/>
            <Order OrderDate="2006-05-10T12:35:49"/>
        </Orders>
    </Customer>
    <Customer CustomerID="4567" ContactName="Bill" CompanyName="Microsoft">
        <Orders>
            <Order OrderDate="2006-03-12T18:32:39"/>
            <Order OrderDate="2006-05-11T17:56:12"/>
        </Orders>
    </Customer>
</Customers>';

EXECUTE sp_xml_preparedocument @docHandle OUTPUT, @xmlDocument;

SELECT Id,
    ParentId,
    NodeType,
    LocalName,
    Prefix,
    NameSpaceUri,
    DataType,
    Prev,
    [Text]
FROM OPENXML(@docHandle, N'/Customers/Customer');

EXECUTE sp_xml_removedocument @docHandle;
GO
```

Listing 11-7 begins by declaring an `int` variable to hold the XML document handle and an `nvarchar(max)` variable to hold the string representation of the XML document to be parsed:

```
DECLARE @docHandle INT;
DECLARE @xmlDocument NVARCHAR(MAX);
SELECT @xmlDocument =
N'<Customers>
    <Customer CustomerID="1234" ContactName="Larry" CompanyName="APress">
        <Orders>
            <Order OrderDate="2006-04-25T13:22:18"/>
            <Order OrderDate="2006-05-10T12:35:49"/>
        </Orders>
    </Customer>
    <Customer CustomerID="4567" ContactName="Bill" CompanyName="Microsoft">
        <Orders>
            <Order OrderDate="2006-03-12T18:32:39"/>
            <Order OrderDate="2006-05-11T17:56:12"/>
        </Orders>
    </Customer>
</Customers>';
```

Next the code calls `sp_xml_preparedocument` to parse the XML text and cache it in memory as an XML node tree structure:

```
EXECUTE sp_xml_preparedocument @docHandle OUTPUT, @xmlDocument
```

Then the code uses `OPENXML` to `SELECT` all of the nodes that match the XPath expression pattern /Customers/Customer:

```
SELECT Id,
    ParentId,
    NodeType,
    LocalName,
    Prefix,
    NameSpaceUri,
    DataType,
    Prev,
    [Text]
FROM OPENXML(@docHandle, N'/Customers/Customer');
```

Finally it calls `sp_xml_removedocument` with the document handle previously generated to get rid of the in-memory XML document:

```
EXECUTE sp_xml_removedocument @docHandle;
GO
```

■**Caution** Always call `sp_xml_removedocument` to free memory used by XML documents created with `sp_xml_createdocument`. Any XML documents created with `sp_xml_createdocument` remain in memory until `sp_xml_removedocument` is called or the SQL Server service is restarted.

The OPENXML query returns the results in edge table format, as shown in Figure 11-1.

	Id	ParentId	NodeType	LocalName	Prefix	NameSpaceUri	DataType	Prev	Text
1	2	0	1	Customer	NULL	NULL	NULL	NULL	NULL
2	3	2	2	CustomerID	NULL	NULL	NULL	NULL	NULL
3	20	3	3	#text	NULL	NULL	NULL	NULL	1234
4	4	2	2	ContactName	NULL	NULL	NULL	NULL	NULL
5	21	4	3	#text	NULL	NULL	NULL	NULL	Larry
6	5	2	2	CompanyName	NULL	NULL	NULL	NULL	NULL
7	22	5	3	#text	NULL	NULL	NULL	NULL	APress
8	6	2	1	Orders	NULL	NULL	NULL	NULL	NULL
9	7	6	1	Order	NULL	NULL	NULL	NULL	NULL
10	8	7	2	OrderDate	NULL	NULL	NULL	NULL	NULL
11	23	8	3	#text	NULL	NULL	NULL	NULL	2006-04-25T13:22:18

Figure 11-1. *Results of the OPENXML query in Listing 11-7*

By adding a WITH clause to the OPENXML query in Listing 11-7, you can specify an explicit schema for the resulting rowset. This technique is demonstrated in Listing 11-8. The differences between Listings 11-8 and 11-7 are shown in bold.

Listing 11-8. *OPENXML and WITH Clause, Explicit Schema*

```
DECLARE @docHandle INT;
DECLARE @xmlDocument NVARCHAR(MAX);
SET @xmlDocument =
N'<Customers>
    <Customer CustomerID="1234" ContactName="Larry" CompanyName="APress">
```

```
        <Orders>
            <Order OrderDate="2006-04-25T13:22:18"/>
            <Order OrderDate="2006-05-10T12:35:49"/>
        </Orders>
    </Customer>
    <Customer CustomerID="4567" ContactName="Bill" CompanyName="Microsoft">
        <Orders>
            <Order OrderDate="2006-03-12T18:32:39"/>
            <Order OrderDate="2006-05-11T17:56:12"/>
        </Orders>
    </Customer>
</Customers>';

EXECUTE sp_xml_preparedocument @docHandle OUTPUT, @xmlDocument;

SELECT CustomerID,
    CustomerName,
    CompanyName,
    OrderDate
FROM OPENXML(@docHandle, N'/Customers/Customer/Orders/Order')
    WITH (CustomerID NCHAR(4) N'../../@CustomerID',
        CustomerName NVARCHAR(50) N'../../@ContactName',
        CompanyName NVARCHAR(50) N'../../@CompanyName',
        OrderDate DATETIME);

EXECUTE sp_xml_removedocument @docHandle;
GO
```

Figure 11-2 shows the result of this OPENXML query.

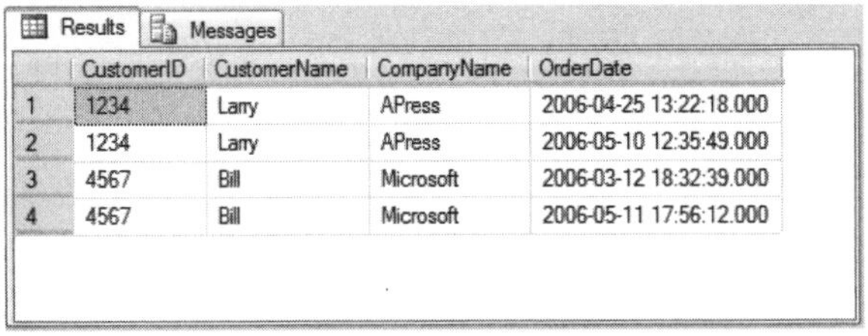

	CustomerID	CustomerName	CompanyName	OrderDate
1	1234	Larry	APress	2006-04-25 13:22:18.000
2	1234	Larry	APress	2006-05-10 12:35:49.000
3	4567	Bill	Microsoft	2006-03-12 18:32:39.000
4	4567	Bill	Microsoft	2006-05-11 17:56:12.000

Figure 11-2. *Results of OPENXML with explicit schema declaration*

The OPENXML WITH clause can also use the schema from an existing table to format the relational result set. This is demonstrated in Listing 11-9. The differences between Listing 11-9 and 11-8 are shown in bold text.

Listing 11-9. *OPENXML with WITH Clause, Existing Table Schema*

```
DECLARE @docHandle INT;
DECLARE @xmlDocument NVARCHAR(MAX);
SET @xmlDocument =
N'<Customers>
    <Customer CustomerID="1234" ContactName="Larry" CompanyName="APress">
      <Orders>
          <Order OrderDate="2006-04-25T13:22:18"/>
          <Order OrderDate="2006-05-10T12:35:49"/>
      </Orders>
    </Customer>
    <Customer CustomerID="4567" ContactName="Bill" CompanyName="Microsoft">
      <Orders>
          <Order OrderDate="2006-03-12T18:32:39"/>
          <Order OrderDate="2006-05-11T17:56:12"/>
      </Orders>
    </Customer>
</Customers>';

EXECUTE sp_xml_preparedocument @docHandle OUTPUT, @xmlDocument;

CREATE TABLE #OrderInfo (CustomerID NCHAR(4) NOT NULL,
    CustomerName NVARCHAR(50) NOT NULL,
    CompanyName NVARCHAR(50) NOT NULL,
    OrderDate NVARCHAR(50) NOT NULL,
    PRIMARY KEY(CustomerID, CustomerName, CompanyName, OrderDate));

INSERT INTO #OrderInfo (CustomerID, CustomerName, CompanyName, OrderDate)
SELECT CustomerID,
    CustomerName,
    CompanyName,
    OrderDate
```

```
FROM OPENXML(@docHandle, N'/Customers/Customer/Orders/Order')
    WITH (CustomerID NCHAR(4) N'../../@CustomerID',
        CustomerName NVARCHAR(50) N'../../@ContactName',
        CompanyName NVARCHAR(50) N'../../@CompanyName',
        OrderDate DATETIME);

SELECT CustomerID,
    CustomerName,
    CompanyName,
    OrderDate
FROM #OrderInfo;

DROP TABLE #OrderInfo;

EXECUTE sp_xml_removedocument @docHandle;
GO
```

Figure 11-3 shows the results of the sample `OPENXML` query using an existing table to format the results.

Results | Messages

	CustomerID	CustomerName	CompanyName	OrderDate
1	1234	Larry	APress	Apr 25 2006 1:22PM
2	1234	Larry	APress	May 10 2006 12:35PM
3	4567	Bill	Microsoft	Mar 12 2006 6:32PM
4	4567	Bill	Microsoft	May 11 2006 5:56PM

Figure 11-3. *Sample OPENXML query using an existing table to format results*

The xml Data Type

SQL Server's legacy XML functionality can be a bit cumbersome and somewhat clunky to use at times. Fortunately, SQL Server 2005 includes much tighter XML integration with its new `xml` data type. The `xml` data type can be used to declare variables or columns of a table. T-SQL `xml` variables and columns have built-in methods that allow you to query and modify nodes, and they can be associated with XML schemas to create typed `xml` instances. This section discusses both typed and untyped `xml` instances in T-SQL.

The T-SQL `xml` data type can hold complete XML documents or XML fragments. An XML document has to have a top-level root element, while an XML fragment does not.

The stored internal representation of an XML document or fragment stored in an xml variable or column maxes out at 2GB of storage. The xml type can be used anywhere other types are used, including

- The return type of a function

- The parameter type for functions and stored procedures

- Variable declarations

- Column declarations

- CAST and CONVERT functions

Untyped xml

Untyped xml variables and columns are created by following them with the keyword xml in the declaration, as shown in Listing 11-10.

Listing 11-10. *Untyped xml Variable and Column Declarations*

```
DECLARE @x XML;
CREATE TABLE XmlPurchaseOrders(PoNum INT NOT NULL PRIMARY KEY,
    XmlPO XML);
```

Populating an xml variable or column with an XML document or fragment requires a simple assignment statement. Char, varchar, nchar, nvarchar, varbinary, text, and ntext data can be implicitly or explicitly converted to xml. Some rules apply when converting from one of these types to xml:

- The XML parser treats nvarchar, nchar, and ntext data as a two-byte Unicode-encoded XML document or fragment.

- Char, varchar, and text data are treated as a single-byte-encoded XML document or fragment. The code page of the source string, variable, or column is used for encoding by default.

- The content of varbinary data is passed directly to the XML parser, which accepts it as a stream. If the varbinary XML data is Unicode-encoded, the byte-order mark/encoding information must be included in the varbinary data. If no byte-order mark/encoding information is included, the default of UTF-8 is used.

■**Note** The binary data type can also be implicitly or explicitly converted to xml, but it must be the exact length of the data it contains. The extra padding applied to binary variables and columns when the data they contain is too short can cause errors in the XML parsing process. Use the varbinary data type when you need to convert binary data to XML.

Listing 11-11 demonstrates implicit conversion from nvarchar to the xml data type. The CAST function can be used to make the conversion explicit.

Listing 11-11. *Populating an Untyped xml Variable*

```
DECLARE @x XML;

SELECT @x =   N'<?xml version="1.0" ?>
        <Address>
            <Latitude>47.642737</Latitude>
            <Longitude>-122.130395</Longitude>
            <Street>ONE MICROSOFT WAY</Street>
            <City>REDMOND</City>
            <State>WA</State>
            <Zip>98052</Zip>
            <Country>US</Country>
        </Address>';

SELECT @x;
```

Typed xml

To create a typed xml variable or column in SQL Server 2005, you must first create an XML schema collection with the CREATE XML SCHEMA COLLECTION statement, which looks like the following:

```
CREATE XML SCHEMA COLLECTION [ schema_name. ] xml_schema_name
AS xml_schema
```

- *Schema_name* is the name of the SQL Server schema to create the XML schema in.

- *Xml_schema_name* is the name SQL Server will use to reference the XML schema collection.

- *Xml_schema* is the XML schema. The *xml_schema* can be a char, varchar, nchar, nvarchar, varbinary, or xml constant or variable.

You can alter or drop an XML schema collection as well. The ALTER XML SCHEMA COLLECTION allows you to add schema components to a specified schema collection. The format is the following:

```
ALTER XML SCHEMA COLLECTION [ schema_name. ] xml_schema_name
ADD schema_component
```

Like the CREATE statement, *schema_name* is the SQL Server schema and *xml_schema_name* is the name SQL Server uses to reference the XML schema collection. *Schema_component* is the schema component to insert into the XML schema collection.

The format of the DROP statement, to remove an XML schema collection from the server, is the following:

```
DROP XML SCHEMA COLLECTION [ schema_name. ] xml_schema_name
```

The DOCUMENT and CONTENT keywords represent *facets* that you can use to constrain typed xml instances. Using the DOCUMENT facet in your typed xml variable or column declarations constrains your typed XML data so that it must contain only one top-level root element. The CONTENT facet allows zero or more top-level elements. CONTENT is the default if neither is specified explicitly.

Listing 11-12 demonstrates how to turn the untyped xml variable from Listing 11-11 into a typed XML xml instance. The differences between this listing and the previous one are in bold text.

Listing 11-12. *Creating a Typed xml Variable*

```
CREATE XML SCHEMA COLLECTION AddressSchemaCollection
    AS N'<?xml version="1.0" encoding="utf-16" ?>
    <xsd:schema xmlns:xsd="http://www.w3.org/2001/XMLSchema">
        <xsd:element name="Address">
            <xsd:complexType>
                <xsd:sequence>
                    <xsd:element name="Latitude" type="xsd:decimal" />
                    <xsd:element name="Longitude" type="xsd:decimal" />
                    <xsd:element name="Street" type="xsd:string" />
                    <xsd:element name="City" type="xsd:string" />
                    <xsd:element name="State" type="xsd:string" />
                    <xsd:element name="Zip" type="xsd:string" />
                    <xsd:element name="Country" type="xsd:string" />
                </xsd:sequence>
            </xsd:complexType>
        </xsd:element>
    </xsd:schema>';
GO
```

```
DECLARE @x XML (CONTENT AddressSchemaCollection);

SELECT @x =   N'<?xml version="1.0" ?>
        <Address>
            <Latitude>47.642737</Latitude>
            <Longitude>-122.130395</Longitude>
            <Street>ONE MICROSOFT WAY</Street>
            <City>REDMOND</City>
            <State>WA</State>
            <Zip>98052</Zip>
            <Country>US</Country>
        </Address>';


SELECT @x;

DROP XML SCHEMA COLLECTION AddressSchemaCollection;
GO
```

The first step in creating a typed xml instance is to create an XML schema collection:

```
CREATE XML SCHEMA COLLECTION AddressSchemaCollection
    AS N'<?xml version="1.0" encoding="utf-16" ?>
    <xsd:schema xmlns:xsd="http://www.w3.org/2001/XMLSchema">
        <xsd:element name="Address">
            <xsd:complexType>
                <xsd:sequence>
                    <xsd:element name="Latitude" type="xsd:decimal" />
                    <xsd:element name="Longitude" type="xsd:decimal" />
                    <xsd:element name="Street" type="xsd:string" />
                    <xsd:element name="City" type="xsd:string" />
                    <xsd:element name="State" type="xsd:string" />
                    <xsd:element name="Zip" type="xsd:string" />
                    <xsd:element name="Country" type="xsd:string" />
                </xsd:sequence>
            </xsd:complexType>
        </xsd:element>
    </xsd:schema>';
GO
```

■Tip The World Wide Web Consortium (W3C) maintains the standards for XML schemas. The XML Schema recommendations are available at `http://www.w3.org/TR/xmlschema-1/` and `http://www.w3.org/TR/xmlschema-2/`. These W3C recommendations are excellent starting points for creating your own XML schemas.

The next step is to declare the variable as `xml` type, but with an XML schema collection specification included:

```
DECLARE @x XML (CONTENT AddressSchemaCollection);
```

The XML data, conforming to the schema in the XML schema collection, is assigned to the `xml` variable:

```
SELECT @x =   N'<?xml version="1.0" ?>
    <Address>
        <Latitude>47.642737</Latitude>
        <Longitude>-122.130395</Longitude>
        <Street>ONE MICROSOFT WAY</Street>
        <City>REDMOND</City>
        <State>WA</State>
        <Zip>98052</Zip>
        <Country>US</Country>
    </Address>';
```

Finally, to prove that you just populated a typed `xml` variable, SELECT it. DROP the `xml` schema collection to clean up:

```
SELECT @x;

DROP XML SCHEMA COLLECTION AddressSchemaCollection;
GO
```

xml Data Type Methods

The `xml` data type has several methods for querying and modifying `xml` data. The built-in methods are shown in Table 11-4.

Table 11-4. *xml Data Type Methods*

Method	Result
query(*XQuery*)	Performs an *XQuery* query against an xml instance. Returns the result as an untyped xml instance.
value(*XQuery*, *Sql_Type*)	Performs an *XQuery* against an xml instance and returns a scalar value of the specified *Sql_Type*.
exist(*XQuery*)	Performs an *XQuery* against an xml instance and returns one of the following bit values: • 1 if the *XQuery* expression returns a nonempty result • 0 if the *XQuery* expression returns an empty result • NULL if the xml instance is NULL
modify(*XML_DML*)	Performs an *XML_DML* statement to modify an xml instance.
nodes(*XQuery*) as *table_name*(*column_name*)	Performs an *XQuery* against an xml instance and returns matching nodes as a SQL result set. *Table_name* and *column_name* specify the name of a virtual table to hold the nodes returned.

This section discusses each of the xml data type methods in turn. Code samples presented in this section use the AdventureWorks database.

The query() Method

The xml data type query() method accepts an XQuery string as its only parameter. This method returns all nodes matching the XQuery as an untyped xml instance. Conveniently enough, Microsoft was kind enough to provide us with sample typed xml data in the Resume column of the HumanResources.JobCandidate table. Though all of its xml is well-formed with a single root element, the Resume column is faceted with the default of CONTENT.

Listing 11-13 shows how to use the query() method to retrieve names from the resumes in the HumanResources.JobCandidate table.

Listing 11-13. *Using the query() Method on the HumanResources.JobCandidate Resume XML*

```
SELECT Resume.query(N'declare namespace
    ns="http://schemas.microsoft.com/sqlserver/2004/07/adventure-works/Resume";
    /ns:Resume/ns:Name') AS [NameXML]
FROM HumanResources.JobCandidate;
```

The first thing to notice is that a namespace is declared inside the XQuery. This is done because the Resume column xml data declares a namespace. In fact, the namespace declaration used in the XQuery is exactly the same as the declaration used in the xml data. The declaration section of the XQuery looks like this:

```
declare namespace ns="http://schemas.microsoft.com/sqlserver/2004/07/adventure-➥
    works/Resume";
```

The actual query portions of both XQuery strings are small by comparison:

```
/ns:Resume/ns:Name
```

A sample of the results of the code in Listing 11-13 looks like the following (reformatted for easy reading):

```
<ns:Name xmlns:ns="http://schemas.microsoft.com/sqlserver/2004/07/adventure-➥
    works/Resume">
    <ns:Name.Prefix>Mr.</ns:Name.Prefix>
    <ns:Name.First>Stephen</ns:Name.First>
    <ns:Name.Middle>Y </ns:Name.Middle>
    <ns:Name.Last>Jiang</ns:Name.Last>
    <ns:Name.Suffix />
</ns:Name>

<ns:Name xmlns:ns="http://schemas.microsoft.com/sqlserver/2004/07/adventure-➥
    works/Resume">
    <ns:Name.Prefix>M.</ns:Name.Prefix>
    <ns:Name.First>Thierry</ns:Name.First>
    <ns:Name.Middle />
    <ns:Name.Last>D'Hers</ns:Name.Last>
    <ns:Name.Suffix />
</ns:Name>

<ns:Name xmlns:ns="http://schemas.microsoft.com/sqlserver/2004/07/adventure-➥
    works/Resume">
    <ns:Name.Prefix>M.</ns:Name.Prefix>
    <ns:Name.First>Christian</ns:Name.First>
    <ns:Name.Middle />
    <ns:Name.Last>Kleinerman</ns:Name.Last>
    <ns:Name.Suffix />
</ns:Name>
```

■**Tip** SQL Server 2005 implements a subset of the W3C XQuery standard. Chapter 12 discusses SQL Server's XPath and XQuery implementations in detail. If you're just getting started with XQuery, additional resources include the W3C standard, available at `http://www.w3.org/TR/2004/WD-xquery-20040723/`, and BOL at `http://msdn2.microsoft.com/en-us/library/ms189919.aspx`.

The value() Method

The `xml` data type `value()` method performs an XQuery against an `xml` object and returns a scalar result. The scalar result of `value()` is cast to the T-SQL data type specified in the call to `value()`. The sample code in Listing 11-14 uses the `value()` method to retrieve all last names from the job applicant resumes.

Listing 11-14. *xml Data Type value() Method Sample*

```
SELECT Resume.value (N'declare namespace
    ns="http://schemas.microsoft.com/sqlserver/2004/07/adventure-works/Resume";
    (/ns:Resume/ns:Name/ns:Name.Last)[1]', 'nvarchar(max)') AS [LastName]
FROM HumanResources.JobCandidate;
```

Like the `query()` method described previously, the `value()` method sample XQuery begins by declaring a namespace:

```
declare namespace
    ns="http://schemas.microsoft.com/sqlserver/2004/07/adventure-works/Resume";
```

The actual query portion of the XQuery looks like this:

```
(/ns:Resume/ns:Name/ns:Name.Last)[1]
```

Because `value()` returns a scalar value, the query is enclosed in parentheses with [1] following it to force the return of a singleton value. The second parameter to `value()` is the T-SQL data type that `value()` will cast the result to, in this case `nvarchar(max)`. `Value()` cannot cast the result to a SQLCLR user-defined type, `xml`, `image`, `text`, `ntext`, or `sql_variant` data type. The results of the query in Listing 11-14 are shown in Figure 11-4.

Figure 11-4. *Result of xml data type value() method sample*

The exist() Method

The xml data type exist() method is useful for determining if a node exists or if an existing node value meets a specific criteria. The example in Listing 11-15 uses the exist() method in a SELECT query to return all job candidates with a bachelor's degree level of education.

Listing 11-15. *xml Data Type exist() Method Example*

```
SELECT Resume.query (N'declare namespace
    ns="http://schemas.microsoft.com/sqlserver/2004/07/adventure-works/Resume";
    /ns:Resume/ns:Name') AS [NameXML]
FROM HumanResources.JobCandidate
WHERE Resume.exist (N'declare namespace
    ns="http://schemas.microsoft.com/sqlserver/2004/07/adventure-works/Resume";
    /ns:Resume/ns:Education/ns:Edu.Level [.="Bachelor"]') = 1;
```

The first part of the query borrows from the query() method example in Listing 11-13 to retrieve matching job candidate names:

```
SELECT Resume.query (N'declare namespace
    ns="http://schemas.microsoft.com/sqlserver/2004/07/adventure-works/Resume";
    /ns:Resume/ns:Name') AS [NameXML]
FROM HumanResources.JobCandidate
```

The exist() method in the WHERE clause determines the xml match criteria. Like the previous sample queries, the XQuery query in Listing 11-15 begins by declaring a namespace:

```
declare namespace
    ns="http://schemas.microsoft.com/sqlserver/2004/07/adventure-➥
    works/Resume";
```

The query itself compares the Edu.Level node text to the string Bachelor:

```
/ns:Resume/ns:Education/ns:Edu.Level [.="Bachelor"]'
```

If there is a match, the query returns a result and the exist() method returns 1. If there is no match there will be no result returned by the XQuery and the exist() method will return 0. If the xml is NULL, exist() will return NULL. The query limits the results to only matching resumes by returning only those where exist() returns 1.

The sample query returns four job candidates whose education credentials match the criteria, as shown here (formatted for easier reading):

```
<ns:Name xmlns:ns="http://schemas.microsoft.com/sqlserver/2004/07/adventure-➥
    works/Resume">
    <ns:Name.Prefix />
    <ns:Name.First>Shai</ns:Name.First>
    <ns:Name.Middle />
    <ns:Name.Last>Bassli</ns:Name.Last>
    <ns:Name.Suffix />
</ns:Name>

<ns:Name xmlns:ns="http://schemas.microsoft.com/sqlserver/2004/07/adventure-➥
    works/Resume">
    <ns:Name.Prefix>Mr.</ns:Name.Prefix>
    <ns:Name.First>Max</ns:Name.First>
    <ns:Name.Middle />
    <ns:Name.Last>Benson</ns:Name.Last>
    <ns:Name.Suffix />
</ns:Name>
```

```
<ns:Name xmlns:ns="http://schemas.microsoft.com/sqlserver/2004/07/adventure-➥
    works/Resume">
    <ns:Name.Prefix>Mr.</ns:Name.Prefix>
    <ns:Name.First>Krishna</ns:Name.First>
    <ns:Name.Middle />
    <ns:Name.Last>Sunkammurali</ns:Name.Last>
    <ns:Name.Suffix />
</ns:Name>

<ns:Name xmlns:ns="http://schemas.microsoft.com/sqlserver/2004/07/adventure-➥
    works/Resume">
    <ns:Name.Prefix>Mr.</ns:Name.Prefix>
    <ns:Name.First>Stephen</ns:Name.First>
    <ns:Name.Middle>Y </ns:Name.Middle>
    <ns:Name.Last>Jiang</ns:Name.Last>
    <ns:Name.Suffix />
</ns:Name>
```

The nodes() Method

The nodes() method of the xml data type retrieves XML content in relational format. The nodes() method returns a rowset with logical copies of the xml nodes returned by the specified XQuery. Listing 11-16 retrieves product names and IDs for those that have the word *Alloy* in the <Material> node of their CatalogDescription. The table queried is Production.ProductModel. Notice that the CROSS APPLY operator is required to perform the nodes() method on all rows of the Production.ProductModel table.

Listing 11-16. *xml Data Type nodes() Example*

```
SELECT ProductModelId, Name, Specs.query('.') AS Result
FROM Production.ProductModel
CROSS APPLY CatalogDescription.nodes( 'declare namespace
    ns = "http://schemas.microsoft.com/sqlserver/2004/07/adventure-
    works/ProductModelDescription";
    /ns:ProductDescription/ns:Specifications/Material/text()[contains(.,"Alloy")]')
        AS NodeTable(Specs);
```

The first part of the SELECT query retrieves the product model ID and name and the results of the nodes() method via the query() method:

```
SELECT ProductModelId, Name, Specs.query('.') AS Result
FROM Production.ProductModel
```

One restriction of the nodes() method is that the relational results generated cannot be retrieved directly; they can only be accessed via the exist(), nodes(), query(), and value() xml data type methods, or with the IS NULL and IS NOT NULL operators.

The nodes() method is cross-applied to generate the final result set. The XQuery used begins by declaring a namespace:

```
declare namespace ns = "http://schemas.microsoft.com/sqlserver/2004/07/adventure-
    works/ProductModelDescription";
```

The query portion retrieves xml items in which the <Material> node text contains the word *Alloy*:

```
/ns:ProductDescription/ns:Specifications/Material/text()[contains(.,"Alloy")]
```

The results generated by this query look like Table 11-5.

Table 11-5. *xml Data Type nodes() Method Results*

ProductModelId	Name	Result
19	Mountain-100	Aluminum Alloy
23	Mountain-500	Aluminum Alloy
28	Road-450	Aluminum Alloy

The modify() Method

The xml data type modify() method can be used to modify the content of an xml variable or column. The modify() method allows you to insert, delete, or update xml content. The main restriction on the modify() method is that it must be used in a variable SET statement or in the SET clause of an UPDATE statement. The example in Listing 11-17 demonstrates the modify() method on an untyped xml variable.

■Tip Although the SELECT and SET statements are similar in their functionality when applied to variables, the modify() method of the xml data type will not work in SELECT statements—even SELECT statements that assign values to variables. Use the SET statement as demonstrated in Listing 11-17 to use the modify() method on an xml variable.

Listing 11-17. *xml Data Type modify() Method Example*

```
DECLARE @x XML;

SELECT @x = N'<?xml version="1.0" ?>
    <Address>
        <Street>1 MICROSOFT WAY</Street>
        <City>REDMOND</City>
        <State>WA</State>
        <Zip>98052</Zip>
        <Country>US</Country>
        <Website>http://www.microsoft.com</Website>
    </Address>';

SELECT @x;

SET @x.modify ('insert (
    <CompanyName>Microsoft Corporation</CompanyName>,
    <Url>http://msdn.microsoft.com</Url>,
    <UrlDescription>Microsoft Developer&apos;s Network</UrlDescription>
)
into (/Address)[1] ');

SET @x.modify(' replace value of (/Address/Street/text())[1]
    with "ONE MICROSOFT WAY"
');

SET @x.modify('
    delete /Address/Website
');

SELECT @x;
```

The sample begins by creating an xml variable and assigning XML content to it:

```
DECLARE @x XML;

SELECT @x = N'<?xml version="1.0" ?>
    <Address>
        <Street>1 MICROSOFT WAY</Street>
        <City>REDMOND</City>
        <State>WA</State>
        <Zip>98052</Zip>
        <Country>US</Country>
        <Website>http://www.microsoft.com</Website>
    </Address>';

SELECT @x;
```

The modify() method insert statement inserts three new nodes into the xml variable, right below the top-level <Address> node:

```
SET @x.modify ('insert (
    <CompanyName>Microsoft Corporation</CompanyName>,
    <Url>http://msdn.microsoft.com</Url>,
    <UrlDescription>Microsoft Developer&apos;s Network</UrlDescription>
)
into (/Address)[1] ');
```

The replace value of statement specified in the next modify() method updates the content of the <Street> node with the street address our good friends at Microsoft prefer: ONE MICROSOFT WAY instead of 1 MICROSOFT WAY.

```
SET @x.modify(' replace value of (/Address/Street/text())[1]
    with "ONE MICROSOFT WAY"
');
```

Finally the modify() method delete statement is used to remove the old <Website> tag from the xml variable's content:

```
SET @x.modify('
    delete /Address/Website
');

SELECT @x;
```

The results of this example look like this (formatted for easier reading):

```
Before:
    <Address>
        <Street>1 MICROSOFT WAY</Street>
        <City>REDMOND</City>
        <State>WA</State>
        <Zip>98052</Zip>
        <Country>US</Country>
        <Website>http://www.microsoft.com</Website>
    </Address>

After:
    <Address>
        <Street>ONE MICROSOFT WAY</Street>
        <City>REDMOND</City>
        <State>WA</State>
        <Zip>98052</Zip>
        <Country>US</Country>
        <CompanyName>Microsoft Corporation</CompanyName>
        <Url>http://msdn.microsoft.com</Url>
        <UrlDescription>Microsoft Developer's Network</UrlDescription>
    </Address>
```

XML Indexes

SQL Server provides XML indexes to increase the efficiency of querying and manipulation of xml data type columns. The process of converting XML data to relational format is known as *shredding*. XML indexes are preshredded representations of SQL Server xml data. SQL Server provides two forms of XML indexes:

- *Primary XML index*: An XML column can have a single primary XML index declared on it. In order to create a primary XML index on a table's xml column, a clustered index must be in place on a primary key column for the table.

- *Secondary XML index*: Secondary XML indexes can also be created on a table's xml column. The three types of secondary XML indexes are the following:

- PATH: Optimizes the secondary XML index for XPath and XQuery path expressions by creating an index on path and node values built on the columns of the primary XML index. The path and node values are used as key columns for efficient path seek operations.

- VALUE: Optimizes the secondary XML index for queries by value. This type of index is based on the node values and paths of the primary XML index.

- PROPERTY: Optimizes the secondary XML index for queries that retrieve data from the table based on the value of nodes or paths in the xml column. This type of secondary index is created on the primary key of the base table, node paths, and node values of the primary XML index.

In order to create secondary XML indexes on an xml column, a primary XML index must already exist on that column.

Consider the example XQuery FLWOR expression in Listing 11-18 that retrieves the last, first, and middle names of all job applicants in the HumanResources.JobCandidate table with an education level of Bachelor.

■**Tip** XQuery FLWOR expressions like this one are described in greater detail in Chapter 12.

Listing 11-18. *Retrieving Job Candidates with Bachelor's Degrees*

```
SELECT Resume.query('declare namespace ns =
    "http://schemas.microsoft.com/sqlserver/2004/07/adventure-works/Resume";
for $m in /ns:Resume
where $m/ns:Education/ns:Edu.Level[. = "Bachelor" ]
return <Name>
    {
        data(($m/ns:Name/ns:Name.Last)[1]),
        data(($m/ns:Name/ns:Name.First)[1]),
        data(($m/ns:Name/ns:Name.Middle)[1])
    }
</Name>')
FROM HumanResources.JobCandidate;
GO
```

The results of this query look like the following:

```
<Name>Bassli Shai </Name>
<Name>Benson Max </Name>
<Name>Sunkammurali Krishna </Name>
<Name>Jiang Stephen Y </Name>
```

The results, however, are not as important as what's going on *under the hood*. This XQuery query is returning the last, first, and middle names of all candidates for which the Edu.Level node contains the value Bachelor. As shown in Figure 11-5, the execution cost of this query is 27.7855.

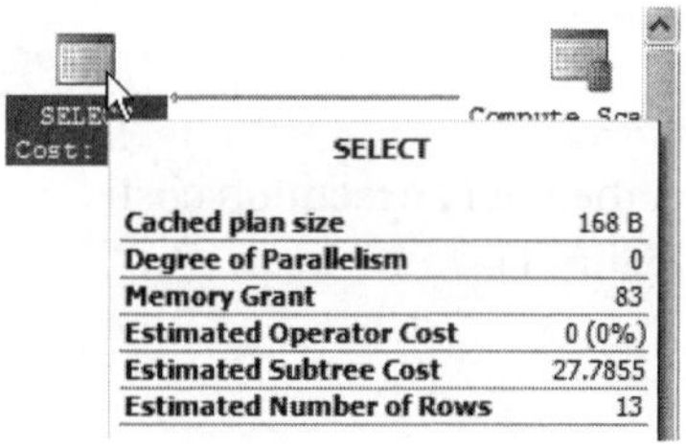

Figure 11-5. *Execution cost of query*

By far the most expensive part of this query is the XML Reader with XPath Filter step, with a cost of 13.052, as shown in Figure 11-6. Two of these steps occur in the query execution plan at a cost of 13.052 each, accounting for 94 percent of the total cost of the query execution plan.

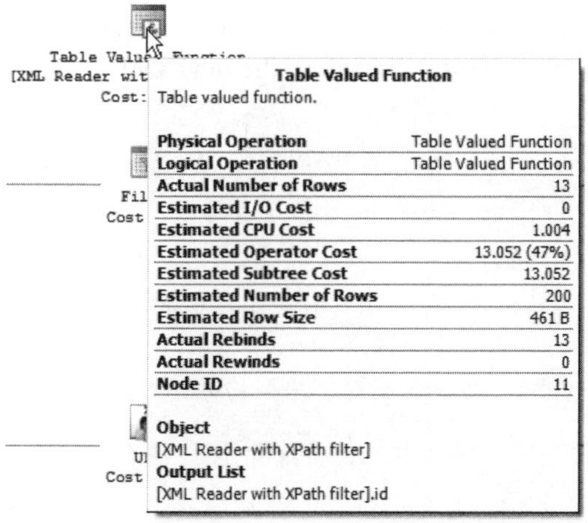

Figure 11-6. *XML Reader with XPath Filter step of the query plan*

Adding XML indexes to this column of the HumanResources.JobCandidate table will significantly improve the query performance. Listing 11-19 demonstrates adding a primary and secondary XML index to the Resume column.

Listing 11-19. *Adding XML Indexes to the Resume Column*

```
CREATE PRIMARY XML INDEX PXML_JobCandidate
ON HumanResources.JobCandidate (Resume);
GO

CREATE XML INDEX IXML_Education
ON HumanResources.JobCandidate (Resume)
USING XML INDEX PXML_JobCandidate
FOR PATH;
GO
```

With the primary and secondary XML indexes in place, the query execution cost drops significantly from 27.7855 to 0.337566, as shown in Figure 11-7.

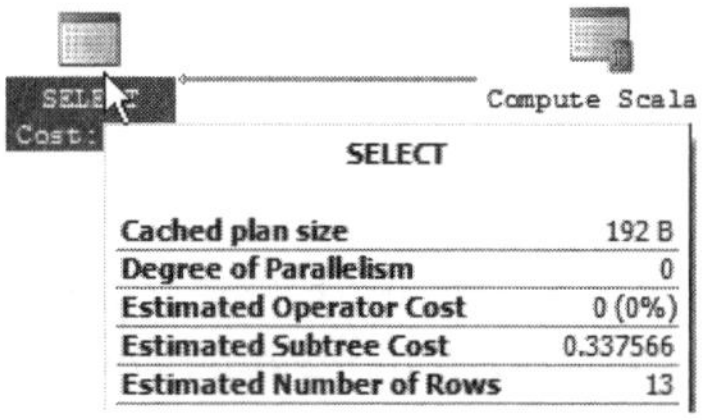

Figure 11-7. *Query execution cost with XML indexes in place*

This greater efficiency is brought about by the XML Reader with XPath Filter step being replaced with an efficient Clustered Index Seek step based on the new XML indexes, as shown in Figure 11-8.

Query 1: Query cost	**Clustered Index Seek**	
SELECT Resume.query('	Scanning a particular range of rows from a clustered index.	
Clustered Index Seek	**Physical Operation**	Clustered Index Seek
tureWorks].[sys].[xml_index]	**Logical Operation**	Clustered Index Seek
Cost: 10 %	**Actual Number of Rows**	13
	Estimated I/O Cost	0.0038657
	Estimated CPU Cost	0.0002455
	Estimated Operator Cost	0.0342139 (10%)
	Estimated Subtree Cost	0.0342139
UDX	**Estimated Number of Rows**	1
Cost: 0 %	**Estimated Row Size**	25 B
	Actual Rebinds	0
	Actual Rewinds	0
	Ordered	True
	Node ID	28

Figure 11-8. *Efficient Clustered Index Seek step using the XML indexes*

The CREATE PRIMARY XML INDEX statement in the example creates a primary XML index on the Resume column of the HumanResources.JobCandidate table. This is a prerequisite for creating the secondary XML index that will provide significant performance increase. The following is the general format for the CREATE PRIMARY XML INDEX statement:

```
CREATE PRIMARY XML INDEX index_name
ON [ database_name. ][ schema_name. ] table_name ( xml_column_name )
[ WITH ( xml_index_option [ , ... n ] ) ] ;
```

The *index_name* is the name to assign to the primary XML index on creation. *Table_name* specifies the name of the table to create the index on; it can be preceded by the *database_name* and *schema_name* as well. The *xml_column_name* is the name of the xml data type column on which the XML index will be created.

The optional WITH clause of this statement allows you to specify a variety of XML index creation options:

- PAD_INDEX = { ON | OFF }: This option specifies index padding. The default is OFF.

- FILLFACTOR = *fill_factor*: The FILLFACTOR option indicates how full the leaf level index pages should be made during index creation or rebuild. Values of 0 and 100 for *fill_factor* are equivalent. The FILLFACTOR option is used in conjunction with the PAD_INDEX option.

- SORT_IN_TEMPDB = { ON | OFF }: The SORT_IN_TEMPDB option specifies that intermediate sort results are stored in TEMPDB. By default, SORT_IN_TEMPDB is set to OFF and intermediate sort results are stored in the local database.

- STATISTICS_NORECOMPUTE = { ON | OFF }: The STATISTICS_NORECOMPUTE option determines whether distribution statistics are automatically recomputed. The default is OFF.

- `DROP_EXISTING = { ON | OFF }`: This option specifies that the preexisting XML index of the same name should be dropped before creating the index. The default is `OFF`.

- `ALLOW_ROW_LOCKS = { ON | OFF }`: This option allows SQL Server to use row locks when accessing the XML index. The default is `ON`.

- `ALLOW_PAGE_LOCKS = { ON | OFF }`: This option allows SQL Server to use page locks when accessing the XML index. The default is `ON`.

- `MAXDOP = max_degree_parallelism`: This option determines the maximum degree of parallelism SQL Server can use during the index operation. `Max_degree_parallelism` can be one of the following values:

  - 0 (uses up to the maximum number of processors available)

  - 1 (uses only one processor; no parallel processing)

  - 2–64 (restricts the number of processors used for parallel processing to the number specified or less)

  The default `MAXDOP` value is 0. Parallel index operations are available only in the Enterprise Edition of SQL Server 2005.

The secondary XML index is created with the `CREATE XML INDEX` statement, which has the following format:

```
CREATE XML INDEX index_name
ON [ database_name. ][ schema_name. ] table_name ( xml_column_name )
USING XML INDEX primary_xml_index_name
FOR { VALUE | PATH | PROPERTY }
[ WITH ( xml_index_option [ , ... n ] ) ];
```

As with the `CREATE PRIMARY XML INDEX` statement, the *index_name* specifies the name of the XML index. The *table_name* is the name of the table on which the XML index will be created; it can be preceded by a *schema_name* and/or *database_name*. The *xml_column_name* is the name of the xml data type column on which the XML index will be built.

The `USING XML INDEX` clause specifies the name of the primary XML index to use in building the secondary XML index. The `FOR` clause determines the type of secondary XML index that will be created. This can be a `VALUE`, `PATH`, or `PROPERTY` type as described previously. The optional `WITH` clause can be used to specify the same set of XML index creation options that can be used with the `CREATE PRIMARY XML INDEX` option.

XSL Transformations

As defined by the W3C, *XSL Transformations* (XSLT) is a language designed for the sole purpose of "transforming XML documents into other XML documents." The XSLT 1.0 standard is available at `http://www.w3.org/TR/xslt`. SQL Server 2005 provides access to XSL Transformations via a combination of the built-in `xml` data type and the SQLCLR `XslCompiledTransform` class.

XSLT can be used in SQL Server as a means of transforming your relational data into an HTML page or other XML document, via the `SELECT` statement's `FOR XML` clause. Listing 11-20 demonstrates the first step in the process: using `FOR XML` to convert relational data to an `xml` variable data type instance.

Listing 11-20. *Using FOR XML to Convert Relational Data to Populate an xml Variable*

```
DECLARE @xml XML;
SELECT @xml = (
    SELECT p.ProductNumber AS '@Id',
        p.Name AS 'Name',
        p.Color AS 'Color',
        p.ListPrice AS 'ListPrice',
        p.SizeUnitMeasureCode AS 'Size/@UOM',
        p.Size AS 'Size',
        p.WeightUnitMeasureCode AS 'Weight/@UOM',
        p.Weight AS 'Weight',
        (
            SELECT COALESCE(SUM(i.Quantity), 0)
            FROM Production.ProductInventory i
            WHERE i.ProductID = p.ProductID
        ) AS 'QuantityOnHand'
    FROM Production.Product p
    WHERE FinishedGoodsFlag = 1
    ORDER BY p.Name
    FOR XML PATH ('Product'),
        ROOT ('Products')
);
```

The resulting xml document looks like the following sample:

```
<Products>
    ...
    <Product Id="FR-M94B-38">
        <Name>HL Mountain Frame - Black, 38</Name>
        <Color>Black</Color>
        <ListPrice>1349.6000</ListPrice>
        <Size UOM="CM ">38</Size>
        <Weight UOM="LB ">2.68</Weight>
        <QuantityOnHand>834</QuantityOnHand>
    </Product>
    <Product Id="FR-M94B-42">
        <Name>HL Mountain Frame - Black, 42</Name>
        <Color>Black</Color>
        <ListPrice>1349.6000</ListPrice>
        <Size UOM="CM ">42</Size>
        <Weight UOM="LB ">2.72</Weight>
        <QuantityOnHand>0</QuantityOnHand>
    </Product>
    ...
</Products>
```

The next step is to create the XSLT style sheet to specify the transformation and assign it to an xml data type variable. Listing 11-21 demonstrates a simple XSLT style sheet to convert our XML data to XHTML.

Listing 11-21. *XSLT Style Sheet to Convert Data to HTML*

```
DECLARE @xslt XML;
SELECT @xslt = N'<?xml version="1.0" encoding="utf-16"?>
<xsl:stylesheet version="1.0"
    xmlns:xsl="http://www.w3.org/1999/XSL/Transform">
<xsl:template match="/Products">
<html>
    <head>
        <title>AdventureWorks Product Listing Report</title>
        <style type="text/css">
```

```
        tr.row-heading {
            background-color: 000099;
            color: ffffff;
            font-family: tahoma, arial, helvetica, sans-serif;
            font-size: 12px;
        }
        tr.row-light {
            background-color: ffffff;
            font-family: tahoma, arial, helvetica, sans-serif;
            font-size: 12px;
        }
        tr.row-dark {
            background-color: 00ffff;
            font-family: tahoma, arial, helvetica, sans-serif;
            font-size: 12px;
        }
        td.col-right {
            text-align: right;
        }
    </style>
</head>
<body>
    <table>
        <tr class="row-heading">
            <th>ID</th>
            <th>Product Name</th>
            <th>On Hand</th>
            <th>List Price</th>
            <th>Color</th>
            <th>Size</th>
            <th>Weight</th>
        </tr>
        <xsl:for-each select="Product">
            <xsl:element name="tr">
                <xsl:choose>
                    <xsl:when test="position() mod 2 = 0">
                        <xsl:attribute name="class">row-light</xsl:attribute>
                    </xsl:when>
                    <xsl:otherwise>
                        <xsl:attribute name="class">row-dark</xsl:attribute>
                    </xsl:otherwise>
                </xsl:choose>
```

```
            <td><xsl:value-of select="@Id"/></td>
            <td><xsl:value-of select="Name"/></td>
            <td class="col-right">
                <xsl:value-of select="QuantityOnHand"/>
            </td>
            <td class="col-right"><xsl:value-of select="ListPrice"/></td>
            <td><xsl:value-of select="Color"/></td>
            <td class="col-right">
                <xsl:value-of select="Size"/>
                <xsl:value-of select="Size/@UOM"/>
            </td>
            <td class="col-right">
                <xsl:value-of select="Weight"/>
                <xsl:value-of select="Weight/@UOM"/>
            </td>
        </xsl:element>
    </xsl:for-each>
    </table>
    </body>
</html>
</xsl:template>
</xsl:stylesheet>';
```

■**Tip** I won't delve into the details of XSLT style sheet definitions in this book, but information can be found at the official W3C XSLT 1.0 standard site: http://www.w3.org/TR/xslt. Also, the book *Beginning XSLT* by Jeni Tennison (Apress, 2004) offers a detailed discussion of XSLT technology.

The final step is to create a .NET SQLCLR stored procedure to accept the raw XML data and the XSLT style sheet, perform the XSL transformation, and write the results to an XHTML file. The SQLCLR stored procedure code is shown in Listing 11-22.

Listing 11-22. *VB 2005 SQLCLR Stored Procedure for XSLT Transformation*

```
Imports System.Data.SqlTypes
Imports System.Xml
Imports System.Xml.Xsl
```

```
Namespace APress.Samples
    Partial Public Class XSLT
        <Microsoft.SqlServer.Server.SqlProcedure()> _
        Public Shared Sub XmlToHtml(ByVal RawXml As SqlXml, _
            ByVal XslStyleSheet As SqlXml, _
            ByVal OutputPage As SqlString)

            ' Create and load the XslCompiledTransform object
            Dim xslt As New XslCompiledTransform()
            Dim xmldoc1 As New XmlDocument()
            xmldoc1.LoadXml(XslStyleSheet.Value)
            xslt.Load(xmldoc1)

            ' Create and load the Raw XML document
            Dim xml As New XmlDocument()
            xml.LoadXml(RawXml.Value)

            ' Create the XmlTextWriter for output to HTML document
            Dim htmlout As New XmlTextWriter(OutputPage.Value, _
                System.Text.Encoding.Unicode)

            ' Perform the transformation
            xslt.Transform(xml, htmlout)

            ' Close the XmlTextWriter
            htmlout.Close()
        End Sub
    End Class
End Namespace
```

The first few lines of Listing 11-22 import the required .NET 2.0 namespaces and declare the APress.Samples namespace:

```
Imports System.Data.SqlTypes
Imports System.Xml
Imports System.Xml.Xsl

Namespace APress.Samples
```

The next section of code declares the requisite class and defines the signature of the stored procedure XmlToHtml. The stored procedure accepts three parameters: the raw input XML, the XSLT style sheet, and the name of the output file:

```
Partial Public Class XSLT
    <Microsoft.SqlServer.Server.SqlProcedure()> _
    Public Shared Sub XmlToHtml(ByVal RawXml As SqlXml, _
        ByVal XslStyleSheet As SqlXml, _
        ByVal OutputPage As SqlString)
```

Inside the XmlToHtml procedure, the first step is to create a .NET 2.0 XslCompiledTransform object and populate it with the style sheet passed in as a parameter:

```
' Create and load the XslCompiledTransform object
Dim xslt As New XslCompiledTransform()
Dim xmldoc1 As New XmlDocument()
xmldoc1.LoadXml(XslStyleSheet.Value)
xslt.Load(xmldoc1)
```

Then the procedure creates an XmlDocument to hold the raw XML input passed in as a parameter:

```
' Create and load the Raw XML document
Dim xml As New XmlDocument()
xml.LoadXml(RawXml.Value)
```

Finally, the procedure creates an XmlTextWriter to output the results of the transformation. Then the actual transformation is performed, and the results are written to the file whose name was specified as the third parameter:

```
' Create the XmlTextWriter for output to HTML document
Dim htmlout As New XmlTextWriter(OutputPage.Value, _
    System.Text.Encoding.Unicode)

' Perform the transformation
xslt.Transform(xml, htmlout)

' Close the XmlTextWriter
htmlout.Close()
    End Sub
    End Class
End Namespace
```

Tip Because the result is output to an XHTML file in the file system, the assembly created needs `EXTERNAL_ACCESS` permissions. These can be set from the Project Properties page in Visual Studio, or specified manually in the `CREATE ASSEMBLY` statement.

Once the assemblies are installed and the `@xml` and `@xslt` variables are defined as shown in Listings 11-20 and 11-21, the `XmlToHtml` stored procedure is ready to run, as shown in Listing 11-23.

Listing 11-23. *Executing the XmlToHtml Stored Procedure*

```
EXECUTE XmlToHtml @xml, @xslt, 'c:\adventureworks-inventory.html';
```

The result is output to the `adventureworks-inventory.html` file. Figure 11-9 shows what the results look like in Internet Explorer.

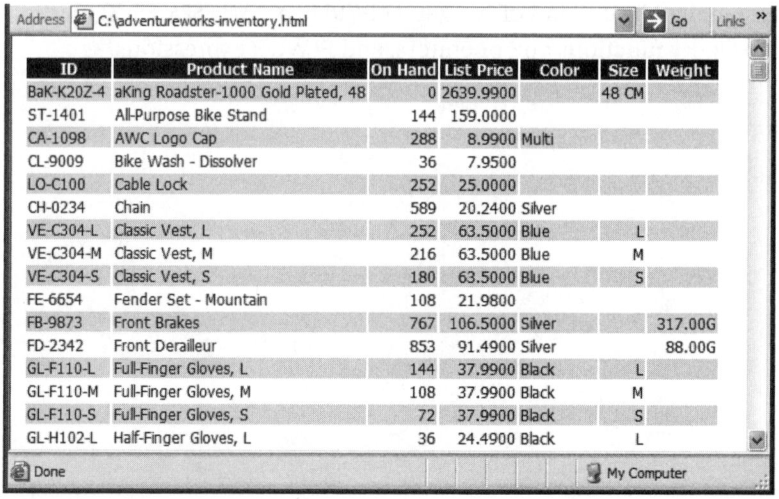

ID	Product Name	On Hand	List Price	Color	Size	Weight
BaK-K20Z-4	aKing Roadster-1000 Gold Plated, 48	0	2639.9900		48 CM	
ST-1401	All-Purpose Bike Stand	144	159.0000			
CA-1098	AWC Logo Cap	288	8.9900	Multi		
CL-9009	Bike Wash - Dissolver	36	7.9500			
LO-C100	Cable Lock	252	25.0000			
CH-0234	Chain	589	20.2400	Silver		
VE-C304-L	Classic Vest, L	252	63.5000	Blue	L	
VE-C304-M	Classic Vest, M	216	63.5000	Blue	M	
VE-C304-S	Classic Vest, S	180	63.5000	Blue	S	
FE-6654	Fender Set - Mountain	108	21.9800			
FB-9873	Front Brakes	767	106.5000	Silver		317.00G
FD-2342	Front Derailleur	853	91.4900	Silver		88.00G
GL-F110-L	Full-Finger Gloves, L	144	37.9900	Black	L	
GL-F110-M	Full-Finger Gloves, M	108	37.9900	Black	M	
GL-F110-S	Full-Finger Gloves, S	72	37.9900	Black	S	
GL-H102-L	Half-Finger Gloves, L	36	24.4900	Black	L	

Figure 11-9. *Result of XmlToHtml procedure*

Summary

This chapter discussed SQL Server 2005 integrated XML functionality. The chapter began with a discussion of legacy XML functionality carried forward, and in some cases improved upon, from SQL Server 2000. I then discussed the new SQL Server 2005 `xml` data type and the functionality implemented to help you take advantage of this new level of XML integration.

Topics covered include the following:

- The SELECT statement's legacy FOR XML clause and the new SQL Server 2005 enhancements to FOR XML, particularly the built-in support for XPath in SQL Server 2005's FOR XML AUTO clause.

- The legacy OPENXML rowset provider.

- SQL Server 2005's new xml data type, including support for untyped XML and typed XML.

- The xml data type methods: query(), value(), exist(), modify(), and nodes().

- Primary and secondary XML indexes.

- Using the SQLCLR with the xml data type and FOR XML to perform XSLT transformations.

The next chapter provides an introduction to SQL Server's XPath and XQuery support, including a more detailed discussion of FOR XML PATH, WITH XMLNAMESPACES, XQuery data types, XPath and XQuery functions and operators, and FLWOR expressions.

■ ■ ■

CHAPTER 12

XQuery and XPath

As described in Chapter 11, SQL Server 2005 presents a new level of XML integration. As part of that integration SQL Server provides the new xml data type and new options for converting relational data to XML format via the SELECT query's FOR XML PATH clause. This chapter discusses how to get the most out of SQL Server's implementation of the powerful and flexible XPath and XQuery standards.

The XML data model represents a departure from the relational model SQL Server developers know well. The XML model is not a replacement for the relational model, but it does nicely complement relational data. Operational data is best represented by tables, because relational databases are composed of tables. XML structures data hierarchically (and with considerable texture), making it very useful for sharing and processing many kinds of data, especially data of the hierarchical and semistructured varieties. Relational tables and XML do not need to be used exclusively of each other. Data stored in tables is commonly converted to XML format to make it easy to communicate with web services and other applications over networks. And highly structured XML data from a remote data source often needs to be stored and queried locally in relational tables. The new SQL Server 2005 xml data type and XML-specific query and conversion tools represent a marriage of relational database and XML technologies. The first step to getting the most out of that technology is to define the terms I'll be using throughout this chapter.

■Note XPath and XQuery are big topics that can easily consume an entire book. This chapter is not meant to be a comprehensive guide to XPath and XQuery, but rather an introduction to SQL Server's XPath and XQuery implementations, which are both subsets of their respective standards (the W3C's XPath 1.0 and XQuery 1.0). In addition to the discussion in this chapter, Appendix B covers the XML Schema data types used by SQL Server XQuery, and Appendix C lists the definitions for XML-, XPath-, and XQuery-related words that are introduced in this chapter.

X-Lingo

The W3C is a standards body that generates "standards, guidelines, software, and tools" to ensure interoperability on the World Wide Web. One the most widely recognized of the W3C standards is the XML 1.0 specification, currently in its fourth edition and freely available at `http://www.w3.org/TR/2006/REC-xml-20060816/#sec-intro`. *XML* is a (somewhat contrived) acronym for *Extensible Markup Language*. According to the W3C, XML was designed as a "simple, very flexible text format derived from SGML (ISO 8879)."

After the widespread acceptance of XML, it was recognized that there was a need for tools to retrieve portions of XML documents. In 1999, the W3C proposed the XML Path Language (XPath) as a language for "addressing parts of an XML document . . ." SQL Server implements a subset of the W3C XPath 1.0 standard, available at `http://www.w3.org/TR/xpath`.

Additional requirements for complex querying and manipulation of portions of XML data were addressed with the W3C's XML Query Language (XQuery) recommendation in 2003. XQuery is the specification for a query language that "uses the structure of XML intelligently" to express queries across many different types of XML data. SQL Server implements a subset of the W3C XQuery 1.0 standard, available at `http://www.w3.org/TR/2006/PR-xquery-20061121/`.

THE XML, XPATH, XQUERY RELATIONSHIP

What's the relationship between XML, XPath, and XQuery? Specifically, XML is described by the W3C as a "subset of the Standard Generalized Markup Language (SGML)" (`http://www.w3.org/TR/2006/REC-xml-20060816/`). SGML is a metalanguage for defining other languages, called *markup languages*, and markup languages are simply that: languages for marking up text, both to organize it and to provide instructions for processing it. Both SGML and XML provide for structuring data in a plain-text, tree-based fashion, using markup "tags" to indicate the hierarchical relationship of the data. In fact, though XML is only a subset of SGML, it satisfies most needs and has largely superseded SGML, even for traditional text markup.

The original XPath 1.0 is a standard language designed to integrate common functionality of Extensible Stylesheet Language Transformations (XSLT) and the XML Pointer (XPointer) standards. XPath 2.0 is a superset of XPath 1.0, providing a more expressive data model with a richer set of data types than XPath 1.0.

XQuery 1.0 is an extension to XPath 2.0. Any valid XPath 2.0 expression will run on and return the same result in XQuery 1.0. Some of the major differences between XQuery 1.0 and XPath 2.0 include FLWOR expressions (XPath supports only a small subset) described later in the chapter, query prolog, and some other functionality.

In addition, SQL Server 2005 supports XML DML (XML Data Manipulation Language) statements that can be applied to the `xml` data type. Don't worry if you're not familiar with these topics; I cover all of them in detail in this chapter.

SQLXML defines Microsoft's XML integration with SQL Server. Note that Microsoft's SQLXML is not the same as the ANSI *SQL/XML*, defined in Part 14 of the ANSI SQL:2003 standard (http://www.ansi.org). After ANSI SQL:2003 was approved, the ANSI working group immediately went to work changing SQL/XML to better integrate XPath and XQuery, effectively adding functionality we SQL Server programmers already have in SQL Server 2005.

XPath and FOR XML PATH

XPath 1.0 is used in SQL Server in conjunction with the FOR XML PATH clause of the SELECT statement to specify the structure of the XML result. Because it is used specifically to define the structure of an XML result, the FOR XML PATH XPath functionality is limited in its functionality. Specifically, you cannot use features that contain certain filter criteria or use absolute paths. Briefly, here are the restrictions:

- A FOR XML PATH XPath expression may not begin or end with the / step operator, and it may not begin with, end with, or contain //.

- FOR XML PATH XPath expressions cannot specify axis specifiers such as child:: or parent::.

- The "." (context node) and ".." (context node parent) axis specifiers are also not allowed.

- The functions defined in Part 4 of the XPath specification, "Core Function Library," are not allowed.

- Predicates, which are used to filter result sets, are not allowed. [position()=4] is an example of a predicate.

Basically the FOR XML PATH XPath subset allows you to specify the structure of the resulting XML, relative to the implicit root node. By default the root node of the result is named row. In general, XPath 1.0 features that can be used to locate specific nodes, return sets of nodes, or filter result sets are not allowed with FOR XML PATH.

By default, FOR XML PATH is *element-centric*, meaning results are defined in terms of element nodes. Consider the query in Listing 12-1.

Listing 12-1. *Simple FOR XML PATH Query Using XPath*

```
SELECT ContactID AS 'Person/ID',
    FirstName AS 'Person/Name/First',
    MiddleName AS 'Person/Name/Middle',
    LastName AS 'Person/Name/Last',
    EmailAddress AS 'Person/Email'
FROM Person.Contact
FOR XML PATH;
```

The result of this query looks like the partial results shown here:

```
<row>
    <Person>
        <ID>1</ID>
        <Name>
            <First>Gustavo</First>
            <Last>Achong</Last>
        </Name>
        <Email>gustavo0@adventure-works.com</Email>
    </Person>
</row>
<row>
    <Person>
        <ID>2</ID>
        <Name>
            <First>Catherine</First>
            <Middle>R.</Middle>
            <Last>Abel</Last>
        </Name>
        <Email>catherine0@adventure-works.com</Email>
    </Person>
</row>
...
```

XPath expressions follow the column names in the SELECT statement:

```
SELECT ContactID AS 'Person/ID',
    FirstName AS 'Person/Name/First',
    MiddleName AS 'Person/Name/Middle',
    LastName AS 'Person/Name/Last',
    EmailAddress AS 'Person/Email';
```

XPath expressions are defined as a path separated by *step operators*. The step operator
(/) indicates that a node is a child of the preceding node. For instance, the XPath expression Person/ID in the example indicates that a node named ID will be created as a child of
the node named Person.

XPath Attributes

Alternatively, you can define a relational column as an attribute of a node. Listing 12-2,
which is a modified version of Listing 12-1, demonstrates this.

Listing 12-2. *FOR XML Defining XML Attributes*

```
SELECT ContactID AS 'Person/@ID',
    EmailAddress AS 'Person/@Email',
    FirstName AS 'Person/Name/First',
    MiddleName AS 'Person/Name/Middle',
    LastName AS 'Person/Name/Last'
FROM Person.Contact
FOR XML PATH;
```

The bolded portion of the SELECT statement in Listing 12-1 generates XML attributes
of the ID and EMAIL nodes by preceding their names in the XPath expression with the @
symbol:

```
SELECT ContactID AS 'Person/@ID',
    EmailAddress AS 'Person/@Email',
```

In this sample, ID and Email are attributes of the Person element of the result. The
(partial) results of Listing 12-1 look like this:

```
<row>
    <Person ID="1" Email="gustavo0@adventure-works.com">
        <Name>
            <First>Gustavo</First>
            <Last>Achong</Last>
        </Name>
    </Person>
</row>
```

```
<row>
    <Person ID="2" Email="catherine0@adventure-works.com">
        <Name>
            <First>Catherine</First>
            <Middle>R.</Middle>
            <Last>Abel</Last>
        </Name>
    </Person>
</row>
...
```

Columns Without Names and Wildcards

Some of the other XPath expression features you can use with FOR XML PATH include columns without names and wildcard expressions, which are turned into inline content. The sample in Listing 12-3 demonstrates this.

Listing 12-3. *FOR XML Defining XML Attributes*

```
SELECT ContactID AS '*',
    ',' + EmailAddress,
    FirstName AS 'Person/Name/First',
    MiddleName AS 'Person/Name/Middle',
    LastName AS 'Person/Name/Last'
FROM Person.Contact
FOR XML PATH;
```

In this example, the XPath expression for ContactID is the wildcard character *. The second column is defined as '*' + EmailAddress so the column has no name. Both of these columns are turned into inline content, as shown in the following (partial) results:

```
<row>
    1,gustavo0@adventure-works.com
    <Person>
        <Name>
            <First>Gustavo</First>
            <Last>Achong</Last>
        </Name>
    </Person>
</row>
```

```
<row>
    2,catherine0@adventure-works.com
    <Person>
        <Name>
            <First>Catherine</First>
            <Middle>R.</Middle>
            <Last>Abel</Last>
        </Name>
    </Person>
</row>
...
```

Element Grouping

As you saw in the previous examples, FOR XML groups together nodes that have the same parent elements. For instance, the First, Middle, and Last elements are all children of the Name element. They are grouped together in all of the examples because of this. However, as shown in Listing 12-4, this is not the case when these elements are separated by an element with a different parent. Consider Listing 12-4.

Listing 12-4. *Two Elements with a Common Parent Element Separated*

```
SELECT ContactID AS 'Person/@ContactID',
    EmailAddress AS 'Person/Email',
    FirstName AS 'Person/Name/First',
    MiddleName AS 'Person/Name/Middle',
    Phone AS 'Person/Phone',
    LastName AS 'Person/Name/Last'
FROM Person.Contact
FOR XML PATH;
```

The results of this query include a new Phone element as a child of the Person element. Because this new element is positioned between the Person/Name/Middle and Person/Name/Last elements, FOR XML creates two separate Person/Name elements: one to encapsulate the First and Middle elements, and another to encapsulate the Last element, as shown in these results:

```
<row>
    <Person ContactID="1">
        <Email>gustavo0@adventure-works.com</Email>
        <Name>
            <First>Gustavo</First>
        </Name>
        <Phone>398-555-0132</Phone>
        <Name>
            <Last>Achong</Last>
        </Name>
    </Person>
</row>
<row>
    <Person ContactID="2">
        <Email>catherine0@adventure-works.com</Email>
        <Name>
            <First>Catherine</First>
            <Middle>R.</Middle>
        </Name>
        <Phone>747-555-0171</Phone>
        <Name>
            <Last>Abel</Last>
        </Name>
    </Person>
</row>
...
```

The data() Function

FOR XML PATH XPath includes a function called data(). If the column name is specified as data(), the value is treated as an atomic value in the generated XML. If the next item generated is also an atomic value, FOR XML PATH appends a space to the end of the data returned. This is useful for using subqueries to create lists of items, as in Listing 12-5, which demonstrates use of the data() function.

Listing 12-5. *The FOR XML PATH XPath data() Function*

```
SELECT DISTINCT soh.SalesPersonID AS 'SalesPerson/@ID',
    (
        SELECT soh2.SalesOrderID AS 'data()'
        FROM Sales.SalesOrderHeader soh2
        WHERE soh2.SalesPersonID = soh.SalesPersonID
        FOR XML PATH ('')
    ) AS 'SalesPerson/@Orders',
    c.FirstName AS 'SalesPerson/Name/First',
    c.MiddleName AS 'SalesPerson/Name/Middle',
    c.LastName AS 'SalesPerson/Name/Last',
    c.EmailAddress AS 'SalesPerson/Email'
FROM Sales.SalesOrderHeader soh
INNER JOIN Person.Contact c
    ON c.ContactID = soh.SalesPersonID
WHERE soh.SalesPersonID IS NOT NULL
FOR XML PATH;
```

This sample retrieves all `SalesPerson` ID numbers from the `Sales.SalesOrderHeader` table (eliminating `NULL`s for simplicity) and retrieves their names in the main query. The subquery uses the `data()` function to retrieve a list of each salesperson's sales order numbers and places them in the attribute of the `SalesPerson` element named `Orders`. A sample of the results is shown here:

```
<row>
    <SalesPerson ID="284" Orders="46982 47004 47062 47969 48084 49078 49134 49452
        49892 50244 50686 50722 51170 51737 51811 51815 51837 51861 53461 53512
        53519 55274 57056 57058 57177 57185 58908 58968 59044 59064 61198 63161
        63173 63229 63242 63254 65201 67203 69551">
        <Name>
            <First>John</First>
            <Last>Emory</Last>
        </Name>
        <Email>john16@adventure-works.com</Email>
    </SalesPerson>
</row>
```

```
<row>
    <SalesPerson ID="288" Orders="53485 53492 53502 53554 53588 53594 57059 58915
        59045 61180 61245 63203 69553 69564 71874 71926">
        <Name>
            <First>Julie</First>
            <Middle>P.</Middle>
            <Last>Estes</Last>
        </Name>
        <Email>julie0@adventure-works.com</Email>
    </SalesPerson>
</row>
...
```

XPath and NULL

In all of the preceding examples, FOR XML PATH mapped SQL NULLs to a missing element or attribute. Consider the results of Listing 12-1 for Mr. Achong. Because his MiddleName in the table is NULL, the Name/Middle element is missing from the results:

```
<row>
    <Person>
        <ID>1</ID>
        <Name>
            <First>Gustavo</First>
            <Last>Achong</Last>
        </Name>
        <Email>gustavo0@adventure-works.com</Email>
    </Person>
</row>
```

If you want SQL NULL-valued elements and attributes to appear in the final results, use FOR XML's ELEMENTS XSINIL option as shown in Listing 12-6.

Listing 12-6. *FOR XML with ELEMENTS XSINIL Option*

```
SELECT ContactID AS 'Person/ID',
    FirstName AS 'Person/Name/First',
    MiddleName AS 'Person/Name/Middle',
    LastName AS 'Person/Name/Last',
    EmailAddress AS 'Person/Email'
FROM Person.Contact
FOR XML PATH, ELEMENTS XSINIL;
```

Mr. Achong's result now looks like the results shown here:

```
<row xmlns:xsi="http://www.w3.org/2001/XMLSchema-instance">
    <Person>
        <ID>1</ID>
        <Name>
            <First>Gustavo</First>
            <Middle xsi:nil="true" />
            <Last>Achong</Last>
        </Name>
        <Email>gustavo0@adventure-works.com</Email>
    </Person>
</row>
```

Notice the addition of the xsi namespace to the root element. The Name/Middle element now appears with the xsi:nil attribute set to true indicating it is a NULL.

WITH XMLNAMESPACES

Namespace support is provided by the WITH XMLNAMESPACES option as shown in Listing 12-7.

Listing 12-7. *FOR XML PATH and WITH XMLNAMESPACES Option*

```
WITH XMLNAMESPACES('http://www.apress.com/xml/sampleSqlXmlNameSpace' as ns)
SELECT ContactID AS 'ns:Person/ID',
    FirstName AS 'ns:Person/Name/First',
    MiddleName AS 'ns:Person/Name/Middle',
    LastName AS 'ns:Person/Name/Last',
    EmailAddress AS 'ns:Person/Email'
FROM Person.Contact
FOR XML PATH;
```

The WITH XMLNAMESPACES option in this example declares a namespace called ns: with the URI http://www.apress.com/xml/sampleSqlXmlNameSpace. FOR XML PATH then adds the namespace prefix to the Person element, as shown in the sample results:

```
<row xmlns:ns="http://www.apress.com/xml/sampleSqlXmlNameSpace">
    <ns:Person>
        <ID>1</ID>
        <Name>
            <First>Gustavo</First>
            <Last>Achong</Last>
        </Name>
        <Email>gustavo0@adventure-works.com</Email>
    </ns:Person>
</row>
```

Node Tests

In addition to these options, the FOR XML PATH XPath implementation supports node tests. The following node tests are supported:

- text() turns the string value of a column into a text node.

- comment() turns the string value of a column into an XML comment.

- node() turns the string value of a column into inline XML content; it is the same as using the wildcard * as the name.

- processing-instruction(name) turns the string value of a column into an XML processing instruction with the specified name.

Listing 12-8 demonstrates use of XPath node tests as column names in a FOR XML PATH query.

Listing 12-8. *FOR XML PATH Using XPath Node Tests*

```
SELECT NameStyle AS 'processing-instruction(nameStyle)',
    ContactID AS 'Person/@ID',
    ModifiedDate AS 'comment()',
    Phone AS 'text()',
```

```
    FirstName AS 'Person/Name/First',
    MiddleName AS 'Person/Name/Middle',
    LastName AS 'Person/Name/Last',
    EmailAddress AS 'Person/Email'
FROM Person.Contact
FOR XML PATH;
```

The results look like this:

```
<row>
    <?nameStyle 0?>
    <Person ID="1" />
    <!--2005-05-16T16:33:33.060-->
    398-555-0132
    <Person>
        <Name>
            <First>Gustavo</First>
            <Last>Achong</Last>
        </Name>
        <Email>gustavo0@adventure-works.com</Email>
    </Person>
</row>
...
```

In this example, the NameStyle column value is turned into an XML processing instruction called nameStyle; the ModifiedDate column is turned into an XML comment; and the contact Phone is turned into a text node.

XQuery and the XML Data Type

XQuery represents the most advanced XML querying language to date. Designed as an extension to the W3C XPath 2.0 standard, XQuery is a case-sensitive, declarative, functional language with a rich type system based on the XDM data model. The SQL Server 2005 xml data type supports querying of XML data using a subset of XQuery via the query() method. I start this section with a discussion of XQuery basics.

Expressions and Sequences

XQuery introduces several advances on the concepts introduced by XPath and other previous XML querying tools. The most important concepts in XQuery are *expressions* and *sequences*. A sequence is an ordered collection of items; either nodes or atomic values.

■**Note** *Ordered*, as it applies to sequences, does not necessarily mean numeric or alphabetic order. Sequences can be in document order, creation order, or another order. The roughly analogous XPath 1.0 structure was known as a *set*, a name that implies ordering was unimportant. Unlike the relational model, however, order is extremely important to XML. In XML the ordering of nodes and other data in storage provides additional context and can be just as important as the data itself. The XQuery sequence was redefined to ensure that the importance of proper ordering is recognized. There are some other differences, which I cover later in this section.

Sequences are denoted by enclosing one of the following in parentheses:

- Lists of items separated by the comma operator (,)

- Range expressions

- Filter expressions

■**Note** Range expressions and the range expression keyword to are not supported in SQL Server 2005 XQuery. If you are converting an XQuery with range expressions like (1 to 10), you will have to modify it to run on SQL Server 2005.

A sequence created as a list of items separated by the comma operator might look like the following:

```
(1, 2, 3, 4, (5, 6), 7, 8, (), 9, 10)
```

The comma operator evaluates each of the items in the sequence and concatenates the result. Sequences cannot be nested, so any sequences within sequences are "flattened out." Also, the empty sequence (a sequence containing no items, denoted by empty parentheses: ()) is eliminated. Evaluation of the previous sample sequence results in the following sequence of ten items:

```
(1, 2, 3, 4, 5, 6, 7, 8, 9, 10)
```

Notice that the nested sequence (5, 6) has been flattened out, and the empty sequence () is removed during evaluation.

■**Note** SQL Server 2005 XQuery does not support the W3C-specified sequence operators union, intersect, and except. If you are porting XQuery code that uses these operators, it will have to be modified to run on SQL Server 2005.

If one of the operands is an empty sequence, or if the first operand is greater than the second operand, the result is an empty sequence. Another method of generating a sequence is with a *filter expression*. The filter expression is a primary expression followed by zero or more predicates. An example of a filter expression to generate a sequence might look like the following:

```
(//Coordinates/*/text())
```

An important property of sequences is that a sequence of one item is indistinguishable from a singleton atomic value. So the sequence (1.0) is equivalent to the singleton atomic value 1.0.

Sequences come in three flavors: empty sequences, homogeneous sequences, and heterogeneous sequences. *Empty sequences* are sequences that contain no items. As mentioned before, the empty sequence is annotated with a set of empty parentheses, ().

Homogeneous sequences are sequences of one or more items of the same, or compatible, types. The examples already given are all examples of homogenous sequences.

Heterogeneous sequences are sequences of two or more items of incompatible types, or singleton atomic types and nodes. The following is an example of a heterogeneous sequence:

```
("Harry", 299792458, xs:date("2006-12-29Z"))
```

SQL Server does not allow heterogeneous sequences that mix nodes with singleton atomic values. Trying to use the following sequence results in an error:

```
(<tag/>, "you are it!")
```

■**Tip** *Singleton atomic values* are defined as values that are in the value space of the atomic types. The *value space* is the complete set of values that can be expressed with a given type. For instance, the complete value space for the xs:boolean type is true and false. Singleton atomic values are indivisible, for purposes of the XML Schema standard. Values that fall into this space are decimals, integers, dates, strings, and other primitive data types.

Primary expressions are the building blocks of XQuery. An expression in XQuery evaluates to a singleton atomic value or sequence. Primary expressions can be any of several different items:

- *Literals*, which include string and numeric data type literals. String literals can be enclosed in either single quotes or double quotes and may contain the XML-defined entity references >, <, &, ", and ', or Unicode character references such as € which represents the euro (€) symbol.

- *Variable references*, which are XML qualified names (QNames) preceded by a $ sign. A variable reference is defined by its local name. Note that SQL Server 2005 does not support variable references with a namespace URI prefix, which are defined under the W3C standard. An example of a variable reference is $count.

- *Parenthesized expressions*, which are expressions enclosed in parentheses. Parenthesized expressions are often used to force a specific order of operator evaluation. For instance, in the expression (3 + 4) * 2, the parentheses force the addition to be performed before the multiplication.

- *Context item expressions*, which are expressions that evaluate to the context item. The context item can be either a node or an atomic value.

- *Function calls*, which are composed of a QName followed by a list of arguments in parentheses. Function calls can reference either built-in functions or user-declared functions.

The query() Method

The query() method can be used to query xml variables or xml-typed columns in tables, as demonstrated in Listing 12-9.

Listing 12-9. *query() Method Against an xml Column*

```
SELECT Resume.query('//*:Name.First,
    //*:Name.Middle,
    //*:Name.Last,
    //*:Edu.Level')
FROM HumanResources.JobCandidate;
```

This simple XQuery query retrieves all first names, middle names, last names, and education levels for AdventureWorks job candidates. The results for one candidate look like this:

```
<p1:Name.First xmlns:p1 =
        "http://schemas.microsoft.com/sqlserver/2004/07/adventure-works/Resume">
    Shai
</p1:Name.First>
<p2:Name.Middle xmlns:p2 =
        "http://schemas.microsoft.com/sqlserver/2004/07/adventure-works/Resume" />
<p3:Name.Last xmlns:p3 =
        "http://schemas.microsoft.com/sqlserver/2004/07/adventure-works/Resume">
    Bassli
</p3:Name.Last>
<p4:Edu.Level xmlns:p4 =
        "http://schemas.microsoft.com/sqlserver/2004/07/adventure-works/Resume">
    Bachelor
</p4:Edu.Level>
```

The example demonstrates a few key XQuery concepts:

- The first is the // axis at the beginning of the location paths. This axis notation is defined as shorthand for /descendant-or-self::node()/, which will be described in more detail in the next section. This particular axis retrieves all nodes with a name that matches the location step, regardless of where it occurs in the XML being queried.

- In the example, the four node tests specified are Name.First, Name.Middle, Name.Last, and Edu.Level. All nodes with the names that match the node tests are returned no matter where they occur in the XML.

- The * namespace qualifier is a wildcard that matches any namespace occurring in the XML. Each node in the result node sequence includes an xmlns namespace declaration.

- This XQuery query is composed of four different paths denoting the four different node sequences to be returned. They are separated by commas.

I build on the previous example with a discussion of location paths.

Location Paths

The *location path* determines which nodes should be returned via XQuery. Following a location path from left to right generally takes you down and to the right in your XML node tree (there are exceptions, of course, which I discuss in the section on axis specifiers). If the first character of the path expression is a single solidus (/), the path expression is an absolute location path, meaning it starts at the root of the XML. Listing 12-10 demonstrates an absolute location path.

Tip The left-hand / actually stands for a conceptual root node that encompasses your XML input. The conceptual root node doesn't actually exist and cannot be viewed in your XML input, nor accessed and manipulated directly. It's this conceptual root node that allows XQuery to properly process XML fragments that are not well-formed (i.e., XML with multiple root nodes) as input.

Listing 12-10. *Absolute Location Path*

```
DECLARE @x XML;
SELECT @x = N'<?xml version = "1.0"?>
<Geocode>
    <Info ID = "1">
        <Coordinates Resolution = "High">
            <Latitude>37.859609</Latitude>
            <Longitude>-122.291673</Longitude>
        </Coordinates>
        <Location Type = "Business">
            <Name>APress, Inc.</Name>
        </Location>
    </Info>
    <Info ID = "2">
        <Coordinates Resolution = "High">
            <Latitude>37.423268</Latitude>
            <Longitude>-122.086345</Longitude>
        </Coordinates>
        <Location Type = "Business">
            <Name>Google, Inc.</Name>
        </Location>
    </Info>
</Geocode>';
SELECT @x.query(N'/Geocode/Info/Coordinates');
```

This code sample defines an `xml` variable and creates an XML document with geocoding data for a couple of well-known businesses. The XQuery uses an absolute location path to retrieve a node sequence of the latitude and longitude coordinates for the entire document. The results look like this:

```
<Coordinates Resolution="High">
  <Latitude>37.859609</Latitude>
  <Longitude>-122.291673</Longitude>
</Coordinates>
<Coordinates Resolution="High">
  <Latitude>37.423268</Latitude>
  <Longitude>-122.086345</Longitude>
</Coordinates>
```

A relative location path is specified by excluding the leading solidus, as in the following modification to Listing 12-10:

```
SELECT @x.query(N'Geocode/Info/Coordinates');
```

And, as previously mentioned, using a double solidus (//) in the lead position returns nodes that match the node test anywhere they occur in the document. This change to Listing 12-10 demonstrates this:

```
SELECT @x.query(N'//Geocode/Info/Coordinates');
```

In addition, the wildcard character * can be used to match any node by name. The following example retrieves the root node, all of the nodes on the next level, and all `Coordinates` nodes below that:

```
SELECT @x.query(N'//*/*/Coordinates');
```

Because the XML document in the example is a simple one, all the variations of Listing 12-10 return the same result.

The solidus character by itself without a node test is a special case path option. This returns everything from the root node down. Changing the `SELECT` in Listing 12-10 to the following demonstrates this:

```
SELECT @x.query(N'/');
```

Node Tests

The node tests in the previous example are simple name node tests. To match, the nodes must have the same names as those specified in the node tests. In addition to name node tests, SQL Server 2005 XQuery supports four node *kind* tests as listed in Table 12-1.

■**Tip** Keep in mind that XQuery, like XML, is case-sensitive. This means your node tests and other identifiers must all be of the proper case. The identifier PersonalID, for instance, does not match personalid in XML or in XQuery. Also note that your database collation case-sensitivity settings do not affect XQuery queries.

Table 12-1. *Supported Node Tests*

Node Kind Test	Description
comment()	Returns true for a comment node only.
node()	Returns true for any kind of node.
processing-instruction("*name*")	Returns true for a processing instruction node. *Name* is an optional string literal. If it is included, only processing instruction nodes with that name are returned; if not included, all processing instructions are returned.
text()	Returns true for a text node only.

SQL Server 2005 XQuery does not support the other node kind tests specified in the XQuery specification. Specifically the schema-element(), element(), attribute(), and document-node() kind tests are not implemented. The XQuery-specified node *type* tests that let you query nodes based on their associated type information are also not implemented in SQL Server 2005.

Listing 12-11 demonstrates use of the processing-instruction() node test to retrieve the processing instruction from the root level of a document for one product model.

Listing 12-11. *Sample processing-instruction() Node Test*

```
SELECT CatalogDescription.query(N'/processing-instruction()') AS Processing_Instr
FROM Production.ProductModel
WHERE ProductModelID = 19;
```

The following is the result of this query:

```
<?xml-stylesheet href="ProductDescription.xsl" type="text/xsl"?>
```

The sample can be modified to retrieve all XML comments from the source by using the comment() node test, as in Listing 12-12.

Listing 12-12. Sample comment() Node Test

```
SELECT CatalogDescription.query(N'//comment()') AS Comments
FROM Production.ProductModel
WHERE ProductModelID = 19;
```

The results of this query look like the following:

```
<!-- add one or more of these elements... one for each specific product in
this product model -->
<!-- add any tags in <specifications> -->
```

Listing 12-13 demonstrates use of the node() node test to retrieve the specifications for product model 19.

Listing 12-13. *Sample node() Node Test*

```
SELECT CatalogDescription.query(N'//*:Specifications/node()') AS Specifications
FROM Production.ProductModel
WHERE ProductModelID = 19;
```

Here is the result of this query (formatted for easy reading):

```
These are the product specifications.
<Material>Almuminum Alloy</Material>
<Color>Available in most colors</Color>
<ProductLine>Mountain bike</ProductLine>
<Style>Unisex</Style>
<RiderExperience>Advanced to Professional riders</RiderExperience>
```

Namespaces

You might notice that the first node of the previous result is not enclosed in XML tags. This node is a text node located in the `<Specifications>` node being queried. You might also notice that the * namespace wildcard mentioned previously is used in this query. This is used because namespaces are declared in the XML of the `CatalogDescription` column. Specifically the root node declaration looks like this:

```
<p1:ProductDescription xmlns:p1="http://schemas.microsoft.com/sqlserver/2004/07/➥
    adventure-works/ProductModelDescription"
    xmlns:wm="http://schemas.microsoft.com/sqlserver/2004/07/adventure-➥
    works/ProductModelWarrAndMain"
    xmlns:wf="http://www.adventure-works.com/schemas/OtherFeatures"
    xmlns:html="http://www.w3.org/1999/xhtml"
    ProductModelID="19"
    ProductModelName="Mountain 100">
```

The `Specifications` node of the XML document is declared with the `p1` namespace in the document. Not using a namespace in the query at all, as shown in Listing 12-14, results in an empty sequence being returned (no matching nodes).

Listing 12-14. *Querying the CatalogDescription with No Namespaces*

```
SELECT CatalogDescription.query(N'//Specifications/node()') AS Specifications
FROM Production.ProductModel
WHERE ProductModelID = 19;
```

In addition to the wildcard namespace specifier, you can use the XQuery prolog to define namespaces for use in your query. Listing 12-15 shows how the previous example can be modified to include the `p1` namespace with a namespace declaration in the prolog.

Listing 12-15. *Prolog Namespace Declaration*

```
SELECT CatalogDescription.query(N'declare namespace
    p1="http://schemas.microsoft.com/sqlserver/2004/07/adventure-works/
    ProductModelDescription";
    //p1:Specifications/node()')
FROM Production.ProductModel
WHERE ProductModelID = 19;
```

The keywords `declare namespace` allow you to declare specific namespaces that will be used in the query. Alternatively you can declare a default namespace as in Listing 12-16.

Listing 12-16. *Prolog Default Namespace Declaration*

```
SELECT CatalogDescription.query(N'declare default element namespace
    "http://schemas.microsoft.com/sqlserver/2004/07/adventure-works/➥
    ProductModelDescription";
    //Specifications/node()')
FROM Production.ProductModel
WHERE ProductModelID = 19;
```

Declaring a default namespace with the declare default element namespace keywords allows you to eliminate namespace prefixes in your location paths (for steps that fall within the scope of the default namespace, of course). The result of Listing 12-15 and Listing 12-16 is the same as the result of the sample in Listing 12-13:

```
These are the product specifications.
<Material>Almuminum Alloy</Material>
<Color>Available in most colors</Color>
<ProductLine>Mountain bike</ProductLine>
<Style>Unisex</Style>
<RiderExperience>Advanced to Professional riders</RiderExperience>
```

SQL Server has several predeclared namespaces that can be used in your queries. With the exception of the xml namespace you can redeclare these namespaces in your queries. The predeclared namespaces are listed in Table 12-2.

Table 12-2. *SQL Server Predeclared XQuery Namespaces*

Namespace	URI	Description
fn	http://www.w3.org/2005/xpath-functions	XQuery 1.0, XPath 2.0, XSLT 2.0 functions and operators namespace
sqltypes	http://schemas.microsoft.com/sqlserver/2004/sqltypes	SQL Server 2005 to base type mapping namespace
xdt	http://www.w3.org/2005/xpath-datatypes/	XQuery 1.0/XPath 2.0 data types namespace
xml	http://www.w3.org/XML/1998/namespace	Default XML namespace
xs	http://www.w3.org/2001/XMLSchema	XML Schema namespace
xsi	http://www.w3.org/2001/XMLSchema-instance	XML Schema instance namespace

The W3C-specified local functions namespace, `local` (`http://www.w3.org/2005/`
`xquery-local-functions`), is not predeclared in SQL Server.

Another useful namespace is `http://www.w3.org/2005/xqt-errors`, which is the namespace for XPath and XQuery function and operator error codes. In the XQuery documentation, this URI is bound to the namespace `err`, though this is not mandatory.

Axis Specifiers

Axis specifiers define the direction of movement of a location path step relative to the current context node. The XQuery standard defines several axis specifiers, which can be defined as *forward axes* or *reverse axes*. SQL Server 2005 supports a subset of these axis specifiers listed in Table 12-3.

Table 12-3. *SQL 2005 Supported Axis Specifiers*

Axis Name	Direction	Description
`child::`	Forward	Retrieves the children of the current context node.
`descendant::`	Forward	Retrieves all descendents of the current context node, recursive style. This includes children of the current node, children of the children, etc.
`self::`	Forward	Contains just the current context node.
`descendant-or-self::`	Forward	Contains the context node and children of the current context node.
`attribute::`	Forward	Returns the specified attribute(s) of the current context node. This axis specifier may be abbreviated as `@`.
`parent::`	Reverse	Returns the parent of the current context node. This axis specifier may be abbreviated as "`..`".

In addition, the primary expression "`.`" is the *context-item expression*. It returns the current context item (which can be either a node or an atomic value).

■**Note** The following axes, defined as *optional axes* by the XQuery 1.0 specification, are not supported by SQL Server 2005: `following-sibling::`, `following::`, `ancestor::`, `preceding-sibling::`, `preceding::`, `ancestor-or-self::`, and the deprecated `namespace::` axis. If you are porting XQuery queries from other sources, they may have to be modified to avoid these axis specifiers.

In all of the examples so far, the axis has been omitted, and the default axis of `child::` is used in each step. Because `child::` is the default axis, the two queries in Listing 12-17 are equivalent.

Listing 12-17. *Query With and Without Default Axes*

```
SELECT CatalogDescription.query(N'//*:Specifications/node()') AS Specifications
FROM Production.ProductModel
WHERE ProductModelID = 19;


SELECT CatalogDescription.query(N'//child::*:Specifications/child::node()')
    AS Specifications
FROM Production.ProductModel
WHERE ProductModelID = 19;
```

Listing 12-18 demonstrates the use of the parent:: axis to retrieve Coordinates nodes from the sample XML.

Listing 12-18. *Sample Using the parent:: Axis*

```
DECLARE @x XML;
SELECT @x = N'<?xml version = "1.0"?>
<Geocode>
    <Info ID = "1">
        <Coordinates Resolution = "High">
            <Latitude>37.859609</Latitude>
            <Longitude>-122.291673</Longitude>
        </Coordinates>
        <Location Type = "Business">
            <Name>APress, Inc.</Name>
        </Location>
    </Info>
    <Info ID = "2">
        <Coordinates Resolution = "High">
            <Latitude>37.423268</Latitude>
            <Longitude>-122.086345</Longitude>
        </Coordinates>
        <Location Type = "Business">
            <Name>Google, Inc.</Name>
        </Location>
    </Info>
</Geocode>';
SELECT @x.query(N'//Location/parent::node()/Coordinates');
```

This particular XQuery locates all Location nodes, then uses the parent:: axis to retrieve the parent nodes (Info nodes), and finally returns the Coordinates nodes, which are children of the Info nodes. The result looks like this:

```
<Coordinates Resolution="High">
  <Latitude>37.859609</Latitude>
  <Longitude>-122.291673</Longitude>
</Coordinates>
<Coordinates Resolution="High">
  <Latitude>37.423268</Latitude>
  <Longitude>-122.086345</Longitude>
</Coordinates>
```

Dynamic XML Construction

We previously talked about the history of XQuery 1.0. It's based on XPath 2.0, which is in turn based on XPath 1.0. The XPath 1.0 standard was designed to consolidate the best features of both XSLT and XPointer. One of the benefits of XQuery's lineage is the ability to query XML and dynamically construct well-formed XML documents from the results. Consider the example in Listing 12-19.

Listing 12-19. *XQuery Dynamic XML Construction*

```
DECLARE @x XML;
SELECT @x = N'<?xml version = "1.0"?>
<Geocode>
    <Info ID = "1">
        <Location Type = "Business">
            <Name>APress, Inc.</Name>
        </Location>
    </Info>
    <Info ID = "2">
        <Location Type = "Business">
            <Name>Google, Inc.</Name>
        </Location>
    </Info>
</Geocode>';
SELECT @x.query(N'<Companies>
    {
        //Info/Location/Name
    }
</Companies>');
```

This query returns an XML document that looks like this:

```
<Companies>
    <Name>APress, Inc.</Name>
    <Name>Google, Inc.</Name>
</Companies>
```

The dynamic construction in the XQuery example looks like this:

```
<Companies>
    {
        //Info/Location/Name
    }
</Companies>
```

The `<Companies>` opening and closing tags in the XQuery act as the root tag for the resulting XML document. The content of the query, known as the *content expression*, consists of the location path to retrieve the nodes. The content expression is wrapped in curly braces inside the `<Companies>` tags:

```
    {
        //Info/Location/Name
    }
```

■**Tip** Need to output curly braces in your XML output? You can escape them by doubling them up in your query: {{ and }}.

You can also use the `element` and `attribute` dynamic constructors to build your XML result, as demonstrated in Listing 12-20.

Listing 12-20. *Element and Attribute Dynamic Constructors*

```
DECLARE @x XML;
SELECT @x = N'<?xml version = "1.0"?>
<Geocode>
    <Info ID = "1">
        <Location Type = "Business">
            <Name>APress, Inc.</Name>
            <Address>
```

```
                    <Street>2560 Ninth St, Ste 219</Street>
                    <City>Berkeley</City>
                    <State>CA</State>
                    <Zip>94710-2500</Zip>
                    <Country>US</Country>
                </Address>
            </Location>
        </Info>
</Geocode>';
SELECT @x.query(N'element Companies
    {
        element FirstCompany
        {
            attribute CompanyID
            {
                (//Info/@ID)[1]
            },
            (//Info/Location/Name)[1]
        }
    }');
```

This query uses dynamic constructors to build the following XML result:

```
<Companies>
    <FirstCompany CompanyID="1">
        <Name>APress, Inc.</Name>
    </FirstCompany>
</Companies>
```

The element Companies dynamic element constructor creates the root <Companies>
node. The FirstCompany node is constructed as a child node:

```
element Companies
{
    element FirstCompany
    {
        ...
    }
}
```

The content expressions of the FirstCompany elements are where the real action takes place:

```
element FirstCompany
{
    attribute CompanyID
    {
        (//Info/@ID)[1]
    },
    (//Info/Location/Name)[1]
}
```

The CompanyID dynamic attribute constructor retrieves the ID attribute from the first Info node. The predicate [1] in the path ensures that only the first //Info/@ID is returned. This path location could also be written like this:

```
//Info[1]/@ID
```

The second path location retrieves the first Name node for the first Location node of the first Info node. Again the [1] predicate ensures only the first matching node is returned. The path is equivalent to the following:

```
//Info[1]/Location[1]/Name[1]
```

To retrieve the second node, change the predicate to [2], and so on.

Tip By definition, a predicate that evaluates to a numeric singleton value (such as the integer constant 1) is referred to as a *numeric predicate*. The predicate truth value is true only when the context position is equal to the numeric predicate expression. When the numeric predicate is 3, for instance, the predicate truth value is true only for the third context position. This is a handy way to limit the results of an XQuery query to a single specific node.

XQuery Comments

XQuery comments (not to be confused with *XML comment nodes*) are used to document your queries inline. They can be included in XQuery expressions by enclosing them with the (: and :) symbols (just like the smiley face emoticon). Comments can be used in your XQuery expressions anywhere ignorable white space is allowed, and they can be nested. Comments have no effect on query processing. The following example modifies the query in Listing 12-19 to include XQuery comments:

```
SELECT @x.query(N'<Companies>  (: This is the root node :)
    {
        //Info/Location/Name (: Retrieves all company names (: ALL of them :) :)
    }
</Companies>');
```

You will see comments in some of the examples later in this chapter.

Data Types

XQuery maintains the string value and typed value for all nodes in the referenced XML. The type of a node is defined in the XML schema collection associated with the xml variable or column. As an example, the built-in AdventureWorks Production.ManuInstructionsSchemaCollection XML schema collection defines the LocationID attribute of the Location element as an xsd:integer:

```
<xsd:attribute name="LocationID" type="xsd:integer" use="required" />
```

Every instance of this attribute in the XML of the Instructions column of the Production.ProductModel table must conform to the requirements of this data type. Typed data can also be manipulated according to the functions and operators defined for this type. For untyped XML, the typed data is defined as xdt:untypedAtomic. A listing of XDM data types available to SQL Server via XQuery is given in Appendix B.

Predicates

An XQuery *predicate* is an expression that evaluates to one of the xs:boolean values true or false. In XQuery predicates are used to filter the results of a node sequence, discarding nodes from the sequence that don't meet the specified criteria. Predicates limit the results by converting the result of the predicate expression into an xs:boolean value, referred to as the *predicate truth value*. The predicate truth value is determined for each item of the input sequence according to the following rules:

1. If the type of the expression is numeric, the predicate truth value is true if the value of the predicate expression is equal to the context position; otherwise, for a numeric predicate, the predicate truth value is false.

2. If the type of the expression is a string, the predicate is false if the length of the expression is 0. For a string type expression with a length greater than 0, the predicate truth value is true.

3. If the type of the expression is xs:boolean, the predicate truth value is the value of the expression.

4. If the expression results in an empty sequence, the predicate truth value is false.

5. If the value of the predicate expression is a node sequence, the predicate truth value is true if the sequence contains at least one node; otherwise it is false.

Queries that include a predicate return only nodes in a sequence for which the predicate truth value evaluates to true. Predicates are composed of expressions, conveniently referred to as *predicate expressions*, enclosed in square brackets ([ ]). You can specify multiple predicates in a path, and they are evaluated in order of occurrence from left to right.

■**Note** The XQuery specification says that multiple predicates are evaluated from left to right, but it also gives some wiggle room for vendors to perform predicate evaluations in other orders, allowing them to take advantage of vendor-specific features such as indexes and other optimizations. You don't have to worry too much about the internal evaluation order of predicates though. No matter what order predicates are actually evaluated in, the end results have to be the same as if the predicates were evaluated left to right.

Value Comparison Operators

As mentioned, the basic function of predicates is to filter results. Results are filtered by specified comparisons, and XQuery offers a rich set of comparison operators. These operators fall into three main groups: value comparison operators, general comparison operators, and node comparison operators. Value comparison operators compare singleton atomic values only. Trying to compare sequences with the value comparison operators results in an error. The value comparison operators are listed in Table 12-4.

Table 12-4. *Value Comparison Operators*

Operator	Description
eq	Equality operator
ne	Not equals operator
lt	Less than operator
le	Less than or equal to operator
gt	Greater than operator
ge	Greater than or equal to operator

Value comparisons follow a specific set of rules:

1. The operands are atomized.

2. If either atomized operand is an empty sequence, the result is an empty sequence.

3. If either atomized operand is a sequence with a length greater than 1, an error is raised.

4. If either atomized operand is of type xs:untypedAtomic, it is cast to xs:string.

5. If the operands have compatible types, they are compared using the appropriate operator. If the comparison of the two operands using the chosen operator evaluates to true, the result is true; otherwise the result is false. If the operands have incompatible types, an error is thrown.

Consider the value comparison examples in Listing 12-21.

Listing 12-21. *Value Comparison Examples*

```
DECLARE @x XML;
SELECT @x = N'<?xml version = "1.0" ?>
<Animal>
    Cat
</Animal>';
SELECT @x.query(N'9 eq 9.0                     (: 9 is equal to 9.0 :)');
SELECT @x.query(N'4 gt 3                        (: 4 is greater than 3 :)');
SELECT @x.query(N'(/Animal/text())[1] lt "Dog" (: Cat is less than Dog :)') ;
```

The result of these queries is the following:

```
true
true
true
```

Listing 12-22 demonstrates a value comparison between two incompatible types.

Listing 12-22. *Incompatible Type Value Comparison*

```
DECLARE @x XML;
SELECT @x = N'';
SELECT @x.query(N'3.141592 eq "Pi"') ;
```

The result of comparing the xs:decimal value 3.141592 to the xs:string value Pi is an error because xs:decimal and xs:string are incompatible types:

```
Msg 2234, Level 16, State 1, Line 4
XQuery [query()]: The operator "eq" cannot be applied to "xs:decimal" and
"xs:string" operands.
```

General Comparison Operators

General comparisons are existential comparisons that work on operand sequences of any length. *Existential* simply means that if one atomized value from the first operand sequence fulfills a value comparison with at least one atomized value from the second operand sequence, the result is true. The general comparison operators will look familiar to programmers who are versed in other languages, particularly C# and other C-style languages. They are listed in Table 12-5.

Table 12-5. *General Comparison Operators*

Operator	Description
=	Equal
!=	Not equal
<	Less than
>	Greater than
<=	Less than or equal
>=	Greater than or equal

Listing 12-23 demonstrates a selection of general comparisons.

Listing 12-23. *General Comparison Examples*

```
DECLARE @x xml;
SELECT @x = '';
SELECT @x.query('(3.141592, 1) = (2, 3.141592)'              (: true :) ');
SELECT @x.query('(1.0, 2.0, 3.0) = 1'                        (: true :) ');
SELECT @x.query('("Joe", "Harold") < "Adam"'                 (: false :) ');
SELECT @x.query('xs:date("1999-01-01Z") < xs:date("2006-01-01Z")'   (: true :)');
```

The result is the following:

```
true
true
false
true
```

Here's how the general comparison operators work. The first query compares the sequence (3.141592, 1) and (2, 3.141592) using the = operator. The comparison atomizes the two operand sequences and compares them using the rules for the equivalent value comparison operators. Since the atomic value 3.141592 exists in both sequences, the equality test result is true.

The second example compares the sequence (1.0, 2.0, 3.0) to the atomic value 1. The atomic values 1.0 and 1 are compatible types and are equal, so the equality test result is true. The third query returns false because neither of the atomic values "Joe" or "Harold" are lexically less than the atomic value "Adam".

The final example compares two xs:date values. Since the date 1999-01-01 is less than the date 2006-01-01, the result is true.

Unlike the homogenous sequences in Listing 12-22, a heterogeneous sequence is one that combines nodes and atomic values, or atomic values of incompatible types (such as xs:string and xs:decimal). Trying to perform a general comparison with a heterogeneous sequence causes an error on SQL Server. Listing 12-24 demonstrates.

Listing 12-24. *General Comparison with Heterogeneous Sequence*

```
DECLARE @x xml;
SELECT @x = '';
SELECT @x.query('(xs:date("2006-10-09Z"), 6.02E23) > xs:date("2007-01-01Z")');
```

The error generated by Listing 12-23 looks like the following:

```
Msg 9311, Level 16, State 1, Line 3
XQuery [query()]: Heterogeneous sequences are not allowed in '>', found 'xs:double'
and 'xs:date'.
```

XQUERY DATE FORMAT

SQL Server's XQuery implementation has a special requirement concerning `xs:date`, `xs:time`, `xs:dateTime`, and derived types. Per the subset of the ISO 8601 standard that SQL Server uses, date and time values must include a time zone. SQL Server strictly enforces this rule. Not including a time zone in values of one of these types in an XQuery expression will result in a "Static simple type validation" error. The time zone must follow a date or time value and can be either of the following:

1. The capital letter *Z* which stands for the *zero meridian* in UTC (Coordinated Universal Time). The zero meridian runs through Greenwich, England.

2. An offset from the zero meridian in the format [+/-]hh:mm. For instance, the U.S. Eastern Time zone would be indicated as -05:00.

Here are a few sample ISO 8601 formatted dates and times acceptable to SQL Server, with descriptions:

- *1999-05-16Z*: May 16, 1999, no time, UTC time zone

- *09:15:00-05:00*: No date, 9:15 AM, U.S. and Canada Eastern Time zone

- *2003-12-25T20:00:00-08:00*: December 25, 2003, 8:00 PM, U.S. and Canada Pacific Time zone

- *2004-07-06T23:59:59.987+01:00*: July 6, 2004, 11:59:59.987 PM (.987 is fractional seconds), Central European Time zone

If you are trying to run third-party samples from other books (or even from the XQuery standard), you may have to modify `xs:date` values to include a time zone. Keep this in mind when building new XQuery expressions or converting existing expressions to SQL Server.

SQL Server does not allow heterogeneous sequences that mix nodes and atomic values, as demonstrated in Listing 12-25.

Listing 12-25. *Mixing Nodes and Atomic Values in Sequences*

```
DECLARE @x xml;
SELECT @x = '';
SELECT @x.query('(1, <myNode>Testing</myNode>)');
```

Trying to mix and match nodes and atomic values in a sequence like this results in an error message like the following:

```
Msg 2210, Level 16, State 1, Line 3
XQuery [query()]: Heterogeneous sequences are not allowed: found 'xs:integer +'
and 'element(myNode,xdt:untyped)'
```

Node Comparisons

The third type of comparison that XQuery allows is the *node comparison*. Node comparisons allow you to compare XML nodes in document order. The node comparison operators are listed in Table 12-6.

Table 12-6. *Node Comparison Operators*

Operator	Description
is	Node identity equality
<<	Left node precedes right node
>>	Left node follows right node

The is operator compares two nodes to each other and returns true if the left node is the same node as the right node. Note that this is not a test of the equality of node contents but rather of the actual nodes themselves. Consider the sample node comparisons in Listing 12-26.

Listing 12-26. *Node Comparison Samples*

```
DECLARE @x xml;
SET @x = N'<?xml version = "1.0"?>
<Root>
    <NodeA>Test Node</NodeA>
    <NodeA>Test Node</NodeA>
    <NodeB>Test Node</NodeB>
</Root>';
SELECT @x.query('((/Root/NodeA)[1] is (//NodeA)[1])        (: true :)');
SELECT @x.query('((/Root/NodeA)[1] is (/Root/NodeA)[2])    (: false :)');
SELECT @x.query('((/Root/NodeA)[2] << (/Root/NodeB)[1])    (: true :)');
```

The results are the following:

```
true
false
true
```

The first query uses the is operator to compare (/Root/NodeA)[1] to itself. The [1] numeric predicate at the end of the path ensures that only a single node is returned for comparison. The right-hand and left-hand expressions must both evaluate to a singleton or empty sequence. The result of this comparison is true only because (/Root/NodeA)[1] is the exact same node returned by the (//NodeA)[1] path on the right-hand side of the operator.

The second query compares (/Root/NodeA)[1] with (/Root/NodeA)[2]. Even though the two nodes have the same name and the same content, they are in fact different nodes. Because they are different nodes, the is operator returns false.

The final query retrieves the second NodeA node with the path (/Root/NodeA)[2]. Then it uses the << operator to determine if this node precedes the NodeB node from the path (/Root/NodeB)[1]. Since the second NodeA precedes the NodeB in document order, the result of this comparison is true.

A node comparison results in an xs:boolean value or to an empty sequence if one of the operands results in an empty sequence. This is demonstrated in Listing 12-27.

Listing 12-27. *Node Comparison That Evaluates to an Empty Sequence*

```
DECLARE @x xml;
SELECT @x = N'<?xml version = "1.0"?>
<Root>
    <NodeA>Test Node</NodeA>
</Root>';
SELECT @x.query('((/Root/NodeA)[1] << (/Root/NodeZ)[1])    (: empty sequence :)');
```

The result of the node comparison is an empty sequence because the right-hand path expression evaluates to an empty sequence (because no node named NodeZ exists in the XML document).

Conditional Expressions (if . . . then . . . else)

As shown in the previous examples, XQuery returns xs:boolean values or empty sequences as the result of comparisons. XQuery also provides the conditional if...then...else expression to return an expression based on the xs:boolean value of another expression. The format for the XQuery conditional expression is the following:

```
if (test-expression)
then then-expression
else else-expression
```

In this syntax *test-expression* represents the conditional expression that is evaluated, the result of which will determine the returned result. When evaluating *test-expression*, the following rules apply:

1. If *test-expression* results in an empty sequence, the result is false.

2. If *test-expression* results in an xs:boolean value, the result is the xs:boolean value of the expression.

3. If *test-expression* results in a sequence of one or more nodes, the result is true.

4. If these fail, a static error is raised.

If *test-expression* evaluates to true, *then-expression* is returned. If *test-expression* evaluates to false, *else-expression* is returned.

The XQuery conditional is a declarative expression. Unlike the C# if...else statement or VB's If...Then...Else construct, XQuery's conditional if...then...else doesn't represent a branch in procedural logic or a change in program flow. It acts like a function that accepts a conditional expression as input and returns an expression as a result. In this respect, XQuery's if . . . then . . . else has more in common with the SQL CASE expression than with the if statement in procedural languages. In the XQuery if . . . then . . . else, syntax parentheses are required around the test-expression, and the else keyword is mandatory.

Arithmetic Expressions

XQuery arithmetic expressions support the usual mathematical operations found in most programming languages, including the following:

- Multiplication (*)

- Division (div)

- Addition (+)

- Subtraction (-)

- Modulo (mod)

INTEGER DIVISION IN XQUERY

SQL Server 2005 XQuery does not support the idiv integer division operator. The XQuery specification defines idiv for variables $x and $y as equivalent to the expression $x div $y cast as xs:integer. If you need to convert XQuery code that uses the idiv operator to SQL Server, you can use the following idiv-equivalent expression:

($arg1 div $arg2) cast as xs:integer?

XQuery also supports the unary plus (+) and unary minus (-) operators. Because the solidus character (forward slash) is used as a path separator in XQuery, the division operator is specified as div. The modulo operator, mod, returns the remainder of division.

Of the supported operators, unary plus and unary minus operators have the highest precedence. Multiplication, division, and modulo are the next highest. Binary addition and subtraction have the lowest precedence. Parentheses can be used to force the evaluation order of mathematical operations.

XQuery Functions

XQuery provides several built-in functions defined in the XQuery Functions and Operators specification (sometimes referred to as "F&O"), which is available at http://www.w3.org/TR/xquery-operators/. The built-in functions are in the predeclared namespace fn:.

Tip The fn: namespace does not have to be specified when calling a built-in function. Some people leave it off to improve readability of their code.

SQL Server 2005–supported built-in XQuery functions are listed in Table 12-7.

Table 12-7. *Supported Built-In XQuery Functions*

Function	Description
fn:avg(x)	Returns the average of the sequence of numbers x. Example: fn:avg((10, 20, 30, 40, 50)) returns 30.
fn:ceiling(n)	Returns the smallest number without a fractional part that is not less than n. Example: fn:ceiling(1.1) returns 2.
fn:concat(s_1, s_2, ...)	Concatenates zero or more strings and returns the concatenated string as a result. Example: fn:concat("hi", ",", "how are you?") returns "hi, how are you?".
fn:contains(s_1, s_2)	Returns true if the string s_1 contains the string s_2. Example: fn:contains("fish", "is") returns true.
fn:count(x)	Returns the number of items in the sequence x. Example: fn:count((1, 2, 4, 8, 16)) returns 5.
fn:data(a)	Returns the typed value of each item specified by the argument a. Example: fn:data((3.141592, "hello")) returns "3.141592 hello".
fn:distinct-values (x)	Returns the sequence x with duplicate values removed. Example: fn:distinct-values((1, 2, 3, 4, 5, 4, 5)) returns "1 2 3 4 5".
fn:empty(i)	Returns true if i is an empty sequence; returns false otherwise. Example: fn:empty((1, 2, 3)) returns false.
fn:expanded-QName(u, l)	Returns an xs:QName. The arguments u and l represent the xs:QName's namespace URI and local name, respectively.
fn:false()	Returns the xs:boolean value false. Example: fn:false() returns false.
fn:floor(n)	Returns the largest number without a fractional part that is not greater than n. Example: fn:floor(1.1) returns 1.
fn:id(x)	Returns the sequence of element nodes with ID values that match one or more of the IDREF values supplied in x. The parameter x is treated as a white space–separated sequence of tokens.
fn:last()	Returns the index number of the last item in the sequence being processed. The first index in the sequence has an index of 1.
fn:local-name(n)	Returns the local name, without the namespace URI, of the specified node n.
fn:local-name-from-QName(q)	Returns the local name part of the xs:QName argument q. The value returned is an xs:NCName.
fn:max(x)	Returns the item with the highest value from the sequence x. Example: fn:max((1.0, 2.5, 9.3, 0.3, -4.2)) returns 9.3.
fn:min(x)	Returns the item with the lowest value from the sequence x. Example: fn:min(("x", "q", "u", "e", "r", "y")) returns "e".

Function	Description
fn:not(*b*)	Returns true if the effective Boolean value of *b* is false; returns false if the effective Boolean value is true. Example: fn:not(xs:boolean("true")) returns false.
fn:namespace-uri(*n*)	Returns the namespace URI of the specified node *n*.
fn:namespace-uri-from-QName(*q*)	Returns the namespace URI part of the xs:QName argument *q*. The value returned is an xs:NCName.
fn:number(*n*)	Returns the numeric value of the node indicated by *n*. Example: fn:number("/Root/NodeA[1]").
fn:position()	Returns the index number of the context item in the sequence currently being processed.
fn:round(*n*)	Returns the number closest to *n* that does not have a fractional part. Example: fn:round(10.5) returns 11.
fn:string(*a*)	Returns the value of the argument *a*, expressed as an xs:string. Example: fn:string(3.141592) returns "3.141592".
fn:string-length(*s*)	Returns the length of the string *s*. Example: fn:string-length("abcdefghij") returns 10.
fn:substring(*s*, *m*, *n*)	Returns *n* characters from the string *s*, beginning at position *m*. If *n* is not specified, all characters from position *m* to the end of the string are returned. The first character in the string is position 1. Example: fn:substring("Money", 2, 3) returns "one".
fn:sum(*x*)	Returns the sum of the sequence of numbers in *x*. Example: fn:sum((1, 4, 9, 16, 25)) returns 55.
fn:true()	Returns the xs:boolean value true. Example: fn:true() returns true.

In addition, two functions from the sql: namespace are supported. The sql:column("*column_name*") function allows you to expose and bind SQL Server relational column data in XQuery queries. Listing 12-28 demonstrates the sql:column function.

Listing 12-28. *The sql:column Function*

```
DECLARE @x xml;
SELECT @x = N'';
SELECT @x.query(N'<Name>
    <ID>{ sql:column("p.ContactID") }</ID>
    <FullName>
        { sql:column("p.FirstName"),
        sql:column("p.MiddleName"),
        sql:column("p.LastName") }
```

```
    </FullName>
</Name>')
FROM Person.Contact p
WHERE p.ContactID <= 5
ORDER BY p.ContactID;
```

The result of this example is a set of XML documents with the ContactID and full name of the first five contacts from the Person.Contact table:

```
<Name><ID>1</ID><FullName>Gustavo Achong</FullName></Name>
<Name><ID>2</ID><FullName>Catherine R. Abel</FullName></Name>
<Name><ID>3</ID><FullName>Kim Abercrombie</FullName></Name>
<Name><ID>4</ID><FullName>Humberto Acevedo</FullName></Name>
<Name><ID>5</ID><FullName>Pilar Ackerman</FullName></Name>
```

The sql:variable("*variable_name*") function goes another step, allowing you to expose T-SQL variables in XQuery. Listing 12-29 gives an example of combining the sql:column and sql:variable functions in one XQuery query.

Listing 12-29. *XQuery sql:column and sql:variable Functions Example*

```
/* 10% discount */
DECLARE @discount NUMERIC(3, 2);
SELECT @discount = 0.10;
DECLARE @x xml;
SELECT @x = '';
SELECT @x.query('<Product>
    <Model-ID> { sql:column("ProductModelID") }</Model-ID>
        <Name> { sql:column("Name") }</Name>
        <Price> { sql:column("ListPrice") } </Price>
        <DiscountPrice>
            { sql:column("ListPrice") -
            (sql:column("ListPrice") * sql:variable("@discount") ) }
        </DiscountPrice>
</Product>
')
FROM Production.Product p
WHERE ProductModelID = 30;
```

The XQuery generates XML documents using the `sql:column` function to retrieve the `ListPrice` from the `Production.Product` table. It also uses the `sql:variable` function to calculate a discount price for the items retrieved. This is what a sample of the results looks like (formatted for easier reading):

```
<Product>
    <Model-ID>30</Model-ID>
    <Name>Road-650 Red, 58</Name>
    <Price>782.99</Price>
    <DiscountPrice>704.691</DiscountPrice>
</Product>
<Product>
    <Model-ID>30</Model-ID>
    <Name>Road-650 Red, 60</Name>
    <Price>782.99</Price>
    <DiscountPrice>704.691</DiscountPrice>
</Product>
...
```

Constructors and Casting

XQuery types provide constructor functions to dynamically create instances of the type. The constructor functions are of the format: `xs:TYP(value)`, where `TYP` is the XQuery type. Most of the XQuery types have constructor functions; however, the following types do not have constructors in SQL Server XQuery: `xs:yearMonthDuration`, `xs:dayTimeDuration`, `xs:QName`, `xs:NMTOKEN`, and `xs:NOTATION`.

The following are examples of XQuery constructor functions:

```
xs:boolean("1")     (: returns true :)
xs:integer(1234)    (: returns 1234 :)
xs:float(9.8723E+3) (: returns 9872.3 :)
xs:NCName("my-id")  (: returns the NCName "my-id" :)
```

Numeric types can be implicitly cast to their base types (or other numeric types) by XQuery to ensure proper results of calculations. The process of implicit casting is known as *type promotion*. For instance, in the following sample expression, the `xs:integer` type value is implicitly cast to a `xs:decimal` to complete the calculation:

```
xs:integer(100) + xs:decimal(100.99)
```

> **Note** Only numeric types can be implicitly cast. String and other types cannot be implicitly cast by XQuery.

Explicit casting is performed by using the cast as keywords. Examples of explicit casting include the following:

```
xs:string("98d3f4") cast as xs:hexBinary?   (: 98d3f4 :)
100 cast as xs:double?                       (: 1.0E+2 :)
"0" cast as xs:boolean?                       (: true :)
```

The ? after the target data type is the *optional occurrence indicator*. It is used to indicate that an empty sequence is allowed. SQL Server XQuery requires the ? after the cast as expression. SQL Server BOL provides a detailed description of the XQuery type casting rules at http://msdn2.microsoft.com/en-us/library/ms191231.aspx.

The instance of Boolean operator allows you to determine the type of a singleton value. The operator takes a singleton value on its left-hand side, and a type on its right. The xs:boolean value true is returned if the atomic value represents an instance of the specified type. The following examples demonstrate the instance of operator:

```
10 instance of xs:integer     (: returns true :)
100 instance of xs:decimal    (: returns true :)
"hello" instance of xs:bytes  (: returns false :)
```

The ? optional occurrence indicator can be appended after the data type to indicate that the empty sequence is allowable (though it is not mandatory as with the cast operator), as in this example:

```
9.8273 instance of xs:double?    (: returns true :)
```

FLWOR Expressions

FLWOR expressions provide a way to iterate over a sequence and bind intermediate results to variables. *FLWOR* is an acronym for the keywords that define this type of expression: for, let, where, order by, and return. This section discusses XQuery's powerful FLWOR expressions.

> **Note** SQL Server 2005 XQuery does not support the let keyword.

for and return

The for and return keywords have long been a part of XPath, though in not nearly so powerful a form as the XQuery FLWOR expression. The for keyword specifies that a variable is iteratively bound to the results of the specified path expression. The result of this iterative binding process is known as a *tuple stream*. The XQuery for expression is roughly analogous to the T-SQL SELECT statement. The for keyword must, at a minimum, have a matching return clause after it. The sample in Listing 12-30 demonstrates a basic for expression.

Listing 12-30. *Basic XQuery for . . . return*

```
SELECT CatalogDescription.query(N'declare namespace ns =
    "http://schemas.microsoft.com/sqlserver/2004/07/adventure-works/➥
        ProductModelDescription";
    for $spec in //ns:ProductDescription/ns:Specifications/*
    return $spec/text()') AS Description
FROM Production.ProductModel
WHERE ProductModelID = 19;
```

The for clause iterates through all elements returned by the path expression. It then binds the elements to the $spec variable. The tuple stream that is bound to $spec consists of the following:

```
$spec = <Material>Almuminum Alloy</Material>
$spec = <Color>Available in most colors</Color>
$spec = <ProductLine>Mountain bike</ProductLine>
$spec = <Style>Unisex</Style>
$spec = <RiderExperience>Advanced to Professional riders</RiderExperience>
```

The return clause applies the text() function to the variable to return the text node of each element as it is bound to $spec. The results look like this (the results are not produced with a line feed or other separator between them; I separated them here for easy reading):

```
Almuminum Alloy
Available in most colors
Mountain bike
Unisex
Advanced to Professional riders
```

The sample can be modified to return an XML result, using the techniques described previously in the "Dynamic XML Construction" section. Listing 12-31 demonstrates.

Listing 12-31. *XQuery for . . . return with XML Result*

```
SELECT CatalogDescription.query(N'declare namespace ns =
    "http://schemas.microsoft.com/sqlserver/2004/07/adventure-works/➥
        ProductModelDescription";
    for $spec in //ns:ProductDescription/ns:Specifications/*
    return <detail> { $spec/text() } </detail>') AS Description
FROM Production.ProductModel
WHERE ProductModelID = 19;
```

The constructed XML result looks like this:

```
<detail>Almuminum Alloy</detail>
<detail>Available in most colors</detail>
<detail>Mountain bike</detail>
<detail>Unisex</detail>
<detail>Advanced to Professional riders</detail>
```

XQuery allows you to bind multiple variables in the for clause. When you bind multiple variables, the result is the Cartesian product of all possible values of the variables. SQL Server programmers will recognize the Cartesian product as being roughly equivalent to the SQL CROSS JOIN operator. Listing 12-32 modifies the previous example further to generate the Cartesian product of the Specifications and Warranty child node text.

Listing 12-32. *XQuery Cartesian Product with for Expression*

```
SELECT CatalogDescription.query(N'declare namespace ns =
    "http://schemas.microsoft.com/sqlserver/2004/07/adventure-works/➥
        ProductModelDescription";
    for $spec in //ns:ProductDescription/ns:Specifications/*,
        $feat in //ns:ProductDescription/*:Features/*:Warranty/node()
    return <detail> { $spec/text() } + { $feat/. cast as xs:string? } </detail>')
    AS Description
FROM Production.ProductModel
WHERE ProductModelID = 19;
```

The $spec variable is bound to the same nodes as shown previously. The $feat variable is added as a second variable binding in the for clause. Specifically it is bound to the child nodes of the Warranty element, which are the following:

```
<p1:WarrantyPeriod>3 years</p1:WarrantyPeriod>
<p1:Description>parts and labor</p1:Description>
```

The Cartesian product of the text nodes of these two tuple streams consists of ten possible combinations. The final result of the XQuery is the following:

```
<detail>Almuminum Alloy + 3 years</detail>
<detail>Almuminum Alloy + parts and labor</detail>
<detail>Available in most colors + 3 years</detail>
<detail>Available in most colors + parts and labor</detail>
<detail>Mountain bike + 3 years</detail>
<detail>Mountain bike + parts and labor</detail>
<detail>Unisex + 3 years</detail>
<detail>Unisex + parts and labor</detail>
<detail>Advanced to Professional riders + 3 years</detail>
<detail>Advanced to Professional riders + parts and labor</detail>
```

A bound variable can be used immediately after it is bound, even in the same for clause. Listing 12-33 demonstrates.

Listing 12-33. *Using a Bound Variable in the for Clause*

```
SELECT CatalogDescription.query(N'declare namespace ns =
    "http://schemas.microsoft.com/sqlserver/2004/07/adventure-works/➥
        ProductModelDescription";
    for $spec in //ns:ProductDescription/ns:Specifications,
        $color in $spec/Color
    return <color> { $color/text() } </color>') AS Color
FROM Production.ProductModel
WHERE ProductModelID = 19;
```

In this example, the $spec variable is bound to the Specifications node. It is then used in the same for clause to bind a value to the variable $color. The result is the following:

```
<color>Available in most colors</color>
```

where

The where keyword specifies an optional clause to filter tuples generated by the for clause. The expression in the where clause is evaluated for each tuple and those for which the effective Boolean value evaluates to false are discarded from the final result. Listing 12-34 demonstrates use of the where clause to limit the results to only those tuples that contain the letter *A*.

Listing 12-34. *where Clause Demonstration*

```
SELECT CatalogDescription.query(N'declare namespace ns =
    "http://schemas.microsoft.com/sqlserver/2004/07/adventure-works/➥
        ProductModelDescription";
    for $spec in //ns:ProductDescription/ns:Specifications/*
    where $spec[contains(., "A")]
    return <detail> { $spec/text() } </detail>') AS Detail
FROM Production.ProductModel
WHERE ProductModelID = 19
```

The result includes only those items that contain the letter *A*, as shown here:

```
<detail>Almuminum Alloy</detail>
<detail>Available in most colors</detail>
<detail>Advanced to Professional riders</detail>
```

The functions and operators described previously in this chapter (such as contains in the example) can be used in the where clause expression to limit results as required by your application.

order by

The order by clause is an optional clause of the FLWOR statement. The order by clause reorders the tuple stream generated by the for clause, using criteria you specify. The order by criteria consists of one or more ordering specifications that are made up of an expression and an optional order modifier. Ordering specifications are evaluated from left to right.

The optional order modifier is either ascending or descending to indicate the direction of ordering. The default is ascending, as shown in Listing 12-35.

Listing 12-35. *The order by Clause*

```
SELECT CatalogDescription.query(N'declare namespace ns =
    "http://schemas.microsoft.com/sqlserver/2004/07/adventure-works/➥
        ProductModelDescription";
    for $spec in //ns:ProductDescription/ns:Specifications/*
    order by $spec/. descending
    return <detail> { $spec/text() } </detail>') AS Detail
FROM Production.ProductModel
WHERE ProductModelID = 19;
```

The sample uses the order by clause to sort the results in descending (reverse) order. The results look like this:

```
<detail>Unisex</detail>
<detail>Mountain bike</detail>
<detail>Available in most colors</detail>
<detail>Almuminum Alloy</detail>
<detail>Advanced to Professional riders</detail>
```

Summary

This chapter expanded the discussion of XML in Chapter 11. In particular, I focused on the SQL Server implementations of XPath and XQuery, including the following topics:

- A more detailed discussion of the SELECT statement's FOR XML PATH clause

- The WITH XMLNAMESPACES keywords

- Node tests and axis specifiers

- XQuery predicates

- XML Schema data types

- Conditional and arithmetic expressions

- Value, general, and node comparisons

- XQuery functions and operators

- Data type instance constructors

- FLWOR expressions

More information on XML Schema data types is provided in Appendix B, and a short list of XQuery- and XML-specific terms and definitions is provided in Appendix C.

The next chapter discusses SQL Server system metadata and how to programmatically access it via T-SQL. System views, including ANSI-defined information schema views, SQL Server catalog views, compatibility views, and useful system functions will all be discussed.

CHAPTER 13

■ ■ ■

SQL Metadata

Sometimes you need to know the structure of your database and tables. Consider administrative applications such as Microsoft SQL Server Management Studio that need to retrieve metadata for many different types of database objects. Under the hood, applications that rely on SQL Bulk Load APIs, such as the bcp (bulk-copy program) utility, have to address database columns by their ordinal position. Robust applications can use SQL metadata to automatically retrieve this information so users on the client-side can continue to specify the destination columns by name.

Whether it's for an administrative application, bulk loading, or a dynamic query that needs to run against several different tables, SQL metadata can provide structure and definition information for database objects. SQL Server 2005 provides several methods of retrieving metadata.

■Note *Metadata* is simply "data that describes data." SQL Server 2005 databases are "self-describing." The data describing the objects, structures, and relationships that comprise the database is stored within the database itself. This data describing the database design and structure is called *metadata*.

Catalog Views

Catalog views are the Microsoft-recommended method of retrieving metadata. Catalog views represent an improvement over methods of retrieving metadata offered by previous versions of SQL Server. Catalog views provide serverwide metadata for all databases in a server. There are several different catalog views, which Microsoft conveniently categorizes for us. Many of the catalog views are geared toward server and database administration as opposed to application development. Table 13-1 describes a subset of the SQL Server 2005 catalog views that are most useful for T-SQL programming and SQL Server application development.

Table 13-1. *Catalog Views Commonly Used for Application Development*

Catalog Views	View Type	Description
CLR Assembly Catalog Views		
sys.assemblies	Databasewide	Returns a row with the name, assembly_id, and other descriptive information for each assembly in the database.
sys.assembly_files	Databasewide	Returns a row with assembly_id, name, file_id, and file content for each file that makes up the assemblies in the database. INNER JOIN with the sys.assemblies catalog view on the assembly_id column to get the assembly names.
sys.assembly_references	Databasewide	Returns a row with assembly_id and referenced_assembly_id for each pair of assemblies that reference one another in the database. INNER JOIN with the sys.assemblies catalog view on the assembly_id column to get the assembly names.
Databases and Files Catalog Views		
sys.backup_devices	Serverwide	Returns a row with name, type, type_description, and physical_name for each backup device registered on a server with sp_adddumpdevice or through SSMS.
sys.databases	Serverwide	Returns a row with name, database_id, owner_sid, creation_date, and other descriptive information for each database on a server.
sys.database_files	Databasewide	Returns a row with file_id, type, name, physical_name, and other metadata for each database file that corresponds to the current database.
sys.database_mirroring	Serverwide	Returns a row with database_id, mirroring_guid, mirroring_state, and other mirroring metadata for each database on a server. If database mirroring is not enabled or the database is not online, NULLs are returned for all columns except database_id. INNER JOIN with the sys.databases catalog view on the database_id column to get the database names.

Catalog Views	View Type	Description
sys.database_recovery_status	Serverwide	Returns the recovery status of each database on a server. If the database is not started, SQL Server will attempt to start it. INNER JOIN with the sys.databases catalog view on the database_id column to get the database names. The user must have VIEW ANY DATABASE permissions, ALTER ANY DATABASE permissions, CREATE DATABASE permissions in the master database, or be the owner of a database to see a row for that database in this catalog view.
sys.master_files	Serverwide	Returns a row with database_id, file_id, type, name, and other descriptive information for each file corresponding to every database on a server, as stored in the master database. INNER JOIN with the sys.databases catalog view on the database_id column to get the database names.
Object Catalog Views		
sys.allocation_units	Databasewide	Returns a row with allocation_unit_id, type, total_pages, used_pages, and other metadata for each allocation unit in a database.
sys.assembly_modules	Databasewide	Returns a row containing object_id, assembly_id, assembly_class, assembly_method, and other information for each SQLCLR procedure, function, or trigger in a database.
sys.check_constraints	Databasewide	Returns a row with information about each check constraint in a database, including columns indicating the parent_column_id of the check constraint, and whether the check constraint is disabled, not for replication, not trusted, and more.
sys.columns	Databasewide	Returns a row containing object_id, name, column_id, system_type_id, user_type_id, and other descriptive information for each column in all tables, views, table-valued functions, and other objects that have columns in a database. Use the object_id column and the OBJECT_ID() function in your query WHERE clause to narrow the results down to a single object.

Continued

Table 13-1. *Continued*

Catalog Views	View Type	Description
sys.computed_columns	Databasewide	Returns a row for each column in a database that is a computed column. The rows returned contain the same columns as the sys.columns catalog view plus an additional column with the definition for the computed column and bit flags indicating whether the column is persisted and/or uses the default database collation. Use the object_id column and the OBJECT_ID() function in your query WHERE clause to narrow the results to computed columns of a single object.
sys.default_constraints	Databasewide	Returns a row for each default constraint in a database. Each row contains the same columns as the sys.objects catalog view plus additional columns indicating the parent_column_id, the constraint definition, and a bit flag indicating whether the constraint name was generated by the system. Use the parent_object_id column and the OBJECT_ID() function in your query WHERE clause to narrow the results to default constraints of a single object.
sys.events	Databasewide	Returns a row containing object_id, type, type_desc, and a bit flag indicating whether the event is a trigger or a notification event for each event that fires a trigger or event notification in a database. INNER JOIN with the sys.objects catalog view on the object_id column to get information about the trigger or event notification object. INNER JOIN these results to the sys.objects catalog view again, on the parent_object_id column, to determine which database object the trigger or event notification is tied to.
sys.event_notifications	Databasewide	Returns a row containing name, object_id, parent_class, and other metadata for each event notification object in a database. INNER JOIN on the sys.objects catalog view on the parent_id column to get information about the parent object of the event notification. A parent_id of 0 means the database itself is the parent object.

Catalog Views	View Type	Description
sys.extended_procedures	Databasewide	Returns a row for each extended stored procedure installed in the database. Each row contains the same columns as the sys.objects catalog view plus an additional column with the dll_name for the extended stored procedure. Querying sys.extended_procedures from any database context other than the master database results in zero rows being returned.
sys.foreign_keys	Databasewide	Returns a row for each foreign key constraint in the database. Each row contains the same columns as the sys.objects catalog view plus referenced_object_id, key_index_id, and other additional columns. INNER JOIN on the sys.objects catalog view on the parent_object_id to get information about the parent object. INNER JOIN on sys.objects with the referenced_object_id to get information about the referenced object.
sys.foreign_key_columns	Databasewide	Returns a row containing constraint_object_id, constraint_column_id, and additional descriptive information for each column (or set of columns) that compose a foreign key. INNER JOIN with the sys.foreign_keys catalog view on the constraint_object_id column to get information about the foreign key constraint. Join with the sys.objects catalog view on the parent_object_id column or the referenced_column_id column to get information about the parent or referenced column information, respectively.
sys.fulltext_indexes	Databasewide	Returns a row containing object_id, unique_index_id, full_text_catalog_id, and other metadata for each full-text index in the database.
sys.fulltext_index_columns	Databasewide	Returns a row with object_id, column_id, type_column_id, and language_id for each column that is part of a full-text index.
sys.identity_columns	Databasewide	Returns a row for each column that is an identity column. Each row contains all the same columns defined in the sys.columns catalog view plus a seed_value, increment_value, last_value, and is_not_for_replication bit flag.

Continued

Table 13-1. *Continued*

Catalog Views	View Type	Description
sys.indexes	Databasewide	Returns a row for each index, clustered index, or heap of a table, view, or table-valued function in the database. Each row contains an object_id, name, index_id, type, and other descriptive metadata about the index. Use the object_id column and the OBJECT_ID() function in your query WHERE clause to narrow the results to a singular tabular object.
sys.index_columns	Databasewide	Returns a row for each column that makes up an index, clustered index, or unordered table in the database. Columns returned include object_id, index_id, index_column_id, and others. INNER JOIN with the sys.tables catalog view on the object_id column to retrieve information about the table the index columns are part of.
sys.key_constraints	Databasewide	Returns a row for each primary key or unique constraint in a database. Each row returned includes all columns from the sys.objects catalog view plus a unique_index_id and a bit flag indicating whether the constraint was named by the system. INNER JOIN with the sys.tables catalog view on the parent_object_id column to get information about the table the constraint is declared on.
sys.numbered_procedures	Databasewide	Returns a row for each numbered procedure in a database. This does not include the base procedure, which is numbered 1. Note that numbered procedures are deprecated in SQL Server 2005 and should not be used for future development.
sys.numbered_procedure_parameters	Databasewide	Returns a row for each parameter of all numbered procedures in a database. This does not include the base procedure, numbered 1. Numbered procedures are deprecated in SQL Server 2005 and should not be used for future development.
sys.objects	Databasewide	Returns a row for all schema-scoped user-defined objects in a database. Columns returned include name, object_id, principal_id, schema_id, type, and others. Several other catalog views inherit their structure from the sys.objects catalog view. The built-in OBJECT_ID(), OBJECT_NAME(), and OBJECTPROPERTY() functions can all be used on objects listed by sys.objects.

Catalog Views	View Type	Description
sys.parameters	Databasewide	Returns a row with object_id, name, parameter_id, system_type_id, and other descriptive metadata for each parameter of all objects that accept parameters in a database. This catalog view also returns a row for the return value of scalar user-defined functions.
sys.partitions	Databasewide	Returns a row containing partition_id, object_id, index_id, and other descriptive information for each partition of all tables and indexes in the database. All tables and indexes have at least one implicit partition, even if no partitions are explicitly declared.
sys.procedures	Databasewide	Returns a row for each procedure in a database, including stored procedures, extended procedures, replication-filter-procedures, and SQLCLR procedures. Each row contains the same columns as sys.objects plus bit flags that indicate whether the procedure is autoexecuted, execution of the procedure is replicated, replication is only done when the transaction can be serialized, or the procedure skips constraints that are identified as NOT FOR REPLICATION.
sys.service_queues	Databasewide	Returns a row for each service queue in a database. The columns returned are inherited from the sys.objects catalog view, plus additional columns including max_readers, activation_procedure, execute_as_principal_id, and bit flags indicating whether send, receive, enqueue, and retention are enabled.
sys.sql_dependencies	Databasewide	Returns a row containing class, class_desc, object_id, column_id, and other descriptive information for each dependency on a referenced object. This catalog view is designed to track database object dependencies on a by-name basis.
sys.sql_modules	Databasewide	Returns a row for each SQL language module. The results include stored procedures, replication-filter procedures, views, DML triggers, SQL scalar functions, inline-table-valued functions, table-valued functions, rules, and defaults. The rows returned include object_id, definition, execute_as_principal_id, and several bit flags indicating various option settings during the creation of each module.

Continued

Table 13-1. *Continued*

Catalog Views	View Type	Description
sys.stats	Databasewide	Returns a row containing object_id, name, stats_id columns, and auto_created, user_created, and no_recompute bit flag columns for each statistic of a tabular object, including tables, views, and table-valued functions.
sys.stats_columns	Databasewide	Returns a row with object_id, stats_id, stats_column_id, and column_id for each column that is part of a sys.stats statistic for each tabular object, including tables, views, and table-valued functions.
sys.synonyms	Databasewide	Returns a row for each synonym defined in a database. The columns returned include all columns from the sys.objects catalog view plus a base_object_name column.
sys.tables	Databasewide	Returns a row for each user-defined table in a database. This catalog view inherits all columns from the sys.objects catalog view and adds several additional columns, including lob_data_space_id, filestream_data_space_id, max_column_id_used, text_in_row_limit, and several additional bit flag columns.
sys.triggers	Databasewide	Returns a row for each trigger (type TA or TR) in the database. This includes DDL triggers, which are not schema-scoped and therefore not visible in sys.objects. Columns returned include name, object_id, parent_class, parent_class_desc, parent_id, and others.
sys.trigger_events	Databasewide	Returns a row for each event that fires a trigger. Note that this does not include event notifications, which can be accessed via the sys.event_notifications catalog view. The columns returned are inherited from the sys.events catalog view, with two additional bit flag columns: is_first and is_last.
sys.views	Databasewide	Returns a row for each view in the database. The columns returned inherit from the sys.objects catalog view, with the addition of several bit flag columns including is_replicated, has_replication_filter, has_opaque_metadata, and others.

Catalog Views	View Type	Description
Scalar Types Catalog Views		
sys.assembly_types	Databasewide	Returns a row for each SQLCLR user-defined type in a database. This catalog view inherits its columns from the sys.types catalog view, with the addition of assembly_id, assembly_class, is_binary_ordered, is_fixed_length, and other columns.
sys.types	Databasewide	Returns a row with name, system_type_id, user_type_id, schema_id, principal_id, and other descriptive information for each system or user-defined type in a database.
XML Schemas Catalog Views		
sys.column_xml_schema_collection_usage	Databasewide	Returns a row containing object_id, column_id, and xml_collection_id for each column that is validated by an XML schema.
sys.parameter_xml_schema_collection_usages	Databasewide	Returns a row with object_id, parameter_id, and xml_collection_id for each parameter that is validated by an XML schema.
sys.xml_indexes	Databasewide	Returns one row per XML index in a database. The results returned contain all rows from the sys.indexes catalog view, plus the additional columns using_xml_index_id, secondary_type, and secondary_type_desc.
sys.xml_schema_attributes	Databasewide	Returns a row for each XML schema component that is an attribute. Result columns are inherited from the sys.xml_schema_components catalog view plus the additional is_default_fixed, must_be_qualified, and default_value columns.
sys.xml_schema_collections	Databasewide	Returns a row containing xml_schema_collection_id, schema_id, principal_id, name, create_date, and modify_date columns for each XML schema collection.
sys.xml_schema_component_placements	Databasewide	Returns a row with xml_component_id, placement_id, placed_xml_component_id, and additional descriptive metadata columns for each placement for XML schema components.
sys.xml_schema_components	Databasewide	Returns a row containing xml_component_id, xml_collection_id, xml_namespace_id, name, and additional descriptive information columns for each component of XML schemas in a database.

Continued

Table 13-1. *Continued*

Catalog Views	View Type	Description
sys.xml_schema_elements	Databasewide	Returns a row for each schema element that is a Type, symbol space E. The results inherit columns from the sys.xml_schema_components catalog view, plus additional columns, including default_value, is_default_fixed, is_nillable, and several other bit flag columns indicating the various options that can be set for these schema elements.
sys.xml_schema_facets	Databasewide	Returns a row for each facet of xml type definitions. *Facet* is an XML term for a restriction on content. The columns returned include xml_component_id, facet_id, kind, kind_desc, is_fixed, and value.
sys.xml_schema_model_groups	Databasewide	Returns a row for each schema element that is a Model-Group, symbol space M. The results returned include all columns from the sys.xml_schema_components catalog view plus the additional columns compositor and compositor_desc.
sys.xml_schema_namespaces	Databasewide	Returns a row containing xml_collection_id, name, and xml_namespace_id columns for each XSD-defined XML namespace.
sys.xml_schema_types	Databasewide	Returns a row for each XML schema component that is a Type, symbol space T. The results returned include all columns from the sys.xml_schema_components catalog view plus additional bit flag columns indicating various settings of the Type.
sys.xml_schema_wildcard_namespaces	Databasewide	Returns a row with xml_component_id and namespace for each enumerated namespace of XML wildcards.
sys.xml_schema_wildcards	Databasewide	Returns a row for each XML schema component that is an Attribute-Wildcard (symbol space N, kind of V) or an Element-Wildcard (symbol space N, kind of W). The result columns are inherited from sys.xml_schema_components with the additional columns process_content, process_content_desc, and disallow_namespaces.

■**Note** In addition to the catalog views listed in Table 13-1, which are commonly used in application development, SQL Server 2005 includes dozens of additional catalog views, dynamic management views, and replication views. These additional views are useful for specific database and server administrative/management functions, but the focus of this section is application development, and the world of server administration and management is a book unto itself. BOL provides good starter information on the additional catalog views, dynamic management views, and replication views available in SQL Server. This information can be found online at `http://msdn2.microsoft.com/en-us/library/ms177862.aspx`.

As an example of how these catalog views might be used, consider the previous suggestion of a bulk-loading application. The Bulk Load APIs require that target columns be referenced by number, but there are some disadvantages to this approach:

- Being a T-SQL developer, it's a safe bet that you are used to specifying columns by name, not number.

- A simple schema change, such as dropping a column or rebuilding a table, can change the ordinal position numbers of the columns, causing all kinds of problems.

- Using column numbers instead of names means that you have to hard-wire the numbers into your application, tying it to the structure of a very specific table. This means it will be useless as a general-purpose tool for multiple tables.

Using `sys.columns`, your application can dynamically determine the column names and their associated numbers with a simple query like the sample in Listing 13-1.

Listing 13-1. *Using sys.columns Catalog View*

```
USE AdventureWorks;
GO

SELECT c.name, c.column_id
FROM sys.columns c
WHERE c.object_id = OBJECT_ID('Person.Contact')
ORDER BY c.column_id;
```

The results of this query look like Figure 13-1.

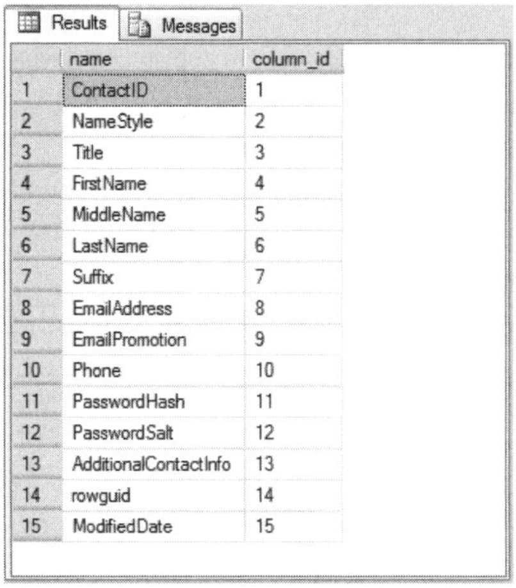

	name	column_id
1	ContactID	1
2	NameStyle	2
3	Title	3
4	FirstName	4
5	MiddleName	5
6	LastName	6
7	Suffix	7
8	EmailAddress	8
9	EmailPromotion	9
10	Phone	10
11	PasswordHash	11
12	PasswordSalt	12
13	AdditionalContactInfo	13
14	rowguid	14
15	ModifiedDate	15

Figure 13-1. *Results of query in Listing 13-1*

In addition to the column_id number, or ordinal position of each column, other information such as the data type, precision and scale, collation, and default can all be retrieved from the `sys.columns` catalog view, providing an opportunity to make bulk loading and other dynamic applications even more robust. Even more information can be gathered by joining the `sys.columns` catalog view against other catalog views such as `sys.objects` and `sys.tables`. Listing 13-2 demonstrates using the `sys.tables` and `sys.columns` catalog views to retrieve column and table information.

Listing 13-2. *Joining sys.schemas, sys.tables, and sys.columns*

```
USE AdventureWorks;
GO

SELECT s.name AS Schema_Name,
    t.name AS Table_Name,
    c.name AS Column_Name,
    c.column_id
FROM sys.schemas s
INNER JOIN sys.tables t
    ON s.schema_id = t.schema_id
INNER JOIN sys.columns c
    ON t.object_id = c.object_id
WHERE s.name = N'Person'
    AND t.name = N'Contact'
ORDER BY c.column_id;
```

This query joins the `sys.schemas` catalog view to the `sys.tables` catalog view on the `schema_id` column, and also joins the `sys.tables` catalog view to the `sys.columns` catalog view on the `object_id` column. The `WHERE` clause narrows the result down to the schema named `Person` and the table named `Contact`. The results are shown in Figure 13-2.

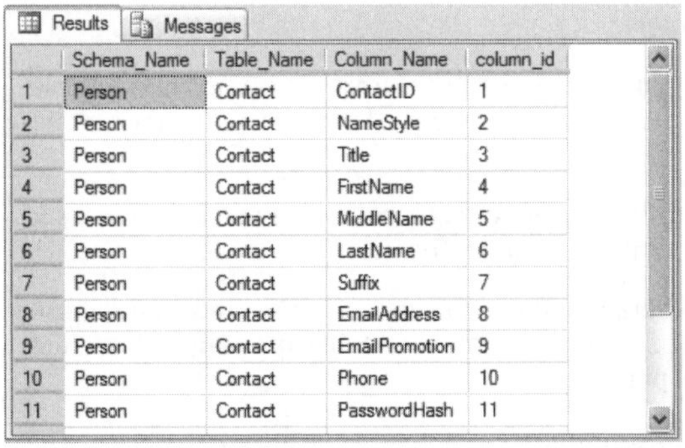

	Schema_Name	Table_Name	Column_Name	column_id
1	Person	Contact	ContactID	1
2	Person	Contact	NameStyle	2
3	Person	Contact	Title	3
4	Person	Contact	FirstName	4
5	Person	Contact	MiddleName	5
6	Person	Contact	LastName	6
7	Person	Contact	Suffix	7
8	Person	Contact	EmailAddress	8
9	Person	Contact	EmailPromotion	9
10	Person	Contact	Phone	10
11	Person	Contact	PasswordHash	11

Figure 13-2. *Result of Listing 13-2*

Catalog views present an excellent way (and indeed, the recommend way) to dynamically retrieve metadata from SQL Server. Catalog views are the preferred method for accessing SQL Server 2005 metadata since they provide the most detailed SQL Server–specific information of any of the available methods for retrieving metadata.

INFORMATION_SCHEMA Views

`INFORMATION_SCHEMA` views provide another method of retrieving metadata in SQL Server 2005. Defined by the SQL-92 standard, `INFORMATION_SCHEMA` views provide the advantage of being cross-platform compatible with other SQL-92–compliant database platforms. One of the major disadvantages is that they do not give platform-specific metadata like SQLCLR assembly information. Also, unlike some of the catalog views that are server-wide, all `INFORMATION_SCHEMA` views are database-specific. The `INFORMATION_SCHEMA` views are listed in Table 13-2.

Table 13-2. *INFORMATION_SCHEMA Views List*

Name	Description
CHECK_CONSTRAINTS	Returns a row of descriptive information for each check constraint in the current database.
COLUMN_DOMAIN_USAGE	Returns a row of metadata for each column in the current database that has an alias data type.
COLUMN_PRIVILEGES	Returns a row of information for each column in the current database with a privilege that has been granted by, or granted to, the current user of the database.
COLUMNS	Returns descriptive information for each column that can be accessed by the current user in the current database.
CONSTRAINT_COLUMN_USAGE	Returns one row of metadata for each column in the current database that has a constraint defined on it, on each table-type object for which the current user has permissions.
CONSTRAINT_TABLE_USAGE	Returns one row of information for each table in the current database that has a constraint defined on it, for which the current user has permissions.
DOMAIN_CONSTRAINTS	Returns a row of descriptive information for each alias data type in the current database that the current user can access, and which has a rule bound to it.
DOMAINS	Returns a row of descriptive metadata for each alias data type in the current data type that the current user can access.
KEY_COLUMN_USAGE	Returns a row of metadata for each column that is constrained by a key, for which the current user has permissions, in the current database.
PARAMETERS	Returns a row of descriptive information for each parameter for all user-defined functions and stored procedures that can be accessed by the current user in the current database. For user-defined functions the results also contain a row with return value information.
REFERENTIAL_CONSTRAINTS	Returns a row of metadata for each FOREIGN KEY constraint defined in the current database, on objects for which the current user has permissions.
ROUTINE_COLUMNS	Returns a row of descriptive information for each column returned by table-valued functions defined in the current database. This INFORMATION_SCHEMA view only returns information about TVFs for which the current user has access.
ROUTINES	Returns a row of metadata for each stored procedure and function in the current database that is accessible to the current user.
SCHEMATA	Returns a row of information for each schema defined in the current database.
TABLE_CONSTRAINTS	Returns a row of metadata for each table constraint in the current database, on table-type objects for which the current user has permissions.
TABLE_PRIVILEGES	Returns a row of descriptive metadata for each table privilege that is either granted by, or granted to, the current user in the current database.

Name	Description
TABLES	Returns a row of metadata for each table in the current database for which the current user has permissions.
VIEW_COLUMN_USAGE	Returns a row of information for each column in the current database that is used in a view definition, on objects for which the current user has permissions.
VIEW_TABLE_USAGE	Returns a row of information for each table in the current database, for which the current user has permissions, that is used in a view.
VIEWS	Returns a row of metadata for each view in the current database that can be accessed by the current user.

■**Note** Some of the changes in SQL Server 2005 can break backward-compatibility with SQL Server 2000 or SQL Server 7.0 INFORMATION_SCHEMA views and applications that rely on them. Also note that SQL Server 6.5 and earlier did not implement INFORMATION_SCHEMA views. Check BOL for specific change information at http://msdn2.microsoft.com/en-us/library/ms186778.aspx if your application uses INFORMATION_SCHEMA and requires backward-compatibility.

You could easily convert the example in Listing 13-1 to use the INFORMATION_SCHEMA. COLUMNS view instead of sys.columns. This is demonstrated in Listing 13-3.

Listing 13-3. *Using INFORMATION_SCHEMA.COLUMNS View*

```
USE AdventureWorks;
GO

SELECT c.Column_Name, c.Ordinal_Position
FROM Information_Schema.Columns c
WHERE c.Table_Schema = 'Person'
    AND c.Table_Name = 'Contact'
ORDER BY c.Ordinal_Position;
```

INFORMATION_SCHEMA views are useful for applications that require cross-platform or high levels of ANSI compatibility. Because they are ANSI compliant, INFORMATION_SCHEMA views do not report a lot of platform-specific metadata, such as SQLCLR assembly metadata and SQL Server-specific data type information.

Compatibility Views

SQL Server 2005 provides yet another set of views to retrieve metadata, known as *compatibility views*. Compatibility views are provided for backward-compatibility only, and Microsoft recommends replacing references to them with catalog views as soon as possible. The following is a list of the SQL Server 2005 compatibility views:

- sysallocunits
- sysbinobjs
- syscerts
- sysclsobjs
- sysconvgroup
- sysdbreg
- sysdesend
- sysfiles1
- sysguidrefs
- syshobts
- sysiscols
- syslogshippers
- sysnsobjs
- sysobjvalues
- sysprivs
- sysremsvcbinds
- sysrowsetcolumns
- sysrowsets

- sysasymkeys
- sysbinsubobjs
- syschildinsts
- syscolpars
- sysdbfiles
- sysdercv
- sysendpts
- sysftinds
- syshobtcolumns
- sysidxstats
- syslnklgns
- sysmultiobjrefs
- sysobjkeycrypts
- sysowners
- sysqnames
- sysrmtlgns
- sysrowsetrefs
- sysrts

- sysscalartypes

- sysserefs

- syssqlguides

- sysusermsgs

- sysxlgns

- sysxmlcomponent

- sysxmlplacement

- sysxsrvs

- sysschobjs

- syssingleobjrefs

- systypedsubobjs

- syswebmethods

- sysxmitqueue

- sysxmlfacet

- sysxprops

The previous example of retrieving column names and numbers can be performed using the syscolumns compatibility view as well. Listing 13-4 provides a sample.

Listing 13-4. *Using the syscolumns Compatibility View*

```
USE AdventureWorks;
GO

SELECT c.name, c.colid
FROM dbo.syscolumns c
WHERE c.id = OBJECT_ID('Person.Contact')
ORDER BY c.colid;
```

As previously mentioned, the compatibility views are provided for backward-compatibility with previous versions of SQL Server only. As such, you can expect them to be removed in a future version of SQL Server. Don't use them for new development; and convert your upgraded scripts to use catalog views as soon as possible.

System Stored Procedures

SQL Server 2005 implements system stored procedures to support ODBC data dictionary functions. The system stored procedures supported are listed in Table 13-3.

Table 13-3. *System Stored Procedures to Retrieve Metadata*

System Stored Procedure	Description
sp_column_privileges	Returns column privileges for a single table
sp_columns	Returns column information for one or more specified tables or views
sp_databases	Returns a list of databases that exist on, or are accessible through, the SQL Server
sp_fkeys	Returns foreign key information for a specified table
sp_pkeys	Returns primary key information for a specified table
sp_server_info	Returns information about a SQL Server instance
sp_special_columns	Returns the set of columns that uniquely identify rows in a table
sp_sproc_columns	Returns column information for a stored procedure or user-defined function
sp_statistics	Returns a list of all indexes and statistics on a table or indexed view
sp_stored_procedures	Returns a list of stored procedures, user-defined functions, and extended procedures
sp_table_privileges	Returns a list of table permissions for one or more specified tables
sp_tables	Returns a list of all objects that can be queried—that is, all objects that can appear in the FROM clause of a query

Listing 13-5 demonstrates using the sp_columns system stored procedure to retrieve column information for a table.

Listing 13-5. *Using sp_columns System Stored Procedure*

```
USE AdventureWorks;
GO

EXECUTE dbo.sp_columns @table_owner = 'Person', @table_name = 'Contact';
```

The results are shown in Figure 13-3.

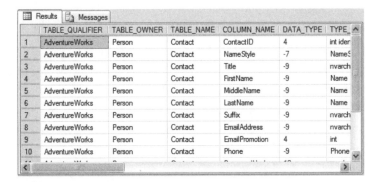

Figure 13-3. *Results of sp_columns on Person.Contact table*

Summary

This chapter covered SQL Server 2005 metadata views and stored procedures:

- Catalog views, which are new to SQL Server 2005 and are the preferred method of retrieving SQL Server metadata

- INFORMATION_SCHEMA views, which provide an ANSI-compliant method for retrieving metadata, though they provide less platform-specific information than catalog views

- Backward-compatible compatibility views, which should be upgraded to catalog views as soon as possible

- System stored procedures, which are used by system drivers to retrieve metadata

SQL Server 2005 provides more options for retrieving database and system metadata than any prior SQL Server release. The self-describing nature of SQL Server databases and database objects, and the SQL Server metadata catalog views, make it particularly easy to create administrative tools or any other type of application that needs to know database and database object structures and properties.

The next chapter discusses one of the newest tools for SQL Server programming, SQLCLR.

■■■

CHAPTER 14

SQLCLR Programming

One of the most prominent new enhancements to SQL Server 2005 is the integrated SQLCLR. The SQLCLR is a SQL Server–specific version of the .NET Common Language Runtime that allows you to run .NET code in the database. SQLCLR programming is a broad subject that could easily fill an entire book, and in fact it does. *Pro SQL Server 2005 Assemblies* by Robin Dewson and Julian Skinner (Apress, 2005) is an excellent resource for in-depth coverage of SQLCLR programming. This chapter will discuss the methods used to extend SQL Server functionality in the past and explain the basics of the new SQLCLR programming model.

The Old Way

In previous versions of SQL Server, developers could extend SQL Server functionality by writing extended stored procedures. Writing high-quality extended stored procedures requires a strong knowledge of the Open Data Services (ODS) library and the poorly documented C-style Extended Stored Procedure API. Anyone who's ever attempted the old style of extended stored procedure programming can tell you it's a complex undertaking, where a single misstep can easily result in memory leaks and/or corruption of the SQL Server process space. Also the threading model used by extended stored procedures requires SQL Server to rely on the operating system to control threading and concurrency. This can also lead to issues, such as unresponsiveness of extended stored procedure code.

■**Caution** Extended stored procedures have been deprecated in SQL Server 2005. Use the SQLCLR instead of extended stored procedures for SQL Server 2005 development.

Earlier SQL Server releases allowed you to create OLE Automation server objects via the sp_OACreate stored procedure. Creating OLE Automation servers can be just as complex as extended stored procedure programming (if not more so). The sp_OACreate method is also notorious for memory leaks.

Another option in previous versions of SQL Server was to code all business logic exclusively in business objects that were physically and logically separate from the database. While this method is preferred by many developers and administrators, it can result in extra network traffic and a less robust security model than can be achieved through tight integration with SQL Server security.

The SQLCLR Way

The introduction of the SQLCLR programming model in SQL Server 2005 provides several advantages over the older methods of extending SQL Server functionality via extended stored procedures, OLE Automation, or external business objects. These advantages include the following:

- Your managed codebase runs on the SQLCLR .NET Framework, which is tightly integrated into SQL Server itself. This means that SQL Server can properly manage threading, memory usage, and other resources accessed via SQLCLR code.

- The tight integration of the SQLCLR into SQL Server means that SQL Server can provide a robust security model for running code, and maintain stricter control over database objects and external resources accessed by the SQLCLR code.

- The SQLCLR is more thoroughly documented in more places than the Extended Stored Procedure API ever was (or presumably ever will be).

- The SQLCLR does not tie you to the C language–based Extended Stored Procedure API. In theory the SQLCLR programming model does not tie you to any one specific language (although Microsoft currently supports only VB 2005, C#, and C++ SQLCLR programming).

- The SQLCLR allows access to all of the familiar .NET namespaces, data types, and managed objects.

- The SQLCLR introduces SQL Server–specific namespaces that allow direct access to the underlying SQL Server databases and resources, which can be used to limit or reduce network traffic generated by using external business objects.

There's a misperception in some quarters that the SQLCLR is a replacement for T-SQL altogether. I can't speak with authority about Microsoft's plans for the future, but as it stands now the SQLCLR is not a *replacement* for T-SQL, but rather a supplement that works hand-in-hand with T-SQL to make SQL Server 2005 more powerful than ever. So when should you use SQLCLR code in your database? There are no hard and fast rules concerning this, but here are some general guidelines:

- Existing extended stored procedures on older versions of SQL Server are excellent candidates for conversion to SQL Server 2005 SQLCLR assemblies, that is, if the functionality provided isn't already part of SQL Server 2005 T-SQL (i.e., encryption).

- Code that accesses external server resources, such as calls to `xp_cmdshell`, are also excellent candidates for conversion to the more secure SQLCLR assemblies.

- T-SQL code that performs a lot of complex calculations and string manipulations can make strong candidates for conversion to SQLCLR assemblies primarily because procedural compiled code can often outperform T-SQL in these areas.

- Highly procedural code with a lot of processing steps might be considered for conversion.

- Clients that pull a lot of data across the wire and perform a lot of processing on that data might be considered for conversion. You might first consider these business objects for conversion to T-SQL stored procedures, especially if they don't perform a lot of processing on the data in question.

Here are some general guidelines for items that should *not* be converted to SQLCLR assemblies:

- Clients that pull small amounts of data across the wire, or that pull a lot of data across the wire but perform no processing on that data, are good candidates for conversion to T-SQL stored procedures instead of SQLCLR assemblies.

- T-SQL code and stored procedures that do not perform complex calculations and string manipulations should not be converted to SQLCLR assemblies.

- T-SQL can be expected to always perform set-based operations on data stored in the database faster than the SQLCLR.

As with T-SQL stored procedures, the decision to use the SQLCLR in your databases, and to what extent, depends on your organizational policies and procedures. The recommendations I present here are guidelines of instances that make good business cases for conversion of existing code and creation of new code.

SQLCLR Assemblies

SQLCLR exposes .NET managed code to SQL Server via *assemblies*. An assembly is compiled into a .NET managed code dynamic link library (DLL), which can then be registered with SQL Server using the `CREATE ASSEMBLY` statement. Publicly accessible members of classes within the assemblies are then referenced in the appropriate CREATE statements, which are described later in this section.

Creating a SQLCLR assembly requires the following:

- Designing and programming a .NET class(es) that publicly exposes the appropriate members

- Compiling the .NET class(es) into managed code DLL manifest files containing the assembly

- Registering the assemblies with SQL Server via the CREATE ASSEMBLY statement

- Registering the appropriate assembly members via the appropriate CREATE FUNCTION, CREATE PROCEDURE, CREATE TYPE, CREATE TRIGGER, or CREATE AGGREGATE statements

The SQLCLR provides additional SQL Server–specific namespaces, classes, and attributes to facilitate assembly programming. Visual Studio 2005 also includes a new SQL Server Project project type that assists in quickly creating assemblies. To create a new assembly using Visual Studio 2005, do the following:

1. Select File ➤ New Project from the menu.

2. Select your .NET language of choice (currently supported languages are Visual Basic, C#, and Visual C++) and choose the SQL Server Project installed template from the Database submenu of the New Project dialog, as shown in Figure 14-1.

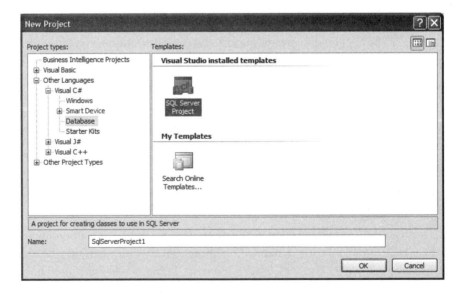

Figure 14-1. *Visual Studio 2005 New Project dialog*

3. You will be prompted with a dialog to select a database connection for the project, as shown in Figure 14-2. You may be prompted to turn on SQLCLR debugging for the connection. This is required if you want to test your assemblies in Debug mode.

Figure 14-2. *Add Database Reference dialog*

4. Next highlight the project name in the Solution Explorer pane and right-click. Then choose a type of SQLCLR item to add to the solution (User-Defined Function, Stored Procedure, etc.), as shown in Figure 14-3.

5. Visual Studio will automatically generate a template for the item you select in the language of your choice, complete with the appropriate Imports statements (using in C#).

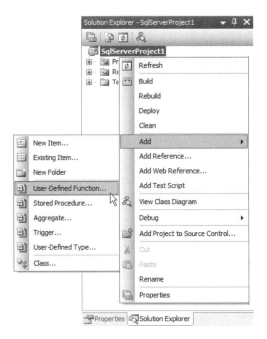

Figure 14-3. *Adding a new SQLCLR item to your project*

In addition to the standard .NET namespaces and classes, the SQLCLR implements some SQL Server–specific namespaces and classes to simplify interfacing your code with SQL Server. Some of the most commonly used namespaces include the following:

- The System namespace, which includes the base .NET data types and the Object class from which all .NET classes inherit

- The System.Data namespace, which contains the DataSet class and other classes for ADO.NET data management

- The System.Data.SqlClient namespace, which contains the SQL Server–specific ADO.NET data provider

- The Microsoft.SqlServer.Server namespace, which contains the SqlContext and SqlPipe classes that allow assemblies to communicate with SQL Server

- The System.Data.SqlTypes namespace, which contains SQL Server data types, which is important because (unlike the standard .NET data types) these types can be set to SQL NULL

Once the assembly is created and compiled, it is registered with SQL Server via the CREATE ASSEMBLY statement:

```
CREATE ASSEMBLY assembly_name
[ AUTHORIZATION owner_name ]
FROM { <client_assembly_specifier> | <assembly_bits> [ , ... n ] }
[ WITH PERMISSION_SET = { SAFE | EXTERNAL_ACCESS | UNSAFE } ] ;
```

The CREATE ASSEMBLY statement requires you to specify the following:

- The assembly_name is a valid SQL Server identifier and must be unique within the database.

- The owner_name is the name of a user or role to designate as the owner of the assembly. If AUTHORIZATION is specified, the current user must be a member of the role specified or have IMPERSONATE permissions for the user specified. If the AUTHORIZATION clause is left out, the default is the current user.

- The client_assembly_specifier is a full local or UNC network path to the DLL manifest file containing the assembly. This option cannot be specified if the current logged-in user is being impersonated.

- Assembly_bits represents the binary value of the assembly (as a varbinary), and can be used instead of client_assembly_specifier. Assembly_bits is the assembly and its dependent assemblies.

- The WITH PERMISSION_SET clause specifies a set of code access permissions to grant the assembly.

  - The SAFE permission set is the most restrictive and prevents the assembly from accessing system resources outside of SQL Server. SAFE is the default.

  - EXTERNAL_ACCESS allows assemblies to access some external resources, such as files, network, the registry, and environment variables.

  - UNSAFE permission allows assemblies unlimited access to external resources, including the ability to execute unmanaged code.

SQLCLR User-Defined Functions

SQLCLR user-defined functions can return scalar values or tablelike result sets. SQLCLR user-defined functions that return scalar values are similar to standard .NET functions. A SQLCLR function requires that you apply the SqlFunction attribute to the main function as shown in Listing 14-1. I explain more about the SqlFunction attribute later in this section. Listing 14-1 demonstrates a sample scalar user-defined function that accepts a value representing a temperature in degrees Fahrenheit and converts it to degrees Celsius.

Listing 14-1. *Sample SQLCLR User-Defined Function Temperature Converter*

```
Imports System
Imports System.Data
Imports System.Data.SqlClient
Imports System.Data.SqlTypes
Imports Microsoft.SqlServer.Server

Namespace APress.Samples
    Partial Public Class Sql
        <SqlFunction(DataAccess:=DataAccessKind.None, _
            IsDeterministic:=True)> _
        Public Shared Function Fahrenheit2Celsius(ByVal f As SqlDouble) As SqlDouble
            Dim c As New SqlDouble
            c = (5.0 / 9.0) * (f - 32.0)
            Return c
        End Function
    End Class
End Namespace
```

The first part of the listing is standard SQLCLR boilerplate; it specifies the required namespaces to import:

```
Imports System
Imports System.Data
Imports System.Data.SqlClient
Imports System.Data.SqlTypes
Imports Microsoft.SqlServer.Server
```

Next the code designates a namespace; in this case I've decided to call it APress.Samples:

```
Namespace APress.Samples
```

Then the class is declared. Microsoft .NET 2.0 introduces the concept of *partial classes*, allowing you to break up the declaration of a single class into multiple source files. While there is only a single source file, it's the code that Visual Studio generates automatically—and it doesn't hurt anything:

```
Partial Public Class Sql
```

The `Public Shared` (public static for C#) function is then declared. The `SqlFunction` attribute is applied with two attributes set. The `DataAccess` attribute is set to `DataAccessKind.None`, indicating the function does not read data from system tables using the in-process data provider. The `IsDeterministic` function is set to `True` to indicate that the function is deterministic in nature:

```
<SqlFunction(DataAccess:=DataAccessKind.None, _
    IsDeterministic:=True)> _
Public Shared Function Fahrenheit2Celsius(ByVal f As SqlDouble) As SqlDouble
    Dim c As New SqlDouble
    c = (5.0 / 9.0) * (f - 32.0)
    Return c
End Function
```

The function itself accepts a `SqlDouble` Fahrenheit temperature, then calculates and returns a `SqlDouble` Celsius temperature.

Tip It's considered best practice to use the SQL Server data types for parameters and return values (i.e., SqlDouble, SqlInt32, SqlString, etc.). Standard .NET data types have no concept of NULL and will error out if a NULL value is passed in as a parameter, calculated within the function, or returned from the function.

After the assembly is installed via the `CREATE ASSEMBLY` statement, the function is set up with the `CREATE FUNCTION` statement with the `EXTERNAL NAME` option:

```
CREATE FUNCTION dbo.Fahrenheit2Celsius (@f FLOAT)
RETURNS FLOAT
WITH EXECUTE AS CALLER
AS
EXTERNAL NAME
    Fahrenheit2Celsius.[Fahrenheit2Celsius.APress.Samples.Sql].Fahrenheit2Celsius
GO
```

At this point the function can be called like any other user-defined function:

```
SELECT dbo.Fahrenheit2Celsius(100.0);
```

■**Tip** You can automate the process of compiling your assembly, registering it with SQL Server, and installing the SQLCLR user-defined function with Visual Studio's Build ➤ Deploy. You can also test the SQLCLR user-defined function with the Visual Studio Debug ➤ Start Debugging option.

As mentioned previously, SQLCLR user-defined functions also allow table-style results to be returned to the caller. Table-valued SQLCLR user-defined functions are a little more complex, as demonstrated in Listing 14-2.

Listing 14-2. *Retrieving Yahoo RSS Feed Top News Stories*

```
Imports System
Imports System.Data
Imports System.Data.SqlClient
Imports System.Data.SqlTypes
Imports Microsoft.SqlServer.Server
Imports System.Xml
Imports System.Runtime.InteropServices

Namespace APress.Samples
    Partial Public Class Sql
        <SqlFunction(IsDeterministic:=False, _
            DataAccess:=DataAccessKind.None, _
            TableDefinition:="title nvarchar(256), link nvarchar(256), " & _
                "pubdate datetime, description nvarchar(max)", _
            FillRowMethodName:="GetRow")> _
        Public Shared Function GetYahooNews() As IEnumerable
            Dim xmlsource As New _
                XmlTextReader("http://rss.news.yahoo.com/rss/topstories")
            Dim newsxml As New XmlDocument
            newsxml.Load(xmlsource)
            xmlsource.Close()
            Return newsxml.SelectNodes("//rss/channel/item")
        End Function

        Private Shared Sub GetRow(ByVal o As Object, _
            <Out()> ByRef title As SqlString, _
            <Out()> ByRef link As SqlString, _
            <Out()> ByRef pubdate As SqlDateTime, _
            <Out()> ByRef description As SqlString)
```

```
        Dim element As XmlElement
        element = DirectCast(o, XmlElement)
        title = element.SelectSingleNode("./title").InnerText
        link = element.SelectSingleNode("./link").InnerText
        pubdate = CType(element.SelectSingleNode("./pubDate").InnerText, _
            DateTime)
        description = element.SelectSingleNode("./description").InnerText
    End Sub
  End Class
End Namespace
```

This example retrieves the Yahoo Top News Stories RSS feed and returns the result as a table. Before we step through the source listing, we need to address security since this function accesses the Internet. Because the function needs to access an external resource, it requires EXTERNAL_ACCESS permissions. In order to deploy a nonsafe assembly, one of two sets of conditions must be met:

- The database must be marked TRUSTWORTHY, and the user installing the assembly must have EXTERNAL_ACCESS ASSEMBLY or UNSAFE ASSEMBLY permission.

- The assembly must be signed with an asymmetric key or certificate associated with a login that has proper permissions.

To meet the first set of requirements, do the following:

- Execute the ALTER DATABASE AdventureWorks SET TRUSTWORTHY ON; statement.

- In Visual Studio, select Project Properties ➤ Database and change the Permission Level to External.

This code listing also begins with the Imports statements. This function requires the addition of the System.Xml namespace in order to parse the RSS feed, and System.Runtime.InteropServices in order to use the <Out()> attribute on parameters in the fill-row method, described later in this section:

```
Imports System
Imports System.Data
Imports System.Data.SqlClient
Imports System.Data.SqlTypes
Imports Microsoft.SqlServer.Server
Imports System.Xml
Imports System.Runtime.InteropServices
```

Like the previous example, this one declares the APress.Samples namespace and the public Sql partial class:

```
Namespace APress.Samples
    Partial Public Class Sql
```

The primary public function again requires the SqlFunction attribute be declared. This time there are several additional attributes that need to be declared with it:

```
<SqlFunction(IsDeterministic:=False, _
    DataAccess:=DataAccessKind.None, _
    TableDefinition:="title nvarchar(256), link nvarchar(256), " & _
        "pubdate datetime, description nvarchar(max)", _
    FillRowMethodName:="GetRow")> _
```

The IsDeterministic attribute is set to False this time since the contents of the RSS feed are not deterministic. Anytime you rely on an external source for your data, the results will most likely be nondeterministic. Since the function does not read data from system tables using the in-process data provider, the DataAccess attribute is set to DataAccessKind.None. The SQLCLR table-valued function requires the additional TableDefinition attribute, which defines the structure of the result set. It also needs the FillRowMethodName attribute, which designates the fill-row method. The *fill-row method* is a user method that converts each element of an IEnumerable object into a SQL Server result set row:

```
Public Shared Function GetYahooNews() As IEnumerable
    Dim xmlsource As New _
        XmlTextReader("http://rss.news.yahoo.com/rss/topstories")
    Dim newsxml As New XmlDocument
    newsxml.Load(xmlsource)
    xmlsource.Close()
    Return newsxml.SelectNodes("//rss/channel/item")
End Function
```

The public function is declared to return an IEnumerable result. This particular function opens an XmlTextReader that retrieves the Yahoo Top News Stories RSS feed and loads it into an XmlDocument. It then uses the SelectNodes method to retrieve the news story summaries from the RSS feed. The SelectNodes method returns an XmlNodeList, which implements IEnumerable. The fill-row method is fired once for each element of the XmlNodeList:

```
        Private Shared Sub GetRow(ByVal o As Object, _
            <Out()> ByRef title As SqlString, _
            <Out()> ByRef link As SqlString, _
            <Out()> ByRef pubdate As SqlDateTime, _
            <Out()> ByRef description As SqlString)
            Dim element As XmlElement
            element = DirectCast(o, XmlElement)
            title = element.SelectSingleNode("./title").InnerText
            link = element.SelectSingleNode("./link").InnerText
            pubdate = CType(element.SelectSingleNode("./pubDate").InnerText, _
                DateTime)
            description = element.SelectSingleNode("./description").InnerText
        End Sub
    End Class
End Namespace
```

The GetRow method is declared as a Visual Basic Sub that returns no value. The method communicates with SQL Server via its parameters. The first parameter is an Object passed by value; in this case it will be an XmlElement. The remaining parameters correspond to the columns of the result set. These parameters are passed by reference and should have the <Out()> attribute applied to them as shown. The sample GetRow method casts the first parameter to an XmlElement. It then uses the SelectSingleNode method and InnerText property to retrieve the proper text from individual child nodes of the XmlElement, assigning each to the proper columns of the result set along the way.

The SQLCLR table-valued function can be called like this:

```
SELECT title, link, pubdate, description
FROM dbo.GetYahooNews();
```

The results are similar to Figure 14-4.

	title	link	pubdate	description
1	Bush unsatisfied with Iraq war progress (AP)	http://us.r...	2006-10-25 23:03:46.000	<p><a href="http://us.rd.yal
2	Report: S.Korea to ban entry from North (AP)	http://us.r...	2006-10-25 23:35:02.000	<p><a href="http://us.rd.yal
3	Defiant Iraqi PM disavows timetable (AP)	http://us.r...	2006-10-25 23:02:42.000	<p><a href="http://us.rd.yal
4	Md. Senate candidates bicker in debate (AP)	http://us.r...	2006-10-25 22:58:18.000	<p><a href="http://us.rd.yal
5	Pentagon eyes major spending for Guantanamo trials (Reute...	http://us.r...	2006-10-25 20:20:36.000	<p><a href="http://us.rd.yal
6	Fla. killer executed for 5 1990 murders (AP)	http://us.r...	2006-10-25 22:56:04.000	<p><a href="http://us.rd.yal
7	Study: Scans may find lung cancer sooner (AP)	http://us.r...	2006-10-25 23:00:00.000	<p><a href="http://us.rd.yal
8	Lance Bass' boyfriend target of threats (AP)	http://us.r...	2006-10-25 22:54:04.000	<p><a href="http://us.rd.yal
9	Tupperware takes on a new role: art (AP)	http://us.r...	2006-10-25 22:50:13.000	<p><a href="http://us.rd.yal
10	Game 4 of World Series postponed by rain (AP)	http://us.r...	2006-10-25 23:00:59.000	<p><a href="http://us.rd.yal
11	NJ court grants gay couples equal marriage rights (Reuters)	http://us.r...	2006-10-25 21:23:12.000	<p><a href="http://us.rd.yal
12	Bush warns Iraqis that American patience has limits (Reuters)	http://us.r...	2006-10-25 20:04:23.000	<p><a href="http://us.rd.yal
13	Russian nuclear project snags Iran sanctions deal (Reuters)	http://us.r...	2006-10-25 19:34:31.000	<p><a href="http://us.rd.yal
14	U.S. troops on active duty call for Iraq withdrawal (Reuters)	http://us.r...	2006-10-25 13:50:06.000	<p><a href="http://us.rd.yal

Figure 14-4. *Sample GetYahooNews function results*

SQLCLR Stored Procedures

SQLCLR stored procedures provide an alternative to extend SQL Server functionality when T-SQL stored procedures just won't do. Of course, like other SQLCLR functionality, there is a certain amount of overhead involved with SQLCLR stored procedures, and you can expect them to be less efficient than comparable T-SQL code for set-based operations. On the other hand, if you need to access .NET functionality or external resources, or have code that is computationally intensive, SQLCLR stored procedures can provide an excellent choice.

Listing 14-3 shows how to use the SQLCLR to retrieve operating system environment variables and return them as a recordset via stored procedure.

Listing 14-3. *Retrieving Environment Variables with a SQLCLR Stored Procedure*

```
Imports System
Imports System.Data
Imports System.Data.SqlClient
Imports System.Data.SqlTypes
Imports Microsoft.SqlServer.Server

Namespace APress.Samples
    Partial Public Class Sql
        <SqlProcedure()> _
        Public Shared Sub GetEnvironmentVars()
            Try
                Dim environmentList As New SortedList
                For Each de As DictionaryEntry In _
                    Environment.GetEnvironmentVariables()
                    environmentList(de.Key) = de.Value
                Next
                Dim record As New SqlDataRecord( _
                    New SqlMetaData("VarName", SqlDbType.NVarChar, 1024), _
                    New SqlMetaData("VarValue", SqlDbType.NVarChar, 4000))
                SqlContext.Pipe.SendResultsStart(record)
                For Each de As DictionaryEntry In environmentList
                    record.SetValue(0, de.Key)
                    record.SetValue(1, de.Value)
                    SqlContext.Pipe.SendResultsRow(record)
                Next
                SqlContext.Pipe.SendResultsEnd()
```

```
        Catch ex As Exception
            SqlContext.Pipe.Send(ex.Message)
        End Try
    End Sub
  End Class
End Namespace
```

As with the other SQLCLR assemblies, appropriate namespaces are imported at the top:

```
Imports System
Imports System.Data
Imports System.Data.SqlClient
Imports System.Data.SqlTypes
Imports Microsoft.SqlServer.Server
```

Like the other SQLCLR assemblies, I'm declaring the APress.Samples namespace and the Sql partial class:

```
Namespace APress.Samples
    Partial Public Class Sql
```

The GetEnvironmentVars method is declared as a public Sub (void function in C#). The SqlProcedure() attribute is applied to the function to indicate to SQL Server that this is a SQLCLR stored procedure:

```
        <SqlProcedure()> _
        Public Shared Sub GetEnvironmentVars()
```

The body of the stored procedure is wrapped in a Try...Catch block to capture any .NET errors. As the procedure begins, all of the environment variable names and their values are copied from the .NET Hashtable returned by the Environment. GetEnvironmentVariables() functions to a .NET SortedList:

```
        Try
            Dim environmentList As New SortedList
            For Each de As DictionaryEntry In _
                Environment.GetEnvironmentVariables()
                environmentList(de.Key) = de.Value
            Next
```

The procedure uses the SqlContext.Pipe to return results to SQL Server as a result set. The first step to using the SqlContext.Pipe is to set up a SqlRecord with the structure that you wish the result set to take:

```
Dim record As New SqlDataRecord( _
    New SqlMetaData("VarName", SqlDbType.NVarChar, 1024), _
    New SqlMetaData("VarValue", SqlDbType.NVarChar, 4000))
```

Next, you call the SendResultsStart method with the SqlDataRecord to initialize the result set:

```
SqlContext.Pipe.SendResultsStart(record)
```

Then it's a simple matter of looping through the SortedList of environment variable key/value pairs and sending them to the server via the SendResultsRow method:

```
For Each de As DictionaryEntry In environmentList
    record.SetValue(0, de.Key)
    record.SetValue(1, de.Value)
    SqlContext.Pipe.SendResultsRow(record)
Next
```

The SetValue method is called for each column of the SqlRecord to properly set the results, and then SendResultsRow is called on the SqlContext.Pipe for each row. After all results have been sent to the client, the SendResultsEnd method of the SqlContext.Pipe is called to complete the result set and return the SqlContext.Pipe to its initial state:

```
SqlContext.Pipe.SendResultsEnd()
```

Finally, the code finishes with the Catch portion of the Try...Catch block:

```
        Catch ex As Exception
            SqlContext.Pipe.Send(ex.Message)
        End Try
    End Sub
End Class
End Namespace
```

The result of executing the GetEnvironmentVars SQLCLR stored procedure is shown in Figure 14-5.

	VarName	VarValue
7	FP_NO_HOST_CHECK	NO
8	INCLUDE	E:\Program Files\Microsoft Visual Studio .NET 2003\SDK\v1.1\include\
9	LIB	E:\Program Files\Microsoft Visual Studio .NET 2003\SDK\v1.1\Lib\;C:\Program Files\SQLXML...
10	NUMBER_OF_PROCESSORS	1
11	OS	Windows_NT
12	Path	C:\Program Files\MiKTeX 2.5\miktex\bin;C:\WINDOWS\system32;C:\WINDOWS;C:\WINDO...
13	PATHEXT	.COM;.EXE;.BAT;.CMD;.VBS;.VBE;.JS;.JSE;.WSF;.WSH
14	PROCESSOR_ARCHITECT...	x86
15	PROCESSOR_IDENTIFIER	x86 Family 15 Model 7 Stepping 10, AuthenticAMD
16	PROCESSOR_LEVEL	15
17	PROCESSOR_REVISION	070a

Figure 14-5. *SQLCLR stored procedure sample results*

SQLCLR User-Defined Aggregates

User-defined aggregates (UDAs) are an exciting new addition to SQL Server 2005. A UDA is similar to a user-defined function, but it can act on entire sets of data at once, as opposed to one item at a time. UDAs operate like the built-in SQL Server aggregate functions (SUM, AVG, etc.). SQLCLR UDAs, however, have access to .NET functionality and can operate on numeric, character, temporal (datetime), or even user-defined data types. A basic UDA has four mandatory methods:

- The UDA calls its Init method when the SQL engine prepares to aggregate. The code in this method can reset temporary variables to their start state, initialize buffers, and perform other initialization functions.

- The Accumulate method is called as each row is processed, allowing you to aggregate the data passed in. The Accumulate method might increment a counter, add a row's value to a running total, or possibly perform other more complex processing on a row's data.

- The Merge method is invoked when SQL Server decides to use parallel processing to complete an aggregate. If the query engine decides to use parallel processing it will create multiple instances of your UDA and call the Merge method to join the results into a single aggregation.

- The Terminate method is the final method of the UDA. It is called after all rows have been processed and any aggregates created in parallel have been merged. The Terminate method returns the final result of the aggregation to the query engine.

THE 8,000-BYTE LIMITATION

Each instance of a SQLCLR UDA has a serialization limit of 8,000 bytes in the current version of SQL Server. Because of this, certain tasks are harder to perform using a SQLCLR UDA. Creating an array, hash table, or other structure to hold intermediate results during an aggregation (such as aggregates that calculate statistical mode or median) can cause your UDA to very quickly run up against the 8,000-byte limit and throw an exception for large datasets. Consider the following sample T-SQL query that calculates the statistical median of the TotalDue column of the Sales.SalesOrderHeader table:

```
USE AdventureWorks;
GO


WITH CalcTotalDueMedian (Num, TotalDue)
AS
(
    SELECT ROW_NUMBER() OVER (ORDER BY TotalDue) AS Num, TotalDue
    FROM Sales.SalesOrderHeader
)
SELECT AVG(TotalDue) AS Median
FROM CalcTotalDueMedian
WHERE Num IN (
    SELECT MAX(Num + 1)/2
    FROM CalcTotalDueMedian
    UNION
    SELECT MAX(Num + 2)/2
    FROM CalcTotalDueMedian
);
GO
```

The statistical median is the middle value for a set of sorted numbers if there is an odd number of numbers in the set, or the average of the middle two values if there is an even number of numbers in the set. This sample code retrieves all the TotalDue values, sorts them, and numbers them with the ROW_NUMBER function. It then calculates the median as the average of the middle one or two terms. Calculating the median with a SQLCLR UDA would require intermediate storage of a potentially large amount of data. The calculation in the sample could generate a potentially large intermediate result set. The Sales.SalesOrderHeader table, for example, has 31,465 rows in it. These types of calculations are better left to the devices of T-SQL's set-based processing.

The sample UDA in Listing 14-4 determines the range for a group of numbers. The range is the difference between the minimum and maximum values in a set of numbers. The UDA determines the minimum and maximum values of the set of numbers passed in and returns the difference.

Listing 14-4. *Sample Range UDA*

```
Imports System
Imports System.Data
Imports System.Data.SqlClient
Imports System.Data.SqlTypes
Imports Microsoft.SqlServer.Server

Namespace APress.Samples
    <Serializable()> _
    <SqlUserDefinedAggregate(Format.Native)> _
    Public Structure Range

        Private min As SqlDouble
        Private max As SqlDouble

        Public Sub Init()
            Me.min = SqlDouble.Null
            Me.max = SqlDouble.Null
        End Sub

        Public Sub Accumulate(ByVal value As SqlDouble)
            If Not value.IsNull Then
                If Me.min.IsNull OrElse value < Me.min Then
                    Me.min = value
                End If
                If Me.max.IsNull OrElse value > Me.max Then
                    Me.max = value
                End If
            End If
        End Sub
```

```
        Public Sub Merge(ByVal tempRange As Range)
            If (Me.min.IsNull OrElse tempRange.min < Me.min) Then
                Me.min = tempRange.min
            End If
            If (Me.min.IsNull OrElse tempRange.max > Me.max) Then
                Me.max = tempRange.max
            End If
        End Sub

        Public Function Terminate() As SqlDouble
            Dim result As SqlDouble = SqlDouble.Null
            If Not (Me.min.IsNull OrElse Me.max.IsNull) Then
                result = Me.max - Me.min
            End If
            Return result
        End Function
    End Structure
End Namespace
```

The UDA begins, like other SQLCLR assemblies, by importing the proper namespaces:

```
Imports System
Imports System.Data
Imports System.Data.SqlClient
Imports System.Data.SqlTypes
Imports Microsoft.SqlServer.Server
```

Next up is the APress.Samples namespace declaration and the Structure (struct for C#), which represents the UDA. The attributes Serializable and SqlUserDefinedAggregate are applied to the Structure. The Format.Native serialization format is specified as well. Because this is a simple UDA, Format.Native will provide the best performance and will be the easiest to implement. More complex UDAs that use reference types require Format.UserDefined serialization, and must implement the IBinarySerialize interface:

```
Namespace APress.Samples
    <Serializable()> _
    <SqlUserDefinedAggregate(Format.Native)> _
    Public Structure Range
```

Inside the aggregate body, two private variables are declared, min and max, which represent the minimum and maximum values:

```
Private min As SqlDouble
Private max As SqlDouble
```

The mandatory Init method initializes the min and max private variables to SqlDouble.Null:

```
Public Sub Init()
    Me.min = SqlDouble.Null
    Me.max = SqlDouble.Null
End Sub
```

The Accumulate method accepts a SqlDouble value. It first checks that the value is not NULL (NULLs are ignored). Then it checks to see if the value passed in is less than the min variable (or if min is NULL), and if so assigns the value to min. It also checks the value against max and assigns it to max if it is greater (or if max is NULL). In this way the min and max values are determined "on the fly" as the query engine feeds values into the Accumulate method:

```
Public Sub Accumulate(ByVal value As SqlDouble)
    If Not value.IsNull Then
        If Me.min.IsNull OrElse value < Me.min Then
            Me.min = value
        End If
        If Me.max.IsNull OrElse value > Me.max Then
            Me.max = value
        End If
    End If
End Sub
```

The Merge method merges a Range structure that is created in parallel with the current structure. The method accepts a Range structure and compares its min and max variables to those of the current Range structure. It then adjusts the current structure's min and max variables based on the Range structure passed into the method, effectively merging the two results:

```
Public Sub Merge(ByVal tempRange As Range)
    If (Me.min.IsNull OrElse tempRange.min < Me.min) Then
        Me.min = tempRange.min
```

```
            End If
            If (Me.min.IsNull OrElse tempRange.max > Me.max) Then
                Me.max = tempRange.max
            End If
        End Sub
```

The final method of the UDA is the Terminate function, which returns a SqlDouble result. This function checks for NULL min or max results (the UDA will return NULL if either min or max is a NULL). If both min and max are not NULL, the result is the difference between the max and min values:

```
        Public Function Terminate() As SqlDouble
            Dim result As SqlDouble = SqlDouble.Null
            If Not (Me.min.IsNull OrElse Me.max.IsNull) Then
                result = Me.max - Me.min
            End If
            Return result
        End Function
    End Structure
End Namespace
```

A simple test of the UDA is the following query that determines the range of prices paid by customers for AdventureWorks products. Information like this can help AdventureWorks' sales and management teams set optimal price points for their products:

```
SELECT ProductID, dbo.Range(UnitPrice) AS Price_Range
FROM Sales.SalesOrderDetail
WHERE UnitPrice > 0
GROUP BY ProductID;
```

The results of this query look like those in Figure 14-6.

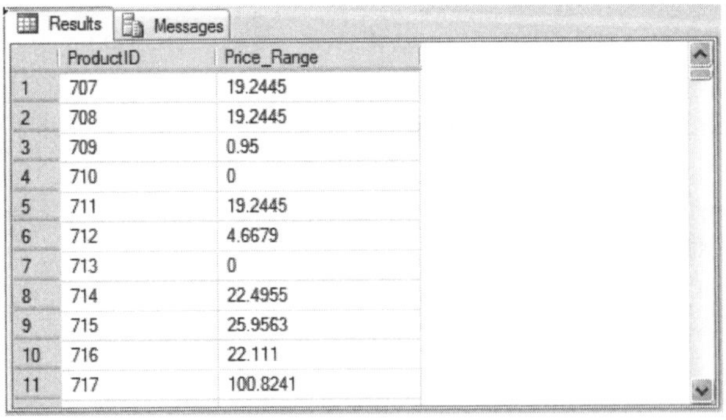

Figure 14-6. *Results of the Range aggregate when applied to unit prices*

When dealing with more complex user-defined aggregates, the SQLCLR imposes some restrictions:

- As mentioned previously, UDAs have a serialization limit of 8,000 bytes total at any given point in a calculation. This can be very limiting if your UDA requires intermediate result storage, or if you intend to use your UDA with strings, complex user-defined types, or .NET reference types such as ArrayLists.

- Any UDA that uses reference (nonvalue) types, such as ArrayLists, SortedLists, and Objects cannot be marked for Format.Native serialization. Such UDAs have to be marked as Format.UserDefined serialization, which means that the UDA must implement the IBinarySerialize interface, including the Read and Write methods. Basically you have to tell SQL Server *how to* serialize your data when using reference types. There is also a performance impact associated with Format.UserDefined serialization as opposed to Format.Native.

- For a UDA, the Terminate method must return the same type of data that the Accumulate method accepts. If these data types do not match, an error will occur. Also, as mentioned previously, it is best practice to use the SQL Server–specific data types, since the standard .NET types tend to choke on NULL values.

■**Tip** The .NET Framework uses Unicode to encode strings and provides no mapping to non-Unicode (i.e., VARCHAR) strings. So, to make a long story short, use NCHAR and NVARCHAR when communicating with SQLCLR assemblies.

SQLCLR User-Defined Types

SQL Server 2000 had built-in support for user-defined data types, but they were limited in scope and functionality. The old-style user-defined data types had the following restrictions:

- They had to be derived from built-in data types.

- Their format and/or range could be restricted by using T-SQL rules.

- They could be assigned a default value.

- They could be declared as NULL or NOT NULL.

SQL Server 2005 provides support for old-style user-defined data types and rules, presumably for backward-compatibility with existing applications. The AdventureWorks database contains examples of old-style user-defined data types, such as the dbo.Phone data type, which is based on the built-in VARCHAR data type.

■**Caution** Rules have been deprecated in SQL Server 2005 and will be removed from a future version. Since rules are the primary method of constraining the values of old-style user-defined data types, it follows that these older user-defined data types might be removed from a future version as well.

SQL Server 2005 supports a far more flexible solution to your custom data type needs in the form of SQLCLR user-defined types (UDTs). SQLCLR user-defined types are backed by the power of the .NET Framework. Common examples of SQLCLR UDTs include mathematical concepts such as points, vectors, complex numbers, and other types not built in to the SQL Server type system.

Complex numbers are a superset of real numbers. They are represented with a "real" part and an "imaginary" part in the format $a+bi$, where a is a real number representing the real part of the value, b is a real number representing the imaginary part, and the literal letter i after the imaginary part stands for the imaginary number i, which is the square root of -1. Complex numbers are often used in the math, science, and engineering fields to solve difficult and sometimes abstract problems. Some examples of complex numbers include: 101.9+3.7i, 98+12i, -19i, and 12+0i (which can also be represented as 12). The example in Listing 14-5 implements complex numbers as a SQLCLR UDT.

Listing 14-5. *Complex Numbers UDT*

```
Imports System.Data.SqlTypes
Imports Microsoft.SqlServer.Server
Imports System.Text.RegularExpressions

Namespace APress.Examples
    <Serializable()> _
    <SqlUserDefinedType(Format.Native, IsByteOrdered:=True)> _
    Public Structure Complex
        Implements INullable

        Public real As Double
        Public imaginary As Double
        Private m_Null As Boolean
```

```vbnet
Private Shared ReadOnly rx As New System.Text.RegularExpressions.Regex( _
    "^(?<Imaginary>[+-]?([0-9]+|[0-9]*\.[0-9]+))[i|I]$|" & _
    "^(?<Real>[+-]?([0-9]+|[0-9]*\.[0-9]+))$|" & _
    "^(?<Real>[+-]?([0-9]+|[0-9]*\.[0-9]+))(?<Imaginary>[+-]?" & _
    "([0-9]+|[0-9]*\.[0-9]+))[i|I]$")


Public Shared Function Parse(ByVal s As SqlString) As Complex
    Dim u As Complex = New Complex
    If s.IsNull Then
        u = Null
    Else
        Dim m As System.Text.RegularExpressions.MatchCollection = _
            rx.Matches(s.Value)
        If (m.Count = 0) Then
            Throw (New FormatException("Invalid Complex Number Format."))
        End If
        Dim real_str As String = m.Item(0).Groups("Real").Value
        Dim imaginary_str As String = m.Item(0).Groups("Imaginary").Value
        If (real_str = "" AndAlso imaginary_str = "") Then
            Throw (New FormatException("Invalid Complex Number Format."))
        End If
        If (real_str = "") Then
            u.real = 0.0
        Else
            u.real = Convert.ToDouble(real_str)
        End If
        If (imaginary_str = "") Then
            u.imaginary = 0.0
        Else
            u.imaginary = Convert.ToDouble(imaginary_str)
        End If
    End If
    Return u
End Function


Public Overrides Function ToString() As String
    Dim sign As String = ""
    If Me.imaginary >= 0.0 Then
        sign = "+"
    End If
    Return Me.real.ToString + sign + Me.imaginary.ToString + "i"
End Function
```

```vb
        Public ReadOnly Property IsNull() As Boolean Implements INullable.IsNull
            Get
                Return m_Null
            End Get
        End Property


        Public Shared ReadOnly Property Null() As Complex
            Get
                Dim h As Complex = New Complex
                h.m_Null = True
                Return h
            End Get
        End Property


        Public Sub New(ByVal r As Double, ByVal i As Double)
            Me.real = r
            Me.imaginary = i
        End Sub


        Public Shared Operator +(ByVal n1 As Complex, ByVal n2 As Complex) As _
            Complex
            Dim u As Complex
            If (n1.IsNull() OrElse n2.IsNull()) Then
                u = Null
            Else
                u = New Complex(n1.real + n2.real, n1.imaginary + n2.imaginary)
            End If
            Return u
        End Operator


        Public Shared Operator /(ByVal n1 As Complex, ByVal n2 As Complex) As _
            Complex
            Dim u As Complex
            If (n1.IsNull() OrElse n2.IsNull()) Then
                u = Null
            Else
                If (n2.real = 0.0 AndAlso n2.imaginary = 0.0) Then
                    Throw New DivideByZeroException("Complex Number Division By ➥
                        Zero Exception.")
                End If
```

```
                    u = New Complex(((n1.real * n2.real) + _
                        (n1.imaginary * n2.imaginary)) / _
                        ((n2.real ^ 2 + n2.imaginary ^ 2)), _
                        ((n1.imaginary * n2.real) - (n1.real * n2.imaginary)) / _
                        ((n2.real ^ 2 + n2.imaginary ^ 2)))
            End If
            Return u
        End Operator

        Public Shared Function CAdd(ByVal n1 As Complex, ByVal n2 As Complex) As _
            Complex
            Return n1 + n2
        End Function

        Public Shared Function Div(ByVal n1 As Complex, ByVal n2 As Complex) As _
            Complex
            Return n1 / n2
        End Function

    End Structure
End Namespace
```

The code begins with the required namespace imports and the namespace declaration for the sample:

```
Imports System.Data.SqlTypes
Imports Microsoft.SqlServer.Server
Imports System.Text.RegularExpressions

Namespace APress.Examples
```

Next is the declaration of the structure that represents an instance of the UDT. The Serializable, Format.Native, and IsByteOrdered:=True attributes/attribute properties are all set on the UDT. In addition, all SQLCLR UDTs must implement the INullable interface. INullable requires that the IsNull and Null properties be defined. Table 14-1 shows a few of the common attributes that are used in SQLCLR UDT definitions.

Table 14-1. *Common SQLCLR UDT Attributes*

AttributeProperty	Value	Description	
Serializable	n/a	n/a	Indicates that the UDT can be serialized and deserialized.
SqlUserDefinedType	Format.Native	n/a	Specifies that the UDT uses native format for serialization. The native format is the most efficient format for serialization/deserialization, but it imposes some limitations. You can only expose .NET value data types as the fields like Char, Integer, etc. You cannot expose reference data types like Strings, Arrays, etc.
	Format.UserDefined	n/a	Specifies that the UDT uses a user-defined format for serialization. When this is specified, your UDT must implement the IBinarySerialize interface and you are responsible for supplying the Write() and Read() methods that serialize and deserialize your UDT.
	IsByteOrdered	True/False	Allows comparisons and sorting of UDT values based on their binary representation. This is also required if you intend to create indexes on columns defined as a SQLCLR UDT type.
	IsFixedLength	True/False	Set to True if the serialized instance of your UDT is a fixed length.
	MaxByteSize	<= 8000	Indicates the maximum size of your serialized UDT instances in bytes. The upper limit for this property is 8,000 bytes.

The code in Listing 14-5 applies the Serializable attribute to the UDT. It also sets the UDT format to Format.IsNative and the UDT IsByteOrdered property to True:

```
<Serializable()> _
<SqlUserDefinedType(Format.Native, IsByteOrdered:=True)> _
Public Structure Complex
    Implements INullable
```

The public and private fields are then declared:

```
Public real As Double
Public imaginary As Double
Private m_Null As Boolean
```

The `real` and `imaginary` public fields represent the real and imaginary parts of the complex number, respectively. The `m_Null` field is a `Boolean` value that is set to `True` if the current instance of the complex type is `NULL`, and `False` otherwise.

The first method declared in the UDT is the `Parse` method (required by all UDTs), which takes a string value from SQL Server and parses it into a complex number. The `Parse` method uses a .NET regular expression to simplify parsing a bit:

```
Private Shared ReadOnly rx As New System.Text.RegularExpressions.Regex( _
    "^(?<Imaginary>[+-]?([0-9]+|[0-9]*\.[0-9]+))[i|I]$|" & _
    "^(?<Real>[+-]?([0-9]+|[0-9]*\.[0-9]+))$|" & _
    "^(?<Real>[+-]?([0-9]+|[0-9]*\.[0-9]+))(?<Imaginary>[+-]?" & _
    "([0-9]+|[0-9]*\.[0-9]+))[i|I]$")

Public Shared Function Parse(ByVal s As SqlString) As Complex
    Dim u As Complex = New Complex
    If s.IsNull Then
        u = Null
    Else
        Dim m As System.Text.RegularExpressions.MatchCollection = _
            rx.Matches(s.Value)
        If (m.Count = 0) Then
            Throw (New FormatException("Invalid Complex Number Format."))
        End If
        Dim real_str As String = m.Item(0).Groups("Real").Value
        Dim imaginary_str As String = m.Item(0).Groups("Imaginary").Value
        If (real_str = "" AndAlso imaginary_str = "") Then
            Throw (New FormatException("Invalid Complex Number Format."))
        End If
        If (real_str = "") Then
            u.real = 0.0
        Else
            u.real = Convert.ToDouble(real_str)
        End If
        If (imaginary_str = "") Then
            u.imaginary = 0.0
        Else
            u.imaginary = Convert.ToDouble(imaginary_str)
```

```
            End If
        End If
        Return u
    End Function
```

The regular expression (*regex*) uses *named groups* to parse the input string into Real and/or Imaginary named groups. If the regex is successful, at least one (if not both) of these named groups will be populated. If unsuccessful, both named groups are empty and a Format Exception is thrown. If at least one of the named groups is properly set, the string representations are converted to Double type and assigned to the appropriate UDT fields. Table 14-2 shows sample input strings and the values assigned to the UDT fields when they are parsed.

Table 14-2. *Complex Number Parsing Samples*

Complex Number	Real	Imaginary	m_Null
100+11i	100.0	11.0	False
99.9	99.9	0.0	False
3.7-9.8i	3.7	-9.8	False
2.1i	0.0	2.1	False
-9-8.2i	-9.0	-8.2	False
NULL	n/a	n/a	True

The ToString method is required for all UDTs as well. This method converts the internal UDT data to its string representation. In the case of complex numbers, ToString needs to perform the following steps:

1. Convert the real part to a string.

2. Append a plus sign (+) if the imaginary part is zero or positive.

3. Append the imaginary part.

4. Append the letter i to indicate it does in fact represent a complex number.

Notice that if the imaginary part is negative, no sign is appended between the real and imaginary parts, since the sign is already included in the imaginary part:

```
Public Overrides Function ToString() As String
    Dim sign As String = ""
    If Me.imaginary >= 0.0 Then
        sign = "+"
    End If
    Return Me.real.ToString + sign + Me.imaginary.ToString + "i"
End Function
```

The IsNull and Null properties are both required by all UDTs. IsNull is a Boolean property that indicates whether a UDT instance is NULL or not. The Null property returns a NULL instance of the UDT type:

```
Public ReadOnly Property IsNull() As Boolean Implements INullable.IsNull
    Get
        Return m_Null
    End Get
End Property

Public Shared ReadOnly Property Null() As Complex
    Get
        Dim h As Complex = New Complex
        h.m_Null = True
        Return h
    End Get
End Property
```

This particular UDT includes a constructor function that accepts two Double type values and creates a UDT instance from them:

```
Public Sub New(ByVal r As Double, ByVal i As Double)
    Me.real = r
    Me.imaginary = i
End Sub
```

■**Tip** For a UDT designed using a Structure, a constructor method is not required. In fact a default constructor (that takes no parameters) is not even allowed. To keep later code simple, a constructor method is used in this example.

To keep this listing short, but highlight the important points, this sample UDT supports only addition and division operations on complex numbers. The UDT overrides the + and / math operators (addition and division). Redefining these operators makes it easier to write and debug additional UDT methods. These overridden .NET math operators are not available to T-SQL code, so that the standard T-SQL math operators will not work on the UDT. Adding and dividing UDT values from T-SQL must be done via explicitly exposed methods of the UDT. These methods in the Complex UDT are CAdd and Div, for complex number addition and division, respectively. Note that CAdd (*complex number add*) was chosen as a method name to avoid conflicts with the T-SQL reserved word ADD.

I won't go too deeply into the inner workings of complex numbers, but these two operators were chosen as samples for this listing because complex number addition is a straightforward operation, while division is a bit more complicated. These two sample methods are declared as Shared (static in C#), so they can be invoked on the UDT data type itself from SQL Server, instead of on an instance of the UDT. The full complex number Complex UDT listing is available in Appendix D.

TO SHARE OR NOT TO SHARE

Shared (static in C#) methods of a UDT are invoked from SQL Server using a format like this:

Complex::CAdd(@n1, @n2)

Nonshared, or *instance*, methods of a UDT are invoked from SQL Server using a format like this:

@n1.CAdd(@n2)

The style of methods you use (shared or instance) is a determination you'll need to make on a case-by-case basis.

The declarations for the addition and division Complex UDT operators are shown here:

```
Public Shared Operator +(ByVal n1 As Complex, ByVal n2 As Complex) As _
    Complex
    Dim u As Complex
    If (n1.IsNull() OrElse n2.IsNull()) Then
        u = Null
    Else
        u = New Complex(n1.real + n2.real, n1.imaginary + n2.imaginary)
    End If
    Return u
End Operator
```

```vb
        Public Shared Operator /(ByVal n1 As Complex, ByVal n2 As Complex) As _
            Complex
            Dim u As Complex
            If (n1.IsNull() OrElse n2.IsNull()) Then
                u = Null
            Else
                If (n2.real = 0.0 AndAlso n2.imaginary = 0.0) Then
                    Throw New DivideByZeroException("Complex Number Division By ➥
                             Zero Exception.")
                End If
                u = New Complex(((n1.real * n2.real) + _
                    (n1.imaginary * n2.imaginary)) / _
                    ((n2.real ^ 2 + n2.imaginary ^ 2)), _
                    ((n1.imaginary * n2.real) - (n1.real * n2.imaginary)) / _
                    ((n2.real ^ 2 + n2.imaginary ^ 2)))
            End If
            Return u
        End Operator

        Public Shared Function CAdd(ByVal n1 As Complex, ByVal n2 As Complex) As _
            Complex
            Return n1 + n2
        End Function

        Public Shared Function Div(ByVal n1 As Complex, ByVal n2 As Complex) As _
            Complex
            Return n1 / n2
        End Function

    End Structure
End Namespace
```

■**Caution** One thing that you need to be aware of any time you invoke a UDT (or any SQLCLR object) from T-SQL is the SQL NULL value. For purposes of the Complex UDT, you take a cue from ANSI SQL and return a NULL result any time a NULL is passed in as a parameter to any UDT method. So a Complex value plus NULL returns NULL, as does a Complex value divided by NULL, and so on. You will notice a lot of code in the full listing that is specifically designed to deal with T-SQL NULLs.

Listing 14-6 demonstrates how the Complex UDT can be used.

Listing 14-6. *Complex Number UDT Demonstration*

```
DECLARE @c COMPLEX
SELECT @c = '+100-10i'
DECLARE @d COMPLEX
SELECT @d = '5i'
SELECT 'ADD: ' + @c.ToString() + ' , ' + @d.ToString(),
    COMPLEX::CAdd(@c, @d).ToString()
SELECT 'DIV: ' + @c.ToString() + ' , ' + @d.ToString(),
    COMPLEX::Div(@c, @d).ToString()
```

The following is the result of this simple test script:

ADD:	100-10i , 0+5i	100-5i
DIV:	100-10i , 0+5i	-2-20i

In addition to the basic operations, the Complex class can be easily extended to support several more advanced complex number operators and functions. The full listing includes all the basic math operators as well as logarithmic and exponential functions (such as Log(), Power(), etc.) and trigonometric and hyperbolic functions (such as Sin(), Cos(), Tanh(), etc.) for complex numbers.

Summary

This chapter discussed SQL Server 2005 assemblies and the different types of SQLCLR objects that can be created. These specific topics were covered:

- SQLCLR usage considerations

- SQLCLR assemblies and security, including SAFE, EXTERNAL_ACCESS, and UNSAFE permission sets

- SQLCLR objects including the following:

  - User-defined functions (scalar and table-valued)

  - Stored procedures

  - User-defined aggregates (UDAs)

  - User-defined types (UDTs)

I provided code samples and some general guidelines for when to use the SQLCLR and when to rely on T-SQL's built-in functionality. The SQLCLR gives you the opportunity to extend SQL Server's capabilities with the full power of the .NET Framework. It is especially useful for accessing external resources that are off-limits to normal T-SQL code; and if properly used it can provide performance gains for code requiring complex calculations and string manipulations.

This chapter served as an introduction to SQLCLR programming. For in-depth SQLCLR programming information, I highly recommend the book *Pro SQL Server 2005 Assemblies* by Robin Dewson and Julian Skinner (Apress, 2005).

The next chapter will introduce client-side .NET connectivity to SQL Server 2005.

CHAPTER 15

■ ■ ■

.NET Client Programming

What's more important? An efficient database, or a well-designed client application to connect to the database? In my estimation they are both equally important. While this book is focused on server-side functionality, the .NET Framework does offer several options to make SQL Server 2005 client connectivity simple and efficient. This chapter discusses using ADO.NET and the .NET SqlClient as a basis for building your own easy-to-use, cutting-edge client applications.

ADO.NET

The System.Data namespaces consist of classes and enumerations that constitute the ADO.NET architecture, the .NET Framework's primary data access method. The .NET architecture provides disconnected data access via the DataSet, DataTable, and DataAdapter classes. The following are some of the more commonly used namespaces for SQL Server data access:

- The System.Data.Common namespace provides access to classes that are shared by .NET Framework data access providers.

- System.Data.Sql contains classes with SQL Server–specific functionality.

- System.Data.SqlTypes provides .NET classes representing native, nullable data types in SQL Server. These SQL Server data types (for the most part) use the same internal representation as SQL Server data types, helping to reduce precision loss problems. Using these types can also help speed up SQL Server connectivity, since it helps eliminate implicit conversions. Table 15-1 lists the .NET SqlTypes and their corresponding native T-SQL data types.

Table 15-1. *System.Data.SqlTypes Reference*

System.Data.SqlTypes Class	Native T-SQL Data Type
SqlBinary	binary, image, timestamp, varbinary
SqlBoolean	bit
SqlByte	tinyint
SqlBytes	image, varbinary(max)
SqlChars	ntext, nvarchar(max), text, varchar(max)
SqlDateTime	datetime, smalldatetime
SqlDouble	float(53)
SqlGuid	uniqueidentifier
SqlInt16	smallint
SqlInt32	int
SqlInt64	bigint
SqlMoney	money, smallmoney
SqlSingle	real, float(24)
SqlString	char, nchar, text, ntext, nvarchar, varchar
SqlXml	xml

■**Note** SqlBytes represents a mutable reference around a Buffer or Stream. SqlChars is a mutable reference around a Char array, SqlStreamChars, or SqlString instance. These types are recommended for large-object (LOB) data types.

- The primary namespace for SQL Server connectivity is System.Data.SqlClient. This namespace includes classes that provide optimized access to SQL Server version 7.0 and higher. The classes in this namespace are designed specifically to take advantage of SQL Server–specific features and won't work with other data sources.

- Microsoft also provides the System.Data.OleDb namespace, which can connect to a variety of data sources, including SQL Server. OLE DB is not as efficient when used against SQL Server, but it is a good option for applications that need to access data on multiple platforms, such as both SQL Server and Microsoft Access.

- The System.Data.Odbc provides managed access to old-fashioned ODBC drivers. ODBC was developed in the early 1990s as a "one-size-fits-all" standard for connecting to a wide array of varied data sources. Because of its mission of standardizing data access across a wide variety of data sources, ODBC provides a generally "plain vanilla" interface that often does not take advantage of most SQL Server or other DBMS platform–specific features. This means ODBC is not as efficient as the SqlClient or OleDb clients but still provides a useful option for connecting to legacy database systems. It is also a proven interface for connecting to a wide variety of data sources such as Excel spreadsheets or other database management systems.

The .NET SqlClient

The .NET SqlClient is the most efficient way to connect to SQL Server from a client application. With the possible exceptions of upgrading legacy code, or designing code that must access non-SQL Server data sources, SqlClient is the client connectivity method of choice.

The main classes for establishing a connection, sending SQL commands, and retrieving results with the SqlClient are listed in Table 15-2.

Table 15-2. *Main SqlClient Classes*

System.Data.SqlClient Class	Description
SqlCommand	An object that represents a SQL Server statement or stored procedure to execute.
SqlCommandBuilder	An object that automatically generates single-table commands to reconcile changes made to an ADO.NET DataSet.
SqlConnection	An object that establishes an open connection to a SQL Server database.
SqlConnectionStringBuilder	An object that creates connection strings used by SqlConnection objects.
SqlDataAdapter	An object that wraps a set of SqlCommands, and a SqlConnection object that can be used to fill a DataSet and update a SQL Server database.
SqlDataReader	An object that provides methods to read a forward-only stream of rows from a SQL Server database.
SqlException	A SQL Server–specific exception class. This class can be used to capture a SQL Server error or warning.
SqlParameter	A parameter to a SqlCommand.
SqlParameterCollection	A collection of SqlParameter objects associated with a SqlCommand.
SqlTransaction	A T-SQL transaction to be made in a SQL Server database.

Listing 15-1 demonstrates `SqlClient` data access with a `SqlDataReader`. This is the type of access you might use in an ASP.NET page to quickly retrieve values for a drop-down list, for example. This sample is written to run as a VB 2005 console application. The SQL Server connection string defined in the `sqlConStr` variable should be modified to suit your local SQL Server environment and security.

Listing 15-1. *SqlDataReader Sample*

```
Imports System.Data.SqlClient

Namespace APress.Samples
    Module DataReaderExample
        Sub Main()
            Dim sqlConStr As String = "DATA SOURCE=(local);" & _
                "INITIAL CATALOG=AdventureWorks;" & _
                "INTEGRATED SECURITY=SSPI;"
            Dim sqlStmt As String = "SELECT DepartmentId, " & _
                "    Name, " & _
                "    GroupName, " & _
                "    ModifiedDate " & _
                " FROM HumanResources.Department " & _
                " ORDER BY DepartmentId"
            Dim sqlCon As SqlConnection = Nothing
            Dim sqlCmd As SqlCommand = Nothing
            Dim sqlDr As SqlClient.SqlDataReader = Nothing
            Try
                sqlCon = New SqlConnection(sqlConStr)
                sqlCon.Open()
                sqlCmd = New SqlCommand(sqlStmt, sqlCon)
                sqlDr = sqlCmd.ExecuteReader()
                Do While sqlDr.Read()
                    Console.WriteLine("{0}" & ControlChars.Tab & _
                        "{1}" & ControlChars.Tab & _
                        "{2}" & ControlChars.Tab & _
                        "{3}", sqlDr.Item("DepartmentId").ToString(), _
                        sqlDr.Item("Name").ToString(), _
                        sqlDr.Item("GroupName").ToString(), _
                        sqlDr.Item("ModifiedDate").ToString())
                Loop
            Catch ex As SqlException
                Console.WriteLine(ex.Message)
```

```
        Finally
            If Not (sqlDr Is Nothing) Then
                sqlDr.Close()
            End If
            If Not (sqlCmd Is Nothing) Then
                sqlCmd.Dispose()
            End If
            If Not (sqlCon Is Nothing) Then
                sqlCon.Dispose()
            End If
        End Try
        Console.Write("Press a Key to Continue...")
        Console.ReadKey()
    End Sub
End Module
End Namespace
```

The example is a very simple VB console application that retrieves the list of departments from the `HumanResources.Department` table of the AdventureWorks database and writes the data to the display. The example begins by importing the `SqlClient` namespace and declaring this module a part of the `APress.Samples` namespace, declaring a VB module and declaring the `Main()` subroutine. Though not required, importing the namespace saves some keystrokes and helps make code more readable by eliminating the need to prefix the `System.Data.SqlClient` classes and enumerations with the namespace:

```
Imports System.Data.SqlClient

Namespace APress.Samples
    Module DataReaderExample
        Sub Main()
```

The subroutine begins by defining the SQL Server connection string and the T-SQL `SELECT` query that will retrieve the department data. The `SqlConnection`, `SqlCommand`, and `SqlDataReader` objects are also declared:

```
            Dim sqlConStr As String = "DATA SOURCE=(local);" & _
                "INITIAL CATALOG=AdventureWorks;" & _
                "INTEGRATED SECURITY=SSPI;"
            Dim sqlStmt As String = "SELECT DepartmentId, " & _
                "    Name, " & _
                "    GroupName, " & _
                "    ModifiedDate " & _
```

```
            " FROM HumanResources.Department " & _
            " ORDER BY DepartmentId"
    Dim sqlCon As SqlConnection = Nothing
    Dim sqlCmd As SqlCommand = Nothing
    Dim sqlDr As SqlClient.SqlDataReader = Nothing
```

The SqlConnection connection string is composed of a series of key/value pairs separated by semicolons like this:

```
DATA SOURCE=(local);INITIAL CATALOG=AdventureWorks;
```

The most commonly used SqlConnection connection string keys are listed in Table 15-3.

Table 15-3. *SqlConnection Connection String Keys*

Connection String Keys	Description
AttachDBFileName	The name of the full path to an attachable primary database file (MDF file).
Connection Timeout	The length of time (in seconds) to wait for a server connection before stopping the attempt.
Data Source	The name or IP address of a SQL Server instance to connect to. Use server\instance format for named instances. A port number can be added to the end of the name or network address with ", port_num".
Encrypt	Encryption, SSL, with SQL Server.
Initial Catalog	The name of the database to connect to once a server connection is established.
Integrated Security	Key set to true, yes, or sspi, Windows Integrated Security for connection. When false or no, SQL Server security is used.
MultipleActiveResultSets	Key, when true, connection multiple active result sets (MARS). When false, all result sets from a batch must be processed before any other batch can be executed on the connection.
Password	The password for the SQL Server account used to log in. Using Integrated Security is recommended over SQL Server account security.
Persist Security Info	Key, when set to false or no, sensitive security information (like password) not returned as part of the connection if the connection has been opened. The recommended setting is false.
User ID	The SQL Server account user ID used to log in. Integrated Security is recommended over SQL Server account security.

The next section of code is enclosed in a Try...Catch block. The SqlConnection is instantiated and opened using the connection string defined previously. Then a SqlCommand is created on the open connection:

```
Try
    sqlCon = New SqlConnection(sqlConStr)
    sqlCon.Open()
    sqlCmd = New SqlCommand(sqlStmt, sqlCon)
```

■**Tip** When connecting to SQL Server from a .NET client application, it's a very good idea to code defensively with Try...Catch blocks. Defensive programming in database client applications can save a lot of headaches down the road. *Defensive programming* simply means trying to anticipate the problems that might occur and make sure your code handles them. Some of the possible errors you might encounter include the following: could not connect to SQL Server; an expected table or other database object does not exist; NULLs are returned when other values are expected.

Next, the ExecuteReader method is called on the SqlCommand and the result is assigned to the SqlDataReader. A Do While loop is used to retrieve rows from the SqlDataReader and display them on the console:

```
sqlDr = sqlCmd.ExecuteReader()
Do While sqlDr.Read()
    Console.WriteLine("{0}" & ControlChars.Tab & _
        "{1}" & ControlChars.Tab & _
        "{2}" & ControlChars.Tab & _
        "{3}", sqlDr.Item("DepartmentId").ToString(), _
        sqlDr.Item("Name").ToString(), _
        sqlDr.Item("GroupName").ToString(), _
        sqlDr.Item("ModifiedDate").ToString())
Loop
```

The Catch block of the Try...Catch captures any SqlExceptions that occur and displays the exception message on the console:

```
Catch ex As SqlException
    Console.WriteLine(ex.Message)
```

The Finally block properly disposes of the SqlDataReader, SqlCommand, and SqlConnection objects. Finally, a "Press a Key to Continue" message is displayed, and the application waits for a key press before exiting:

```
        Finally
            If Not (sqlDr Is Nothing) Then
                sqlDr.Close()
            End If
            If Not (sqlCmd Is Nothing) Then
                sqlCmd.Dispose()
            End If
            If Not (sqlCon Is Nothing) Then
                sqlCon.Dispose()
            End If
        End Try
        Console.Write("Press a Key to Continue...")
        Console.ReadKey()
    End Sub
  End Module
End Namespace
```

The results of the sample application look like the following:

```
1   Engineering              Research and Development      6/1/1998 12:00:00 AM
2   Tool Design              Research and Development      6/1/1998 12:00:00 AM
3   Sales                    Sales and Marketing           6/1/1998 12:00:00 AM
4   Marketing                Sales and Marketing           6/1/1998 12:00:00 AM
5   Purchasing               Inventory Management          6/1/1998 12:00:00 AM
6   Research and Development  Research and Development      6/1/1998 12:00:00 AM
7   Production               Manufacturing                 6/1/1998 12:00:00 AM
8   Production Control       Manufacturing                 6/1/1998 12:00:00 AM
9   Human Resources          Executive General and Admin...  6/1/1998 12:00:00 AM
10  Finance Executive        General and Administration    6/1/1998 12:00:00 AM
11  Information Services      Executive General and Admin...  6/1/1998 12:00:00 AM
12  Document Control         Quality Assurance             6/1/1998 12:00:00 AM
13  Quality Assurance        Quality Assurance             6/1/1998 12:00:00 AM
14  Facilities and Maintenance Executive General and Admin...  6/1/1998 12:00:00 AM
15  Shipping and Receiving   Inventory Management          6/1/1998 12:00:00 AM
16  Executive                Executive General and Admin...  6/1/1998 12:00:00 AM
Press a Key to Continue...
```

The example in Listing 15-1 demonstrates the forward-only read-only SqlDataReader, which provides an efficient interface for retrieving data but is far less flexible than ADO.NET disconnected datasets. Listing 15-2 demonstrates how to use the SqlDataAdapter to fill a DataSet and print the results like the previous example. The differences between Listing 15-2 and the previous example (Listing 15-1) are shown in bold.

Listing 15-2. *Using SqlDataReader to Fill a DataSet*

```vb
Imports System.Data
Imports System.Data.SqlClient

Namespace APress.Samples
    Module DataReaderExample
        Sub Main()
            Dim sqlConStr As String = "DATA SOURCE=(local);" & _
                "INITIAL CATALOG=AdventureWorks;" & _
                "INTEGRATED SECURITY=SSPI;"
            Dim sqlStmt As String = "SELECT DepartmentId, " & _
                "       Name, " & _
                "       GroupName, " & _
                "       ModifiedDate " & _
                " FROM HumanResources.Department " & _
                " ORDER BY DepartmentId"
            Dim sqlDa As SqlClient.SqlDataAdapter = Nothing
            Dim ds As DataSet = Nothing
            Try
                sqlDa = New SqlClient.SqlDataAdapter(sqlStmt, sqlConStr)
                ds = New DataSet
                sqlDa.Fill(ds)
                For Each dr As DataRow In ds.Tables(0).Rows
                    Console.WriteLine("{0}" & ControlChars.Tab & _
                        "{1}" & ControlChars.Tab & _
                        "{2}" & ControlChars.Tab & _
                        "{3}", dr.Item("DepartmentId").ToString(), _
                        dr.Item("Name").ToString(), _
                        dr.Item("GroupName").ToString(), _
                        dr.Item("ModifiedDate").ToString())
                Next
            Catch ex As SqlException
                Console.WriteLine(ex.Message)
```

```
        Finally
            If Not (ds Is Nothing) Then
                ds.Dispose()
            End If
            If Not (sqlDa Is Nothing) Then
                sqlDa.Dispose()
            End If
        End Try
        Console.Write("Press a Key to Continue...")
        Console.ReadKey()
    End Sub
    End Module
End Namespace
```

The first difference is that this sample imports the System.Data namespace, because
the DataSet is a member of System.Data. Again, this is not required, but it does save wear
and tear on your fingers by eliminating the need to prefix System.Data classes and enumerations with the namespace:

```
Imports System.Data
Imports System.Data.SqlClient
```

The namespace, module, and Main() subroutine definition are the same as the previous example. The SQL connection string and query string definitions are also the same.
This sample departs from the first listing by declaring a SqlDataAdapter and a DataSet:

```
        Dim sqlDa As SqlClient.SqlDataAdapter = Nothing
        Dim ds As DataSet = Nothing
```

The code to retrieve the data creates a new SqlDataAdapter and DataSet and then
populates the DataSet via the SqlDataAdpater's Fill method:

```
        Try
            sqlDa = New SqlClient.SqlDataAdapter(sqlStmt, sqlConStr)
            ds = New DataSet
            sqlDa.Fill(ds)
```

The main loop iterates through each DataRow in the one table of the DataSet and
writes the results to the console:

```
For Each dr As DataRow In ds.Tables(0).Rows
    Console.WriteLine("{0}" & ControlChars.Tab & _
        "{1}" & ControlChars.Tab & _
        "{2}" & ControlChars.Tab & _
        "{3}", dr.Item("DepartmentId").ToString(), _
        dr.Item("Name").ToString(), _
        dr.Item("GroupName").ToString(), _
        dr.Item("ModifiedDate").ToString())
Next
```

The remaining code handles exceptions, performs cleanup by disposing of the DataSet and SqlDataAdapter, and waits for a key press before exiting:

```
Catch ex As SqlException
    Console.WriteLine(ex.Message)
Finally
    If Not (ds Is Nothing) Then
        ds.Dispose()
    End If
    If Not (sqlDa Is Nothing) Then
        sqlDa.Dispose()
    End If
End Try
Console.Write("Press a Key to Continue...")
Console.ReadKey()
    End Sub
End Module
End Namespace
```

Parameterized Queries

ADO.NET provides a safe method for passing parameters to a stored procedure or a SQL statement, known as *parameterization*. The classic VB6/VBScript method of concatenating parameter values directly into a long SQL query string is inefficient and potentially unsafe. A concatenated string query might look like this:

```
Dim sqlstmt As String = "SELECT ContactID, FirstName, MiddleName, LastName " & _
    " FROM Person.Contact " & _
    " WHERE LastName = N'" & name & "'"
```

The value of the name variable can contain additional SQL statements, leaving your SQL Server wide open to SQL injection attacks, as in the following:

```
name = "'; DELETE FROM Person.Contact; --"
```

This value for the name variable will result in the following dangerous SQL statement being executed on the server:

```
SELECT ContactID, FirstName, MiddleName, LastName
    FROM Person.Contact
    WHERE LastName = N'';
    DELETE FROM Person.Contact; --'
```

Parameterized queries avoid SQL injection by sending the parameter values to the server separately from the SQL statement. Listing 15-3 demonstrates a parameterized query.

Listing 15-3. *Parameterized SQL Query*

```
Imports System.Data.SqlClient

Namespace APress.Samples
    Module ParameterizedQuery
        Sub Main()
            Dim name As String = "SMITH"
            Dim sqlstmt As String = _
                "SELECT ContactID, FirstName, MiddleName, LastName " & _
                " FROM Person.Contact " & _
                " WHERE LastName = @name"
            Dim sqlcon As SqlConnection = Nothing
            Dim sqlcmd As SqlCommand = Nothing
            Dim sqldr As SqlDataReader = Nothing
            Try
                sqlcon = New SqlConnection("SERVER=(local); " & _
                    "INITIAL CATALOG=AdventureWorks;INTEGRATED SECURITY=SSPI;")
                sqlcon.Open()
                sqlcmd = New SqlCommand(sqlstmt, sqlcon)
                sqlcmd.Parameters.Add("@name", SqlDbType.NVarChar, 50).Value = name
                sqldr = sqlcmd.ExecuteReader()
```

```
            Do While (sqldr.Read())
                Console.WriteLine("{0}" & ControlChars.Tab & _
                    "{1}," & ControlChars.Tab & _
                    "{2}" & ControlChars.Tab & _
                    "{3}" & ControlChars.Tab, _
                    sqldr.Item("ContactID").ToString(), _
                    sqldr.Item("LastName").ToString(), _
                    sqldr.Item("FirstName").ToString(), _
                    sqldr.Item("MiddleName").ToString())
            Loop
        Catch ex As Exception
            Console.WriteLine(ex.Message)
        Finally
            If Not (sqldr Is Nothing) Then
                sqldr.Close()
            End If
            If Not (sqlcmd Is Nothing) Then
                sqlcmd.Dispose()
            End If
            If Not (sqlcon Is Nothing) Then
                sqlcon.Dispose()
            End If
        End Try
        Console.WriteLine("Press any key...")
        Console.ReadKey()
    End Sub
    End Module
End Namespace
```

Listing 15-3 retrieves and prints the contact information for all contacts in the AdventureWorks Person.Contact table whose last name is SMITH. The sample begins by importing the System.Data.SqlClient namespace and declaring the APress.Samples namespace and the VB module and subroutine:

```
Imports System.Data.SqlClient

Namespace APress.Samples
    Module ParameterizedQuery
        Sub Main()
```

The Main() subroutine begins by declaring a variable to hold the parameter value, a parameterized SQL SELECT statement, and the SqlClient SqlConnection, SqlCommand, and SqlDataReader objects:

```
Dim name As String = "SMITH"
Dim sqlstmt As String = _
    "SELECT ContactID, FirstName, MiddleName, LastName " & _
    " FROM Person.Contact " & _
    " WHERE LastName = @name"
Dim sqlcon As SqlConnection = Nothing
Dim sqlcmd As SqlCommand = Nothing
Dim sqldr As SqlDataReader = Nothing
```

The parameterized SQL SELECT statement contains the @name SQL Server named parameter. Next, a connection is established to the AdventureWorks database:

```
Try
    sqlcon = New SqlConnection("SERVER=(local); " & _
        "INITIAL CATALOG=AdventureWorks;INTEGRATED SECURITY=SSPI;")
    sqlcon.Open()
```

Then a SQL SELECT query is created and a value is assigned to the @name parameter:

```
sqlcmd = New SqlCommand(sqlstmt, sqlcon)
sqlcmd.Parameters.Add("@name", SqlDbType.NVarChar, 50).Value = name
```

Every SqlCommand exposes a SqlParameterCollection property called Parameters. The Add method of the Parameters collection allows you to add parameters to the SqlCommand. In this sample, the parameter added is named @name; it is an nvarchar type parameter, and its length is 50. The parameters in the Parameters collection are passed along to SQL Server with the SQL statement when the ExecuteReader, ExecuteScalar, ExecuteNonQuery, or ExecuteXmlReader method of the SqlCommand is called. In this instance the ExecuteReader method is called to return the results via SqlDataReader:

```
sqldr = sqlcmd.ExecuteReader()
```

The Do While loop retrieves and displays each row of the result set from the SqlDataReader:

```
        Do While (sqldr.Read())
            Console.WriteLine("{0}" & ControlChars.Tab & _
                "{1}," & ControlChars.Tab & _
                "{2}" & ControlChars.Tab & _
                "{3}" & ControlChars.Tab, _
                sqldr.Item("ContactID").ToString(), _
                sqldr.Item("LastName").ToString(), _
                sqldr.Item("FirstName").ToString(), _
                sqldr.Item("MiddleName").ToString())
    Loop
```

The last part of the code handles exceptions, proper disposal of SqlClient objects, and pausing for a key press:

```
        Catch ex As Exception
            Console.WriteLine(ex.Message)
        Finally
            If Not (sqldr Is Nothing) Then
                sqldr.Close()
            End If
            If Not (sqlcmd Is Nothing) Then
                sqlcmd.Dispose()
            End If
            If Not (sqlcon Is Nothing) Then
                sqlcon.Dispose()
            End If
        End Try
        Console.WriteLine("Press any key...")
        Console.ReadKey()
    End Sub
End Module
End Namespace
```

■**Tip** In addition to preventing SQL injection attacks, parameterized queries provide greater efficiency than concatenated strings. Parameterized queries can take advantage of SQL Server's built-in query plan caching mechanisms, while concatenated string queries generally will not be able to take advantage of cached query plan reuse. Additionally, a parameter can be specified as an OUTPUT parameter when calling stored procedures. In this case, the stored procedure will return a value to the client application via the OUTPUT parameter.

Nonquery, Scalar, and XML Querying

The examples covered so far in this chapter have all been SQL SELECT queries, which return rows. SQL statements that do not return result sets are classified by .NET as nonqueries. Examples of nonqueries include UPDATE, INSERT, and DELETE statements, as well as DDL statements such as CREATE INDEX and ALTER TABLE statements. The .NET Framework provides the ExecuteNonQuery method of the SqlCommand class to execute nonqueries such as these. The following is an example of the ExecuteNonQuery method in action:

```
sqlcmd = New SqlCommand("CREATE TABLE #temp(Id INT NOT NULL PRIMARY KEY, " & _
    "Name NVARCHAR(50))", sqlcon)
sqlcmd.ExecuteNonQuery()
```

The example creates a temporary table called #temp with two columns. Because the statement is a DDL statement that returns no result set, the ExecuteNonQuery method is used. In addition to queries that return no result sets, some queries return a result set consisting of one row by one column. For these queries .NET provides a shortcut method of retrieving the value. The ExecuteScalar method retrieves the single value returned as a scalar value in a .NET Object. Using this method you can avoid the hassle of creating a SqlDataReader and iterating it to retrieve a single value. The following example demonstrates ExecuteScalar:

```
sqlcmd = New SqlCommand("SELECT COUNT(*) FROM Person.Contact", sqlcon)
Dim count As Object = sqlcmd.ExecuteScalar()
```

■**Caution** If ExecuteScalar is called on a SqlCommand that returns more than one row and/or more than one column, only the first row of the first column is retrieved. Your best bet is to make sure you only call ExecuteScalar on queries that return a single scalar value (one row, one column) to avoid possible confusion and problems down the line.

An additional method of retrieving results in .NET is the ExecuteXmlReader method. This method of the SqlCommand object uses an XmlReader to retrieve the results of a SELECT query with the FOR XML option. Listing 15-4 demonstrates a conversion of the code in Listing 15-3 to use the ExecuteXmlReader method. Differences between this listing and Listing 15-3 are in bold.

Listing 15-4. *ExecuteXmlReader Example*

```
Imports System.Data.SqlClient
Imports System.Xml

Namespace APress.Samples
    Module XmlReaderQuery
        Sub Main()
            Dim name As String = "SMITH"
            Dim sqlstmt As String = "SELECT ContactID, FirstName, " & _
                " COALESCE(MiddleName, '') AS MiddleName, LastName " & _
                " FROM Person.Contact " & _
                " WHERE LastName = @name FOR XML AUTO"
            Dim sqlcon As SqlConnection = Nothing
            Dim sqlcmd As SqlCommand = Nothing
            Dim sqlxr As XmlReader = Nothing
            Try
                sqlcon = New SqlConnection("SERVER=(local); " & _
                    "INITIAL CATALOG=AdventureWorks;INTEGRATED SECURITY=SSPI;")
                sqlcon.Open()
                sqlcmd = New SqlCommand(sqlstmt, sqlcon)
                sqlcmd.Parameters.Add("@name", SqlDbType.NVarChar, 50).Value = name
                sqlxr = sqlcmd.ExecuteXmlReader()
                Do While (sqlxr.Read())
                    Console.WriteLine("{0}" & ControlChars.Tab & _
                        "{1}," & ControlChars.Tab & _
                        "{2}" & ControlChars.Tab & _
                        "{3}" & ControlChars.Tab, _
                        sqlxr.Item("ContactID").ToString(), _
                        sqlxr.Item("LastName").ToString(), _
                        sqlxr.Item("FirstName").ToString(), _
                        sqlxr.Item("MiddleName").ToString())
                Loop
            Catch ex As Exception
                Console.WriteLine(ex.Message)
            Finally
                If Not (sqlxr Is Nothing) Then
                    sqlxr.Close()
                End If
```

```
                      If Not (sqlcmd Is Nothing) Then
                          sqlcmd.Dispose()
                      End If
                      If Not (sqlcon Is Nothing) Then
                          sqlcon.Dispose()
                      End If
                  End Try
                  Console.WriteLine("Press any key...")
                  Console.ReadKey()
              End Sub
          End Module
      End Namespace
```

The first difference between this listing and Listing 15-3 is the import of the System.Xml namespace, since the XmlReader class is being used:

```
Imports System.Data.SqlClient
Imports System.Xml
```

The SQL SELECT statement is also slightly different. For one thing, the COALESCE function is used on the MiddleName column to replace NULL values with an empty string. The FOR XML clause leaves NULL-valued attributes out of the generated XML by default. Missing attributes would generate exceptions while trying to display the results. The FOR XML AUTO clause was also added to the SELECT query to inform SQL Server that it needs to generate an XML result:

```
Dim sqlstmt As String = "SELECT ContactID, FirstName, " & _
    " COALESCE(MiddleName, '') AS MiddleName, LastName " & _
    " FROM Person.Contact " & _
    " WHERE LastName = @name FOR XML AUTO"
```

The loop that displays the results is very similar to the previous example as well. The main difference in this sample is that an XmlReader is used in place of a SqlDataReader:

```
sqlxr = sqlcmd.ExecuteXmlReader()
Do While (sqlxr.Read())
    Console.WriteLine("{0}" & ControlChars.Tab & _
        "{1}," & ControlChars.Tab & _
        "{2}" & ControlChars.Tab & _
        "{3}" & ControlChars.Tab, _
```

```
                    sqlxr.Item("ContactID").ToString(), _
                    sqlxr.Item("LastName").ToString(), _
                    sqlxr.Item("FirstName").ToString(), _
                    sqlxr.Item("MiddleName").ToString())
        Loop
```

The remaining code in the sample performs exception handling and proper cleanup, as in Listing 15-3.

SqlBulkCopy

SQL Server provides tools, such as SQL Server Integration Services (SSIS) and the Bulk Copy Program (bcp), to help populate your databases from external data sources. Sometimes project requirements demand a customized ETL (Extract, Transform, Load) solution. Generally custom ETL solutions are implemented when special processing or transformation of raw input data is required "on the fly." The .NET 2.0 SqlClient implements the SqlBulkCopy class to make designing efficient ETL applications easy. SqlBulkCopy can be used to load data from a database table, an XML table, a flat file, or any other type of data source you choose. The SqlBulkCopy example in Listing 15-5 loads ZIP code data from a tab-delimited flat file into a SQL Server table. Part of the source text file is shown in Table 15-4.

Table 15-4. *Partial Sample Tab-Delimited ZIP Code Data*

ZIP code	Latitude	Longitude	City	State
99546	54.2402	-176.7874	ADAK	AK
99551	60.3147	-163.1189	AKIACHAK	AK
99552	60.3147	-163.1189	AKIAK	AK
99553	55.4306	-162.5581	AKUTAN	AK
99554	62.1172	-163.2376	ALAKANUK	AK
99555	58.9621	-163.1189	ALEKNAGIK	AK

The complete sample ZIP code file is included with the downloadable sample source code ZIP file for this book. The destination table is built with the following script:

```
CREATE TABLE ZipCodes (ZIP CHAR(5) NOT NULL PRIMARY KEY,
    Latitude NUMERIC(8, 4) NOT NULL,
    Longitude NUMERIC(8, 4) NOT NULL,
    City NVARCHAR(50) NOT NULL,
    State CHAR(2) NOT NULL)
GO
```

The code presented in Listing 15-5 uses the SqlBulkCopy class to bulk copy the data from the flat file into the destination table.

Listing 15-5. *SqlBulkCopy Class Example*

```
Imports System
Imports System.Data
Imports System.Data.SqlClient
Imports System.IO

Namespace APress.Samples
    Module ZipImport

        Sub Main()
            Dim sw As New Stopwatch
            sw.Start()
            Dim rowcount As Integer = DoImport()
            sw.Stop()
            Console.WriteLine("{0} Rows Imported in {1} Seconds.", _
                rowcount, (sw.ElapsedMilliseconds / 1000.0))
            Console.WriteLine("Press a Key...")
            Console.ReadKey()
        End Sub

        Function DoImport() As Integer
            Dim sqlcon As String = "DATA SOURCE=(local); " & _
                "INITIAL CATALOG=AdventureWorks;INTEGRATED SECURITY=SSPI;"
            Dim srcfile As String = "C:\ZIPCodes.txt"
            Dim dt As DataTable = Nothing
            Using bulkCopier As New SqlClient.SqlBulkCopy(sqlcon)
                bulkCopier.DestinationTableName = "ZIPCodes"
                Try
                    dt = LoadSourceFile(srcfile)
                    bulkCopier.WriteToServer(dt)
```

```
            Catch ex As SqlException
                Console.WriteLine(ex.Message)
            End Try
        End Using
        Return dt.Rows.Count
    End Function


    Function LoadSourceFile(ByVal srcfile As String) As DataTable
        Dim loadtable As New DataTable
        Dim loadcolumn As New DataColumn
        Dim loadrow As DataRow

        With loadcolumn
            .DataType = Type.GetType("System.String")
            .ColumnName = "ZIP"
            .Unique = True
        End With
        loadtable.Columns.Add(loadcolumn)

        loadcolumn = New DataColumn()
        With loadcolumn
            .DataType = System.Type.GetType("System.Double")
            .ColumnName = "Latitude"
            .Unique = False
        End With
        loadtable.Columns.Add(loadcolumn)

        loadcolumn = New DataColumn()
        With loadcolumn
            .DataType = System.Type.GetType("System.Double")
            .ColumnName = "Longitude"
            .Unique = False
        End With
        loadtable.Columns.Add(loadcolumn)

        loadcolumn = New DataColumn()
        With loadcolumn
            .DataType = System.Type.GetType("System.String")
            .ColumnName = "City"
            .Unique = False
        End With
        loadtable.Columns.Add(loadcolumn)
```

```
            loadcolumn = New DataColumn()
            With loadcolumn
                .DataType = System.Type.GetType("System.String")
                .ColumnName = "State"
                .Unique = False
            End With
            loadtable.Columns.Add(loadcolumn)

            Using sr As New StreamReader(srcfile)
                Dim record As String
                record = sr.ReadLine()
                Do While Not (record Is Nothing)
                    Dim s() As String = record.Split(ControlChars.Tab)
                    loadrow = loadtable.NewRow()
                    loadrow("ZIP") = s(0)
                    loadrow("Latitude") = s(1)
                    loadrow("Longitude") = s(2)
                    loadrow("City") = s(3)
                    loadrow("State") = s(4)
                    loadtable.Rows.Add(loadrow)
                    record = sr.ReadLine()
                Loop
            End Using
            Return loadtable
        End Function
    End Module
End Namespace
```

The code begins by importing required namespaces, declaring the APress.Samples namespace, and declaring the module name. The System.IO namespace is imported for the StreamReader:

```
Imports System
Imports System.Data
Imports System.Data.SqlClient
Imports System.IO

Namespace APress.Samples
    Module ZipImport
```

The import module is divided into three subroutines. The `Main()` subroutine begins by starting a `StopWatch` to time the import process. Then it invokes the `DoImport()` function that performs the actual import. Finally, the `StopWatch` is stopped and the number of rows imported and the number of seconds elapsed are displayed:

```
Sub Main()
    Dim sw As New Stopwatch
    sw.Start()
    Dim rowcount As Integer = DoImport()
    sw.Stop()
    Console.WriteLine("{0} Rows Imported in {1} Seconds.", _
        rowcount, (sw.ElapsedMilliseconds / 1000.0))
    Console.WriteLine("Press a Key...")
    Console.ReadKey()
End Sub
```

The second function, `DoImport()`, begins by defining the SQL Server connection string and the source file name:

```
Function DoImport() As Integer
    Dim sqlcon As String = "DATA SOURCE=(local); " & _
        "INITIAL CATALOG=AdventureWorks;INTEGRATED SECURITY=SSPI;"
    Dim srcfile As String = "C:\ZIPCodes.txt"
```

Next `DoImport()` declares a `DataTable` to hold the source file in memory and a `SqlBulkCopy` object that will perform the actual bulk copy. `DoImport()` calls the `LoadSourceFile()` function to retrieve a `DataTable` with the proper structure, populated with the data from the source file:

```
        Dim dt As DataTable = Nothing
        Using bulkCopier As New SqlClient.SqlBulkCopy(sqlcon)
            bulkCopier.DestinationTableName = "ZIPCodes"
            Try
                dt = LoadSourceFile(srcfile)
```

The populated `DataTable` is passed into the `WriteToServer` method of the `SqlBulkCopy` object. This method copies all the rows in the `DataTable` to the `SqlBulkCopy` object's specified destination table:

```
                    bulkCopier.WriteToServer(dt)
                Catch ex As SqlException
                    Console.WriteLine(ex.Message)
                End Try
            End Using
```

Tip The Using...End Using statement block is new to VB 2005. This statement block automatically disposes of the resources under its control. In the sample code provided, the SqlBulkCopy object is placed under the control of the Using...End Using statement. In practice, Using...End Using behaves just like a shorthand version of a Try...Catch block with a Finally to dispose of the resource(s) under its control.

The DoImport() function ends by returning the total number of rows imported into the DataTable:

```
                Return dt.Rows.Count
            End Function
```

The third and final function is the workhorse of the program. The LoadSourceFile() function accepts the name of the source file to import and returns a properly structured and populated DataTable. The function begins by setting the structure of the DataTable, one DataColumn at a time:

```
        Function LoadSourceFile(ByVal srcfile As String) As DataTable
            Dim loadtable As New DataTable
            Dim loadcolumn As New DataColumn
            Dim loadrow As DataRow

            With loadcolumn
                .DataType = Type.GetType("System.String")
                .ColumnName = "ZIP"
                .Unique = True
            End With
            loadtable.Columns.Add(loadcolumn)

            loadcolumn = New DataColumn()
            With loadcolumn
                .DataType = System.Type.GetType("System.Double")
                .ColumnName = "Latitude"
                .Unique = False
            End With
            loadtable.Columns.Add(loadcolumn)
```

```
loadcolumn = New DataColumn()
With loadcolumn
    .DataType = System.Type.GetType("System.Double")
    .ColumnName = "Longitude"
    .Unique = False
End With
loadtable.Columns.Add(loadcolumn)

loadcolumn = New DataColumn()
With loadcolumn
    .DataType = System.Type.GetType("System.String")
    .ColumnName = "City"
    .Unique = False
End With
loadtable.Columns.Add(loadcolumn)

loadcolumn = New DataColumn()
With loadcolumn
    .DataType = System.Type.GetType("System.String")
    .ColumnName = "State"
    .Unique = False
End With
loadtable.Columns.Add(loadcolumn)
```

LoadSourceFile() next opens up the tab-delimited source file as a StreamReader and reads each line of the file into memory. The tab delimiter is used to split each line of the file into an array of Strings, and each element of the array is assigned to a column of the current row. As each row is filled, it is then added to the DataTable. Finally, after the entire file is read, the full DataTable is returned to the caller as a result:

```
Using sr As New StreamReader(srcfile)
    Dim record As String
    record = sr.ReadLine()
    Do While Not (record Is Nothing)
        Dim s() As String = record.Split(ControlChars.Tab)
        loadrow = loadtable.NewRow()
        loadrow("ZIP") = s(0)
        loadrow("Latitude") = s(1)
        loadrow("Longitude") = s(2)
        loadrow("City") = s(3)
        loadrow("State") = s(4)
```

```
                    loadtable.Rows.Add(loadrow)
                    record = sr.ReadLine()
             Loop
           End Using
           Return loadtable
        End Function
     End Module
End Namespace
```

The results of the `SqlBulkCopy` example will look like the following:

```
41831 Rows Imported in 2.15 Seconds.
Press a Key...
```

A simple `SELECT` statement verifies the destination table is populated:

```
SELECT ZIP, Latitude, Longitude, City, State
FROM ZipCodes;
```

A sample of the results of this query is shown here:

```
ZIP     Latitude   Longitude   City        State
00501   40.9223    -72.6371    HOLTSVILLE  NY
00544   40.9223    -72.6371    HOLTSVILLE  NY
01001   42.1405    -72.7887    AGAWAM      MA
01002   42.3671    -72.4646    AMHERST     MA
01003   42.3695    -72.6359    AMHERST     MA
01004   42.3845    -72.5131    AMHERST     MA
01005   42.3292    -72.1394    BARRE       MA
```

Multiple Active Result Sets

Prior to SQL Server 2005, client-side applications were limited to one open result set per connection to SQL Server. The workaround was to process or cancel all open result sets on a single connection before retrieving a new result set, or to open multiple connections, each with its own single open result.

SQL Server 2005 introduces multiple active result sets (MARS), new functionality that allows you to process multiple open result sets over a single connection.

Listing 15-6 is an attempt to open multiple result sets simultaneously over a single connection to SQL Server.

Listing 15-6. *Trying to Open Two Result Sets Over a Single Connection*

```
Imports System
Imports System.Data
Imports System.Data.SqlClient

Namespace APress.Samples
    Module SqlResultTests

        Sub Main()
            ' Create and open a native SqlClient connection to SQL Server 2005
            Dim sqlcon As New SqlConnection("SERVER=(local);" & _
                "INITIAL CATALOG=AdventureWorks;INTEGRATED SECURITY=SSPI;")
            sqlcon.Open()
            ' Create two SqlCommands to retrieve two result sets
            Dim sqlcmd1 As New SqlCommand( _
                "SELECT DepartmentID, Name, GroupName " & _
                "FROM HumanResources.Department", sqlcon)
            Dim sqlcmd2 As New SqlCommand( _
                "SELECT ShiftID, Name, StartTime, EndTime " & _
                "FROM HumanResources.Shift", sqlcon)
            ' Open the first result set
            Dim sqldr1 As SqlDataReader = sqlcmd1.ExecuteReader()
            ' Open the second result set
            Dim sqldr2 As SqlDataReader = sqlcmd2.ExecuteReader()
            ' Output the results of the first result set
            Console.WriteLine("===========")
            Console.WriteLine("Departments")
            Console.WriteLine("===========")
            While (sqldr1.Read())
                Console.WriteLine(String.Format("{0}" & ControlChars.Tab & "{1}" & _
                    ControlChars.Tab & "{2}", sqldr1.Item("DepartmentID"), _
                    sqldr1.Item("Name"), sqldr1.Item("GroupName")))
            End While
            ' Output the results of the second result set
            Console.WriteLine("======")
            Console.WriteLine("Shifts")
```

```
        Console.WriteLine("======")
        While (sqldr2.Read())
            Console.WriteLine(String.Format("{0}" & ControlChars.Tab & "{1}" & _
                ControlChars.Tab & "{2}" & ControlChars.Tab & "{3}", _
                sqldr2.Item("ShiftID"), sqldr2.Item("Name"), _
                sqldr2.Item("StartTime"), _
                sqldr2.Item("EndTime")))
        End While
        ' Clean up
        sqldr1.Close()
        sqldr2.Close()
        sqlcmd1.Dispose()
        sqlcmd2.Dispose()
        sqlcon.Dispose()
        ' Exit the program
        Console.WriteLine("Press a key to end.")
        Console.ReadKey()
    End Sub

End Module
End Namespace
```

Listing 15-6 begins by importing necessary namespaces and declaring the application namespace and module name for the VB console application:

```
Imports System
Imports System.Data
Imports System.Data.SqlClient

Namespace APress.Samples
    Module SqlResultTests
```

The Sub Main() routine starts by using the SqlClient to open a connection to SQL Server (using Integrated Security). The connection is then opened, and two SqlCommands are created on the connection to retrieve the two result sets:

```
    Sub Main()
        ' Create and open a native SqlClient connection to SQL Server 2005
        Dim sqlcon As New SqlConnection("SERVER=(local);" & _
            "INITIAL CATALOG=AdventureWorks;INTEGRATED SECURITY=SSPI;")
        sqlcon.Open()
        ' Create two SqlCommands to retrieve two result sets
        Dim sqlcmd1 As New SqlCommand( _
```

```
            "SELECT DepartmentID, Name, GroupName " & _
            "FROM HumanResources.Department", sqlcon)
    Dim sqlcmd2 As New SqlCommand( _
            "SELECT ShiftID, Name, StartTime, EndTime " & _
            "FROM HumanResources.Shift", sqlcon)
```

Then the first result set is opened using a `SqlDataReader`:

```
    ' Open the first result set
    Dim sqldr1 As SqlDataReader = sqlcmd1.ExecuteReader()
```

The next line, which attempts to open a second result set over the open connection, throws an invalid operation exception, as shown in Figure 15-1:

```
    ' Open the second result set
    Dim sqldr2 As SqlDataReader = sqlcmd2.ExecuteReader()
```

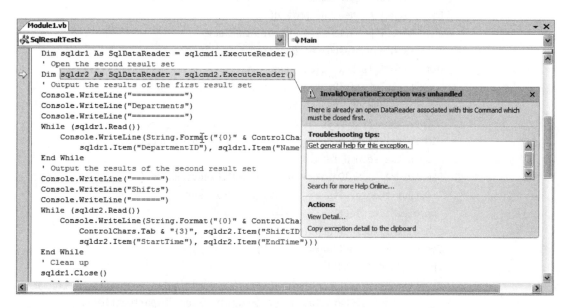

Figure 15-1. *Invalid operation exception—trying to open two result sets over one connection*

The remainder of the code is designed to iterate over the result sets and display the results on the console. Because of the invalid operation exception that's thrown, this part of the code is never reached, however. Take advantage of MARS to allow multiple result sets to be opened simultaneously over a single connection; just add the `MultipleActiveResultSets=TRUE` keyword/value pair to your `SqlConnection` string. Listing 15-7 updates the previous listing to include the `MultipleActiveResultSets` keyword in the connection string.

Listing 15-7. *Enabling MARS on a SqlClient Connection to SQL 2005*

```vb
Imports System
Imports System.Data
Imports System.Data.SqlClient

Namespace APress.Samples
    Module SqlResultTests

        Sub Main()
            ' Create and open a native SqlClient connection to SQL Server 2005
            Dim sqlcon As New SqlConnection("SERVER=(local);" & _
                "INITIAL CATALOG=AdventureWorks;INTEGRATED SECURITY=SSPI;" & _
                "MULTIPLEACTIVERESULTSETS=TRUE;")
            sqlcon.Open()
            ' Create two SqlCommands to retrieve two result sets
            Dim sqlcmd1 As New SqlCommand( _
                "SELECT DepartmentID, Name, GroupName " & _
                "FROM HumanResources.Department", sqlcon)
            Dim sqlcmd2 As New SqlCommand( _
                "SELECT ShiftID, Name, StartTime, EndTime " & _
                "FROM HumanResources.Shift", sqlcon)
            ' Open the first result set
            Dim sqldr1 As SqlDataReader = sqlcmd1.ExecuteReader()
            ' Open the second result set
            Dim sqldr2 As SqlDataReader = sqlcmd2.ExecuteReader()
            ' Output the results of the first result set
            Console.WriteLine("===========")
            Console.WriteLine("Departments")
            Console.WriteLine("===========")
            While (sqldr1.Read())
                Console.WriteLine(String.Format("{0}" & ControlChars.Tab & "{1}" & _
                    ControlChars.Tab & "{2}", sqldr1.Item("DepartmentID"), _
                    sqldr1.Item("Name"), sqldr1.Item("GroupName")))
            End While
```

```
        ' Output the results of the second result set
        Console.WriteLine("======")
        Console.WriteLine("Shifts")
        Console.WriteLine("======")
        While (sqldr2.Read())
            Console.WriteLine(String.Format("{0}" & ControlChars.Tab & "{1}" & _
                ControlChars.Tab & "{2}" & ControlChars.Tab & "{3}", _
                sqldr2.Item("ShiftID"), sqldr2.Item("Name"), _
                sqldr2.Item("StartTime"), _
                sqldr2.Item("EndTime")))
        End While
        ' Clean up
        sqldr1.Close()
        sqldr2.Close()
        sqlcmd1.Dispose()
        sqlcmd2.Dispose()
        sqlcon.Dispose()
        ' Exit the program
        Console.WriteLine("Press a key to end.")
        Console.ReadKey()
    End Sub

    End Module
End Namespace
```

With MultipleActiveResultSets set to True, the code can successfully open two or more result sets over a single connection simultaneously. The code succeeds and generates the output shown in Figure 15-2.

```
c:\                                                             _□×
::::::::::::                                                      ▲
1       Engineering     Research and Development
2       Tool Design     Research and Development
3       Sales   Sales and Marketing
4       Marketing       Sales and Marketing
5       Purchasing      Inventory Management
6       Research and Development        Research and Development
7       Production      Manufacturing
8       Production Control      Manufacturing
9       Human Resources Executive General and Administration
10      Finance Executive General and Administration
11      Information Services    Executive General and Administration
12      Document Control        Quality Assurance
13      Quality Assurance       Quality Assurance
14      Facilities and Maintenance      Executive General and Administration
15      Shipping and Receiving  Inventory Management
16      Executive       Executive General and Administration
::::::
Shifts
::::::
1       Day     1/1/1900 7:00:00 AM     1/1/1900 3:00:00 PM
2       Evening 1/1/1900 3:00:00 PM     1/1/1900 11:00:00 PM
3       Night   1/1/1900 11:00:00 PM    1/1/1900 7:00:00 AM
Press a key to end.                                              ▼
```

Figure 15-2. *Results of MARS sample application*

Summary

Although the focus of this book is on server-side development, a good database is only as useful as the data you get out of it. That's where the client-side application comes in. This chapter discussed the options available for connecting to SQL Server 2005 via .NET 2.0. This chapter specifically talked about the following:

- The .NET System.Data.SqlClient namespace

- The SqlConnection, SqlCommand, SqlDataReader, SqlDataAdapter, XmlReader, and DataSet classes

- SqlConnection connection string options

- The SqlBulkCopy class for bulk loading data into SQL Server

- Multiple Active Result Sets (MARS), the new SQL Server feature that allows you to open multiple result sets simultaneously on a single connection

Although .NET offers other options for connecting to SQL Server, including OLE DB and ODBC, the primary method of connecting to SQL Server (version 7.0 and higher) is encapsulated in the ADO.NET and the System.Data.SqlClient namespace.

The next chapter will discuss SQL Server 2005 HTTP SOAP endpoints.

■ ■ ■

CHAPTER 16

HTTP Endpoints

SQL Server 2000 offered SOAP (Simple Object Access Protocol) web service support via SQLXML. The SQL Server 2000 model relied on a loose coupling of SQL Server and Internet Information Services (IIS), making setup and configuration a bit of a hassle. The end result was that a lot of developers found that creating .NET web services in the middle tier was a far more flexible (and easier to use) solution than the SQL Server 2000/SQLXML/IIS model.

SQL Server 2005 provides native HTTP endpoints to expose your stored procedures as web methods directly from SQL Server via the SOAP protocol. HTTP endpoints are easy to create and administer, and the SQL Server HTTP endpoints model provides tight security integration with SQL Server. HTTP endpoints raise the level of SQL Server functionality from *just* a database management system to a full-fledged application server.

This chapter discusses HTTP endpoint setup and configuration and provides samples to demonstrate how to use HTTP endpoints from your .NET applications.

What Are HTTP Endpoints?

The W3C defines an endpoint as the following:

> *An association between a binding and a network address, specified by a URI, that may be used to communicate with an instance of a service. An endpoint indicates a specific location for accessing a service using a specific protocol and data format.* `(http://www.w3.org/TR/ws-gloss/#defs)`

SQL Server provides built-in support for exposing endpoints over the HTTP protocol, allowing you to access SQL Server stored procedures as SOAP-based web service methods.

■Note SQL Server HTTP endpoints are supported on Windows Server 2003 and Windows XP Service Pack 2. HTTP endpoints are not supported on SQL Server 2005 Express Edition.

The CREATE ENDPOINT Statement

As the keywords suggest, SQL Server 2005's CREATE ENDPOINT statement allows you to create endpoints. The following is the format for creating an HTTP endpoint that exposes your stored procedures and user-defined functions as SOAP web service methods:

```
CREATE ENDPOINT end_point_name
[ AUTHORIZATION login ]
[ STATE = { STARTED | STOPPED | DISABLED } ]
AS HTTP (
    PATH = 'url' ,
    AUTHENTICATION = ( { BASIC | DIGEST | INTEGRATED | NTLM | KERBEROS }
        [ , ... n ] ) ,
    PORTS = ( { CLEAR | SSL } [ , ... n ] )
    [ , SITE = { '*' | '+' | 'web_site' } ]
    [ , CLEAR_PORT = clear_port ]
    [ , SSL_PORT = ssl_port ]
    [ , AUTH_REALM = { 'realm' | NONE } ]
    [ , DEFAULT_LOGON_DOMAIN = { 'domain' | NONE } ]
    [ , COMPRESSION = { ENABLED | DISABLED } ]
)
FOR SOAP (
    [ { WEBMETHOD [ 'namespace' . ] 'method_alias'
        (
            NAME = 'database.schema.proc_name'
            [ , SCHEMA = { NONE | STANDARD | DEFAULT } ]
            [ , FORMAT = { ALL_RESULTS | ROWSETS_ONLY | NONE } ]
        )
      } [ , ... n ] ]
    [ , BATCHES = { ENABLED | DISABLED } ]
    [ , WSDL = { NONE | DEFAULT | 'sp_name' } ]
    [ , SESSIONS = { ENABLED | DISABLED } ]
    [ , LOGIN_TYPE = { MIXED | WINDOWS } ]
    [ , SESSION_TIMEOUT = timeout_interval | NEVER ]
    [ , DATABASE = { 'database_name' | DEFAULT } ]
    [ , NAMESPACE = { 'namespace' | DEFAULT } ]
    [ , SCHEMA = { NONE | STANDARD } ]
    [ , CHARACTER_SET = { SQL | XML } ]
    [ , HEADER_LIMIT = header_limit ]
);
```

■Note The CREATE ENDPOINT statement also supports creating TCP endpoints for Service Broker and database mirroring applications. I focus on HTTP SOAP endpoint creation in this chapter, but the full syntax for the CREATE ENDPOINT statement is available in BOL at http://msdn2.microsoft.com/en-us/library/ms181591.aspx. The full syntax includes all TCP, TSQL, Service Broker, and database mirroring options.

CREATE ENDPOINT Arguments

The base endpoint arguments for the CREATE ENDPOINT statement are the same regardless of the chosen protocol and application. The CREATE ENDPOINT arguments for HTTP SOAP endpoints are listed here:

- *end_point_name* is the name of the endpoint. This name is used to reference and manage the endpoint and must be a valid T-SQL identifier.

- *login* is the SQL Server or Windows login that is assigned ownership of the endpoint at creation time. The default, if the AUTHORIZATION clause is left off, is the caller. If *login* is not the same as the caller, the caller must have IMPERSONATE permission on the specified login.

- The STATE argument specifies the state of the endpoint at creation time. STOPPED is the default. The following are the valid states:

  - STARTED: The endpoint is started and begins listening for connections at creation time.

  - STOPPED: The endpoint is stopped. The server listens for connections on the endpoint when it is STOPPED but returns errors to the client when it receives requests.

  - DISABLED: The server does not listen for connections on the endpoint, and it doesn't respond to requests on the endpoint.

HTTP Protocol Arguments

The HTTP protocol arguments are used in the AS HTTP clause to specify HTTP as the transport protocol. These arguments include the following:

- *url* is a relative uniform resource locator (URL) specification to help SQL Server route HTTP SOAP requests appropriately. For the absolute URL http://www. apress.com/SQLWebService1, the portion specified by PATH = '*url*' would be PATH = '/SQLWebService1'. The portion specified by the SITE option would be www.apress.com.

- The AUTHENTICATION option specifies how the server should authenticate clients. You can specify one or more of the following authentication types:

  - BASIC authentication is specified by the Internet Engineering Task Force (IETF) HTTP 1.1 specification (RFC 2617, http://www.ietf.org/rfc/rfc2617.txt). BASIC authentication is performed via a header containing the Base-64-encoded username and password. SQL Server requires that the PORTS value be set to SSL, that the username and password be mapped to a valid Windows login, and that a Secure Sockets Layer port be used for the connection if BASIC authentication is specified.

  - DIGEST authentication is the second form of authentication specified by the IETF HTTP 1.1 specification. DIGEST authentication hashes the username and password using the MD5 one-way hash algorithm before sending it to the server. The server then compares the hashed credentials sent to it with a hash of the same credentials stored locally. Windows-based DIGEST authentication is only supported over domain controllers that are running under Windows Server 2003, and local user accounts cannot be authenticated using this method. Only valid Windows domain accounts can be authenticated using this method.

  - NTLM, also known as Windows NT Challenge/Response authentication, is the authentication method supported by Windows 95, Windows 98, and Windows NT 4.0 (Server and Workstation). NTLM is a connection-based protocol that is more secure than either BASIC or DIGEST. Windows 2000 and later provide NTLM authentication by means of a Security Support Provider Interface (SSPI).

  - KERBEROS authentication is an Internet-standard authentication protocol developed at the Massachusetts Institute of Technology (http://web.mit.edu/kerberos/). KERBEROS authentication support is provided in Windows 2000 and later by means of an SSPI. When KERBEROS authentication is specified, a Service Principal Name (SPN) must be associated with the account it will be running on. More information on this is available in BOL at http://msdn2.microsoft.com/en-us/library/ms178119.aspx.

- INTEGRATED authentication allows the client to request either KERBEROS or NTLM authentication. If the authentication type specified by the client does not succeed, the server terminates the connection. The server will not fall back and attempt to reauthenticate using the other allowable INTEGRATED authentication method.

More than one authentication method can be specified in a comma-delimited list. If more than one authentication method is specified, the method specified by the client is used.

- The PORTS option specifies the type of listening port the endpoint will use. The following are valid values:

  - CLEAR port type specifies incoming requests must use the HTTP (http://) protocol.

  - SSL port type specifies incoming requests must use the Secure HTTP (https://) protocol.

You may specify both port types for a single endpoint.

- The SITE argument specifies the name of the host computer. The default is the asterisk (*). The following are valid values:

  - The asterisk (*) indicates that the endpoint should listen for all possible hostnames for the computer that are not explicitly reserved. Namespaces may be explicitly reserved using the sp_reserve_http_namespace stored procedure. This procedure is described in BOL at http://msdn2.microsoft.com/en-us/library/ms190614.aspx.

  - The plus sign (+) indicates that the endpoint should listen for all possible hostnames for the computer.

  - An explicit *web_site* name indicates the endpoint should listen for the specified hostname for the computer.

- The CLEAR_PORT option is used when the PORTS = (CLEAR) option has been specified. The *clear_port* value is the port number to be used for HTTP communication. The default is the standard HTTP port number 80.

- The SSL_PORT option is used when the PORTS = (SSL) option has been specified. The *ssl_port* value is the port number to be used for Secure HTTP communication. The default is the standard Secure HTTP port number 443.

- The AUTH_REALM option specifies a hint returned to the client (as part of the HTTP challenge) when AUTHENTICATION = (DIGEST) has been specified. The default is NONE.

- The DEFAULT_LOGON_DOMAIN specifies the default domain to log on when AUTHENTICATION = (BASIC) is specified. The default is NONE.

- The COMPRESSION option tells SQL Server to return a GZip-compressed response when a request specifies GZip compression in its headers. The default is DISABLED.

SOAP Arguments

The SOAP arguments are used in the FOR SOAP clause and are specific to the SOAP protocol configuration for the endpoint. The following are valid arguments:

- WEBMETHOD specifies an alias for a web method exposed via SOAP. The *method_alias* can be preceded by an optional namespace. Note that WEBMETHOD is an optional argument and you can declare an HTTP SOAP endpoint with no web methods. The WEBMETHOD argument has its own list of subarguments:

    - Every WEBMETHOD needs a NAME argument to specify the three-part name of a stored procedure or user-defined function to implement the SOAP web method. Note that the *database* and *schema* parts of the stored procedure or user-defined function name are mandatory.

    - SCHEMA is an optional argument that specifies whether an inline XSD schema is returned for the current web method in the SOAP response. The following are valid values:

        - NONE specifies no inline XSD schema is returned.

        - STANDARD specifies an inline XSD schema is returned.

        - DEFAULT specifies the endpoint SCHEMA setting should be used.

    - FORMAT specifies how results should be returned to the client. The default is ALL_RESULTS. The following are valid FORMAT values:

- ALL_RESULTS specifies that a result set, row count, warnings, and error messages will all be returned to the client as an array of .NET System.Objects.

- ROWSETS_ONLY specifies that only result sets are returned to the client. This option should be used when you want to return a .NET System.Data.DataSet object instead of an Object array.

- NONE suppresses SOAP-specific markup in the response. In this mode, the application is responsible for generating well-formed raw XML. The NONE option has several restrictions and limitations, all of which are described in detail in BOL at http://msdn2.microsoft.com/en-us/library/ms181591.aspx.

- The BATCHES argument enables or disables ad hoc SQL queries on the endpoint via the sql:sqlbatch web method. The sql:sqlbatch method allows parameterized queries, which I will discuss in the section "Executing HTTP Endpoint Ad Hoc Queries." The default is DISABLED.

- The WSDL argument specifies whether the endpoint can generate WSDL documents. The default value of DEFAULT specifies that a WSDL response is generated for WSDL queries to this endpoint. A value of NONE specifies that no WSDL response is generated. Under specific circumstances you can specify a stored procedure (*sp_name*) to generate a modified WSDL document if you need custom WSDL support.

- SESSIONS can be either ENABLED or DISABLED. When enabled, the endpoint can treat multiple SOAP request/response pairs as a single SOAP session. The default is DISABLED.

- LOGIN_TYPE is the SQL Server authentication type for the endpoint and can be either MIXED or WINDOWS. The default is WINDOWS. When MIXED is used, the endpoint must be configured to use SSL.

- SESSION_TIMEOUT specifies an integer time-out value (in seconds) before a SOAP session expires at the server. The default *timeout_interval* is 60 seconds. A value of NEVER indicates SOAP sessions should never time out.

- The DATABASE argument specifies the database context under which the SOAP method should execute. The default is the default database for the login.

- NAMESPACE specifies a namespace for the endpoint. The default namespace is http://tempuri.org. The optional namespace, if included in the WEBMETHOD declaration, overrides this NAMESPACE declaration.

- The SCHEMA argument specifies whether an inline XSD schema should be included in the SOAP responses returned to the client. If set to NONE, no inline XSD schema is included; if set to STANDARD, an inline XSD schema is included in responses. The value specified for SCHEMA in the WEBMETHOD argument overrides this setting on a per-method basis, unless the WEBMETHOD specifies DEFAULT, in which case this endpointwide setting is used. The STANDARD setting is required to map SOAP results to a .NET System.Data.DataSet, and the default is STANDARD.

- CHARACTER_SET can specify either the SQL or XML character set. If SQL is specified, characters that are not valid character references are encoded and returned in the result. If XML is specified, characters are encoded according to the XML specification. The default is XML.

- The HEADER_LIMIT specifies the maximum size of the header section in bytes. The default is 8,192 bytes. If the header section is larger than this limit, the server will generate an error.

Creating an HTTP Endpoint

Before we create our first HTTP endpoint, we need to create stored procedures and user-defined functions that implement the web methods we want to expose. We will create three methods: two stored procedures, and a scalar user-defined function. We will expose all three as web methods.

■**Note** Technically you don't have to create the stored procedures and/or user-defined functions first. You can create the endpoint and add methods later, if you prefer, with the ALTER ENDPOINT statement. However, for our purposes, creating the stored procedures and user-defined functions is as good a place to start as any.

For this demonstration we'll create a stored procedure named Sales. GetSalespersonList. This stored procedure will retrieve a list of all AdventureWorks salespeople's names and their ID numbers. Listing 16-1 is the Sales. GetSalespersonList procedure.

Listing 16-1. *Sales.GetSalespersonList Stored Procedure*

```
USE AdventureWorks;
GO
CREATE PROCEDURE Sales.GetSalespersonList
AS
BEGIN
    SELECT s.SalesPersonID,
        s.LastName + ', ' + s.FirstName + ' ' +
            COALESCE(s.MiddleName, '') AS FullName
    FROM Sales.vSalesPerson s
    ORDER BY s.LastName, s.FirstName, s.MiddleName;
END;
GO
```

While the Sales.GetSalespersonList stored procedure does not accept any parameters, the second method will. For the second method you'll define another stored
procedure that accepts a single salesperson ID number as a parameter and returns a
summary listing of that salesperson's sales. Listing 16-2 is the Sales.GetSalespersonSales
procedure listing.

Listing 16-2. *Sales.GetSalespersonSales Procedure*

```
USE AdventureWorks;
GO
CREATE PROCEDURE Sales.GetSalespersonSales (@SalespersonID INT)
AS
BEGIN
    SELECT soh.SalesOrderID,
        soh.CustomerID,
        soh.OrderDate,
        soh.SubTotal
    FROM Sales.SalesOrderHeader soh
    WHERE soh.SalesPersonID = @SalespersonID
    ORDER BY soh.SalesOrderID;
END;
GO
```

The third method is a scalar user-defined function that also accepts an Adventure-
Works salesperson's ID number and returns the total dollar amount of sales for that
salesperson. Listing 16-3 is the listing for the Sales.GetSalesTotal UDF.

Listing 16-3. *Sales.GetSalesTotal Scalar User-Defined Function*

```
USE AdventureWorks;
GO
CREATE FUNCTION Sales.GetSalesTotal(@SalespersonID INT)
RETURNS MONEY
AS
BEGIN
    RETURN (
        SELECT SUM(soh.SubTotal)
        FROM Sales.SalesOrderHeader soh
        WHERE SalesPersonID = @SalespersonID
    );
END;
GO
```

■**Note** SQL Server HTTP endpoints support exposing stored procedures and scalar UDFs as web methods. Table-valued functions and extended stored procedures, however, cannot be exposed as web methods.

Now that three methods have been implemented, it's time to turn them into SOAP web methods with the CREATE ENDPOINT statement. The CREATE ENDPOINT statement I'll use to expose these three methods is shown in Listing 16-4.

Listing 16-4. *CREATE ENDPOINT Statement*

```
USE AdventureWorks;
GO
CREATE ENDPOINT AdvSalesEndpoint
    STATE = STARTED
AS HTTP
(
    PATH = N'/AdvSalesSql',
    AUTHENTICATION = (INTEGRATED),
    PORTS = (CLEAR),
    SITE = N'*'
)
```

```
FOR SOAP
(
    WEBMETHOD N'GetSalespersonList'
    (
        NAME = N'AdventureWorks.Sales.GetSalespersonList',
        FORMAT = ROWSETS_ONLY
    ),
    WEBMETHOD N'GetSalesPersonSales'
    (
        NAME = N'AdventureWorks.Sales.GetSalesPersonSales',
        FORMAT = ROWSETS_ONLY
    ),
    WEBMETHOD 'GetSalesTotal'
    (
        NAME = N'AdventureWorks.Sales.GetSalesTotal'
    ),
    WSDL = DEFAULT,
    DATABASE = N'AdventureWorks',
    SCHEMA = STANDARD
);
GO
```

The endpoint definition begins by defining the alias AdvSalesEndpoint and setting the endpoint state to STARTED:

```
CREATE ENDPOINT AdvSalesEndpoint
    STATE = STARTED
```

The AS HTTP clause declares HTTP as the endpoint transport protocol. The HTTP arguments define the PATH as /AdvSalesSql and set the AUTHENTICATION type to INTEGRATED. Also the PORTS are set to CLEAR and the SITE is set to *. HTTP port number 80 is used by default:

```
AS HTTP
(
    PATH = N'/AdvWorksSql',
    AUTHENTICATION = (INTEGRATED),
    PORTS = (CLEAR),
    SITE = N'*'
)
```

▌Tip You may run into problems using the default port if you are running IIS and SQL Server 2005 on the same computer. IIS has a habit of intercepting web requests directed at the server before SQL Server can get to them. If you do run into these problems, you can turn IIS off or use a different port number for your HTTP Endpoint. In the previous example you could change the HTTP endpoint port number by using the HTTP CLEAR_PORT argument.

The FOR SOAP clause is where the web methods are mapped to the stored procedures and user-defined functions via the WEBMETHOD arguments:

```
FOR SOAP
(
    WEBMETHOD N'GetSalespersonList'
    (
        NAME = N'AdventureWorks.Sales.GetSalespersonList',
        FORMAT = ROWSETS_ONLY
    ),
    WEBMETHOD N'GetSalesPersonSales'
    (
        NAME = N'AdventureWorks.Sales.GetSalesPersonSales',
        FORMAT = ROWSETS_ONLY
    ),
    WEBMETHOD N'GetSalesTotal'
    (
        NAME = N'AdventureWorks.Sales.GetSalesTotal'
    ),
```

The first WEBMETHOD argument maps a web method named GetSalespersonList to the AdventureWorks.Sales.GetSalespersonList stored procedure. The second and third WEBMETHOD arguments map web methods named GetSalesPersonSales and GetSalesTotal to their respective procedures and user-defined functions. For the two stored procedures, the FORMAT is defined as ROWSETS_ONLY, which allows you to retrieve the results as .NET System.Data.DataSets. The remaining arguments set endpointwide settings. The WSDL argument specifies that the endpoint can generate default WSDL documents. The DATABASE argument sets the default database context to the AdventureWorks database, and the SCHEMA argument is set to STANDARD so that inline XSD schemas will be included in the SOAP responses:

```
    WSDL = DEFAULT,
    DATABASE = N'AdventureWorks',
    SCHEMA = STANDARD
);
GO
```

You can use the SSMS Object Explorer to verify that the HTTP endpoint was created. It will be listed in the Endpoints folder under Server Objects. The newly created HTTP endpoint is shown in Figure 16-1.

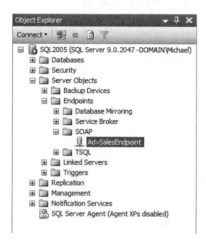

Figure 16-1. *HTTP endpoint in SSMS Object Explorer*

WSDL Documents

The W3C WSDL standard describes an "XML language for describing Web services" (http://www.w3.org/TR/2006/CR-wsdl20-20060327/). SQL Server HTTP endpoints can generate two types of WSDL documents for your web services: a standard WSDL document or a simple WSDL document. The CREATE ENDPOINT statement in Listing 16-4 sets the WSDL argument to DEFAULT, so the endpoint can generate WSDL documents as required. The WSDL documents can be viewed by pointing Internet Explorer at the endpoint URL with a ?wsdl or a ?wsdlsimple parameter like this:

```
http://localhost/AdvSalesSql?wsdl
http://localhost/AdvSalesSql?wsdlsimple
```

The full URL includes the website name, the port number (if ports other than the defaults are used), the relative URL path, and a ?wsdl or ?wsdlsimple parameter. The ?wsdl parameter tells SQL Server to generate a fully decorated XSD schema with complex types, while ?wsdlsimple uses standard simple XSD data types.

Figure 16-2 shows a portion of the WSDL document generated by the sample HTTP endpoint.

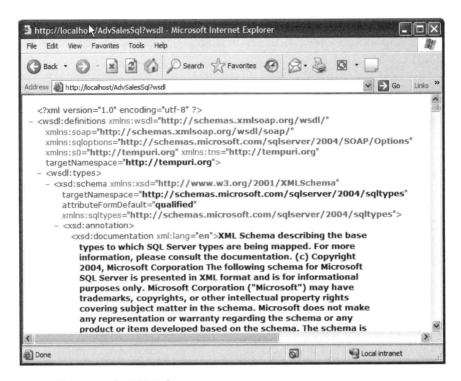

Figure 16-2. *Sample WSDL document*

■**Tip** Internet Explorer is a handy way to view WSDL documents for your HTTP endpoints, but they can be retrieved by other applications using standard HTTP GET requests.

WSDL document details are available from the W3C Web Services Description Working Group home page at http://www.w3.org/2002/ws/desc/.

Creating a Web Service Consumer

Now that you have an HTTP SOAP endpoint with exposed methods configured, it's time to create a web service consumer. Here you'll create a simple web services client with Visual Basic. The first step is to create a new Windows Application project in Visual Studio. Then you'll drag a DataGridView, a ComboBox, a TextBox, and a Button control onto the form, as shown in Figure 16-3.

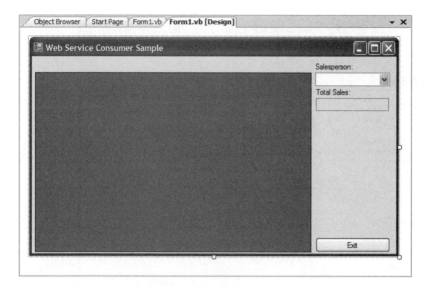

Figure 16-3. *Web services consumer form design*

The next step is to add a web reference to the project. Right-click in the Visual Studio Solution Explorer and choose Add Web Reference from the pop-up menu. The Add Web Reference window then requires you to type in the URL to retrieve the WSDL document from the endpoint and press the Go button. In this instance the URL is `http://localhost/AdvSalesSql?wsdl`. The three web methods exposed by the HTTP endpoint will be displayed. Next, click the Add Reference button to add the web reference. Figure 16-4 shows the Add Web Reference window.

After the Windows form is set up and the web reference has been added to the project, it's a simple matter to add the code to reference the web methods from your Visual Basic code. There are four basic steps that need to be performed to use a web method:

1. Create a web service proxy.

2. Set the proxy security credentials.

3. Invoke the web method.

4. Retrieve the results.

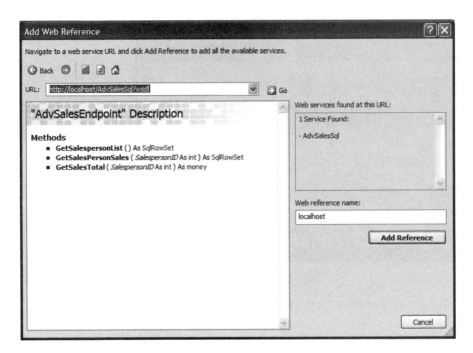

Figure 16-4. *Add Web Reference window*

All of these steps are shown in the VB code in Listing 16-5.

Listing 16-5. *VB Code for Web Service Consumer*

```
Imports System.Data
Imports System.Net

Public Class Form1

    Private Sub Form1_Load(ByVal sender As System.Object, ByVal e As _
        System.EventArgs) _
        Handles MyBase.Load

        ' Create a web service proxy using the SQL Server HTTP endpoint
        Dim proxy As New localhost.AdvSalesEndpoint

        ' Set the integrated security credentials
        proxy.Credentials = CredentialCache.DefaultCredentials
```

```vbnet
        ' Bind the combo box to the results of the web method call
        Me.cboSalesPerson.ValueMember = "SalespersonId"
        Me.cboSalesPerson.DisplayMember = "FullName"

        ' Call the web method
        Me.cboSalesPerson.DataSource = proxy.GetSalespersonList().Tables(0)

    End Sub

    Private Sub cboSalesPerson_SelectedIndexChanged(ByVal sender As System.Object, _
        ByVal e As System.EventArgs) Handles cboSalesPerson.SelectedIndexChanged

        ' Create a web service proxy using the SQL Server HTTP endpoint
        Dim proxy As New localhost.AdvSalesEndpoint

        ' Set the integrated security credentials
        proxy.Credentials = CredentialCache.DefaultCredentials

        ' Bind the data grid view to the results of the web method call
        Me.dgvSales.DataSource = proxy.GetSalesPersonSales(New _
            SqlTypes.SqlInt32(Me.cboSalesPerson.SelectedValue)).Tables(0)

        ' Populate the text box with the results of the second web method call
        Me.txtTotalSales.Text = proxy.GetSalesTotal(New _
            SqlTypes.SqlInt32(Me.cboSalesPerson.SelectedValue)).Value.ToString("C")

    End Sub

    Private Sub btnExit_Click(ByVal sender As System.Object, ByVal e As _
        System.EventArgs) _
        Handles btnExit.Click

        ' Exit the application
        Application.Exit()

    End Sub
End Class
```

The form Load event creates a web service proxy, binds the ComboBox, and then calls the GetSalesPersonList web method to populate the ComboBox. Creating the proxy is as simple as declaring a new instance of the proxy class:

```
' Create a web service proxy using the SQL Server HTTP endpoint
Dim proxy As New localhost.AdvSalesEndpoint
```

The security credentials are set using System.Net.CredentialCache. DefaultCredentials. This assigns the credentials of the currently logged-in user to the proxy object:

```
' Set the integrated security credentials
proxy.Credentials = CredentialCache.DefaultCredentials
```

The ComboBox ValueMember and DisplayMember are assigned the names of the columns in the table returned by the web method:

```
' Bind the combo box to the results of the web method call
Me.cboSalesPerson.ValueMember = "SalespersonId"
Me.cboSalesPerson.DisplayMember = "FullName"
```

Finally, the GetSalespersonList web method is called, and the results are bound to the ComboBox:

```
' Call the web method
Me.cboSalesPerson.DataSource = proxy.GetSalespersonList().Tables(0)


End Sub
```

The ComboBox SelectedIndexChanged event is up next. This event, like the form Load event, creates a web service proxy object and assigns the appropriate security credentials to it using System.Net.CredentialCache.DefaultCredentials:

```
Private Sub cboSalesPerson_SelectedIndexChanged(ByVal sender As System.Object, _
    ByVal e As System.EventArgs) Handles cboSalesPerson.SelectedIndexChanged

    ' Create a web service proxy using the SQL Server HTTP endpoint
    Dim proxy As New localhost.AdvSalesEndpoint

    ' Set the integrated security credentials
    proxy.Credentials = CredentialCache.DefaultCredentials
```

Next, the SelectedIndexChanged event passes the ID number of the selected salesperson to the GetSalesPersonSales web method. It binds the DataGridView to the results returned by the web method:

```
' Bind the data grid view to the results of the web method call
Me.dgvSales.DataSource = proxy.GetSalesPersonSales(New _
    SqlTypes.SqlInt32(Me.cboSalesPerson.SelectedValue)).Tables(0)
```

Then the GetSalesTotal web method is called with the selected salesperson ID as a parameter. The result is formatted as a currency string and displayed in the TextBox:

```
' Populate the text box with the results of the second web method call
Me.txtTotalSales.Text = proxy.GetSalesTotal(New _
    SqlTypes.SqlInt32(Me.cboSalesPerson.SelectedValue)).Value.ToString("C")
```

```
End Sub
```

Finally, the btnExit.Click event exits the application:

```
Private Sub btnExit_Click(ByVal sender As System.Object, ByVal e As _
    System.EventArgs) _
    Handles btnExit.Click

    ' Exit the application
    Application.Exit()

End Sub
```

Figure 16-5 shows a screenshot of the web service consumer application in action.

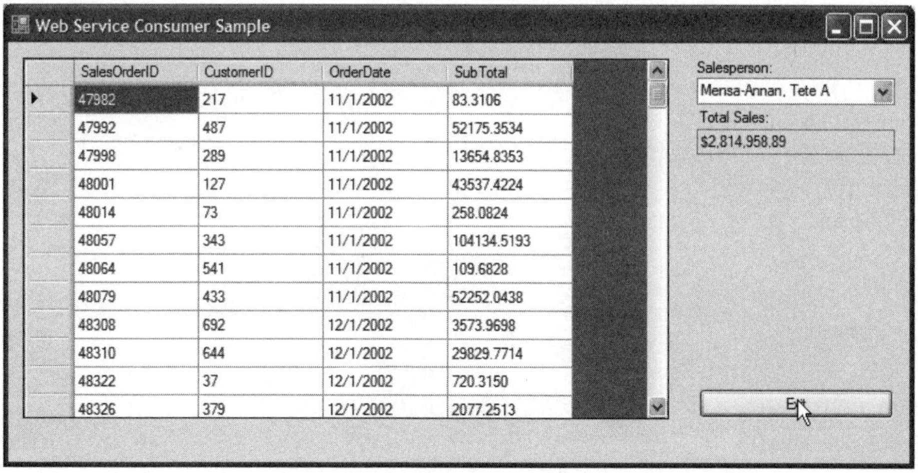

Figure 16-5. *Web method consumer example in action*

In the sample application, selecting a different salesperson from the ComboBox automatically updates the DataGridView and Total Sales TextBox with results from the proper web methods.

As you can see, SQL Server HTTP endpoints make it easy to create and access stored procedure and user-defined function results from user applications.

Executing HTTP Endpoint Ad Hoc Queries

In addition to exposing stored procedures and user-defined functions, SQL Server HTTP endpoints provide the capability of performing ad hoc queries via web methods. You can enable ad hoc querying by specifying BATCHES = ENABLED when you create an HTTP endpoint.

■**Caution** Ad hoc querying of SQL Server via web methods is a powerful feature, but it is also potentially dangerous. If you enable this feature, take extra care to make sure your server is properly secured.

Listing 16-6 creates an HTTP endpoint. No methods are declared explicitly, but the SOAP argument BATCHES is set to ENABLED. Because of this setting, a web method named sqlbatch is implicitly exposed.

Listing 16-6. *Endpoint Declared with Ad Hoc Querying Enabled*

```
CREATE ENDPOINT AdvAdHocEndpoint
    STATE = STARTED
AS HTTP (
    PATH = N'/AdvAdhocSql',
    AUTHENTICATION = (INTEGRATED),
    PORTS = (CLEAR),
    SITE = N'*'
)
FOR SOAP (
    WSDL = DEFAULT,
    DATABASE = N'AdventureWorks',
    SCHEMA = STANDARD,
    BATCHES = ENABLED
);
GO
```

Apart from the fact that this endpoint contains no explicit WEBMETHOD declarations, and the PATH argument is different, this declaration is very similar to the previous example. Once the endpoint is created, a web service consumer can be created to perform ad hoc queries against it. We'll start by creating a simple VB form like before. This one needs a TextBox, a Button, and a DataGridView control. It looks like Figure 16-6.

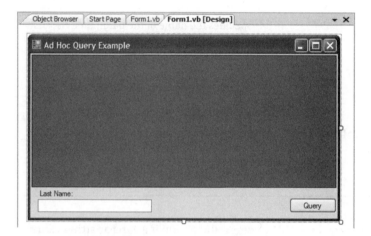

Figure 16-6. *Web method consumer form in design mode*

The sqlbatch Method

When you add the web reference to http://localhost/AdvAdhocSql?wsdl, the only method exposed is the sqlbatch web method. This method takes the following form:

```
sqlbatch ( BatchCommands As String,
    Parameters As ArrayOfSqlParameter ) As SqlResultStream
```

BatchCommands is a string containing the T-SQL statements/queries to be executed. These queries can be parameterized.

Parameters is an array of proxyclass.SqlParameter objects, where proxyclass is your web services proxy class. If your proxy class is named localhost (the default), a SqlParameter object would be declared as the following:

```
Dim p As New localhost.SqlParameter
```

The *Parameters* array represents the parameters to pass in for a parameterized query. If your query does not have parameters, pass Nothing for *Parameters*. Each proxyclass.SqlParameter object exposes a set of properties that need to be set prior to use. Table 16-1 lists some of the most common proxyclass.SqlParameter attributes.

Table 16-1. *Common proxyclass.SqlParameter Properties*

Name	Type	Description
direction	proxyclass.ParameterDirection	Specifies whether the parameter is an Input parameter or an InputOutput parameter.
maxLength	Long	Specifies the max length of the parameter Value.
name	String	Specifies the name of the parameter. Because of XML naming convention requirements, you must leave off the leading @ in the parameter name.
precision	Byte	Specifies the parameter Value precision.
scale	Byte	Specifies the parameter Value scale.
sqlDbType	proxyclass.sqlDbTypeEnum	Determines the type of the parameter. Valid values include all of the SQL valid T-SQL data types, including Int, VarChar, Char, etc.
Value	Object	Specifies the value assigned to the parameter.

The VB code to create a proxyclass.SqlParameter and assign it a varchar string value might look like this:

```
Dim p As New localhost.SqlParameter
p.sqlDbType = localhost.sqlDbTypeEnum.VarChar
p.maxLength = 50
p.name = "LastName"
p.Value = "Smith"
```

The sample in Listing 16-7 demonstrates how to use the sqlbatch web method to perform a simple parameterized query using the HTTP endpoint created in Listing 16-6.

Listing 16-7. *sqlbatch Web Method Client*

```
Imports System.Net
Imports System.Data


Public Class Form1

    Private Sub btnQuery_Click(ByVal sender As System.Object, _
        ByVal e As System.EventArgs) Handles btnQuery.Click
```

```
        ' Create web services proxy class
        Dim proxy As New localhost.AdvAdHocEndpoint

        ' Assign credentials to proxy
        proxy.Credentials = CredentialCache.DefaultCredentials

        ' Define the parameterized query here. Notice the leading @ is left on
        ' the parameter name in the query
        Dim sql As String = "SELECT ContactID, FirstName, MiddleName, LastName " & _
            " FROM Person.Contact " & _
            " WHERE LastName = @LastName"

        ' Create a parameter for the parameterized query
        Dim p As New localhost.SqlParameter
        p.sqlDbType = localhost.sqlDbTypeEnum.VarChar
        p.maxLength = 50
        ' Notice the leading @ is stripped off the parameter name here
        p.name = "LastName"
        p.Value = txtLastName.Text

        ' Call the sqlbatch web method with the query string and parameter array.
        ' Notice we have to create an array and put the parameter in it here
        Dim ds As DataSet = CType(proxy.sqlbatch(sql, _
            New localhost.SqlParameter() {p})(0), DataSet)

        ' Bind the data grid view to the result
        dgvResults.DataSource = ds.Tables(0)
    End Sub
End Class
```

The btnQuery.Click event handler begins like the previous examples. It creates an instance of the web service proxy class and assigns the appropriate security credentials to it:

```
        ' Create web services proxy class
        Dim proxy As New localhost.AdvAdHocEndpoint

        ' Assign credentials to proxy
        proxy.Credentials = CredentialCache.DefaultCredentials
```

Next, it defines a parameterized query string. Notice that the parameter in the query string still has the leading @ sign:

```
' Define the parameterized query here. Notice the leading @ is left on
' the parameter name in the query
Dim sql As String = "SELECT ContactID, FirstName, MiddleName, LastName " & _
    " FROM Person.Contact " & _
    " WHERE LastName = @LastName"
```

Then it creates a single parameter for the query and sets its properties accordingly:

```
' Create a parameter for the parameterized query
Dim p As New localhost.SqlParameter
p.sqlDbType = localhost.sqlDbTypeEnum.VarChar
p.maxLength = 50
' Notice the leading @ is stripped off the parameter name here
p.name = "LastName"
p.Value = txtLastName.Text
```

Notice that in the name property of the parameter, the leading @ sign is stripped off. The next step is to actually call the sqlbatch method and cast the result to a DataSet. The result is actually returned as an array of Objects, and the Object at element zero of the array is the DataSet. This could have been combined with the next step, but I split it up here to make it easier to read:

```
' Call the sqlbatch web method with the query string and parameter array.
' Notice we have to create an array and put the parameter in it here
Dim ds As DataSet = CType(proxy.sqlbatch(sql, _
    New localhost.SqlParameter() { p })(0), DataSet)
```

■**Note** The second parameter of the sqlbatch method is always an array of SqlParameter objects. Even if you are passing just one SqlParameter, it still needs to be a member of an array. In the example, I create an array of SqlParameter and initialize it on the fly with the following statement: New localhost.SqlParameter() { p }.

When using web methods, such as sqlbatch, Visual Studio provides IntelliSense support, as shown in Figure 16-7.

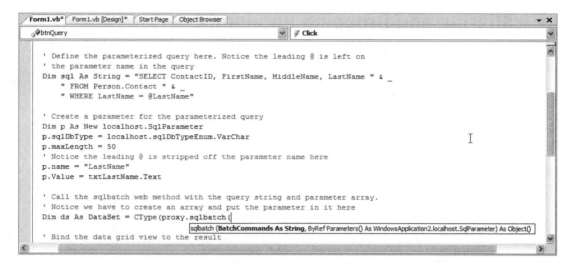

Figure 16-7. *Web method IntelliSense support*

The final step is to bind the results to the DataGridView. The actual rows returned by the query are in DataTable number 0 of the DataSet:

```
' Bind the data grid view to the result
dgvResults.DataSource = ds.Tables(0)
```

To test the application, just enter a last name in the TextBox and press the Query button. All contacts from the Person.Contact table with that last name are returned, as shown in Figure 16-8.

ContactID	FirstName	MiddleName	LastName
11232	Abigail		Smith
2355	Adriana		Smith
17269	Alexander		Smith
10494	Alexandra		Smith
11190	Alexis	L	Smith
15054	Allen		Smith
10721	Alyssa		Smith
15258	Andre		Smith

Ad Hoc Query Example

Last Name:
SMITH   Query

Figure 16-8. *Ad hoc query example in action*

Altering and Dropping Endpoints

You can drop an endpoint with the DROP ENDPOINT statement. The following is the format:

```
DROP ENDPOINT end_point_name;
```

The end_point_name is the name you gave the endpoint when you created it. To drop the endpoint you created for ad hoc queries, you would issue a DROP ENDPOINT statement like this:

```
DROP ENDPOINT AdvAdHocEndpoint;
```

Altering an endpoint requires the ALTER ENDPOINT statement. This statement has a format very similar to CREATE ENDPOINT. The following is the format:

```
ALTER ENDPOINT end_point_name
[ AUTHORIZATION login ]
[ STATE = { STARTED | STOPPED | DISABLED } ]
AS HTTP (
    [ [,] PATH = 'url' ]
    [ [,] AUTHENTICATION = ( { BASIC | DIGEST | INTEGRATED | NTLM | KERBEROS }
        [ , ... n ] ) ]
    [ [,] PORTS = ( { CLEAR | SSL } [ , ... n ] ) ]
    [ [,] SITE = { '*' | '+' | 'web_site' } ]
    [ [,] CLEAR_PORT = clear_port ]
    [ [,] SSL_PORT = ssl_port ]
    [ [,] AUTH_REALM = { 'realm' | NONE } ]
    [ [,] DEFAULT_LOGON_DOMAIN = { 'domain' | NONE } ]
    [ [,] COMPRESSION = { ENABLED | DISABLED } ]
)
FOR SOAP (
    [ [,] { ADD WEBMETHOD [ 'namespace' . ] 'method_alias'
        (
            NAME = 'database.schema.proc_name'
            [ , SCHEMA = { NONE | STANDARD | DEFAULT } ]
            [ , FORMAT = { ALL_RESULTS | ROWSETS_ONLY | NONE } ]
        )
    } [ , ... n ] ]
```

```
[ [,] { ALTER WEBMETHOD [ 'namespace' . ] 'method_alias'
    (
        NAME = 'database.schema.proc_name'
        [ , SCHEMA = { NONE | STANDARD | DEFAULT } ]
        [ , FORMAT = { ALL_RESULTS | ROWSETS_ONLY | NONE } ]
    )
  } [ , ... n ] ]

[ [,] DROP WEBMETHOD [ 'namespace' . ] 'method_alias' [ , ... n ] ]

[ [,] BATCHES = { ENABLED | DISABLED } ]
[ [,] WSDL = { NONE | DEFAULT | 'sp_name' } ]
[ [,] SESSIONS = { ENABLED | DISABLED } ]
[ [,] LOGIN_TYPE = { MIXED | WINDOWS } ]
[ [,] SESSION_TIMEOUT = timeout_interval | NEVER ]
[ [,] DATABASE = { 'database_name' | DEFAULT } ]
[ [,] NAMESPACE = { 'namespace' | DEFAULT } ]
[ [,] SCHEMA = { NONE | STANDARD } ]
[ [,] CHARACTER_SET = { SQL | XML } ]
[ [,] HEADER_LIMIT = header_limit ]
);
```

All the base HTTP endpoint arguments for ALTER ENDPOINT are the same as for CREATE ENDPOINT. These are described earlier in this chapter, so I won't relist them all here. The HTTP-specific arguments are also the same.

The SOAP-specific arguments are where ALTER ENDPOINT and CREATE ENDPOINT part ways. With ALTER ENDPOINT you can use ADD WEBMETHOD to add a new web method to your endpoint; ALTER WEBMETHOD to alter an existing web method; or DROP WEBMETHOD to drop an existing web method. The parameters for ADD WEBMETHOD and ALTER WEBMETHOD are the same as for CREATE ENDPOINT's WEBMETHOD argument. The DROP WEBMETHOD accepts a method_alias.

All of the endpointwide SOAP-specific ALTER ENDPOINT arguments are the same as for CREATE ENDPOINT.

■Tip When you issue an ALTER ENDPOINT, only include arguments that you actually want to change for the endpoint. Any arguments you leave out of the ALTER ENDPOINT statement will retain their current settings.

Summary

In this chapter I discussed SQL Server 2005 HTTP SOAP endpoints, including the following:

- Constructing the CREATE ENDPOINT statement

- Exposing stored procedures and scalar user-defined functions as web methods, both with and without parameters

- Adding a web service proxy to your Visual Studio project

- Accessing the HTTP endpoint web methods from Visual Basic

- Performing ad hoc queries over HTTP endpoints with the sqlbatch method

- Altering and dropping HTTP endpoints

At this point, I'd like to take a moment to thank you for reading this book. I hope you had as much fun reading it as I did writing it for you. I also hope that you find the content useful and informative, and I wish you well in your SQL Server 2005 development and all your other endeavors.

APPENDIX A

■■■

T-SQL Keywords

SQL Server 2005 has 179 reserved keywords. These keywords define the grammar of T-SQL. It's highly recommended that you avoid using these reserved keywords as identifiers when possible, although you can use them as identifiers by delimiting them (with brackets or quotes). The following is a list of the T-SQL reserved keywords:

ADD	CASE	CROSS
ALL	CHECK	CURRENT
ALTER	CHECKPOINT	CURRENT_DATE
AND	CLOSE	CURRENT_TIME
ANY	CLUSTERED	CURRENT_TIMESTAMP
AS	COALESCE	CURRENT_USER
ASC	COLLATE	CURSOR
AUTHORIZATION	COLUMN	DATABASE
BACKUP	COMMIT	DBCC
BEGIN	COMPUTE	DEALLOCATE
BETWEEN	CONSTRAINT	DECLARE
BREAK	CONTAINS	DEFAULT
BROWSE	CONTAINSTABLE	DELETE
BULK	CONTINUE	DENY
BY	CONVERT	DESC
CASCADE	CREATE	DISK

DISTINCT	FULL	LOAD
DISTRIBUTED	FUNCTION	NATIONAL
DOUBLE	GOTO	NOCHECK
DROP	GRANT	NONCLUSTERED
DUMMY	GROUP	NOT
DUMP	HAVING	NULL
ELSE	HOLDLOCK	NULLIF
END	IDENTITY	OF
ERRLVL	IDENTITY_INSERT	OFF
ESCAPE	IDENTITYCOL	OFFSETS
EXCEPT	IF	ON
EXEC	IN	OPEN
EXECUTE	INDEX	OPENDATASOURCE
EXISTS	INNER	OPENQUERY
EXIT	INSERT	OPENROWSET
EXTERNAL	INTERSECT	OPENXML
FETCH	INTO	OPTION
FILE	IS	OR
FILLFACTOR	JOIN	ORDER
FOR	KEY	OUTER
FOREIGN	KILL	OVER
FREETEXT	LEFT	PERCENT
FREETEXTTABLE	LIKE	PIVOT
FROM	LINENO	PLAN

PRECISION	ROWGUIDCOL	TRIGGER
PRIMARY	RULE	TRUNCATE
PRINT	SAVE	TSEQUAL
PROC	SCHEMA	UNION
PROCEDURE	SELECT	UNIQUE
PUBLIC	SESSION_USER	UNPIVOT
RAISERROR	SET	UPDATE
READ	SETUSER	UPDATETEXT
READTEXT	SHUTDOWN	USE
RECONFIGURE	SOME	USER
REFERENCES	STATISTICS	VALUES
REPLICATION	SYSTEM_USER	VARYING
RESTORE	TABLE	VIEW
RESTRICT	TABLESAMPLE	WAITFOR
RETURN	TEXTSIZE	WHEN
REVERT	THEN	WHERE
REVOKE	TO	WHILE
RIGHT	TOP	WITH
ROLLBACK	TRAN	WRITETEXT
ROWCOUNT	TRANSACTION	

T-SQL reserves several symbols for use as math, comparison, bitwise, and other operators. Table A-1 lists these symbols.

Table A-1. *T-SQL Operators*

Operator	Description
+	Add, unary plus, string concatenation
-	Subtract, unary minus
*	Multiply
/	Divide
%	Modulo
&	Bitwise AND
|	Bitwise OR
^	Bitwise XOR (Exclusive OR)
~	Bitwise NOT
=	Equals
>	Greater than
<	Less than
>=, !<	Greater than or equal to, not less than
<=, !>	Less than or equal to, not greater than
<>, !=	Not equal to
--	Single-line comment
/* ... */	Multiline comment

Nonreserved keywords in T-SQL include those that are part of the T-SQL grammar but are not reserved by the language itself. These keywords include system and other built-in function names, data types, and other keywords that are part of the definition of various T-SQL statements.

T-SQL can use the location of these keywords in T-SQL statements to determine the context in which they are being used, so they do not have to be reserved. The following is a list of these keywords:

> ■**Caution** Although you can use most of these nonreserved keywords as identifiers, it is not recommended. Some of these keywords cannot effectively be used as identifiers, although they are not considered "reserved" by Microsoft. An example is the @@ERROR system function, which cannot be redeclared as a variable in your T-SQL code.

$PARTITION	@@PACKET_ERRORS
@@CONNECTIONS	@@PROCID
@@CPU_BUSY	@@REMSERVER
@@CURSOR_ROWS	@@ROWCOUNT
@@DATEFIRST	@@SERVERNAME
@@DBTS	@@SERVICENAME
@@ERROR	@@SPID
@@FETCH_STATUS	@@TEXTSIZE
@@IDENTITY	@@TIMETICKS
@@IDLE	@@TOTAL_ERRORS
@@IO_BUSY	@@TOTAL_READ
@@LANGID	@@TOTAL_WRITE
@@LANGUAGE	@@TRANCOUNT
@@LOCK_TIMEOUT	@@VERSION
@@MAX_CONNECTIONS	ABS
@@MAX_PRECISION	ACOS
@@NESTLEVEL	AGGREGATE
@@OPTIONS	APP_NAME
@@PACK_RECEIVED	APPLICATION
@@PACK_SENT	APPLOCK_MODE

APPLOCK_TEST	CHECKSUM_AGG
ASCII	COL_LENGTH
ASIN	COL_NAME
ASSEMBLY	COLLATIONPROPERTY
ASSEMBLYPROPERTY	COLLECTION
ASYMKEY_ID	COLUMNPROPERTY
ASYMMETRIC	COLUMNS_UPDATED
ATAN	CONTEXT_INFO
ATN2	CONTRACT
AVG	CONVERSATION
BIGINT	COS
BINARY	COT
BINARY_CHECKSUM	COUNT
BINDING	COUNT_BIG
BIT	CREDENTIAL
CAST	CURRENT_REQUEST_ID
CATALOG	CURSOR_STATUS
CATCH	DATABASE_PRINCIPAL_ID
CEILING	DATABASEPROPERTY
CERT_ID	DATABASEPROPERTYEX
CERTIFICATE	DATALENGTH
CERTPROPERTY	DATEADD
CHAR	DATEDIFF
CHARINDEX	DATENAME
CHECKSUM	DATEPART

DAY	ERROR_SEVERITY
DB_ID	ERROR_STATE
DB_NAME	EVENT
DECIMAL	EVENTDATA
DECRYPTBYASYMKEY	EXP
DECRYPTBYCERT	FILE_ID
DECRYPTBYKEY	FILE_IDEX
DECRYPTBYKEYAUTOASYMKEY	FILE_NAME
DECRYPTBYKEYAUTOCERT	FILEGROUP_ID
DECRYPTBYPASSPHRASE	FILEGROUP_NAME
DEGREES	FILEGROUPPROPERTY
DENSE_RANK	FILEPROPERTY
DIALOG	FLOAT
DIFFERENCE	FLOOR
DISABLE	FORMATMESSAGE
ENABLE	FULLTEXT
ENCRYPTBYASYMKEY	FULLTEXTCATALOGPROPERTY
ENCRYPTBYCERT	FULLTEXTSERVICEPROPERTY
ENCRYPTBYKEY	GET
ENCRYPTBYPASSPHRASE	GET_TRANSMISSION_STATUS
ENDPOINT	GETANSINULL
ERROR_LINE	GETDATE
ERROR_MESSAGE	GETUTCDATE
ERROR_NUMBER	GO
ERROR_PROCEDURE	GROUPING

HAS_DBACCESS	LOGIN
HAS_PERMS_BY_NAME	LOGINPROPERTY
HASHBYTES	LOWER
HOST_ID	LTRIM
HOST_NAME	MASTER
IDENT_CURRENT	MAX
IDENT_INCR	MESSAGE
IDENT_SEED	MIN
IMAGE	MONEY
INDEX_COL	MONTH
INDEXKEY_PROPERTY	MOVE
INDEXPROPERTY	NCHAR
INT	NEWID
IS_MEMBER	NEWSEQUENTIALID
IS_SRVROLEMEMBER	NOTIFICATION
ISDATE	NTEXT
ISNULL	NTILE
ISNUMERIC	NUMERIC
JOB	NVARCHAR
KEY_GUID	OBJECT_DEFINITION
KEY_ID	OBJECT_ID
LEN	OBJECT_NAME
LOG	OBJECTPROPERTY
LOG10	OBJECTPROPERTYEX

ORIGINAL_LOGIN	ROW_NUMBER
OUTPUT	ROWCOUNT_BIG
PARSENAME	RTRIM
PARTITION	SCHEMA_ID
PATINDEX	SCHEMA_NAME
PERMISSIONS	SCHEME
PI	SCOPE_IDENTITY
POWER	SEND
PUBLISHINGSERVERNAME	SERVERPROPERTY
QUERY	SERVICE
QUEUE	SESSIONPROPERTY
QUOTENAME	SIGN
RADIANS	SIGNATURE
RAND	SIGNBYASYMKEY
RANK	SIGNBYCERT
REAL	SIN
RECEIVE	SMALLDATETIME
REMOTE	SMALLINT
REPLACE	SMALLMONEY
REPLICATE	SOUNDEX
REVERSE	SPACE
ROLE	SQL_VARIANT
ROUND	SQL_VARIANT_PROPERTY
ROUTE	SQRT

SQUARE	TRIGGER_NESTLEVEL
STATS	TRY
STATS_DATE	TYPE
STDEV	TYPE_ID
STDEVP	TYPE_NAME
STR	TYPEPROPERTY
STUFF	UNICODE
SUBSCRIPTION	UNIQUEIDENTIFIER
SUBSTRING	UPPER
SUM	USER_ID
SUSER_ID	USER_NAME
SUSER_NAME	VAR
SUSER_SID	VARBINARY
SUSER_SNAME	VARCHAR
SYMMETRIC	VARP
SYNONYM	VERIFYSIGNEDBYASMKEY
TAN	VERIFYSIGNEDBYCERT
TERTIARY_WEIGHTS	WORK
TEXT	XACT_STATE
TEXTPTR	XML
TEXTVALID	XML_SCHEMA_NAMESPACE
TIMER	XMLNAMESPACES
TIMESTAMP	YEAR
TINYINT	

In addition to these T-SQL-specific keywords, ANSI SQL:2003 defines several additional keywords as reserved; ODBC has its own set of reserved keywords (important if you are using ODBC for client connectivity); and Microsoft defines several keywords that may be reserved in future versions of SQL Server. Additional care should be taken if you are using a client application with its own list of reserved keywords, such as Microsoft Access. A complete list of SQL Server 2005, ODBC, and other keywords that may be reserved in the future is available in BOL at `http://msdn2.microsoft.com/en-us/library/ms189822.aspx`.

XQuery Data Types

XQuery is a strongly typed language, and the XDM and XML Schema specifications specify several data types that XQuery relies on. This appendix lists the built-in XML Schema–defined data types available to SQL Server XQuery. The W3C provides a complete data type hierarchy diagram in the W3C "XML Schema Part 2: Datatypes Second Edition" specification at http://www.w3.org/TR/xmlschema-2/. The chart in Figure B-1 shows the hierarchy of XML Schema data types supported by SQL Server 2005.

Table B-1 describes the SQL Server–supported XML Schema data types.

Table B-1. *XQuery XML Schema Data Types*

Name	Description
Base Types	
xs:anySimpleType	Represents all simple built-in types.
xs:anyType	Represents all simple and complex built-in types.
Temporal (Time) Types	
xs:date	Represents a Gregorian calendar–based date value exactly one day in length. Represented in the format yyyy-mm-dd[*time_zone*]. *Time_zone* can be a capital Z for *zero-meridian (UTC)*, or in the format +/-hh:mm to represent a UTC offset. An example of a valid xs:date is 2006-12-25Z, which represents December 25, 2006, UTC time. For SQL Server, the *time_zone* component is mandatory.
xs:dateTime	Represents a Gregorian calendar–based date and time value with precision to 1/1,000th of a second. The format is yyyy-mm-ddThh:mm:ss.sss[*time_zone*]. Time is specified using a 24-hour clock. As with xs:date, *time_zone* can be a capital Z (UTC) or a UTC offset in the format +/-hh:mm. A valid xs:dateTime value is 2006-10-30T13:00:59.500-05:00, which represents October 30, 2006, 1:00:59.5 PM, U.S. Eastern Standard Time. For SQL Server, the *time_zone* component is mandatory for xs:dateTime values.
xs:duration	Represents a Gregorian calendar–based temporal (time-based) duration. Represented as PyyyyYmmMddDThhHmmMss.sssS. P0010Y03M12DT00H00M00.000S, for instance, represents 10 years, 3 months, 12 days.

Continued

Table B-1. *Continued*

Name	Description
xs:gDay	Represents a Gregorian calendar–based day. The format is ---dd[*time_zone*] (notice the three preceding hyphen characters). The *time_zone* is optional. A valid xs:gDay value is ---09Z, which stands for the ninth day of the month, UTC time zone.
xs:gMonth	Represents a Gregorian calendar–based month. The format is --mm[*time_zone*] (notice the two preceding hyphen characters). *Time_zone* is optional. A valid xs:gMonth value is --12, which stands for December.
xs:gMonthDay	Represents a Gregorian calendar–based month and day. The format is --mm-dd[*time_zone*] (notice the two preceding hyphens). The *time_zone* for this data type is optional. A valid xs:gMonthDay value is --02-29 for February 29.
xs:gYear	Represents a Gregorian calendar–based year. The format is yyyy[*time_zone*]. The *time_zone* is optional. The year can also have a preceding minus sign indicating a negative year (B.C.E.) as opposed to a positive (C.E.) date. A valid xs:gYear value is -0044 for 44 B.C.E. Notice that all four digits are required in the year representation, even for years that can be normally represented with less than four digits.
xs:gYearMonth	Represents a Gregorian calendar–based year and month. The format is yyyy-mm[*time_zone*]. The *time_zone* for this data type is optional and can be Z or a UTC offset. A valid xs:gYearMonth value is 2001-01 for January 2001.
xs:time	Represents a time value with precision to 1/1,000th of a second, using a 24-hour clock representation. The format is hh:mm:ss.sss[*time_zone*]. As with other temporal data types, *time_zone* can be Z (UTC) or a UTC offset in the format +/-hh:mm. A valid xs:time value is 23:59:59.000-06:00, which represents 11:59:59 PM, U.S. Central Standard Time. The canonical representation of midnight in 24-hour format is 00:00:00.

■**Tip** SQL Server converts all temporal typed values to UTC, so querying the value xs:dateTime ("2006-10-30T13:00:59.500-05:00") returns 2006-10-30T18:00:59.5Z.

Binary Types

xs:base64Binary	Represents Base-64-encoded binary data. Base-64-encoding symbols are defined in RFC 2045 (http://www.ietf.org/rfc/rfc2045.txt) as letters A–Z and a–z, and 0–9, +, /, and trailing = signs. Whitespace characters are also allowed. An example of a valid xs:base64Binary value is the following: QVByZXNzIEJvb2tzIEFuZCBTUUwwgU2VydmVyIDIwMDU=.
xs:hexBinary	Represents hexadecimal-encoded binary data. The symbols defined for encoding data in hexadecimal format are 0–9, A–F, and a–f. Uppercase and lowercase letters A–F are considered equivalent by this data type. A valid xs:hexBinary value is 6170726573732E636F6D.

Name	Description
Boolean Type	
xs:boolean	Represents a boolean binary truth value. The values supported are true, false, or 1 (true), 0 (false). An example of a valid xs:boolean value is true.
Numeric Types	
xs:byte	Represents an 8-bit signed integer in the range -128 to +127.
xs:decimal	Represents an exact decimal value, up to 38 digits in length. These numbers can have up to 28 digits before the decimal point and up to 10 digits after the decimal point. A valid xs:decimal value is 8372.9381.
xs:double	Represents a double-precision floating point value patterned after the IEEE standard representation for floating point types. The representation of values is similar to xs:float values, $nE[+/-]e$, where n is the mantissa followed by the letter E or e and an exponent e. The range of valid values for xs:double is approximately -1.79E+308 to -2.23E-308, 0, and +2.23E-308 to +1.79E+308.
xs:float	Represents an approximate single-precision floating point value per the IEEE 754-1985 standard. The format for values of this type is nEe, where n is a decimal mantissa followed by the letter E or e and an exponent e. The value represents $n \cdot 10^e$. The range for xs:float values is approximately -3.4028e+38 to -1.401298E-45, 0, and +1.401298E-45 to +3.4028e+38. The special values -INF and +INF represent negative and positive infinity. SQL Server does not support the XQuery-specified special value NaN, which stands for "Not a Number." A valid xs:float value is 1.98E+2.

■Tip The xs:double and xs:float data types are considered *approximate* data types. There are many floating point numbers that can be represented exactly in decimal (base-10) notation, but that cannot be represented exactly in the binary (base-2) notation used by the IEEE 754 standard. These numbers are converted and stored as an approximation of the exact value. Do not rely on the exactness of the xs:double and xs:float floating point data types. Also, the IEEE standard specifies the special symbols +INF, -INF, and NaN, which represent positive infinity, negative infinity, and "not a number," respectively. SQL Server XQuery floating point types support +INF and -INF, but no support is provided for NaN.

---

xs:int	Represents a 32-bit signed integer in the range -2147483648 to +2147483647.
xs:integer	Represents an integer value up to 28 digits in length. A valid xs:integer value is 76372.
xs:long	Represents a 64-bit signed integer in the range -9223372036854775808 to +9223372036854775807.
xs:negativeInteger	Represents a negative nonzero integer value derived from the xs:integer type. It can be up to 28 digits in length.

Continued

Table B-1. *Continued*

Name	Description
xs:nonNegativeInteger	Represents a positive or zero integer value derived from the xs:integer type. It can be up to 28 digits in length.
xs:nonPositiveInteger	Represents a negative or zero integer value derived from the xs:integer type. It can be up to 28 digits in length.
xs:positiveInteger	Represents a positive nonzero integer value derived from the xs:integer type. It can be up to 28 digits in length.
xs:short	Represents a 16-bit signed integer in the range -37268 to +32767.
xs:unsignedByte	Represents an unsigned 8-bit integer in the range 0 to +255.
xs:unsignedInt	Represents an unsigned 32-bit integer in the range 0 to +4294967295.
xs:unsignedLong	Represents an unsigned 64-bit integer in the range 0 to +18446744073709551615.
xs:unsignedShort	Represents an unsigned 16-bit integer in the range 0 to +65535.
String Types	
xs:ENTITY	Is equivalent to the ENTITY type from the XML 1.0 standard. The lexical space has the same construction as an xs:NCName.
xs:ENTITIES	Is a space-separated list of ENTITY types.
xs:ID	Is equivalent to the ID attribute type from the XML 1.0 standard. An xs:ID value has the same lexical construction as an xs:NCName.
xs:IDREF	Represents the IDREF attribute type from the XML 1.0 standard. The lexical space has the same construction as an xs:NCName.
xs:IDREFS	Is a space-separated list of IDREF attribute types.
xs:language	Is a language identifier string. This data type represents natural language identifiers as specified by RFC 3066 (http://www.ietf.org/rfc/rfc3066.txt). Language identifiers must conform to the regular expression pattern [a-zA-Z]{1,8}(-[a-zA-Z0-9]{1,8})*. An example of a valid language identifier is tlh, which is the ISO 639-2 identifier for the Klingon language.
xs:Name	Is an XML *name* string. A name string must match the XML-specified production for Name. Per the standard, a Name must begin with a letter, an underscore, or a colon and may then contain a combination of letters, numbers, underscores, colons, periods, hyphens, and various other characters designated in the XML standard as *combining characters* and *extenders*. Refer to the XML standard at http://www.w3.org/TR/2000/WD-xml-2e-20000814#NT-Name for specific information about these additional allowable Name characters.
xs:NCName	Is a noncolonized name. The format for an xs:NCName is the same as for xs:Name but without colon characters.

Name	Description
xs:NMTOKEN	Is an NMTOKEN type from the XML 1.0 standard. An xs:NMTOKEN value is composed of any combination of letters, numbers, underscores, colons, periods, hyphens, and XML combining characters and extenders.
xs:NMTOKENS	Is a space-separated list of xs:NMTOKEN values.
xs:normalizedString	Is an XML *whitespace normalized* string. A whitespace normalized string is one that does not contain the whitespace characters #x9 (tab), #xA (line feed), or #xD (carriage return).
xs:string	Is an XML character string.
xs:token	Is an XML whitespace normalized string with the following additional restrictions on #x20 (space) characters: 1) they can have no leading or trailing spaces, and 2) they cannot contain any sequences of two space characters in a row.

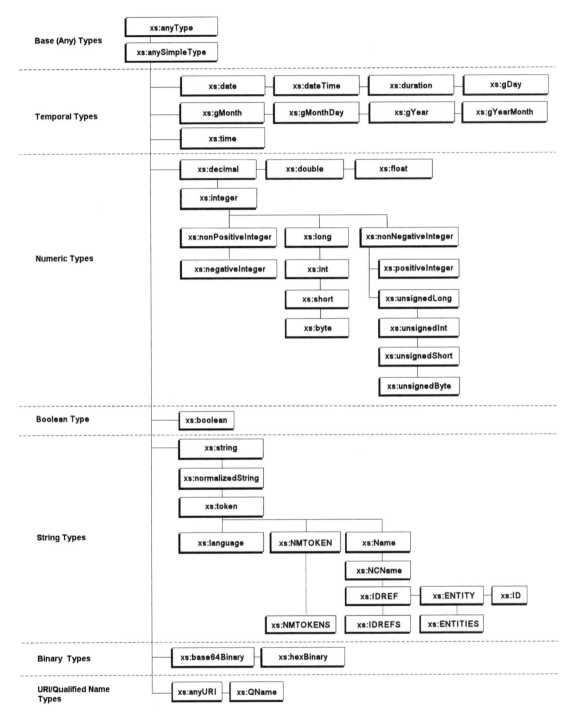

Figure B-1. *SQL Server XQuery data types hierarchy*

XQuery Terms

$\mathbf{X}$Query support in SQL Server 2005 brings with it a whole new vocabulary. This appendix lists some of the commonly used XQuery terms and their definitions.

Atomic data types, list data types, and union data types

Atomic data types are indivisible data types that derive from the xs:anyAtomicType type. Examples include xs:boolean, xs:date, and xs:integer. List data types are types that are constructed of sequences of other types. Union data types are constructed from the *ordered union* of two or more data types, or a restricted subset of a data type. The "XML Schema 1.1 Part 2: Datatypes" specification working draft (http://www.w3.org/TR/xmlschema11-2/#ordinary-built-ins) defines no built-in union data types.

Axis

An axis specifier indicates the relationship between the nodes selected by the location step and the context node. Examples of axis specifiers include child, parent, and ancestor.

Comments

XQuery comments are denoted by the (: and :) delimiters in XQuery queries. XQuery comments are ignored during processing and should not be confused with XML *comment nodes*.

Context item expression

This expression evaluates to the context node.

Context node

The context node is the node currently being processed. Each node of each set/sequence returned by a step in a location path is used in turn as a context node. Subsequent steps define their axes in relation to the current context node. For instance, with the sample XPath expression /Root/Person/Address, the Root node is the first context node. All Person nodes returned below Root become the context node in turn, and the Address nodes are retrieved relative to these context nodes.

Empty sequence

This is an XPath 2.0 and XQuery 1.0 sequence containing zero items.

F&O

This is XQuery Functions and Operators, as defined by the "XQuery 1.0 and XPath 2.0 Functions and Operators" specification, available at `http://www.w3.org/TR/xquery-operators/`.

Facets

Facets are schema components used to constrain data types. A couple of commonly used facets are `whiteSpace` and `length`, which control how whitespace in string values is handled, and restrict values to a specific number of units in length, respectively.

Filter expression

This is a primary expression followed by zero or more predicates.

FLWOR expression

FLWOR is an acronym for the XQuery keywords `for`, `let`, `where`, `order by`, and `return`. FLWOR expressions support iteration and binding variables.

General comparisons

These are existentially quantified XQuery comparisons that may be applied to operand sequences of any length. In general comparisons, the nodes are atomized and the atomic values of both operands are compared using value comparisons. If any of the value comparisons evaluate to `true`, the result is `true`.

Location paths

The *path* is an XPath or XQuery expression that addresses a specific subset of nodes in an XML document. The location path is a series of *steps* separated by the solidus (forward slash) character, evaluated from left to right. Each step generates a sequence of items. Location paths can be relative or absolute. *Absolute* location paths begin with a single solidus character; *relative* location paths do not.

Node comparisons

Node comparisons in XQuery compare nodes by their document order or identity.

Nodes

XPath 2.0 and XQuery 1.0 treat XML data as a hierarchical tree structure, similar to (but not exactly the same as) the Document Object Model (DOM) that web programmers often use to manipulate HTML and XML. XPath and XQuery XML trees are composed of the seven types of nodes defined in the W3C XQuery 1.0 and XPath 2.0 Data Model (XDM), full descriptions of which are available at `http://www.w3.org/TR/xpath-datamodel/#node-identity`. These node types include the following:

- Attribute nodes, which represent XML attributes

- Comment nodes, which encapsulate XML comments

- Document nodes, which encapsulate XML documents

- Element nodes, which encapsulate XML elements

- Namespace nodes, which represent the binding of a namespace URI to a namespace prefix (or the default namespace)

- Processing instruction nodes, which encapsulate processing instructions (PIs)

- Text nodes, which encapsulate XML character content

XPath 1.0 defines the node types it uses in Part 5 of the XPath 1.0 specification. The main difference between XPath 1.0 nodes and XDM nodes is that XPath 1.0 defines the *root node* of a document in place of the *document nodes* of the XDM. Another major difference is that in the XDM, element nodes are either explicitly or implicitly (based on content) assigned type information.

Node test

A node test is a condition that must be true for each node generated by a step. A node test can be based on the name of the node, the kind of node, or the type of node.

Optional occurrence indicator

This is the ? character, when used in conjunction with the cast as keywords. It indicates that the empty sequence is allowed as a result.

Path expression

See *location paths*.

Predicates

A predicate is an expression enclosed in brackets ([ ]) that is used to filter a sequence. The predicate expressions are generally comparison expressions of some sort (equality, inequality, etc.).

Primary expression

This is the basic *primitive* of the XQuery language. A primary expression can be a literal, a variable reference, a context item expression, a data type constructor, or a function call.

Sequences

XPath 2.0 and XQuery 1.0 define sequences as ordered collections of zero or more items. The term *ordered* is important here, as it differentiates a *sequence* from a *set*, which, as most T-SQL programmers know (or quickly come to realize), is unordered. XPath 1.0 defined its results in terms of *node sets*, which are unordered and cannot contain duplicates. XQuery changes this terminology to *node sequences*, which recognize the importance of node order in XML and can contain duplicates.

Shredding

This is the process of converting XML data to relational style rows and columns.

SOAP

Simple Object Access Protocol is an XML-based protocol designed for exchanging structured information in distributed, decentralized environments.

Step

A *step* in XQuery is composed of an axis, a node test, and zero or more predicates. Each step is a part of a path expression that generates a sequence of items and then filters the sequence.

Value comparison

This is a comparison of single values in XQuery.

W3C

The World Wide Web Consortium is a standards body with the stated mission of "developing interoperable technologies . . . to lead the Web to its full potential."

XDM

The XQuery 1.0 and XPath 2.0 Data Model is defined by the W3C at `http://www.w3.org/TR/2006/PR-xpath-datamodel-20061121/`.

XML

Extensible Markup Language is a restricted form of SGML (Standardized General Markup Language) designed to be easily served, received, and processed on the Web.

XML Schema

Part 2 of the XML Schema 1.1 standard defines XML Schema data types, which are the basic data types utilized by XQuery.

XPath

XML Path Language is an expression language designed to allow processing of values that conform to the XDM.

XQuery

XML Query Language is an XML query language designed to retrieve and interpret data from diverse XML sources.

XSL

Extensible Stylesheet Language is a language for expressing style sheets, consisting of a language for transforming XML documents, and an XML vocabulary for specifying formatting semantics.

XSLT

XSL Transformations is a language for transforming XML documents into other XML documents. For instance, XSLT can be used to transform an XML document into an XHTML document.

■■■

Selected T-SQL Source Code Listings

This appendix contains the complete program listings for some of the longer sample programs in Chapters 5, 6, 8, 12, and 16.

Chapter 5

Listing 5-3. *Creating a Numbers Table*

```
-- This SELECT INTO statement uses the T-SQL IDENTITY function to quickly
-- build a Numbers table
SELECT TOP 10000 IDENTITY(INT, 1, 1) AS Num
INTO dbo.Numbers
FROM sys.columns a
    CROSS JOIN sys.columns b;
GO
-- A table isn't a table without a Primary Key
ALTER TABLE dbo.Numbers
    ADD CONSTRAINT PK_Num PRIMARY KEY CLUSTERED (Num);
```

Listing 5-4. *NYSIIS UDF*

```
-- Create the NYSIIS replacement rules table
CREATE TABLE dbo.NYSIIS_Replacements
    (Location NVARCHAR(10) NOT NULL,
    NGram NVARCHAR(10) NOT NULL,
    Replacement NVARCHAR(10) NOT NULL,
    PRIMARY KEY (Location, NGram));
```

```
-- The end-of-name n-gram rules
INSERT INTO NYSIIS_Replacements (Location, NGram, Replacement)
    VALUES (N'End', N'AY', N'YY');
INSERT INTO NYSIIS_Replacements (Location, NGram, Replacement)
    VALUES (N'End', N'DT', N'DD');
INSERT INTO NYSIIS_Replacements (Location, NGram, Replacement)
    VALUES (N'End', N'EE', N'YY');
INSERT INTO NYSIIS_Replacements (Location, NGram, Replacement)
    VALUES (N'End', N'EY', N'YY');
INSERT INTO NYSIIS_Replacements (Location, NGram, Replacement)
    VALUES (N'End', N'IE', N'YY');
INSERT INTO NYSIIS_Replacements (Location, NGram, Replacement)
    VALUES (N'End', N'IY', N'YY');
INSERT INTO NYSIIS_Replacements (Location, NGram, Replacement)
    VALUES (N'End', N'ND', N'DD');
INSERT INTO NYSIIS_Replacements (Location, NGram, Replacement)
    VALUES (N'End', N'NT', N'DD');
INSERT INTO NYSIIS_Replacements (Location, NGram, Replacement)
    VALUES (N'End', N'OY', N'YY');
INSERT INTO NYSIIS_Replacements (Location, NGram, Replacement)
    VALUES (N'End', N'RD', N'DD');
INSERT INTO NYSIIS_Replacements (Location, NGram, Replacement)
    VALUES (N'End', N'RT', N'DD');
INSERT INTO NYSIIS_Replacements (Location, NGram, Replacement)
    VALUES (N'End', N'UY', N'YY');

-- The middle-of-name n-gram rules
INSERT INTO NYSIIS_Replacements (Location, NGram, Replacement)
    VALUES (N'Mid', N'A', N'A');
INSERT INTO NYSIIS_Replacements (Location, NGram, Replacement)
    VALUES (N'Mid', N'E', N'A');
INSERT INTO NYSIIS_Replacements (Location, NGram, Replacement)
    VALUES (N'Mid', N'I', N'A');
INSERT INTO NYSIIS_Replacements (Location, NGram, Replacement)
    VALUES (N'Mid', N'K', N'C');
INSERT INTO NYSIIS_Replacements (Location, NGram, Replacement)
    VALUES (N'Mid', N'M', N'N');
INSERT INTO NYSIIS_Replacements (Location, NGram, Replacement)
    VALUES (N'Mid', N'O', N'A');
INSERT INTO NYSIIS_Replacements (Location, NGram, Replacement)
    VALUES (N'Mid', N'Q', N'G');
```

```
INSERT INTO NYSIIS_Replacements (Location, NGram, Replacement)
    VALUES (N'Mid', N'U', N'A');
INSERT INTO NYSIIS_Replacements (Location, NGram, Replacement)
    VALUES (N'Mid', N'Z', N'S');
INSERT INTO NYSIIS_Replacements (Location, NGram, Replacement)
    VALUES (N'Mid', N'AW', N'AA');
INSERT INTO NYSIIS_Replacements (Location, NGram, Replacement)
    VALUES (N'Mid', N'EV', N'AF');
INSERT INTO NYSIIS_Replacements (Location, NGram, Replacement)
    VALUES (N'Mid', N'EW', N'AA');
INSERT INTO NYSIIS_Replacements (Location, NGram, Replacement)
    VALUES (N'Mid', N'IW', N'AA');
INSERT INTO NYSIIS_Replacements (Location, NGram, Replacement)
    VALUES (N'Mid', N'KN', N'NN');
INSERT INTO NYSIIS_Replacements (Location, NGram, Replacement)
    VALUES (N'Mid', N'OW', N'AA');
INSERT INTO NYSIIS_Replacements (Location, NGram, Replacement)
    VALUES (N'Mid', N'PH', N'FF');
INSERT INTO NYSIIS_Replacements (Location, NGram, Replacement)
    VALUES (N'Mid', N'UW', N'AA');
INSERT INTO NYSIIS_Replacements (Location, NGram, Replacement)
    VALUES (N'Mid', N'SCH', N'SSS');


-- The start-of-name n-gram rules
INSERT INTO NYSIIS_Replacements (Location, NGram, Replacement)
    VALUES (N'Start', N'K', N'C');
INSERT INTO NYSIIS_Replacements (Location, NGram, Replacement)
    VALUES (N'Start', N'KN', N'NN');
INSERT INTO NYSIIS_Replacements (Location, NGram, Replacement)
    VALUES (N'Start', N'PF', N'FF');
INSERT INTO NYSIIS_Replacements (Location, NGram, Replacement)
    VALUES (N'Start', N'PH', N'FF');
INSERT INTO NYSIIS_Replacements (Location, NGram, Replacement)
    VALUES (N'Start', N'MAC', N'MCC');
INSERT INTO NYSIIS_Replacements (Location, NGram, Replacement)
    VALUES (N'Start', N'SCH', N'SSS');
GO
CREATE FUNCTION dbo.fnNYSIIS (@Name NVARCHAR(50))
RETURNS NVARCHAR(50)
WITH RETURNS NULL ON NULL INPUT, SCHEMABINDING
AS
```

```sql
BEGIN
    DECLARE @Result NVARCHAR(50);    -- This will contain our end result
    SELECT @Result = UPPER(@Name);

    -- Replace the start n-gram
    SELECT TOP 1 @Result = STUFF(@Result, 1, LEN(NGram), Replacement)
    FROM dbo.NYSIIS_Replacements
    WHERE Location = N'Start'
        AND SUBSTRING(@Result, 1, LEN(NGram)) = NGram
    ORDER BY LEN(NGram) DESC;

    -- Replace the end n-gram
    SELECT TOP 1 @Result = STUFF(@Result, LEN(@Result) - LEN(NGram) + 1,
        LEN(NGram), Replacement)
    FROM dbo.NYSIIS_Replacements
    WHERE Location = N'End'
        AND SUBSTRING(@Result, LEN(@Result) - LEN(NGram) + 1, LEN(NGram)) = NGram
    ORDER BY LEN(NGram) DESC;

    -- Store the first letter of the name
    DECLARE @first_letter NCHAR(1)
    SELECT @first_letter = SUBSTRING(@Result, 1, 1);

    -- Replace all middle n-grams
    DECLARE @replacement NVARCHAR(10);
    DECLARE @i INT;
    SELECT @i = 1;
    WHILE @i <= LEN(@Result)
    BEGIN
        SELECT @replacement = NULL;

        -- Grab the middle-of-name replacement n-gram
        SELECT TOP 1 @replacement = Replacement
        FROM dbo.NYSIIS_Replacements
        WHERE Location = N'Mid'
            AND SUBSTRING(@Result, @i, LEN(NGram)) = NGram
        ORDER BY LEN(NGram) DESC;

        -- If we found a replacement, apply it
        IF @replacement IS NOT NULL
            SELECT @Result = STUFF(@Result, @i, LEN(@replacement), @replacement);
```

```
    -- Move on to the next n-gram
    SELECT @i = @i + COALESCE(LEN(@replacement), 1);
END;


-- Replace the first character with the first letter we saved at the start
SELECT @Result = STUFF(@Result, 1, 1, @first_letter);


-- Here we apply our special rules for the 'H' character
SELECT @Result =
    STUFF(@Result, Num, 1,
        CASE SUBSTRING(@Result, Num, 1)
            WHEN N'H'
            THEN
                CASE
                    WHEN SUBSTRING(@Result, Num + 1, 1)
                        NOT IN (N'A', N'E', N'I', N'O', N'U')
                        OR SUBSTRING(@Result, Num - 1, 1)
                        NOT IN (N'A', N'E', N'I', N'O', N'U')
                    THEN SUBSTRING(@Result, Num - 1, 1)
                    ELSE N'H'
                END
            ELSE SUBSTRING(@Result, Num, 1)
        END)
FROM dbo.Numbers
WHERE Num <= LEN(@Result);


-- Here we replace the first letter of any sequence of two side-by-side
-- duplicate letters with a period
SELECT @Result =
    STUFF(@Result, Num, 1,
        CASE SUBSTRING(@Result, Num, 1)
            WHEN SUBSTRING(@Result, Num + 1, 1) THEN N'.'
            ELSE SUBSTRING(@Result, Num, 1)
        END)
FROM dbo.Numbers
WHERE Num <= LEN(@Result);


-- Next we replace all periods '.' with an empty string ''
SELECT @Result = REPLACE(@Result, N'.', N'');
```

```
    -- Remove trailing 'S' characters
    WHILE RIGHT(@Result, 1) = N'S'
        SELECT @Result = STUFF(@Result, LEN(@Result), 1, N'');

    -- Remove trailing vowels
    WHILE RIGHT(@Result, 1) = N'A'
        SELECT @Result = STUFF(@Result, LEN(@Result), 1, N'');

    RETURN @Result;
END;
GO
```

Listing 5-5. *Pull Product List Multistatement Table-Valued Function*

```
CREATE FUNCTION dbo.fnProductPullList()
RETURNS @result TABLE (
    SalesOrderID INT NOT NULL,
    ProductID INT NOT NULL,
    LocationID SMALLINT NOT NULL,
    Shelf NVARCHAR(10) NOT NULL,
    Bin TINYINT NOT NULL,
    QuantityInBin SMALLINT NOT NULL,
    QuantityOnOrder SMALLINT NOT NULL,
    QuantityToPull SMALLINT NOT NULL,
    PartialFillFlag CHAR(1) NOT NULL,
    PRIMARY KEY (SalesOrderID, ProductID, LocationID, Shelf, Bin))
WITH SCHEMABINDING
AS
BEGIN
    INSERT INTO @result (
        SalesOrderID,
        ProductID,
        LocationID,
        Shelf,
        Bin,
        QuantityInBin,
        QuantityOnOrder,
        QuantityToPull,
        PartialFillFlag)
```

```
SELECT Order_Details.SalesOrderID,
    Order_Details.ProductID,
    Inventory_Details.LocationID,
    Inventory_Details.Shelf,
    Inventory_Details.Bin,
    Inventory_Details.Quantity,
    Order_Details.OrderQty,
    COUNT(*) AS PullQty,
    CASE WHEN COUNT(*) < Order_Details.OrderQty
        THEN 'Y'
        ELSE 'N'
    END AS PartialFillFlag
FROM
(
    SELECT ROW_NUMBER() OVER (PARTITION BY i.ProductID
        ORDER BY i.ProductID,
            i.LocationID,
            i.Shelf,
            i.Bin) AS Num,
        i.ProductID,
        i.LocationID,
        i.Shelf,
        i.Bin,
        i.Quantity
    FROM
        (
            SELECT ProductID,
                LocationID,
                Shelf,
                Bin,
                Quantity
            FROM Production.ProductInventory
            INNER JOIN dbo.Numbers n
                ON n.Num BETWEEN 1 AND Quantity
        ) i
    INNER JOIN Production.ProductInventory p
        ON i.ProductID = p.ProductID
            AND i.LocationID = p.LocationID
            AND i.Shelf = p.Shelf
            AND i.Bin = p.Bin
) Inventory_Details
```

```
    INNER JOIN
    (
        SELECT ROW_NUMBER() OVER (PARTITION BY o.ProductID
            ORDER BY o.ProductID,
                o.SalesOrderID) AS Num,
            o.ProductID,
            o.SalesOrderID,
            o.OrderQty
        FROM
            (
                SELECT ProductID,
                    SalesOrderID,
                    SalesOrderDetailID,
                    OrderQty
                FROM Sales.SalesOrderDetail
                INNER JOIN dbo.Numbers n
                    ON n.Num BETWEEN 1 AND OrderQty
            ) o
        INNER JOIN Sales.SalesOrderDetail sod
            ON o.SalesOrderID = sod.SalesOrderID
                AND o.SalesOrderDetailID = sod.SalesOrderDetailID
                AND o.ProductID = sod.ProductID
    ) Order_Details
        ON Inventory_Details.ProductID = Order_Details.ProductID
            AND Inventory_Details.Num = Order_Details.Num
    GROUP BY Order_Details.SalesOrderID,
        Order_Details.ProductID,
        Inventory_Details.LocationID,
        Inventory_Details.Shelf,
        Inventory_Details.Bin,
        Inventory_Details.Quantity,
        Order_Details.OrderQty;
    RETURN;
END;
GO
```

Listing 5-6. *Comma-Splitter Inline Table-Valued Function*

```
CREATE FUNCTION dbo.fnCommaSplit (@String NVARCHAR(MAX))
RETURNS TABLE
WITH SCHEMABINDING
AS
RETURN
(
    WITH Splitter(Num, Element)
    AS
    (
        SELECT Num,
            SUBSTRING(@String,
                CASE Num
                    WHEN 1 THEN 1
                    ELSE Num + 1
                END,
                CASE CHARINDEX(N',', @String, Num + 1)
                    WHEN 0 THEN LEN(@String) - Num + 1
                    ELSE CHARINDEX(N',', @String, Num + 1) - Num -
                        CASE
                            WHEN Num > 1 THEN 1
                            ELSE 0
                        END
                END
            ) AS Element
        FROM dbo.Numbers
        WHERE Num <= LEN(@String)
            AND (SUBSTRING(@String, Num, 1) = N','
                OR Num = 1)
    )
    SELECT ROW_NUMBER() OVER (ORDER BY Num) AS Num,
        Element
    FROM Splitter
);
GO
```

Chapter 6

Listing 6-4. *Towers of Hanoi Puzzle*

```
-- This stored procedure displays all the discs in the appropriate
-- towers.
CREATE PROCEDURE dbo.ShowTowers
AS
BEGIN
    -- Each disc is displayed as a series of asterisks (*), centered, with
    -- the appropriate width. Using FULL OUTER JOIN allows us to show all
    -- three towers side by side in a single query.
    SELECT REPLICATE(' ', COALESCE(5 - a.Disc, 0)) +
            REPLICATE('**', COALESCE(a.Disc, 0)) AS Tower_A,
        REPLICATE(' ', COALESCE(5 - b.Disc, 0)) +
            REPLICATE('**', COALESCE(b.Disc, 0)) AS Tower_B,
        REPLICATE(' ', COALESCE(5 - c.Disc, 0)) +
            REPLICATE('**', COALESCE(c.Disc, 0)) AS Tower_C
    FROM #TowerA a
    FULL OUTER JOIN #TowerB b
        ON a.Disc = b.Disc
    FULL OUTER JOIN #TowerC c
        ON a.Disc = b.Disc;
END;
GO


-- This SP moves a single disc from the specified source tower to the
-- specified destination tower.
CREATE PROCEDURE dbo.MoveOneDisc (@Source NCHAR(1),
    @Dest NCHAR(1))
AS
BEGIN
    -- @Top is the smallest disc on the source tower
    DECLARE @Top INT;
    -- We use IF ... ELSE to get the smallest disc from the source tower
    IF @Source = N'A'
```

```
    BEGIN
        -- This gets the smallest disc from Tower A
        SELECT @Top = MIN(Disc)
        FROM #TowerA;
        -- Then we delete it
        DELETE FROM #TowerA
        WHERE Disc = @Top;
    END ELSE IF @Source = N'B'
    BEGIN
        -- This gets the smallest disc from Tower B
        SELECT @Top = MIN(Disc)
        FROM #TowerB;
        -- Then we delete it
        DELETE FROM #TowerB
        WHERE Disc = @Top;
    END ELSE IF @Source = N'C'
    BEGIN
        -- This gets the smallest disc from Tower C
        SELECT @Top = MIN(Disc)
        FROM #TowerC;
        -- Then we delete it
        DELETE FROM #TowerC
        WHERE Disc = @Top;
    END
    -- Print out the disc move performed
    PRINT N'Move Disc #' + CAST(COALESCE(@Top, 0) AS NCHAR(1)) + N' from Tower ' +
        @Source + N' to Tower ' + @Dest;
    -- Perform the move: INSERT the disc from the source tower to the
    -- destination tower
    IF @Dest = N'A'
        INSERT INTO #TowerA (Disc) VALUES (@Top);
    ELSE IF @Dest = N'B'
        INSERT INTO #TowerB (Disc) VALUES (@Top);
    ELSE IF @Dest = N'C'
        INSERT INTO #TowerC (Disc) VALUES (@Top);
    -- Show the towers
    EXECUTE dbo.ShowTowers;
END;
GO
```

```sql
-- This SP moves multiple discs recursively
CREATE PROCEDURE dbo.MoveDiscs (@DiscNum INT,
    @MoveNum INT OUTPUT,
    @Source NCHAR(1) = N'A',
    @Dest NCHAR(1) = N'C',
    @Aux NCHAR(1) = N'B'
)
AS
BEGIN
    -- If the number of discs to move is 0, we're done
    IF @DiscNum = 0
        PRINT N'Done';
    ELSE
    BEGIN
        -- If the number of discs to move is 1, go ahead and move it
        IF @DiscNum = 1
        BEGIN
            -- Increase the move counter
            SELECT @MoveNum = @MoveNum + 1;
            -- And move one disc from source to destination
            EXEC dbo.MoveOneDisc @Source, @Dest
        END
        ELSE
        BEGIN
            DECLARE @n INT
            SELECT @n = @DiscNum - 1
            -- Move (@DiscNum - 1) discs from Source to Auxiliary tower
            EXEC dbo.MoveDiscs @n, @MoveNum OUTPUT, @Source, @Aux, @Dest;
            -- Move 1 Disc from Source to Destination tower
            EXEC dbo.MoveDiscs 1, @MoveNum OUTPUT, @Source, @Dest, @Aux;
            -- Move (@DiscNum - 1) discs from Auxiliary to Destination tower
            EXEC dbo.MoveDiscs @n, @MoveNum OUTPUT, @Aux, @Dest, @Source;
        END;
    END;
END;
GO
```

```
-- This SP creates the three towers and populates Tower A with 5 discs
CREATE PROCEDURE dbo.SolveTowers
AS
BEGIN
    -- SET NOCOUNT ON to eliminate system messages that will clutter up
    -- the Message display
    SET NOCOUNT ON
    -- Create the three towers: Tower A = Source, Tower B = Auxiliary,
    -- Tower C = Destination
    CREATE TABLE #TowerA (Disc INT PRIMARY KEY NOT NULL);
    CREATE TABLE #TowerB (Disc INT PRIMARY KEY NOT NULL);
    CREATE TABLE #TowerC (Disc INT PRIMARY KEY NOT NULL);
    -- Populate Tower A with 5 discs
    INSERT INTO #TowerA (Disc) VALUES (1);
    INSERT INTO #TowerA (Disc) VALUES (2);
    INSERT INTO #TowerA (Disc) VALUES (3);
    INSERT INTO #TowerA (Disc) VALUES (4);
    INSERT INTO #TowerA (Disc) VALUES (5);
    -- Initialize the move number to 0
    DECLARE @MoveNum INT;
    SELECT @MoveNum = 0;
    -- Show the initial state of the towers
    EXECUTE dbo.ShowTowers;
    -- Solve the puzzle. Notice we don't need to specify the parameters with
    -- defaults
    EXECUTE dbo.MoveDiscs 5, @MoveNum OUTPUT;
    -- How many moves did it take?
    PRINT N'Solved in ' + CAST (@MoveNum AS NVARCHAR(10)) + N' moves.';
    -- Drop the temp tables
    DROP TABLE #TowerC;
    DROP TABLE #TowerB;
    DROP TABLE #TowerA;
    -- SET NOCOUNT OFF before we exit
    SET NOCOUNT OFF
END;
GO
-- Solve the puzzle
EXECUTE dbo.SolveTowers;
GO
```

Chapter 8

Listing 8-5. *EncryptByCert and DecryptByCert Sample*

```
CREATE MASTER KEY ENCRYPTION BY PASSWORD = 'Test_P@sswOrd';

CREATE CERTIFICATE TestCertificate
    WITH SUBJECT = 'AdventureWorks Test Certificate',
    EXPIRY_DATE = '10/31/2036';

CREATE SYMMETRIC KEY TestSymmetricKey
    WITH ALGORITHM = TRIPLE_DES
    ENCRYPTION BY CERTIFICATE TestCertificate;

OPEN SYMMETRIC KEY TestSymmetricKey
    DECRYPTION BY CERTIFICATE TestCertificate;

CREATE TABLE #Temp (ContactID   INT PRIMARY KEY,
    FirstName   NVARCHAR(200),
    MiddleName  NVARCHAR(200),
    LastName    NVARCHAR(200),
    eFirstName  VARBINARY(200),
    eMiddleName VARBINARY(200),
    eLastName   VARBINARY(200));

INSERT
    INTO #Temp (ContactID, eFirstName, eMiddleName, eLastName)
    SELECT ContactID,
        EncryptByKey(Key_GUID('TestSymmetricKey'), FirstName),
        EncryptByKey(Key_GUID('TestSymmetricKey'), MiddleName),
        EncryptByKey(Key_GUID('TestSymmetricKey'), LastName)
FROM Person.Contact
    WHERE ContactID <= 100;

UPDATE #Temp
    SET FirstName = DecryptByKey(eFirstName),
        MiddleName = DecryptByKey(eMiddleName),
        LastName = DecryptByKey(eLastName);
```

```
SELECT ContactID,
    FirstName,
    MiddleName,
    LastName,
    eFirstName,
    eMiddleName,
    eLastName
FROM #Temp;

DROP TABLE #Temp;
CLOSE SYMMETRIC KEY TestSymmetricKey;

DROP SYMMETRIC KEY TestSymmetricKey;
DROP CERTIFICATE TestCertificate;
DROP MASTER KEY;
```

Chapter 12

Listing 12-8. *FOR XML PATH Clause Example*

```
SELECT NameStyle AS 'processing-instruction(nameStyle)',
    ContactID AS 'Person/@ID',
    ModifiedDate AS 'comment()',
    Phone AS 'text()',
    FirstName AS 'Person/Name/First',
    MiddleName AS 'Person/Name/Middle',
    LastName AS 'Person/Name/Last',
    EmailAddress AS 'Person/Email'
FROM Person.Contact
FOR XML PATH;
```

Listing 12-20. *Dynamic XML Construction*

```
DECLARE @x XML;
SELECT @x = N'<?xml version = "1.0"?>
<Geocode>
    <Info ID = "1">
        <Location Type = "Business">
            <Name>APress, Inc.</Name>
```

```
            <Address>
                <Street>2560 Ninth St, Ste 219</Street>
                <City>Berkeley</City>
                <State>CA</State>
                <Zip>94710-2500</Zip>
                <Country>US</Country>
            </Address>
        </Location>
    </Info>
</Geocode>';
SELECT @x.query(N'element Companies
    {
        element FirstCompany
        {
            attribute CompanyID
            {
                (//Info/@ID)[1]
            },
            (//Info/Location/Name)[1]
        }
    }');
```

Listing 12-28. *sql:column and sql:variable Function Example*

```
/* 10% discount */
DECLARE @discount NUMERIC(3, 2);
SELECT @discount = 0.10;
DECLARE @x xml;
SELECT @x = '';
SELECT @x.query('<Product>
    <Model-ID> { sql:column("ProductModelID") }</Model-ID>
        <Name> { sql:column("Name") }</Name>
        <Price> { sql:column("ListPrice") } </Price>
        <DiscountPrice>
            { sql:column("ListPrice") -
            (sql:column("ListPrice") * sql:variable("@discount") ) }
        </DiscountPrice>
</Product>
')
FROM Production.Product p
WHERE ProductModelID = 30;
```

Listing 12-34. *XQuery FLWOR Expression Example*

```
SELECT CatalogDescription.query(N'declare namespace ns =
    "http://schemas.microsoft.com/sqlserver/2004/07/adventure-works/➥
        ProductModelDescription";
    for $spec in //ns:ProductDescription/ns:Specifications/*
    order by $spec/. descending
    return <detail> { $spec/text() } </detail>') AS Detail
FROM Production.ProductModel
WHERE ProductModelID = 19;
```

Chapter 16

Listing 16-1. *HTTP Endpoint Example GetSalespersonList Method*

```
USE AdventureWorks;
GO
CREATE PROCEDURE Sales.GetSalespersonList
AS
BEGIN
    SELECT s.SalesPersonID,
        s.LastName + ', ' + s.FirstName + ' ' + COALESCE(s.MiddleName, '')
            AS FullName
    FROM Sales.vSalesPerson s
    ORDER BY s.LastName, s.FirstName, s.MiddleName;
END;
GO
```

Listing 16-2. *HTTP Endpoint Example GetSalespersonSales Method*

```
USE AdventureWorks;
GO
CREATE PROCEDURE Sales.GetSalespersonSales (@SalespersonID INT)
AS
BEGIN
    SELECT soh.SalesOrderID,
        soh.CustomerID,
        soh.OrderDate,
        soh.SubTotal
```

```
    FROM Sales.SalesOrderHeader soh
    WHERE soh.SalesPersonID = @SalespersonID
    ORDER BY soh.SalesOrderID;
END;
GO
```

Listing 16-3. *HTTP Endpoint Example GetSalesTotal Method*

```
USE AdventureWorks;
GO
CREATE FUNCTION Sales.GetSalesTotal(@SalespersonID INT)
RETURNS MONEY
AS
BEGIN
    RETURN (
        SELECT SUM(soh.SubTotal)
        FROM Sales.SalesOrderHeader soh
        WHERE SalesPersonID = @SalespersonID
    );
END;
GO
```

Listing 16-4. *HTTP Endpoint Example CREATE ENDPOINT*

```
USE AdventureWorks;
GO
CREATE ENDPOINT AdvSalesEndpoint
    STATE = STARTED
AS HTTP
(
    PATH = N'/AdvSalesSql',
    AUTHENTICATION = (INTEGRATED),
    PORTS = (CLEAR),
    SITE = N'*'
)
FOR SOAP
(
    WEBMETHOD N'GetSalespersonList'
    (
        NAME = N'AdventureWorks.Sales.GetSalespersonList',
        FORMAT = ROWSETS_ONLY
    ),
```

```
    WEBMETHOD N'GetSalesPersonSales'
    (
        NAME = N'AdventureWorks.Sales.GetSalesPersonSales',
        FORMAT = ROWSETS_ONLY
    ),
    WEBMETHOD 'GetSalesTotal'
    (
        NAME = N'AdventureWorks.Sales.GetSalesTotal'
    ),
    WSDL = DEFAULT,
    DATABASE = N'AdventureWorks',
    SCHEMA = STANDARD
);
GO
```

Listing 16-6. *HTTP Endpoint Ad Hoc Querying*

```
CREATE ENDPOINT AdvAdHocEndpoint
    STATE = STARTED
AS HTTP (
    PATH = N'/AdvAdhocSql',
    AUTHENTICATION = (INTEGRATED),
    PORTS = (CLEAR),
    SITE = N'*'
)
FOR SOAP (
    WSDL = DEFAULT,
    DATABASE = N'AdventureWorks',
    SCHEMA = STANDARD,
    BATCHES = ENABLED
);
GO
```

■ ■ ■

.NET Source Code Listings

This appendix contains complete program listings of the .NET sample programs in Chapters 14, 15, and 16 in C #. Most of the samples throughout this book were written in VB.

Chapter 14

Listing 14-1. *Fahrenheit to Celsius Converter SQLCLR UDF in C#*

```csharp
using System;
using System.Data;
using System.Data.SqlClient;
using System.Data.SqlTypes;
using Microsoft.SqlServer.Server;

namespace APress.Samples {

    public partial class Sql
    {
        [SqlFunction(DataAccess=DataAccessKind.None,
            IsDeterministic=true)]
        public static SqlDouble Fahrenheit2Celsius(SqlDouble f)
        {
            SqlDouble c = new SqlDouble();
            c = (5.0 / 9.0) * (f - 32.0);
            return c;
        }
    };
}
```

Listing 14-2. *GetYahooNews SQLCLR Table-Valued Function in C#*

```csharp
using System;
using System.Data;
using System.Data.SqlClient;
using System.Data.SqlTypes;
using Microsoft.SqlServer.Server;
using System.Xml;
using System.Runtime.InteropServices;
using System.Collections;

namespace APress.Samples {

    public partial class Sql
    {
        [SqlFunction(IsDeterministic=false,
            DataAccess=DataAccessKind.None,
            TableDefinition="title nvarchar(256), link nvarchar(256), " +
                "pubdate datetime, description nvarchar(max)",
            FillRowMethodName="GetRow")]
        public static IEnumerable GetYahooNews()
        {
            XmlTextReader xmlsource = new
                XmlTextReader("http://rss.news.yahoo.com/rss/topstories");
            XmlDocument newsxml = new XmlDocument();
            newsxml.Load(xmlsource);
            xmlsource.Close();
            return newsxml.SelectNodes("//rss/channel/item");
        }

        private static void GetRow(Object o, out SqlString title,
            out SqlString link,
            out SqlDateTime pubdate, out SqlString description)
        {
            XmlElement element;
            element = (XmlElement)o;
            title = element.SelectSingleNode("./title").InnerText;
            link = element.SelectSingleNode("./link").InnerText;
```

```csharp
            pubdate = DateTime.Parse(
                element.SelectSingleNode("./pubDate").InnerText);
            description = element.SelectSingleNode("./description").InnerText;
        }
    };
}
```

Listing 14-3. *Get Environment Variables SQLCLR Stored Procedure in C#*

```csharp
using System;
using System.Data;
using System.Data.SqlClient;
using System.Data.SqlTypes;
using Microsoft.SqlServer.Server;
using System.Collections;

namespace APress.Samples
{
    public partial class Sql
    {
        [Microsoft.SqlServer.Server.SqlProcedure]
        public static void GetEnvironmentVars()
        {
            try
            {
                SortedList environmentList = new SortedList();
                foreach (DictionaryEntry de in
                    Environment.GetEnvironmentVariables())
                {
                    environmentList[de.Key] = de.Value;
                }
                SqlDataRecord record = new SqlDataRecord(new SqlMetaData("VarName",
                    SqlDbType.NVarChar, 1024),
                    new SqlMetaData("VarValue", SqlDbType.NVarChar, 4000));
                SqlContext.Pipe.SendResultsStart(record);
                foreach (DictionaryEntry de in environmentList)
                {
                    record.SetValue(0, de.Key);
                    record.SetValue(1, de.Value);
                    SqlContext.Pipe.SendResultsRow(record);
                }
```

```
                SqlContext.Pipe.SendResultsEnd();
            }
            catch (Exception ex)
            {
                SqlContext.Pipe.Send(ex.Message);
            }
        }
    };
}
```

Listing 14-4. *Range SQLCLR UDA in C#*

```csharp
using System;
using System.Data;
using System.Data.SqlClient;
using System.Data.SqlTypes;
using Microsoft.SqlServer.Server;

namespace APress.Samples
{
    [Serializable]
    [Microsoft.SqlServer.Server.SqlUserDefinedAggregate(Format.Native)]
    public struct Range
    {
        private SqlDouble min;
        private SqlDouble max;

        public void Init()
        {
            this.min = SqlDouble.Null;
            this.max = SqlDouble.Null;
        }

        public void Accumulate(SqlDouble Value)
        {
            if (!Value.IsNull)
            {
                if (this.min.IsNull || Value < this.min)
                    this.min = Value;
```

```
            if (this.max.IsNull || Value > this.max)
                this.max = Value;
        }
    }

    public void Merge(Range tempRange)
    {
        if (this.min.IsNull || tempRange.min < this.min)
            this.min = tempRange.min;
        if (this.min.IsNull || tempRange.max > this.max)
            this.max = tempRange.max;
    }

    public SqlDouble Terminate()
    {
        SqlDouble result = new SqlDouble();
        result = SqlDouble.Null;
        if (!this.min.IsNull && !this.max.IsNull)
            result = this.max - this.min;
        return result;
    }
};
}
```

Listing 14-5 in Chapter 14 is a scaled-down version of the Complex type listed here. The listing in Chapter 14 demonstrates complex number parsing, conversion to string, and the addition and division operators only. The following listing demonstrates the fully featured Complex UDT with built-in constants, all the basic math operators, and several additional complex number logarithmic, trigonometric, and hyperbolic functions.

Listing 14-5. *Complex Number SQLCLR UDT in C#*

```
// The Complex UDT allows you to represent and manipulate complex numbers
// in T-SQL via the SQLCLR.  Complex numbers are represented with the format:
//    a + bi

// Where a is the "real" part of the complex number, b is the "imaginary part", and
// the literal letter "i" is used to represent the imaginary number (square root
// of -1). If b is negative, the format is:
//    a - bi
```

```
// The UDT exposes a few useful constants including:
//    Pi:     The complex number representation of the Pi (3.14159265358979+0i)
//    i:       The complex number representation of the constant i (0+1i)
//    One: The complex number representation of the constant 1 (1+0i)
//    Two: The complex number representation of the constant 2 (2+0i)

// The exposed methods of the UDT include:
//    CAdd(n1, n2):  Adds the complex numbers n1 and n2
//    Sub(n1, n2):     Subtracts the complex number n2 from n1
//    Mult(n1, n2):     Multiplies the complex numbers n1 and n2
//    Div(n1, n2):      Divides the complex number n1 by n2
//    Neg(n1):          Returns the negative of the complex number n1
//    Conj(n1):         Returns the conjugate of the complex number n1
//    Abs(n1):           Returns the absolute value of the complex number n1
//    Exp(n1):           Returns the exponential function of a complex number n1
//    Power(n1, n2):  Returns the result of the complex number n1 to the n2 power
//    Sqrt(n1):          Returns the square root of the complex number n1
//    Ln(n1):             Returns the natural logarithm of the complex number n1
//    Log(n1):           Returns the base-10 logarithm of the complex number n1
//    Sin(n1):           Sine of a complex number
//    Sinh(n1):         Hyperbolic sine of a complex number
//    Cos(n1):          Cosine of a complex number
//    Cosh(n1):         Hyperbolic cosine of a complex number
//    Sec(n1):           Secant of a complex number
//    Sech(n1):         Hyperbolic secant of a complex number
//    Csc(n1):           Cosecant of a complex number
//    Csch(n1):         Hyperbolic cosecant of a complex number
//    Tan(n1):           Tangent of a complex number
//    Tanh(n1):         Hyperbolic tangent of a complex number
//    Cot(n1):           Cotangent of a complex number
//    Coth(n1):         Hyperbolic cotangent of a complex number

using System;
using System.Data.SqlTypes;
using Microsoft.SqlServer.Server;
using System.Text.RegularExpressions;
```

```csharp
namespace APress.Sample
{
    [Serializable]
    [Microsoft.SqlServer.Server.SqlUserDefinedType(Format.Native,
        IsByteOrdered = true)]
    public struct Complex : INullable
    {

        #region "Complex Number UDT Fields/Components"

        public Double real;
        public Double imaginary;
        private bool m_Null;

        #endregion

        #region "Complex Number Parsing, Constructor, and Methods/Properties"

        private static readonly Regex rx = new Regex(
            "^(?<Imaginary>[+-]?([0-9]+|[0-9]*\\.[0-9]+))[i|I]$|" +
            "^(?<Real>[+-]?([0-9]+|[0-9]*\\.[0-9]+))$|" +
            "^(?<Real>[+-]?([0-9]+|[0-9]*\\.[0-9]+))" +
            "(?<Imaginary>[+-]?([0-9]+|[0-9]*\\.[0-9]+))[i|I]$");

        public static Complex Parse(SqlString s)
        {
            Complex u = new Complex();
            if (s.IsNull)
                u = Null;
            else
            {
                MatchCollection m = rx.Matches(s.Value);
                if (m.Count == 0)
                    throw (new FormatException("Invalid Complex Number Format."));
                String real_str = m[0].Groups["Real"].Value;
                String imaginary_str = m[0].Groups["Imaginary"].Value;
                if (real_str == "" && imaginary_str == "")
                    throw (new FormatException("Invalid Complex Number Format."));
                if (real_str == "")
                    u.real = 0.0;
```

```
            else
                u.real = Convert.ToDouble(real_str);
            if (imaginary_str == "")
                u.imaginary = 0.0;
            else
                u.imaginary = Convert.ToDouble(imaginary_str);
        }
        return u;
    }

    public override String ToString()
    {
        String sign = "";
        if (this.imaginary >= 0.0)
            sign = "+";
        return this.real.ToString() + sign + this.imaginary.ToString() + "i";
    }

    public bool IsNull
    {
        get
        {
            return m_Null;
        }
    }

    public static Complex Null
    {
        get
        {
            Complex h = new Complex();
            h.m_Null = true;
            return h;
        }
    }

    public Complex(Double r, Double i)
    {
        this.real = r;
        this.imaginary = i;
        this.m_Null = false;
    }
```

```csharp
#endregion

#region "Useful Complex Number Constants"

// The property "i" is the Complex number 0 + 1i. Defined here because
// it is useful in some calculations

public static Complex i
{
    get
    {
        return new Complex(0, 1);
    }
}

// The property "Pi" is the Complex representation of the number
// Pi (3.141592... + 0i)

public static Complex Pi
{
    get
    {
        return new Complex(Math.PI, 0);
    }
}

// The property "One" is the Complex number representation of the
// number 1 (1 + 0i)

public static Complex One
{
    get
    {
        return new Complex(1, 0);
    }
}

// The property "Two" is the Complex number representation of the
// number 2 (2 + 0i)
```

```csharp
public static Complex Two
{
    get
    {
        return new Complex(2, 0);
    }
}

#endregion

#region "Complex Number Basic Operators"

// Complex number addition

public static Complex operator +(Complex n1, Complex n2)
{
    Complex u;
    if (n1.IsNull || n2.IsNull)
        u = Null;
    else
        u = new Complex(n1.real + n2.real, n1.imaginary + n2.imaginary);
    return u;
}

// Complex number subtraction

public static Complex operator -(Complex n1, Complex n2)
{
    Complex u;
    if (n1.IsNull || n2.IsNull)
        u = Null;
    else
        u = new Complex(n1.real - n2.real, n1.imaginary - n2.imaginary);
    return u;
}

// Complex number multiplication
```

```
public static Complex operator *(Complex n1, Complex n2)
{
    Complex u;
    if (n1.IsNull || n2.IsNull)
        u = Null;
    else
        u = new Complex((n1.real * n2.real) - (n1.imaginary * n2.imaginary),
            (n1.real * n2.imaginary) + (n2.real * n1.imaginary));
    return u;
}


// Complex number division

public static Complex operator /(Complex n1, Complex n2)
{
    Complex u;
    if (n1.IsNull || n2.IsNull)
        u = Null;
    else
    {
        if (n2.real == 0.0 && n2.imaginary == 0.0)
            throw new DivideByZeroException(
                "Complex Number Division By Zero Exception.");
        u = new Complex(((n1.real * n2.real) +
            (n1.imaginary * n2.imaginary)) /
            ((Math.Pow(n2.real, 2) + Math.Pow(n2.imaginary, 2))),
            ((n1.imaginary * n2.real) - (n1.real * n2.imaginary)) /
            ((Math.Pow(n2.real, 2) + Math.Pow(n2.imaginary, 2))));
    }
    return u;
}


// Unary minus operator

public static Complex operator -(Complex n1)
{
    Complex u;
    if (n1.IsNull)
        u = Null;
```

```csharp
    else
        u = new Complex(-n1.real, -n1.imaginary);
    return u;
}


// Exponentation operator

public static Complex operator ^(Complex n1, Complex n2)
{
    Complex u;
    if (n1.IsNull || n2.IsNull)
        u = Null;
    else
        u = Exp(n2 * Ln(n1));
    return u;
}


#endregion

#region "Exposed Mathematical Basic Operator Methods"

// Add complex number n2 to n1

public static Complex CAdd(Complex n1, Complex n2)
{
    return n1 + n2;
}


// Subtract complex number n2 from n1

public static Complex Sub(Complex n1, Complex n2)
{
    return n1 - n2;
}


// Multiply complex number n1 * n2

public static Complex Mult(Complex n1, Complex n2)
{
    return n1 * n2;
}
```

```
// Divide complex number n1 by n2

public static Complex Div(Complex n1, Complex n2)
{
    return n1 / n2;
}

// Returns negated complex number

public static Complex Neg(Complex n1)
{
    return -n1;
}

// Returns conjugate of complex number

public static Complex Conj(Complex n1)
{
    Complex u;
    if (n1.IsNull)
        u = Null;
    else
        u = new Complex(n1.real, -n1.imaginary);
    return u;
}

// Returns absolute value of a complex number

public static Complex Abs(Complex n1)
{
    Complex u;
    if (n1.IsNull)
        u = Null;
    else
        u = new Complex(Math.Sqrt(Math.Pow(n1.real, 2) +
            Math.Pow(n1.imaginary, 2)), 0.0);
    return u;
}

#endregion
```

```csharp
#region "Complex Number Exponentiation, Roots, Powers"

// The exponential function of a complex number

public static Complex Exp(Complex n1)
{
    Complex u;
    if (n1.IsNull)
        u = Null;
    else
        u = new Complex((Math.Exp(n1.real) * Math.Cos(n1.imaginary)),
        (Math.Exp(n1.real) * Math.Sin(n1.imaginary)));
    return u;
}


// Returns the square root of a complex number

public static Complex Sqrt(Complex n1)
{
    return n1 ^ new Complex(0.5, 0);
}


// Raises a complex number n1 to the power n2

public static Complex Power(Complex n1, Complex n2)
{
    return n1 ^ n2;
}


// Complex number natural logarithm

public static Complex Ln(Complex n1)
{
    Complex u;
    if (n1.IsNull)
        u = Null;
    else
        u = new Complex((Math.Log(Math.Pow((Math.Pow(n1.real, 2) +
            Math.Pow(n1.imaginary, 2)), (0.5)))),
                Math.Atan2(n1.imaginary, n1.real));
    return u;
}
```

```csharp
// Complex number base-10 logarithm

public static Complex Log(Complex n1)
{
    return Ln(n1) / Ln(new Complex(10, 0));
}

#endregion

#region "Complex Number Trigonometric and Hyperbolic Functions"

// Sine of a complex number

public static Complex Sin(Complex n1)
{
    return (Exp(n1 * i) - Exp(-n1 * i)) / (Two * i);
}

// Hyperbolic Sine of a complex number

public static Complex Sinh(Complex n1)
{
    return (Exp(n1) - Exp(-n1)) / Two;
}

// Cosine of a complex number

public static Complex Cos(Complex n1)
{
    return (Exp(n1 * i) + Exp(-n1 * i)) / Two;
}

// Hyperbolic cosine of a complex number

public static Complex Cosh(Complex n1)
{
    return (Exp(n1) + Exp(-n1)) / Two;
}

// Tangent of a complex number
```

```csharp
    public static Complex Tan(Complex n1)
    {
        return Sin(n1) / Cos(n1);
    }


    // Hyperbolic tangent of a complex number

    public static Complex Tanh(Complex n1)
    {
        return Sinh(n1) / Cosh(n1);
    }


    // Cotangent of a complex number

    public static Complex Cot(Complex n1)
    {
        return Cos(n1) / Sin(n1);
    }


    // Hyperbolic cotangent of a complex number

    public static Complex Coth(Complex n1)
    {
        return Cosh(n1) / Sinh(n1);
    }


    // Secant of a complex number

    public static Complex Sec(Complex n1)
    {
        return One / Cos(n1);
    }


    // Hyperbolic secant of a complex number

    public static Complex Sech(Complex n1)
    {
        return One / Cosh(n1);
    }


    // Cosecant of a complex number
```

```csharp
public static Complex Csc(Complex n1)
{
    return One / Sin(n1);
}


// Hyperbolic cosecant of a complex number

public static Complex Csch(Complex n1)
{
    return One / Sinh(n1);
}


        #endregion
    }
}
```

Chapter 15

Listing 15-1. *.NET DataReader SQL Client in C#*

```csharp
using System;
using System.Text;
using System.Data.SqlClient;
using System.Collections.Generic;

namespace Apress.Samples
{
    class DataReaderExample
    {
        static void Main(string[] args)
        {
            String sqlConStr = "DATA SOURCE=(local);" +
                "INITIAL CATALOG=AdventureWorks;" +
                "INTEGRATED SECURITY=SSPI;";
            String sqlStmt = "SELECT DepartmentId, " +
                "    Name, " +
                "    GroupName, " +
                "    ModifiedDate " +
                " FROM HumanResources.Department " +
                " ORDER BY DepartmentId";
```

```csharp
SqlConnection sqlCon = null;
SqlCommand sqlCmd = null;
SqlDataReader sqlDr = null;
try
{
    sqlCon = new SqlConnection(sqlConStr);
    sqlCon.Open();
    sqlCmd = new SqlCommand(sqlStmt, sqlCon);
    sqlDr = sqlCmd.ExecuteReader();
    while (sqlDr.Read())
    {
        Console.WriteLine("{0}\t{1}\t{2}\t{3}",
            sqlDr["DepartmentId"].ToString(),
            sqlDr["Name"].ToString(),
            sqlDr["GroupName"].ToString(),
            sqlDr["ModifiedDate"].ToString());
    }
}
catch (SqlException ex)
{
    Console.WriteLine(ex.Message);
}
finally
{
    if (sqlDr != null)
        sqlDr.Close();
    if (sqlCmd != null)
        sqlCmd.Dispose();
    if (sqlCon != null)
        sqlCon.Dispose();
}
Console.Write("Press a Key to Continue...");
Console.ReadKey();
        }
    }
}
```

Listing 15-3. *.NET Parameterized SQL Query in C#*

```csharp
using System;
using System.Data;
using System.Data.SqlClient;
using System.Collections.Generic;

namespace Apress.Samples
{
    class ParameterizedQuery
    {
        static void Main(string[] args)
        {
            String name = "SMITH";
            String sqlstmt = "SELECT ContactID, FirstName, MiddleName, LastName " +
                " FROM Person.Contact " +
                " WHERE LastName = @name";
            SqlConnection sqlcon = null;
            SqlCommand sqlcmd = null;
            SqlDataReader sqldr = null;
            try
            {
                sqlcon = new SqlConnection("SERVER=(local); " +
                    "INITIAL CATALOG=AdventureWorks;INTEGRATED SECURITY=SSPI;");
                sqlcon.Open();
                sqlcmd = new SqlCommand(sqlstmt, sqlcon);
                sqlcmd.Parameters.Add("@name", SqlDbType.NVarChar, 50).Value = name;
                sqldr = sqlcmd.ExecuteReader();
                while (sqldr.Read())
                {
                    Console.WriteLine("{0}\t{1}\t{2}\t{3}",
                        sqldr["ContactID"].ToString(),
                        sqldr["LastName"].ToString(),
                        sqldr["FirstName"].ToString(),
                        sqldr["MiddleName"].ToString());
                }
            }
            catch (Exception ex)
            {
                Console.WriteLine(ex.Message);
            }
```

```
        finally
        {
            if (sqldr != null)
                sqldr.Close();
            if (sqlcmd != null)
                sqlcmd.Dispose();
            if (sqlcon != null)
                sqlcon.Dispose();
        }
        Console.WriteLine("Press any key...");
        Console.ReadKey();
    }
  }
}
```

Listing 5-4. *.NET ExecuteXmlReader Example in C#*

```
using System;
using System.Data;
using System.Xml;
using System.Data.SqlClient;

namespace Apress.Samples
{
    class XmlReaderQuery
    {
        static void Main(string[] args)
        {
            String name = "SMITH";
            String sqlstmt = "SELECT ContactID, FirstName, " +
                " COALESCE(MiddleName, '') AS MiddleName, LastName " +
                " FROM Person.Contact " +
                " WHERE LastName = @name FOR XML AUTO";
            SqlConnection sqlcon = null;
            SqlCommand sqlcmd = null;
            XmlReader sqlxr = null;
            try
```

```csharp
{
    sqlcon = new SqlConnection("SERVER=(local); " +
        "INITIAL CATALOG=AdventureWorks;INTEGRATED SECURITY=SSPI;");
    sqlcon.Open();
    sqlcmd = new SqlCommand(sqlstmt, sqlcon);
    sqlcmd.Parameters.Add("@name", SqlDbType.NVarChar, 50).Value = name;
    sqlxr = sqlcmd.ExecuteXmlReader();
    while (sqlxr.Read())
    {
        Console.WriteLine("{0}\t{1}\t{2}\t{3}",
            sqlxr["ContactID"].ToString(),
            sqlxr["LastName"].ToString(),
            sqlxr["FirstName"].ToString(),
            sqlxr["MiddleName"].ToString());
    }
}
catch (Exception ex)
{
    Console.WriteLine(ex.Message);
}
finally
{
    if (sqlxr != null)
        sqlxr.Close();
    if (sqlcmd != null)
        sqlcmd.Dispose();
    if (sqlcon != null)
        sqlcon.Dispose();
}
Console.WriteLine("Press any key...");
Console.ReadKey();
        }
    }
}
```

Listing 15-5. *.NET SqlBulkCopy Example in C#*

```csharp
using System;
using System.Data;
using System.Xml;
using System.IO;
using System.Data.SqlClient;
using System.Diagnostics;

namespace Apress.Samples
{
    class ZipImport
    {
        private static void Main(string[] args)
        {
            Stopwatch sw = new Stopwatch();
            sw.Start();
            int rowcount = DoImport();
            sw.Stop();
            Console.WriteLine("{0} Rows Imported in {1} Seconds.",
                rowcount, (sw.ElapsedMilliseconds / 1000.0));
            Console.WriteLine("Press a Key...");
            Console.ReadKey();
        }

        private static int DoImport()
        {
            String sqlcon = "DATA SOURCE=(local); " +
                "INITIAL CATALOG=AdventureWorks;INTEGRATED SECURITY=SSPI;";
            String srcfile = "C:\\ZIPCodes.txt";
            DataTable dt = null;
            using (SqlBulkCopy bulkCopier = new SqlBulkCopy(sqlcon))
            {
                bulkCopier.DestinationTableName = "ZIPCodes";
                try
                {
                    dt = LoadSourceFile(srcfile);
                    bulkCopier.WriteToServer(dt);
                }
                catch (SqlException ex)
```

```
            {
                Console.WriteLine(ex.Message);
            }
        }
        return dt.Rows.Count;
    }


    private static DataTable LoadSourceFile(String srcfile)
    {
        DataTable loadtable = new DataTable();
        DataColumn loadcolumn = new DataColumn();
        DataRow loadrow;
        loadcolumn.DataType = Type.GetType("System.String");
        loadcolumn.ColumnName = "ZIP";
        loadcolumn.Unique = true;
        loadtable.Columns.Add(loadcolumn);
        loadcolumn = new DataColumn();
        loadcolumn.DataType = System.Type.GetType("System.Double");
        loadcolumn.ColumnName = "Latitude";
        loadcolumn.Unique = false;
        loadtable.Columns.Add(loadcolumn);
        loadcolumn = new DataColumn();
        loadcolumn.DataType = System.Type.GetType("System.Double");
        loadcolumn.ColumnName = "Longitude";
        loadcolumn.Unique = false;
        loadtable.Columns.Add(loadcolumn);
        loadcolumn = new DataColumn();
        loadcolumn.DataType = System.Type.GetType("System.String");
        loadcolumn.ColumnName = "City";
        loadcolumn.Unique = false;
        loadtable.Columns.Add(loadcolumn);
        loadcolumn = new DataColumn();
        loadcolumn.DataType = System.Type.GetType("System.String");
        loadcolumn.ColumnName = "State";
        loadcolumn.Unique = false;
        loadtable.Columns.Add(loadcolumn);
        using (StreamReader sr = new StreamReader(srcfile))
        {
            String record = sr.ReadLine();
            while (record != null)
```

```
            {
                String [] s = record.Split('\t');
                loadrow = loadtable.NewRow();
                loadrow["ZIP"] = s[0];
                loadrow["Latitude"] = s[1];
                loadrow["Longitude"] = s[2];
                loadrow["City"] = s[3];
                loadrow["State"] = s[4];
                loadtable.Rows.Add(loadrow);
                record = sr.ReadLine();
            }
        }
        return loadtable;
    }
  }
}
```

Listing 15-7. *MARS Client Example in C#*

```
using System;
using System.Data;
using System.Data.SqlClient;

namespace Apress.Samples
{
    class SqlResultTests
    {
        private static void Main(string[] args)
        {
            // Create and open a native SqlClient connection to SQL Server 2005
            SqlConnection sqlcon = new SqlConnection("SERVER=(local);" +
                "INITIAL CATALOG=AdventureWorks;INTEGRATED SECURITY=SSPI;" +
                "MULTIPLEACTIVERESULTSETS=TRUE;");
            sqlcon.Open();

            // Create two SqlCommands to retrieve two result sets
            SqlCommand sqlcmd1 = new SqlCommand("SELECT DepartmentID, Name, " +
                "GroupName FROM HumanResources.Department", sqlcon);
            SqlCommand sqlcmd2 = new SqlCommand("SELECT ShiftID, Name, " +
                "StartTime, EndTime FROM HumanResources.Shift", sqlcon);
```

```
// Open the first result set
SqlDataReader sqldr1 = sqlcmd1.ExecuteReader();

// Open the second result set
SqlDataReader sqldr2 = sqlcmd2.ExecuteReader();

// Output the results of the first result set
Console.WriteLine("===========");
Console.WriteLine("Departments");
Console.WriteLine("===========");
while (sqldr1.Read())
{
    Console.WriteLine(String.Format("{0}\t{1}\t{2}",
        sqldr1["DepartmentID"], sqldr1["Name"],
        sqldr1["GroupName"]));
}

// Output the results of the second result set
Console.WriteLine("======");
Console.WriteLine("Shifts");
Console.WriteLine("======");
while (sqldr2.Read())
{
    Console.WriteLine(String.Format("{0}\t{1}\t{2}\t{3}",
        sqldr2["ShiftID"], sqldr2["Name"], sqldr2["StartTime"],
        sqldr2["EndTime"]));
}

// Clean up
sqldr1.Close();
sqldr2.Close();
sqlcmd1.Dispose();
sqlcmd2.Dispose();
sqlcon.Dispose();

// Exit the program
Console.WriteLine("Press a key to end.");
Console.ReadKey();
        }
    }
}
```

Chapter 16

Listing 16-5. *HTTP Endpoint Consumer in C#*

```csharp
using System;
using System.Net;
using System.Windows.Forms;
using System.Data.SqlClient;

namespace APress.Samples
{
    public partial class Form1 : Form
    {
        public Form1()
        {
            InitializeComponent();
        }

        private void Form1_Load(object sender, EventArgs e)
        {
            // Create a web service proxy using the SQL Server HTTP endpoint
            localhost.AdvSalesEndpoint proxy = new localhost.AdvSalesEndpoint();

            // Set the integrated security credentials
            proxy.Credentials = CredentialCache.DefaultCredentials;

            // Bind the combo box to the results of the web method call
            this.cboSalesPerson.ValueMember = "SalespersonId";
            this.cboSalesPerson.DisplayMember = "FullName";

            // Call the web method
            this.cboSalesPerson.DataSource = proxy.GetSalespersonList().Tables[0];
        }

        private void cboSalesPerson_SelectedIndexChanged(object sender, EventArgs e)
        {
            // Create a web service proxy using the SQL Server HTTP endpoint
            localhost.AdvSalesEndpoint proxy = new localhost.AdvSalesEndpoint();

            // Set the integrated security credentials
            proxy.Credentials = CredentialCache.DefaultCredentials;
```

```csharp
            // Bind the data grid view to the results of the web method call
            this.dgvSales.DataSource = proxy.GetSalesPersonSales(new
                System.Data.SqlTypes.SqlInt32(
                    (int)this.cboSalesPerson.SelectedValue)).Tables[0];

            // Populate the text box with the results of the second web method call
            this.txtTotalSales.Text = proxy.GetSalesTotal(new
                System.Data.SqlTypes.SqlInt32(
                    (int)this.cboSalesPerson.SelectedValue)).Value.ToString("C");
        }

        private void btnExit_Click(object sender, EventArgs e)
        {
            // Exit the application
            Application.Exit();
        }
    }
}
```

Index

▪T

You Need the Companion eBook

Your purchase of this book entitles you to buy the companion PDF-version eBook for only $10. Take the weightless companion with you anywhere.

We believe this Apress title will prove so indispensable that you'll want to carry it with you everywhere, which is why we are offering the companion eBook (in PDF format) for $10 to customers who purchase this book now. Convenient and fully searchable, the PDF version of any content-rich, page-heavy Apress book makes a valuable addition to your programming library. You can easily find and copy code—or perform examples by quickly toggling between instructions and the application. Even simultaneously tackling a donut, diet soda, and complex code becomes simplified with hands-free eBooks!

Once you purchase your book, getting the $10 companion eBook is simple:

❶ Visit **www.apress.com/promo/tendollars/**.

❷ Complete a basic registration form to receive a randomly generated question about this title.

❸ Answer the question correctly in 60 seconds, and you will receive a promotional code to redeem for the $10.00 eBook.

2560 Ninth Street • Suite 219 • Berkeley, CA 94710

eBookshop

THE EXPERT'S VOICE™

Offer valid through 10/23/07